British Columbia

RECREATIONAL

Atlas

SCALE 1 : 600 000
(1 cm = 6 km)

INTRODUCTION

...e is magic in maps. From the comfort of your armchair they will take you ... in memory down byways long forgotten, or lead you on to unknown ...ac...s on trails you have yet to tread. This atlas spreads the broad horizons of British Columbia conveniently before you in a single volume, inviting you to explore, and providing the basic knowledge of location and access that will help you translate imagined journeys into reality.

For the ever-increasing throngs of outdoor enthusiasts, the atlas offers a ready means to orient themselves in the field, to find new places to pursue their interests, or to retrace past trips. Hunters particularly, and fishers and others using the outdoor environment will find it an almost indispensable aid to compliance with provincial regulations. The maps show the definitive bounda-ries of the wildlife management units, the bases of British Columbia's wildlife management program and regulations, revised and up-to-date to the time of p...lication.

But there is much more here than boundaries: topography, place names, roads, trails, elevations, streams, lakes, parks, sanctuaries and places of special interest are all catalogued and mapped. Whatever your interest in the out-doors, whether you hunt, fish, photograph, run rivers, hike, camp, study wildlife, or enjoy the outdoors in some other way, the atlas can be ... ...ide to safe, more pleasant and adventurous outdoor experiences.

Ministry of Environmer

Acknowledgements

This Recreational Atlas was compiled in cooperation with the BRITISH COLUMBIA MINISTRY OF ENVIRONMENT, LANDS AND PARKS which supplied the most recent updates of the official Wildlife Management Unit Boundaries. The Wildlife Branch greatly expanded its contribution of data on the Wildlife Watch program, which promotes the appreciation of wildlife in their natural habitat. BC Parks also contributed information on over one hundred and fifty new Parks and Protected Areas.

For this Edition, we recognize our indebtedness to the following sources for their generous assistance:

Parks Canada
Royal British Columbia Museum
Beautiful British Columbia Magazine
Canadian Forest Products Ltd.
Crestbrook Forest Industries Ltd.
Enso Forest Products Ltd.
Fletcher Challenge Canada Ltd
Galloway Lumber Company Ltd.
Ministry of Tourism and Provincial Secretary
B.C. Forest Service (Ministry of Forests - Regions and Districts)
Ministry of Transportation and Highways - Regions and Districts

Whistler Village
MacMillan Bloedel Ltd.
Northwood Pulp and Timber Ltd.
Pope and Talbot Ltd.
Skeena Cellulose Inc.
Slocan Forest Products Ltd.
Tanizul Timber Ltd.
Weldwood of Canada Ltd.
Westar Timber Ltd.
Western Forest Products
Weyerhaeuser Canada

Information in this atlas is as factual as possible at date of publication. Readers are invited to present suggestions, corrections and/or updates to:

P.T.C. Phototype Composing Ltd.
2647 Anscomb Place
Victoria, B.C.
V8R 2C7
Fax (250) 592-8138

CANADIAN CATALOGUING IN PUBLICATION DATA
P.T.C. Phototype Composing Ltd.
British Columbia Recreational Atlas

Includes Index
ISBN 0-9680772-1-8

1. Recreational areas - British Columbia -
Maps. 2. Wildlife management areas -
British Columbia - Maps. 3. British Columbia -
Description and travel - Guide-books. I. Title
G1171.E63W55 1989   912'.133378'09711   C88-091478-5

Copyright © 1989 P.T.C. Phototype Composing Ltd.
FIRST EDITION: July 1989
SECOND EDITION: July 1990
THIRD EDITION: April 1993
FOURTH EDITION: April 1997

Typesetting and layout by *RAPIDRAFT*, Larry & Elaine Wells, Victoria, B.C.

Printed in Hong Kong

Table of Contents

Key Map and Legend . . . . .Page I–II

National Topographic System Index . . . . .Page III–IV

British Columbia Recreational Atlas Maps . . . . .Page 1–88

BC Ecoprovince Map
Map showing the Ecoprovince classifications of British Columbia . . . . .Page 89

British Columbia Wildlife Watch
Guide to B.C.'s Wildlife Watch program with information on 189 Wildlife Viewing Sites around the
province, including facilities guide, species identification, time of year for best sighting opportunities,
as well as access information to the sites . . . . .Pages 90 - 99

British Columbia Ecological Reserves
139 unique areas of the province which are reserved for the preservation and protection
of rare or endangered plants and animals in their natural habitat . . . . .Pages 100–102

British Columbia's Provincial and National Parks
Locations of B.C.'s 6 National and over 500 Provincial Parks and Protected Areas, facilities guide
for camping, Parks District office contacts, information and contact numbers for BC Parks
new reservation system . . . . .Pages 103–111

Hunting Information
Hunters should refer to the current British Columbia Hunting and Trapping Regulations Synopsis for
information detailing no shooting, limited entry and other regulations governing each Management Unit.
Particulars may be obtained from **Ministry of Environment and Conservation Officer contacts** . . . . .Page 112

Fishing Information
Fishers should refer to the current British Columbia Freshwater Fishing Regulations Synopsis for
information detailing closed areas, class restrictions and other regulations governing each region.
Particulars may be obtained from **Ministry of Environment and Conservation Officer contacts** . . . . .Page 112

BC Forest Service Recreation Sites
There are more than 1000 free recreation sites around the province which are developed and
maintained by the BC Forest Service. For information regarding specific sites, particulars may
be obtained from **District Office contacts** . . . . .Page 113

Ferry Services and Information
Ferry schedules, carrying capacities and reservation contact numbers . . . . .Page 114

British Columbia Gazetteer
Locations of over 10,000 Places, Rivers, Lakes, Streams, Inlets, Bays and Mountains . . . . .Pages 115–141

Helpful Hints for the Back Road Explorer
Safe driving tips, sign identification and road deactivation information . . . . .Page 142

Distance Table of Provincial Destinations
Gives distances between towns and cities in British Columbia . . . . .Inside Back Cover

Civil Aviation Council
The B.C. Air Facilities Map is a valuable guide to air facilities and services throughout the province. Showing some popular
VFR routes through the Canadian Rockies and over the magnificent west coast, the map will help you to organize your flight.
The Air Facilities Map is available from the BC Aviation Council, 303-5360 Airport Road South, Richmond, B.C., V7B 1B4.
TELEPHONE: (604) 278-9330 FAX: (604) 278-8210. Once you have selected your B.C. destinations, official air navigation charts
and publications may be obtained from Transport Canada or from Canadian chart dealers.

ATLAS MAP LAYOUT

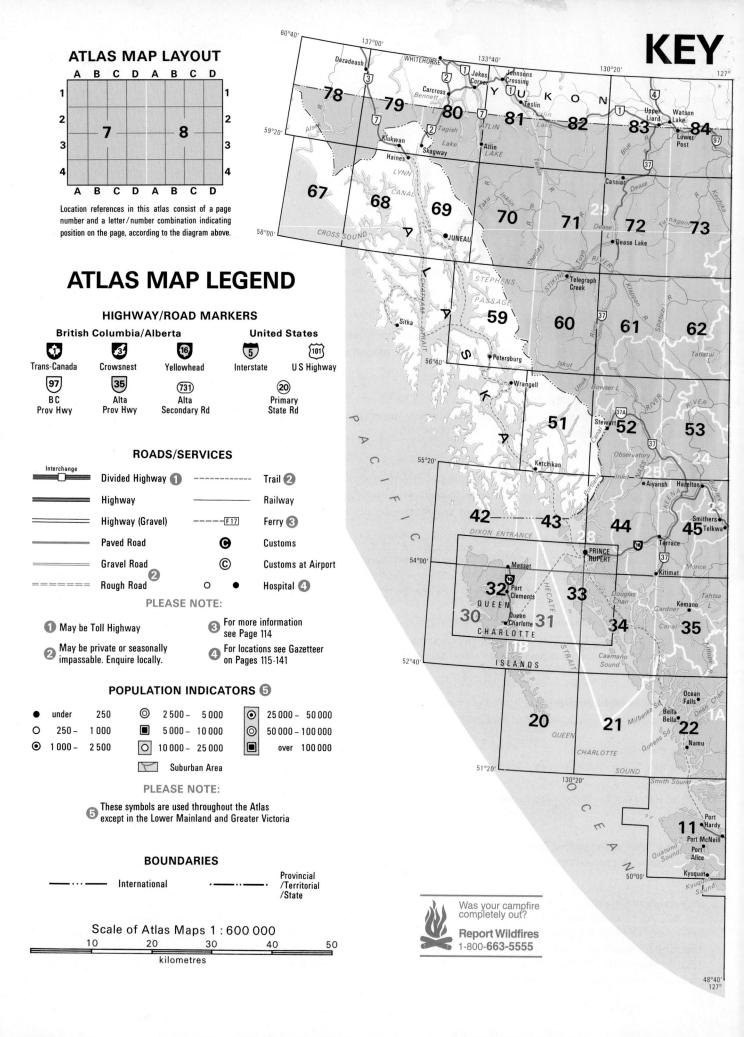

Location references in this atlas consist of a page number and a letter/number combination indicating position on the page, according to the diagram above.

ATLAS MAP LEGEND

HIGHWAY/ROAD MARKERS

British Columbia/Alberta

- Trans-Canada
- Crowsnest
- Yellowhead
- BC Prov Hwy
- Alta Prov Hwy
- Alta Secondary Rd

United States

- Interstate
- US Highway
- Primary State Rd

ROADS/SERVICES

Interchange	
Divided Highway ❶	Trail ❷
Highway	Railway
Highway (Gravel)	Ferry ❸
Paved Road	Ⓒ Customs
Gravel Road	Ⓒ Customs at Airport
Rough Road ❷	○ ● Hospital ❹

PLEASE NOTE:

❶ May be Toll Highway

❷ May be private or seasonally impassable. Enquire locally.

❸ For more information see Page 114

❹ For locations see Gazetteer on Pages 115–141

POPULATION INDICATORS ❺

● under 250	◎ 2 500 – 5 000	◉ 25 000 – 50 000
○ 250 – 1 000	■ 5 000 – 10 000	◎ 50 000 – 100 000
◉ 1 000 – 2 500	▢ 10 000 – 25 000	■ over 100 000
	▱ Suburban Area	

PLEASE NOTE:

❺ These symbols are used throughout the Atlas except in the Lower Mainland and Greater Victoria

BOUNDARIES

— · · · — International

— · — · — Provincial /Territorial /State

Scale of Atlas Maps 1 : 600 000

10   20   30   40   50

kilometres

KEY

MAP

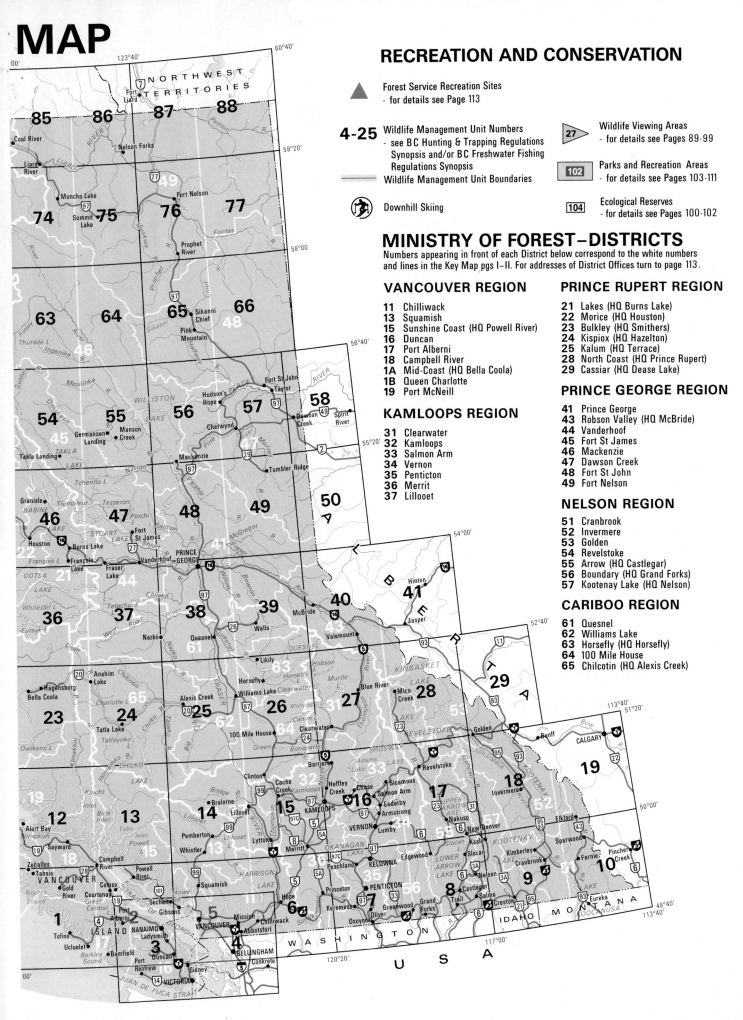

RECREATION AND CONSERVATION

▲ Forest Service Recreation Sites
- for details see Page 113

4-25 Wildlife Management Unit Numbers
- see BC Hunting & Trapping Regulations
Synopsis and/or BC Freshwater Fishing
Regulations Synopsis
— Wildlife Management Unit Boundaries

🚶 Downhill Skiing

▷ **27** Wildlife Viewing Areas
- for details see Pages 89-99

102 Parks and Recreation Areas
- for details see Pages 103-111

104 Ecological Reserves
- for details see Pages 100-102

MINISTRY OF FOREST–DISTRICTS

Numbers appearing in front of each District below correspond to the white numbers and lines in the Key Map pgs I–II. For addresses of District Offices turn to page 113.

VANCOUVER REGION

11 Chilliwack
13 Squamish
15 Sunshine Coast (HQ Powell River)
16 Duncan
17 Port Alberni
18 Campbell River
1A Mid-Coast (HQ Bella Coola)
1B Queen Charlotte
19 Port McNeill

KAMLOOPS REGION

31 Clearwater
32 Kamloops
33 Salmon Arm
34 Vernon
35 Penticton
36 Merrit
37 Lillooet

PRINCE RUPERT REGION

21 Lakes (HQ Burns Lake)
22 Morice (HQ Houston)
23 Bulkley (HQ Smithers)
24 Kispiox (HQ Hazelton)
25 Kalum (HQ Terrace)
28 North Coast (HQ Prince Rupert)
29 Cassiar (HQ Dease Lake)

PRINCE GEORGE REGION

41 Prince George
43 Robson Valley (HQ McBride)
44 Vanderhoof
45 Fort St James
46 Mackenzie
47 Dawson Creek
48 Fort St John
49 Fort Nelson

NELSON REGION

51 Cranbrook
52 Invermere
53 Golden
54 Revelstoke
55 Arrow (HQ Castlegar)
56 Boundary (HQ Grand Forks)
57 Kootenay Lake (HQ Nelson)

CARIBOO REGION

61 Quesnel
62 Williams Lake
63 Horsefly (HQ Horsefly)
64 100 Mile House
65 Chilcotin (HQ Alexis Creek)

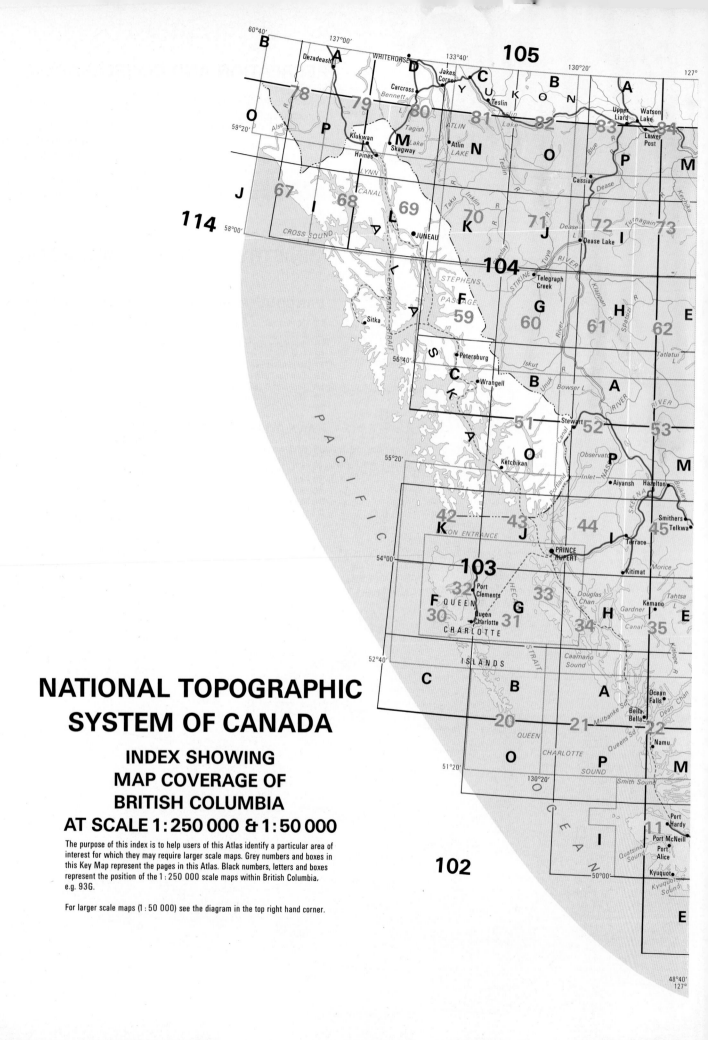

NATIONAL TOPOGRAPHIC SYSTEM OF CANADA

INDEX SHOWING
MAP COVERAGE OF
BRITISH COLUMBIA
AT SCALE 1:250 000 & 1:50 000

The purpose of this index is to help users of this Atlas identify a particular area of interest for which they may require larger scale maps. Grey numbers and boxes in this Key Map represent the pages in this Atlas. Black numbers, letters and boxes represent the position of the 1:250 000 scale maps within British Columbia. e.g. 93G.

For larger scale maps (1:50 000) see the diagram in the top right hand corner.

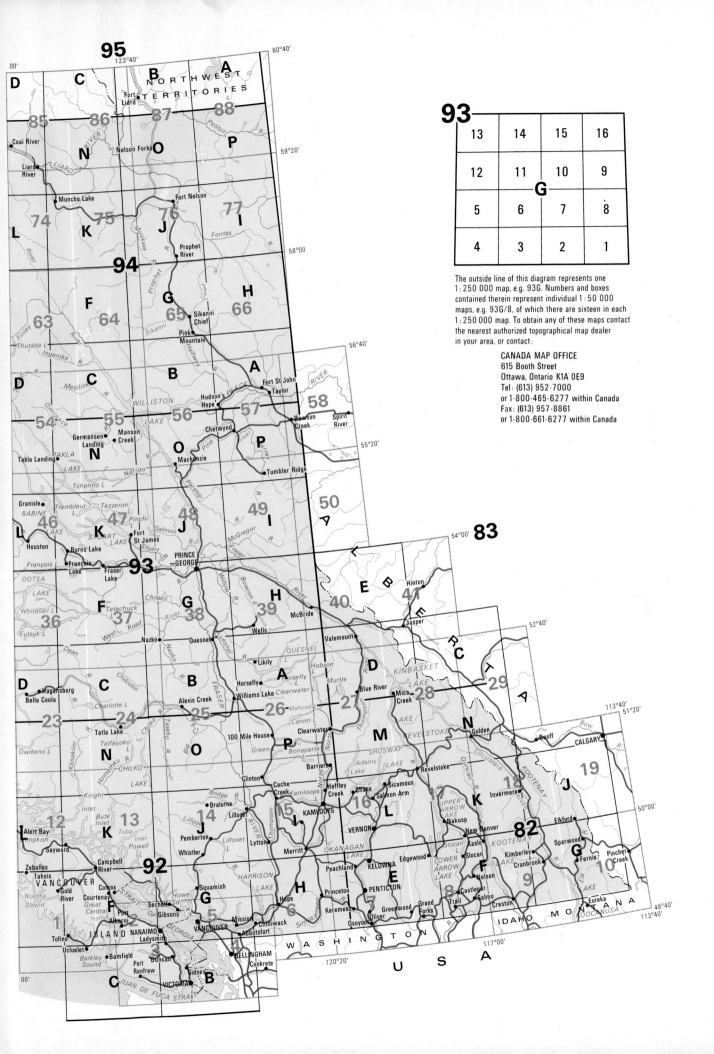

93

13	14	15	16
12	11	10	9
5	6	7	8
4	3	2	1

G

The outside line of this diagram represents one
1:250 000 map, e.g. 93G. Numbers and boxes
contained therein represent individual 1:50 000
maps, e.g. 93G/8, of which there are sixteen in each
1:250 000 map. To obtain any of these maps contact
the nearest authorized topographical map dealer
in your area, or contact:

CANADA MAP OFFICE
615 Booth Street
Ottawa, Ontario K1A 0E9
Tel: (613) 952-7000
or 1-800-465-6277 within Canada
Fax: (613) 957-8861
or 1-800-661-6277 within Canada

IV

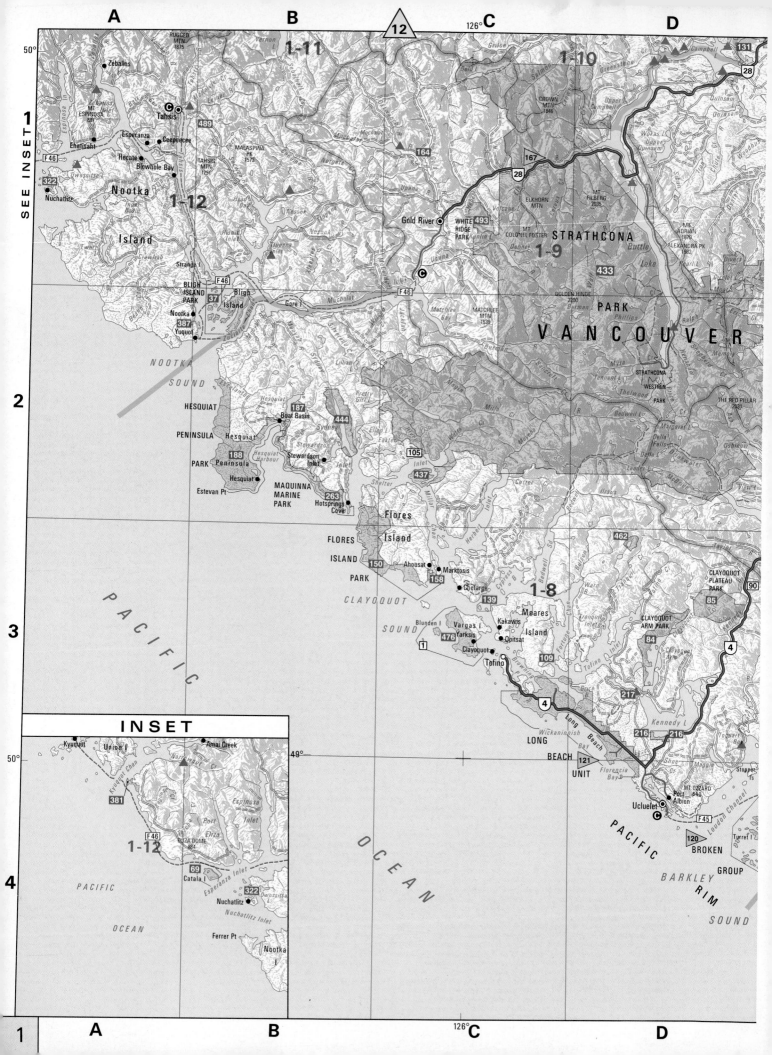

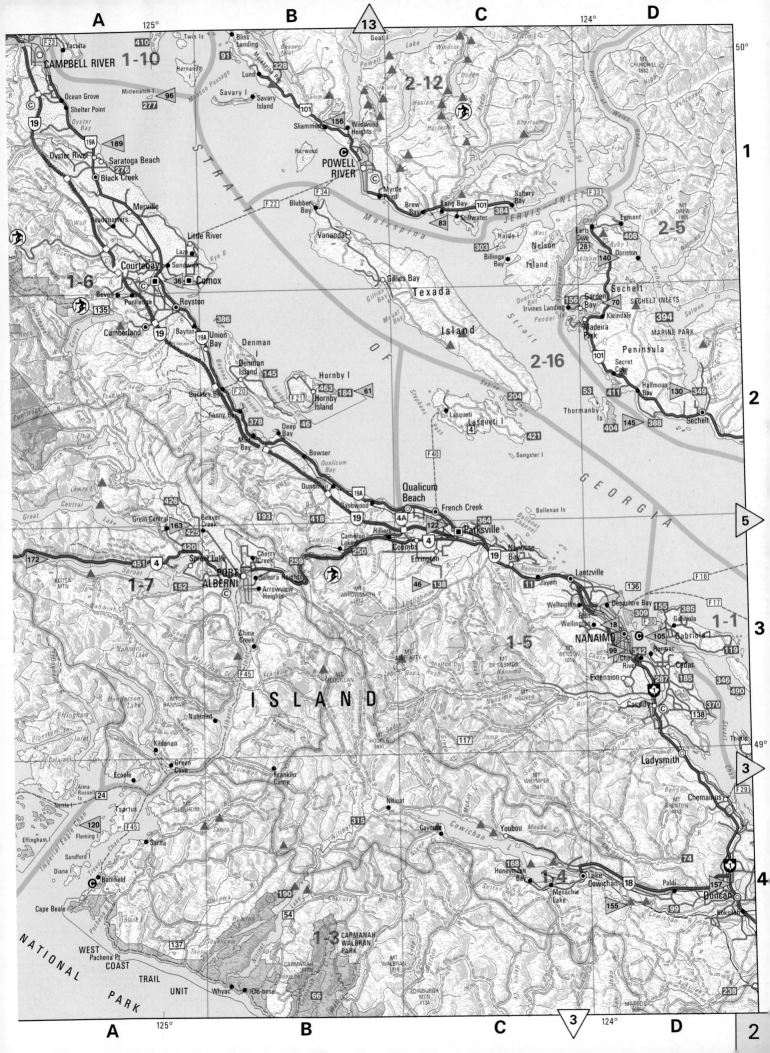

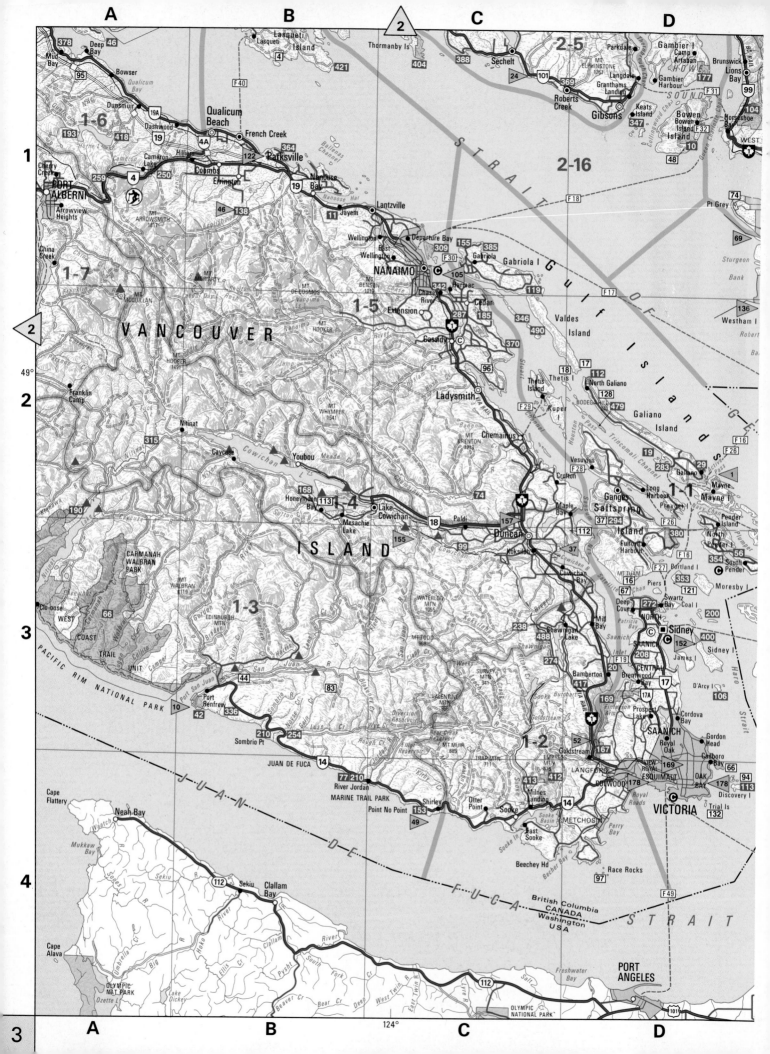

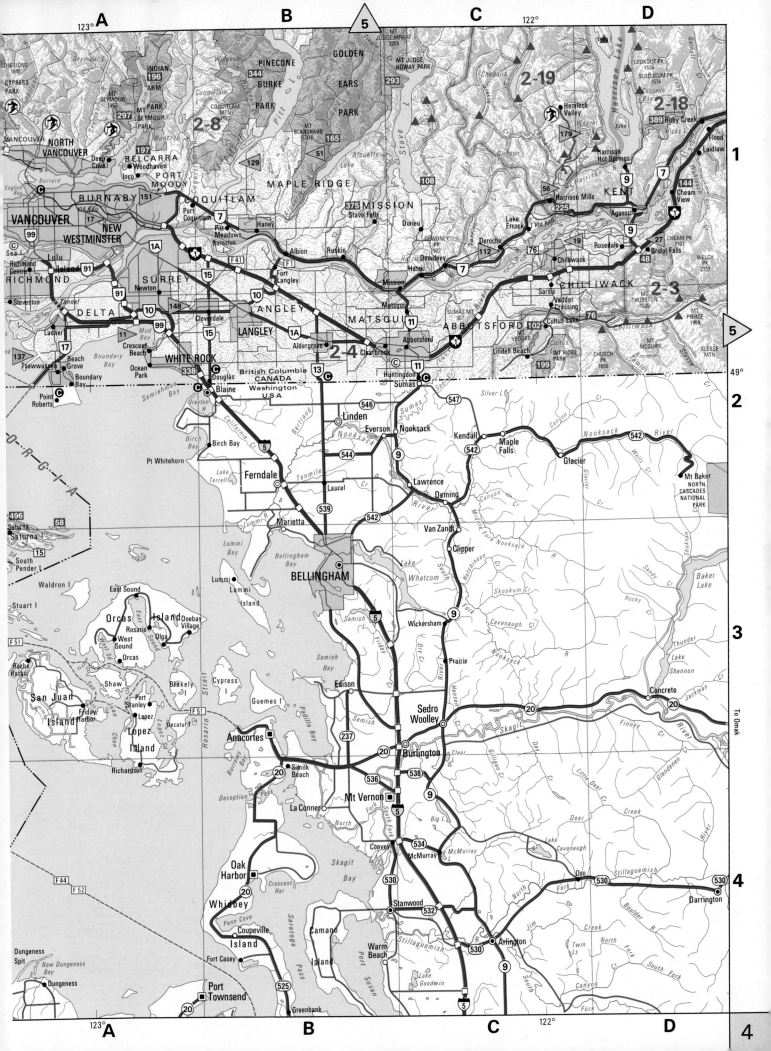

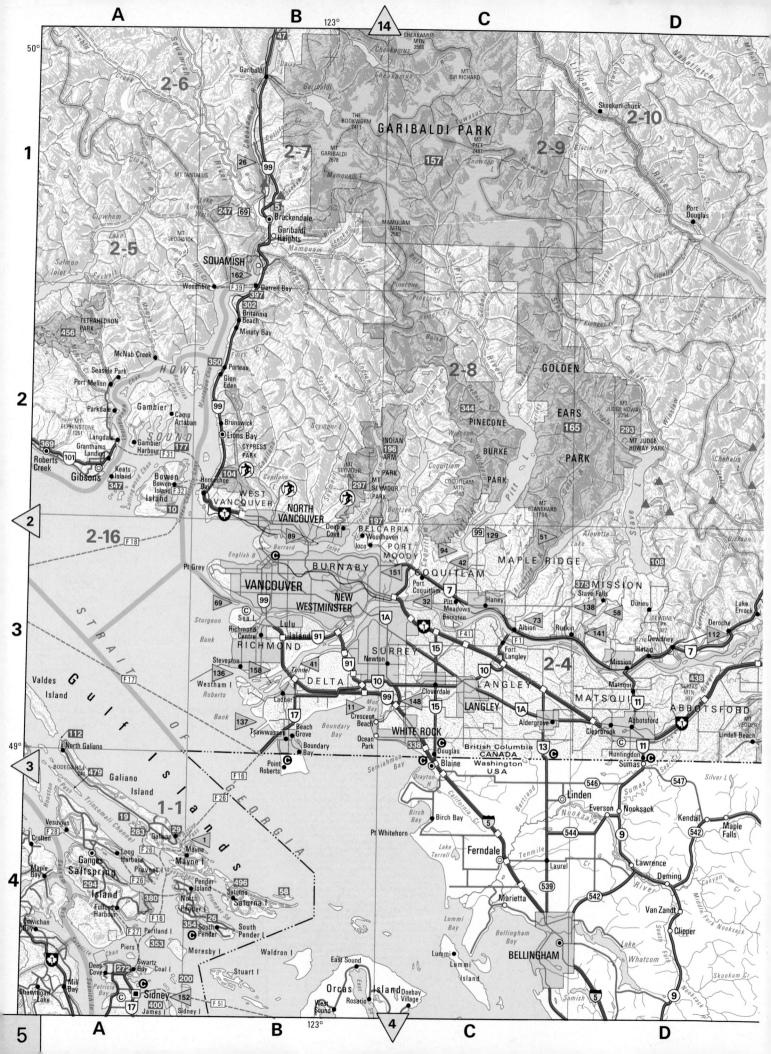

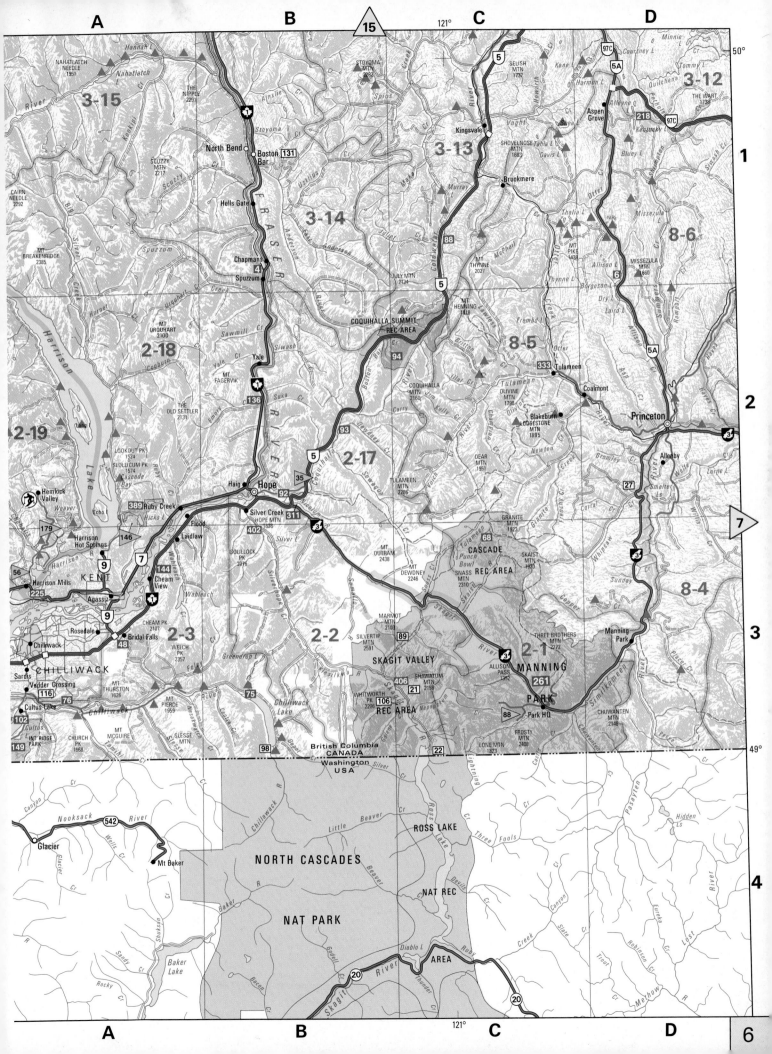

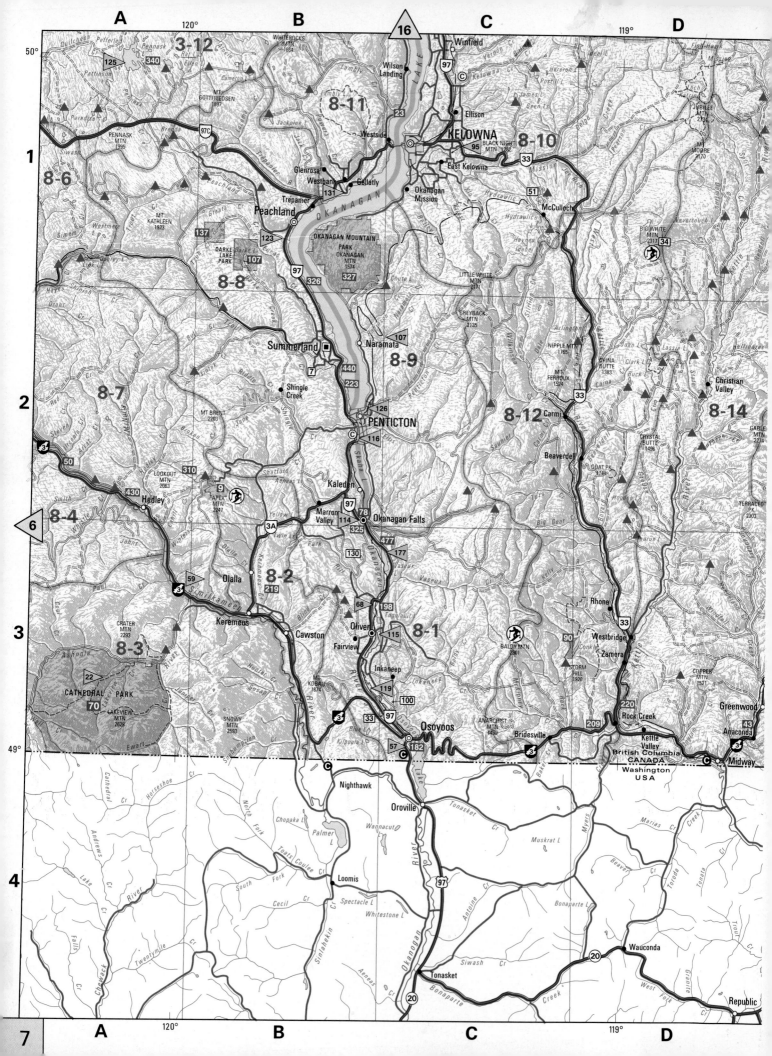

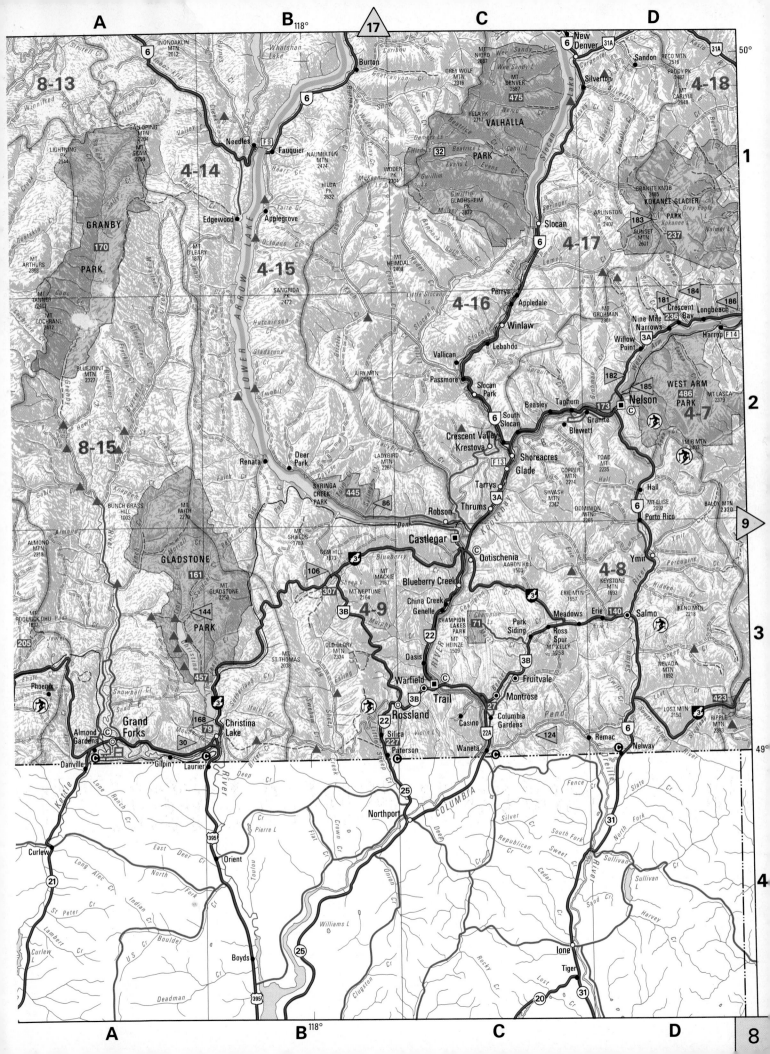

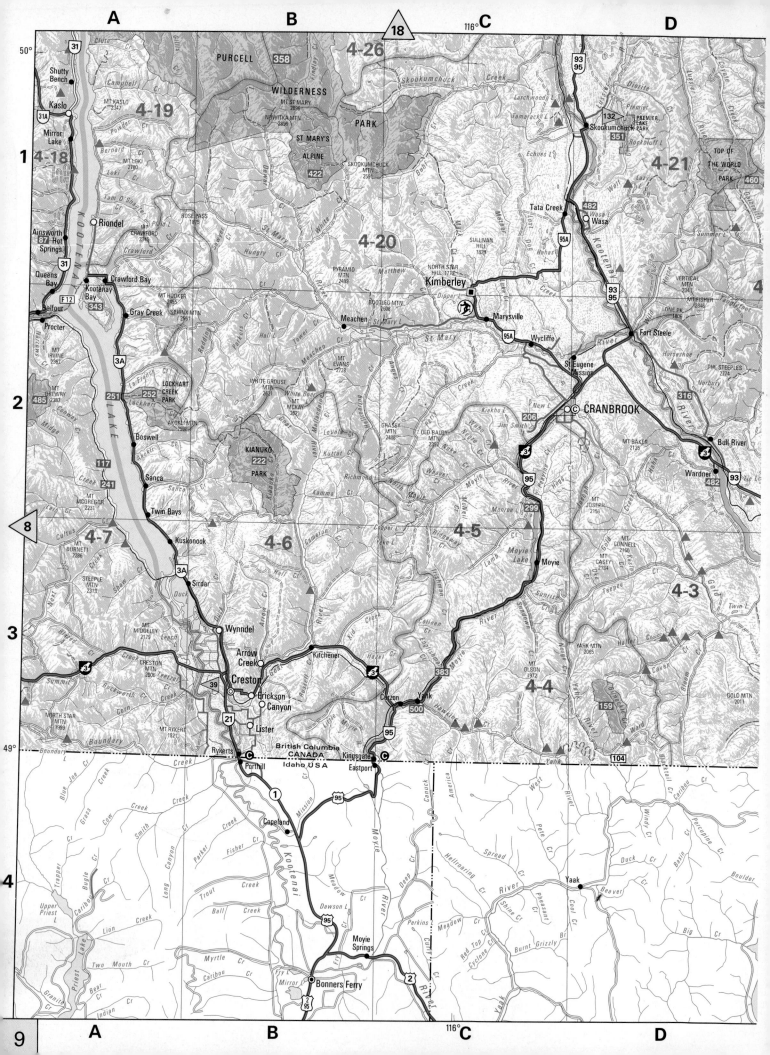

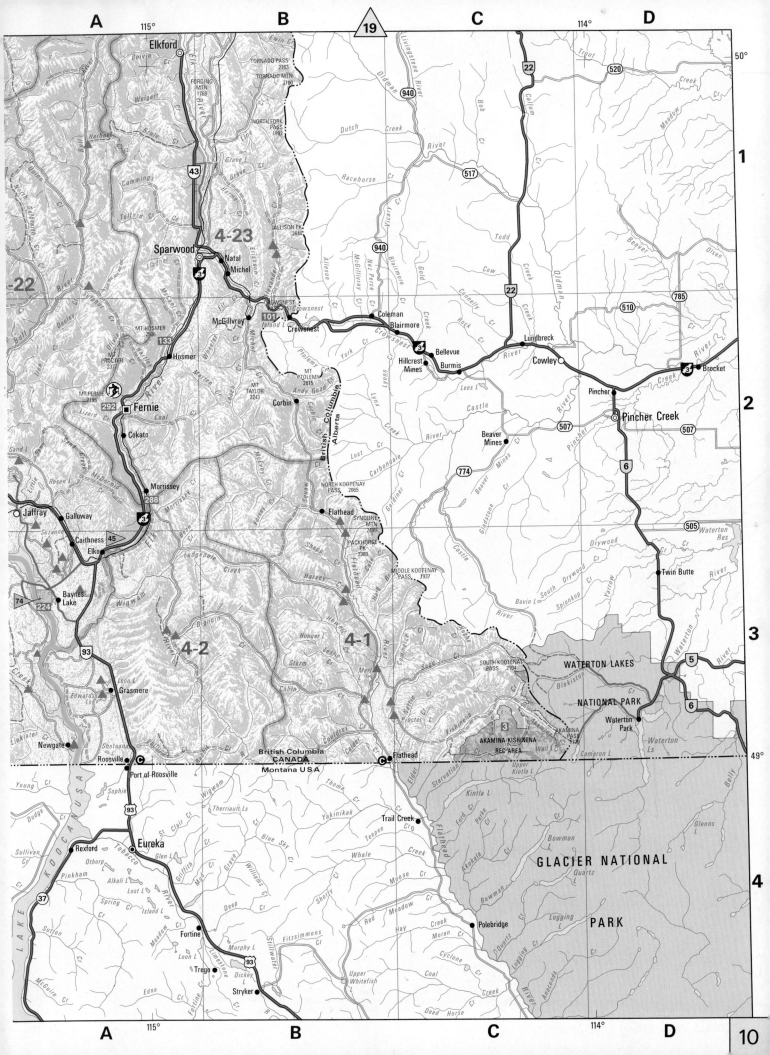

PURCELL WILDERNESS CONSERVANCY

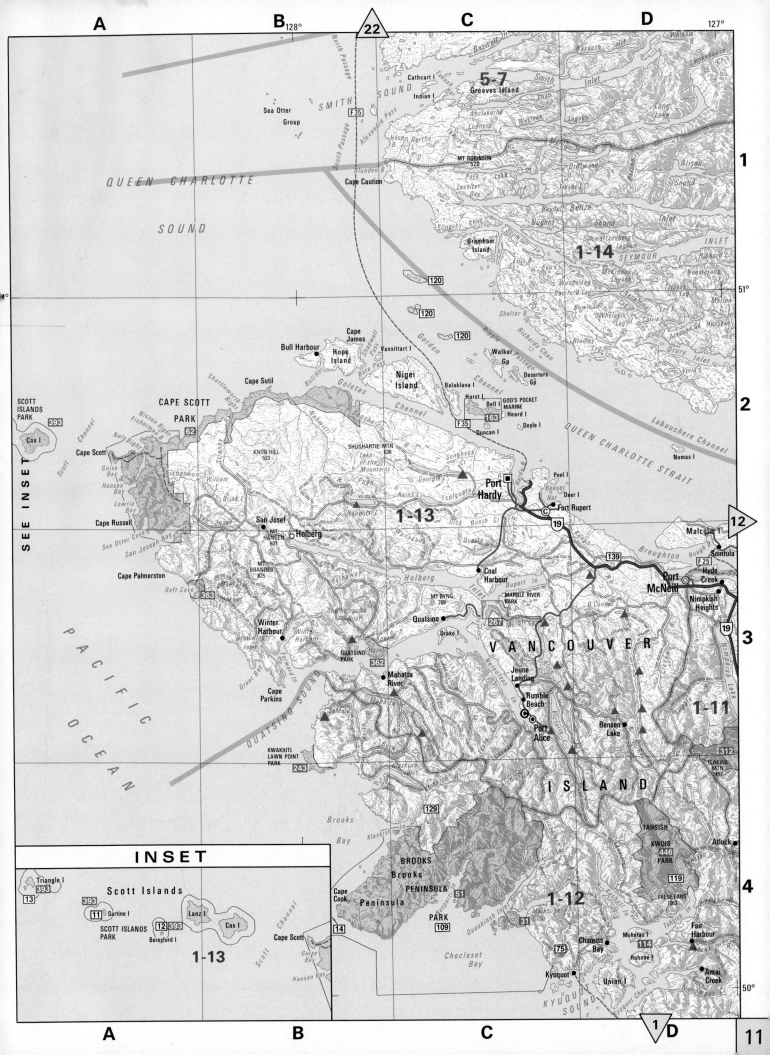

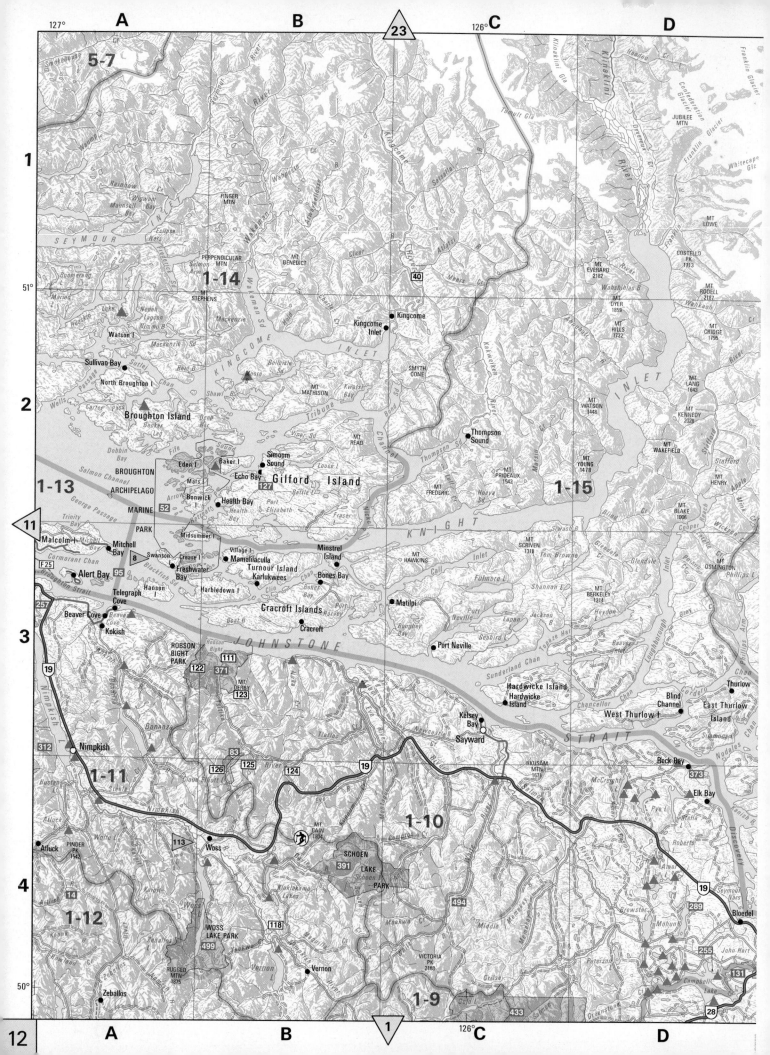

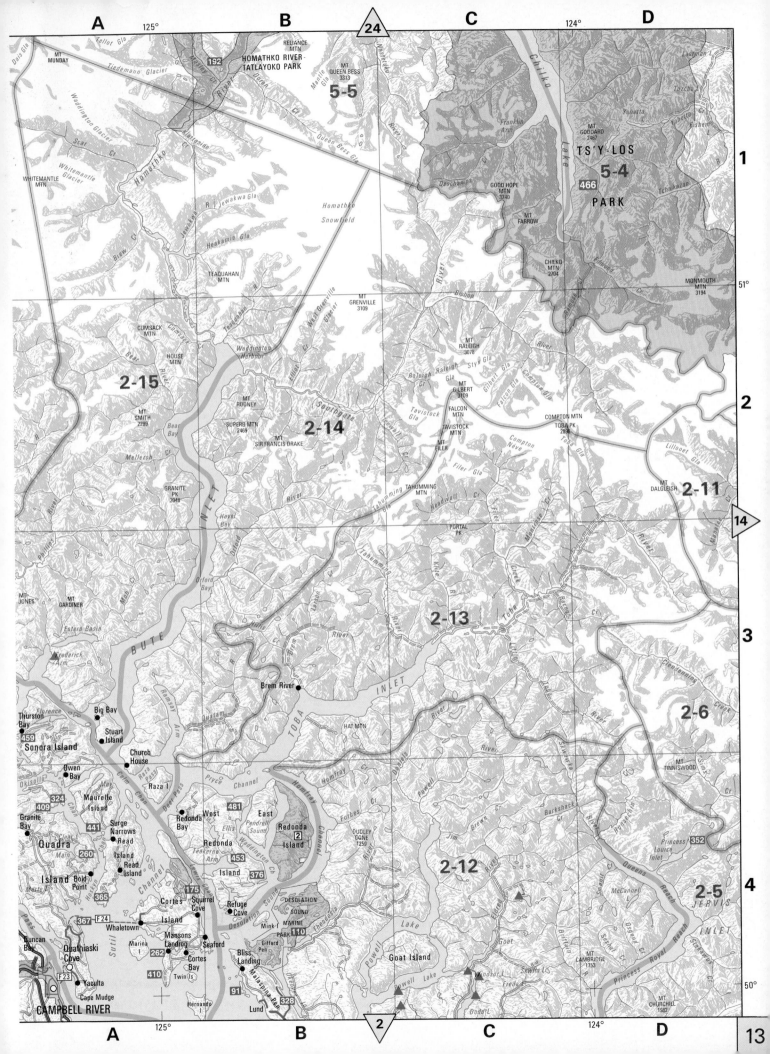

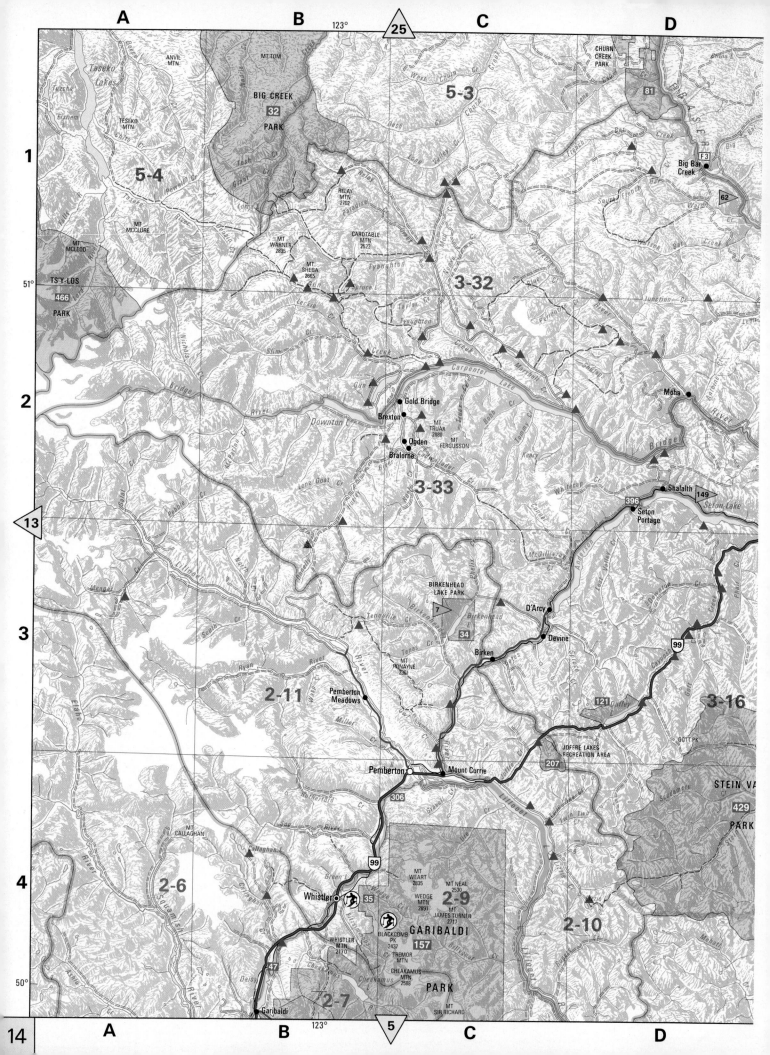

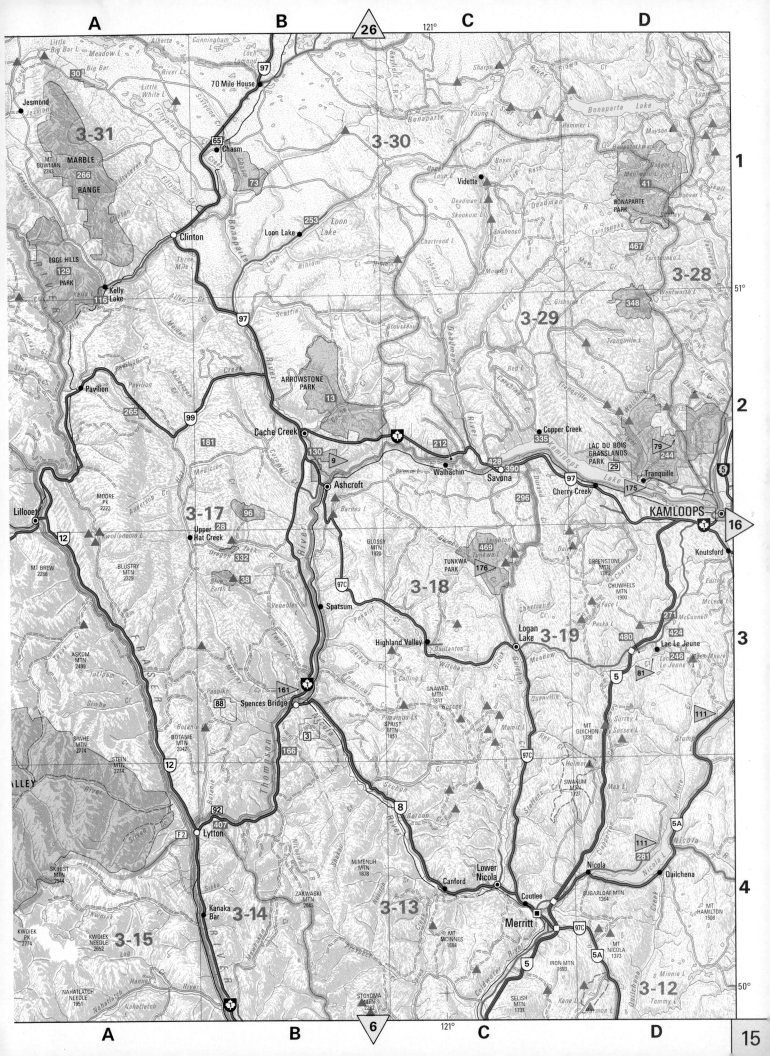

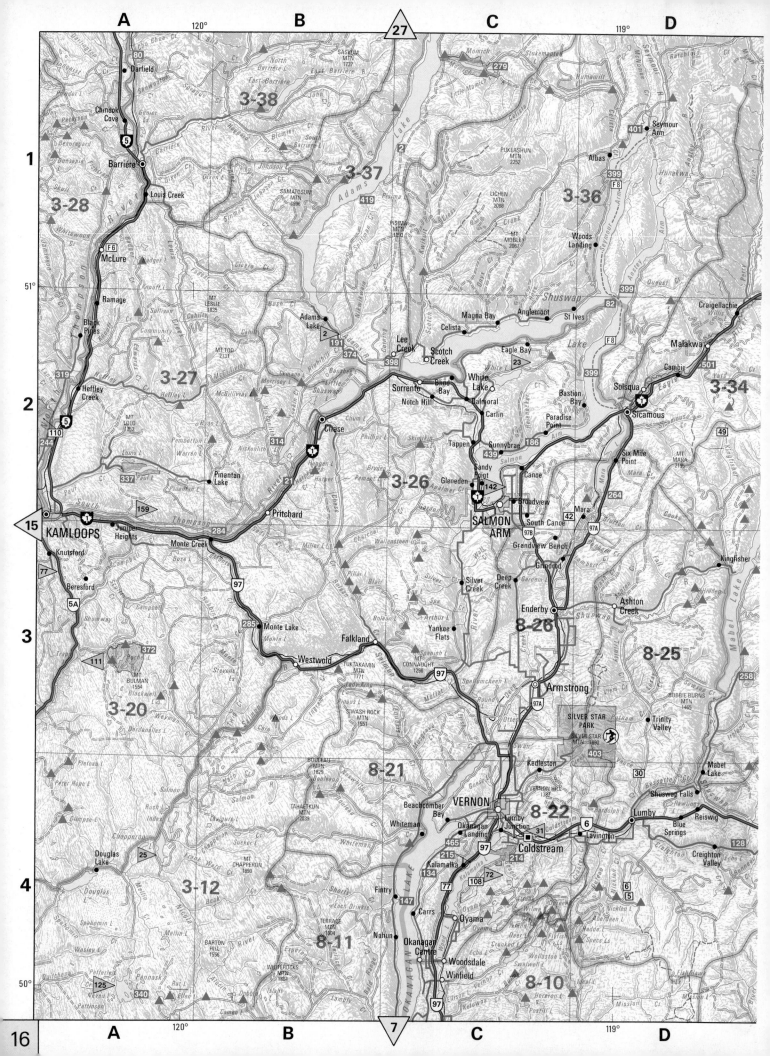

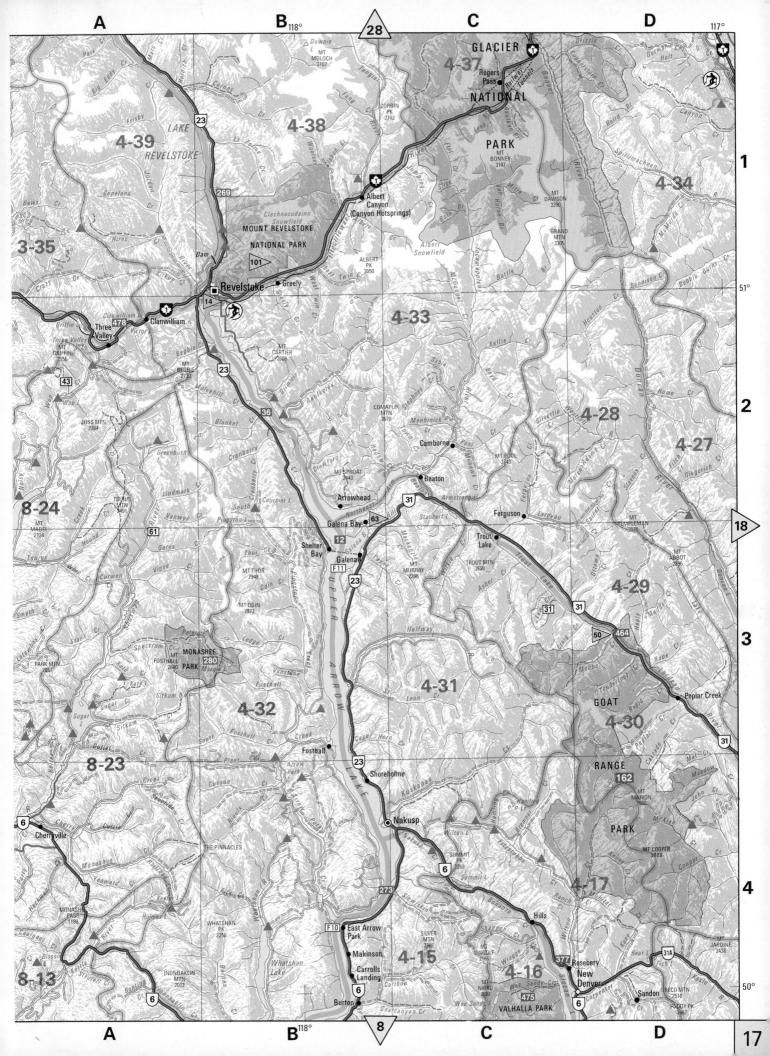

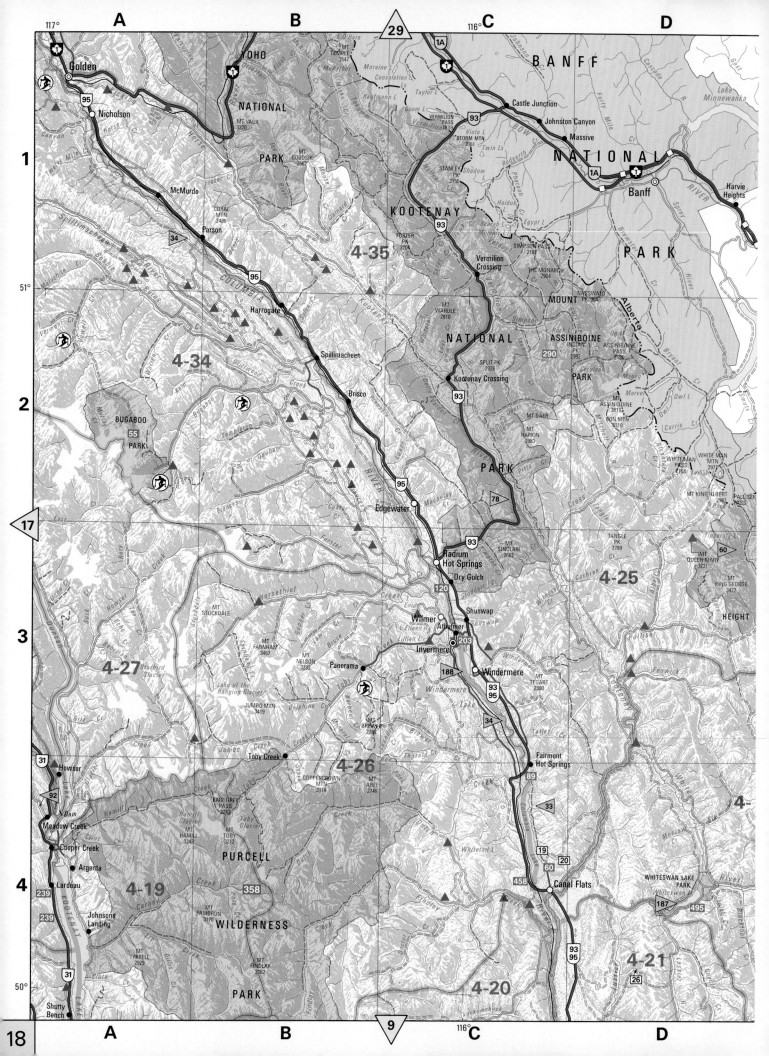

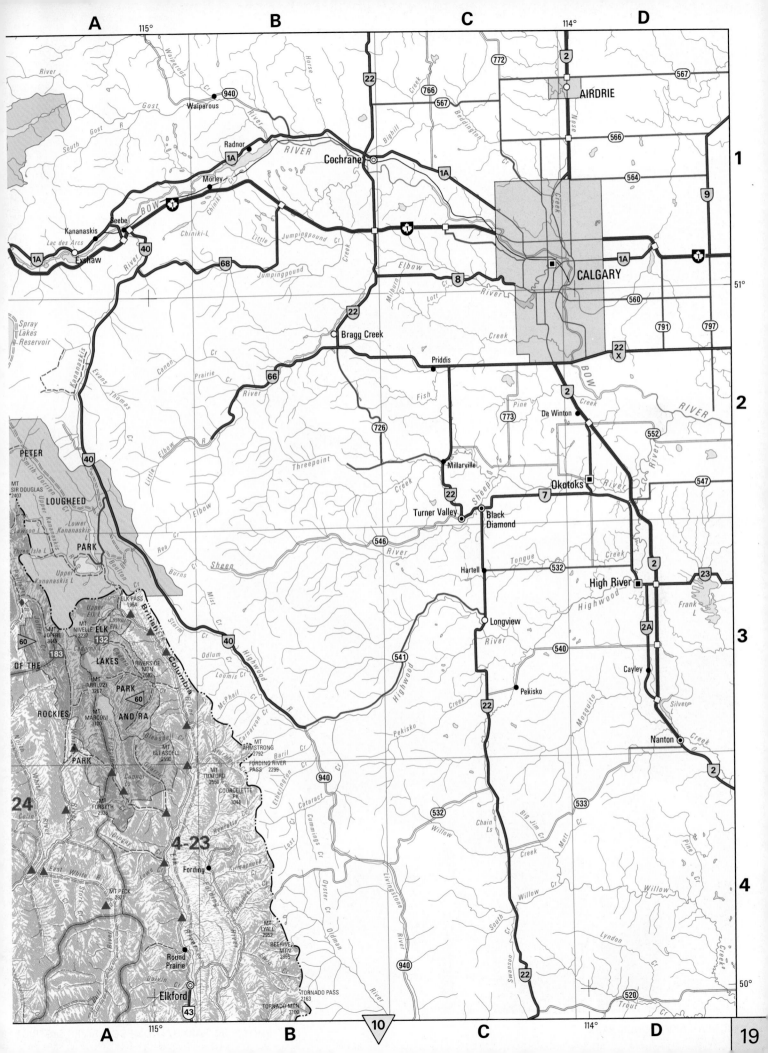

NICOLA LAKE/MONCK PARK

PHOTO: BC PARKS/THOMPSON RIVER DISTRICT

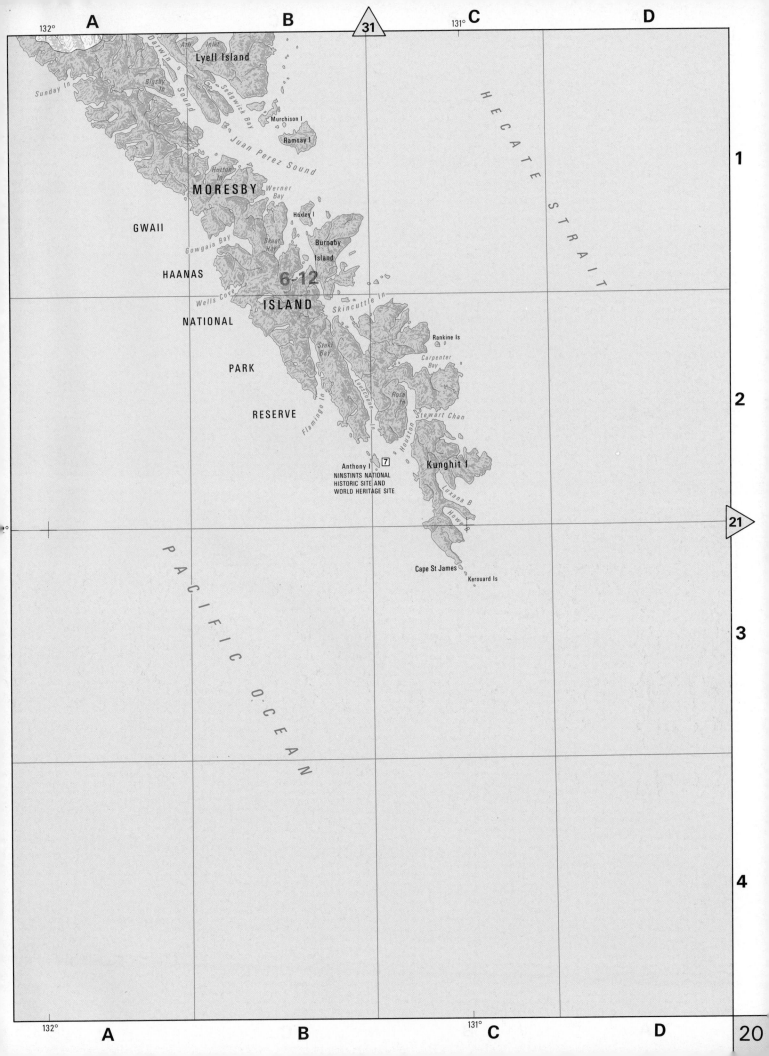

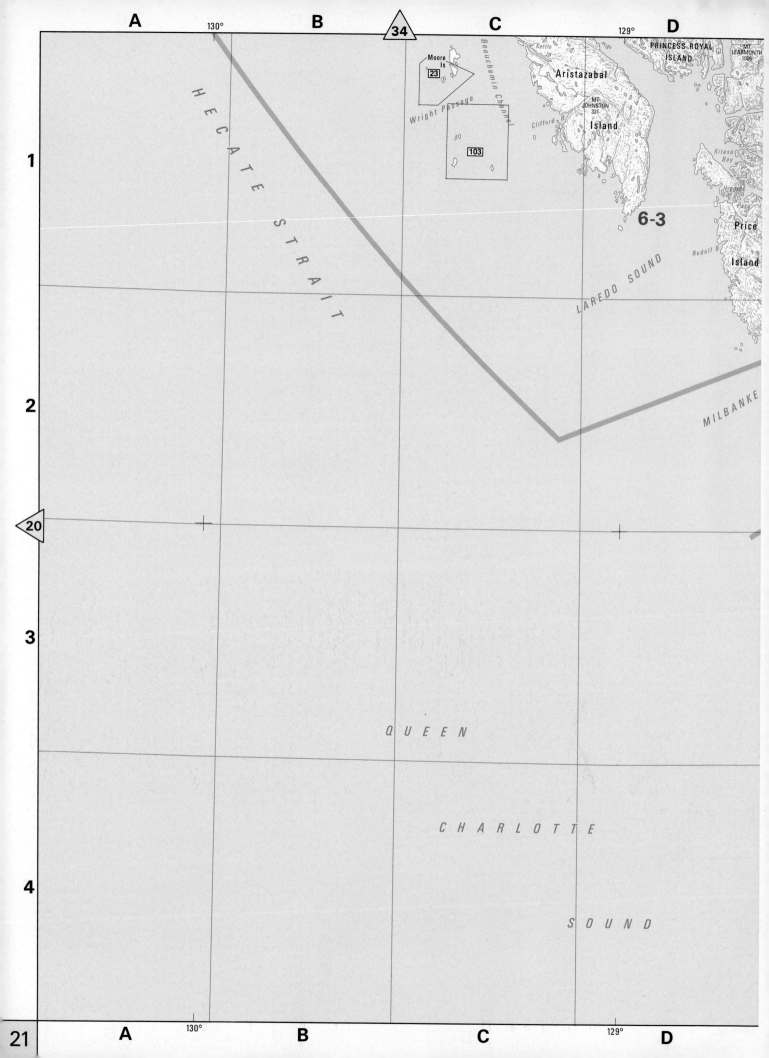

A   130°   B   △34   C   129°   D

PRINCESS ROYAL
ISLAND

MT
LEARMONTH
1006

Kettle In

Aristazabal

Moore
Is
23

Beauchemin Channel

Wright Passage

Clifford B

MT
JOHNSTON
331

Island

Kitasu
Bay

103

6-3

Price

Island

HECATE STRAIT

LAREDO SOUND

Rudolf B

Fass

MILBANKE

△20

1

2

QUEEN

3

CHARLOTTE

4

SOUND

21   A   130°   B   C   129°   D

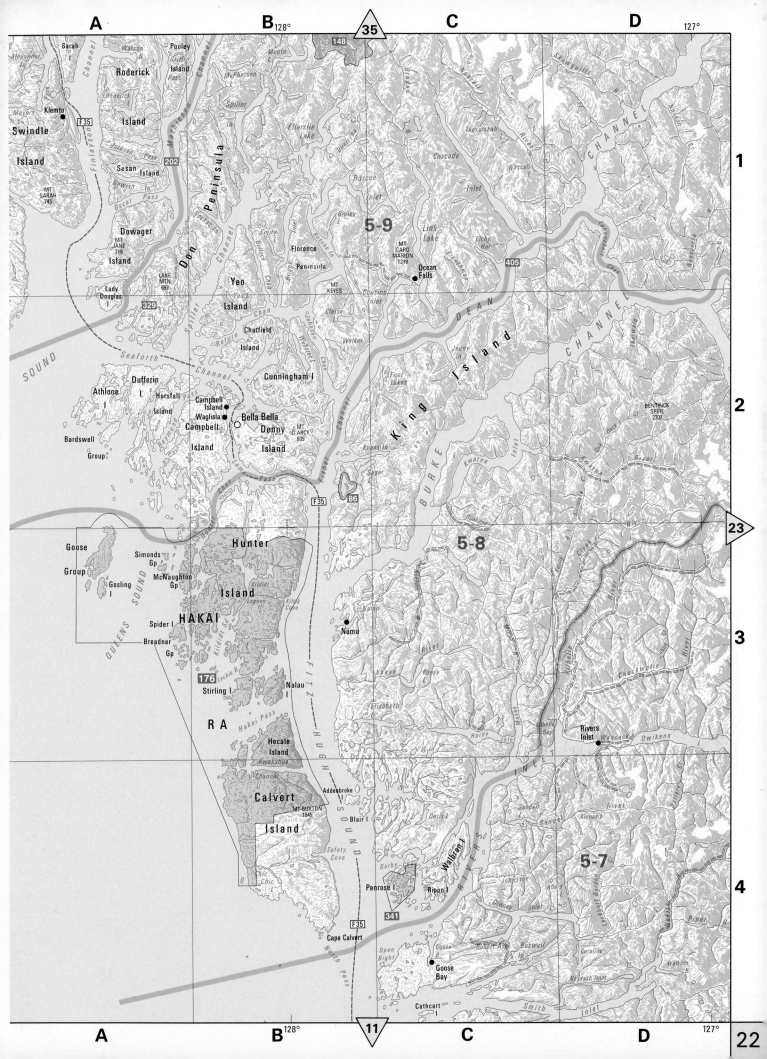

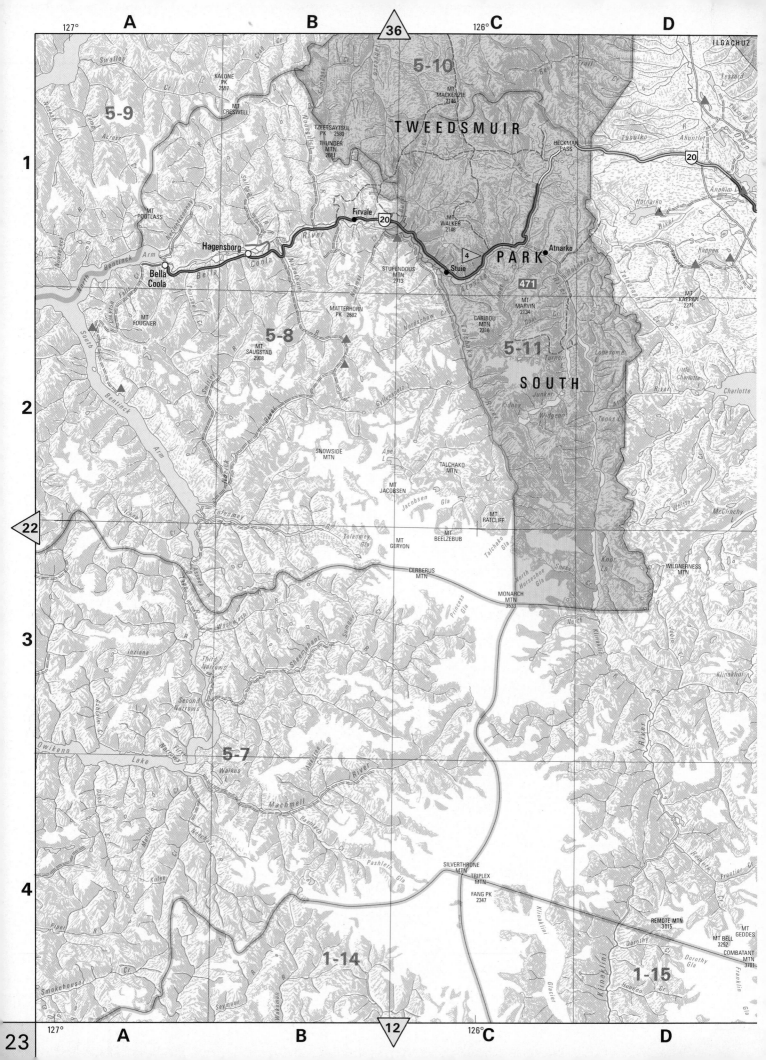

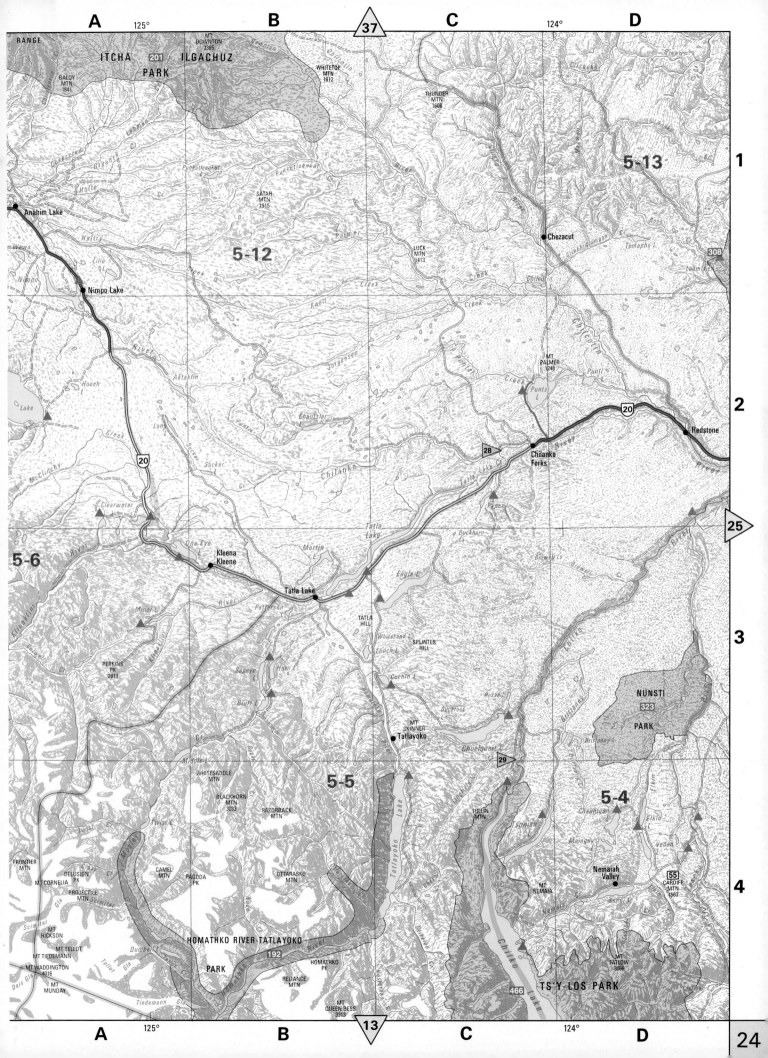

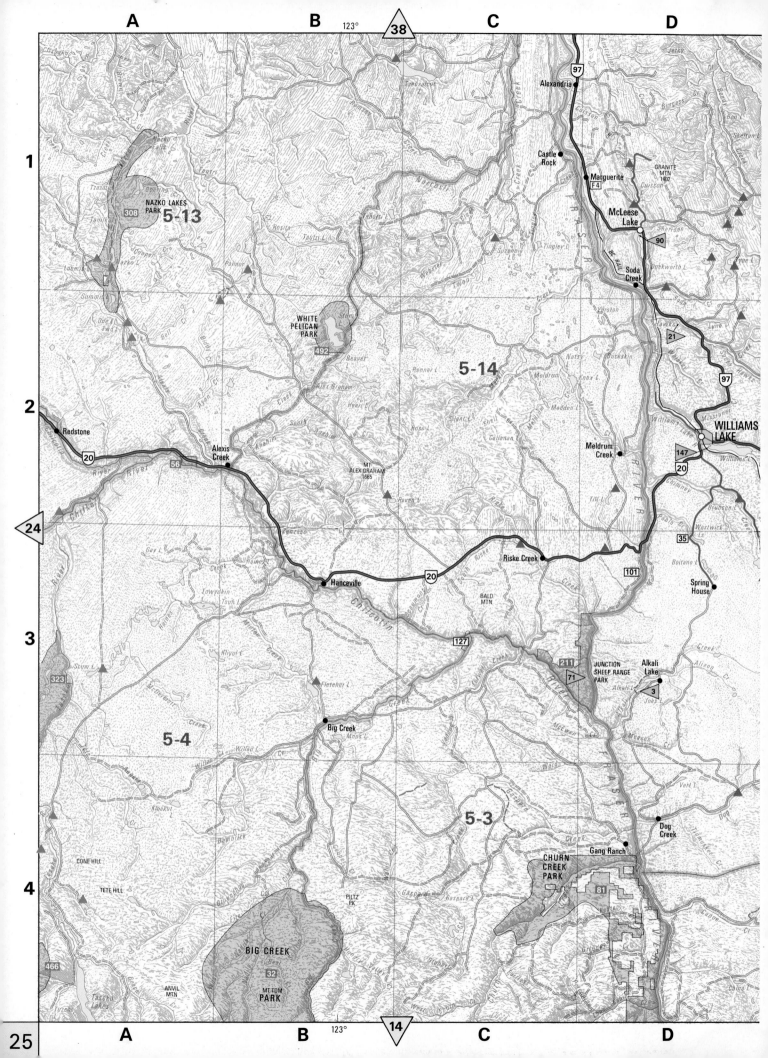

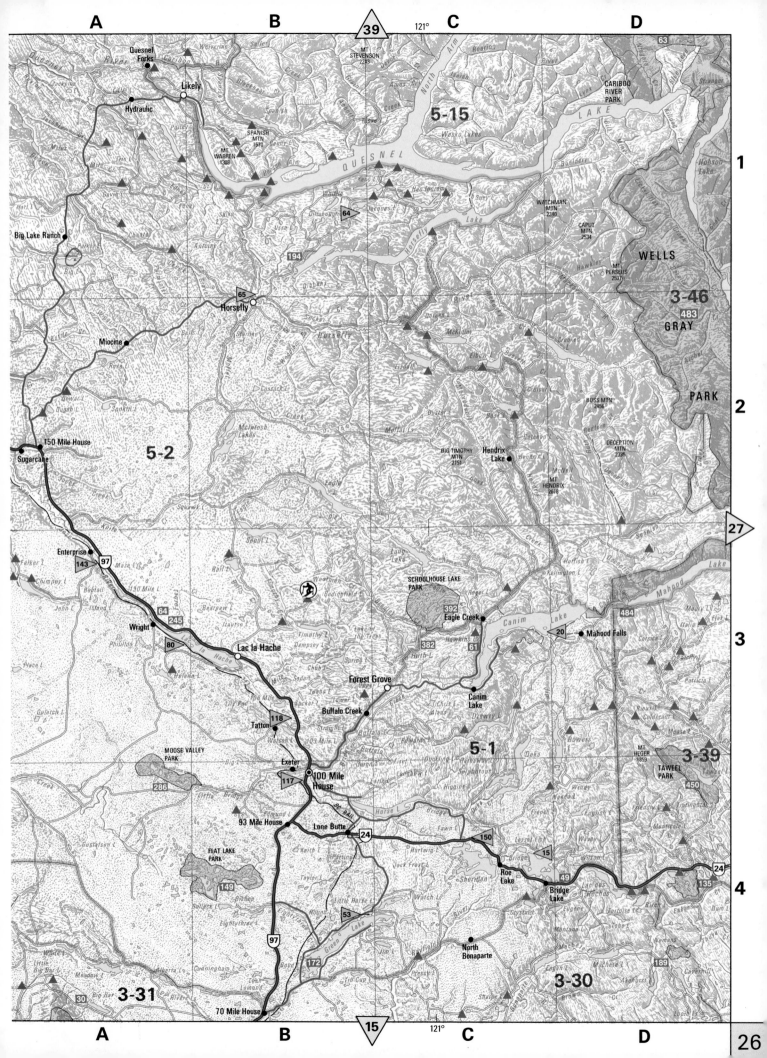

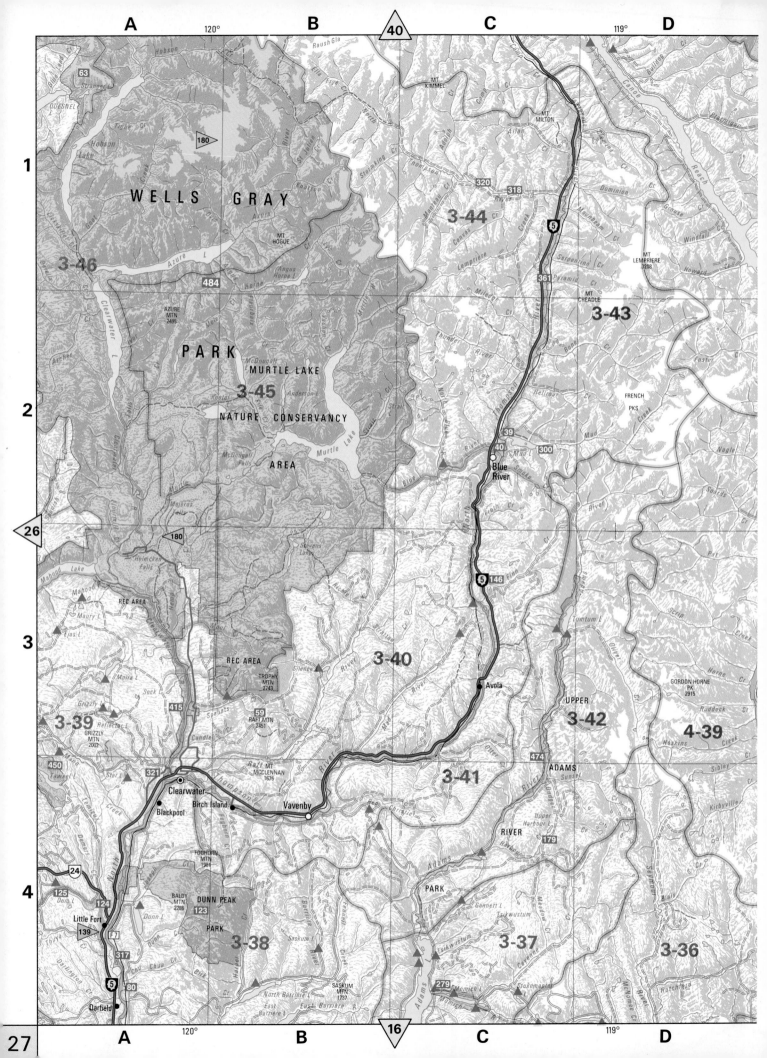

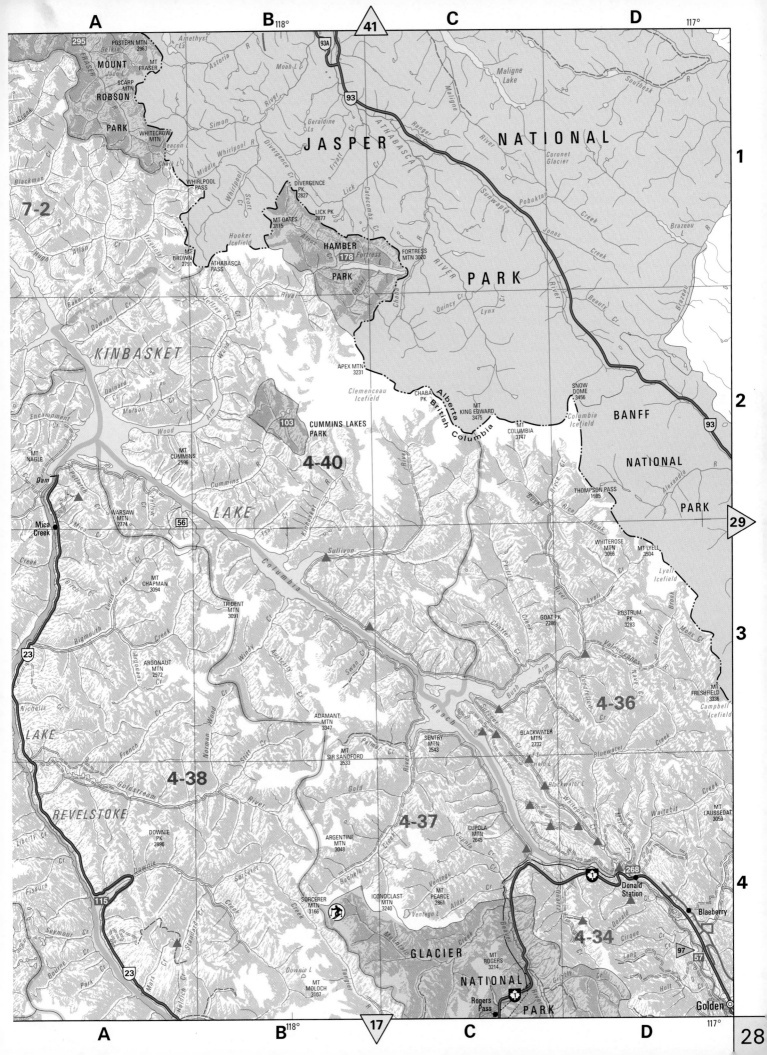

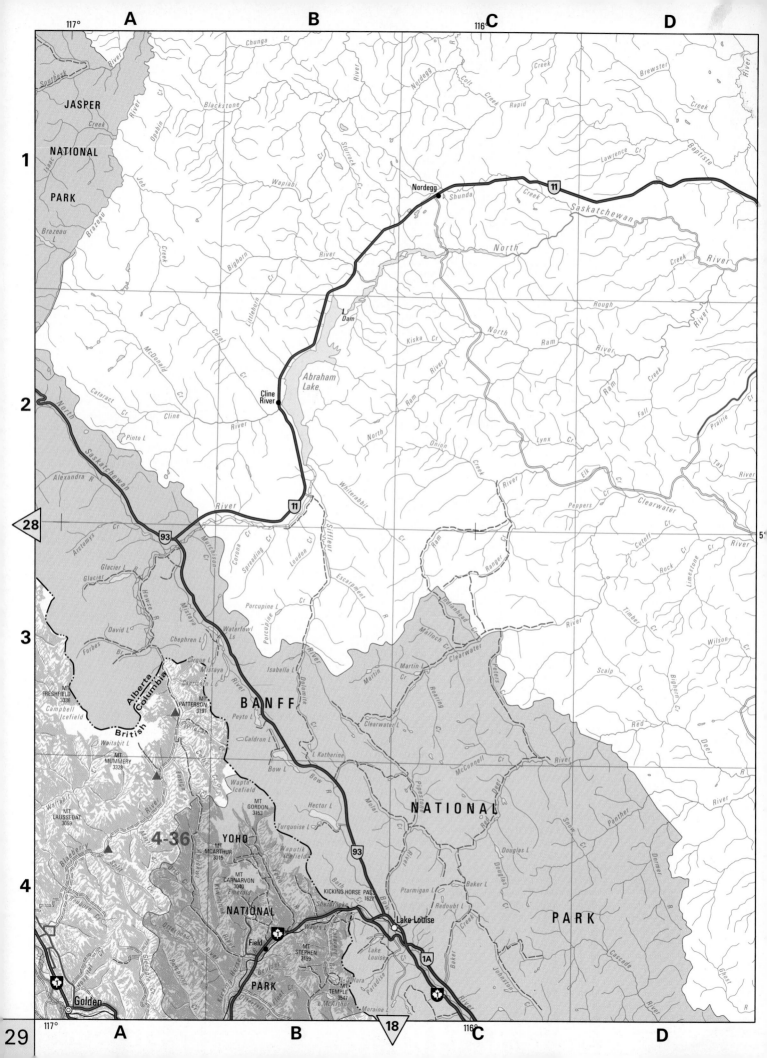

MURTLE LAKE/WELLS GRAY PARK

PHOTO: BC PARKS/THOMPSON RIVER DISTRICT

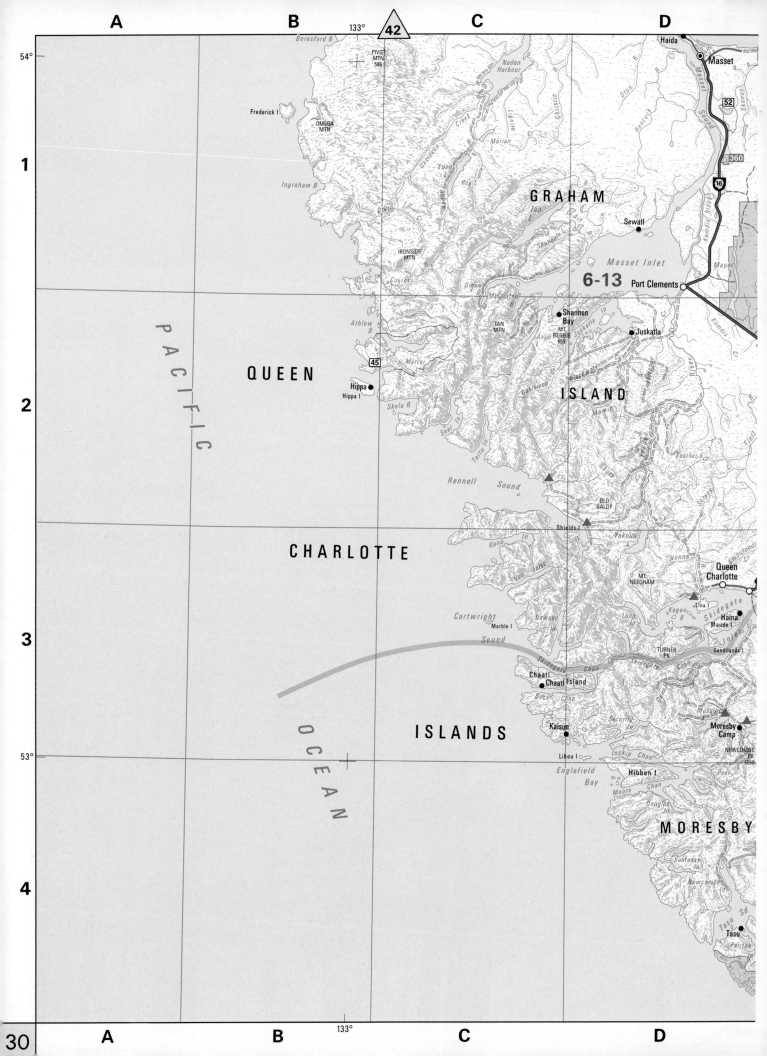

A   B   133°   C   D

54°

GRAHAM

Haida
Masset

52

360

16

1

Beresford B

PIVOT
MTN
586

Frederick I

OMEGA
MTN

Ingraham B

Naden
Harbour

Creek

Eden

Royl L

Ian
L

IRONSIDE
MTN

Coates

Dinan B

McClinton
B

PACIFIC

QUEEN

Athlow
B

TAN
MTN

MT
BEGBIE
659

Mercer

45

Hippa
Hippa I

Skelu B

Seal In

Tartu In

Oatswen

Sewall

Masset Inlet

6-13   Port Clements

Shannon
Bay

Juskatla

ISLAND

2

CHARLOTTE

Rennell   Sound

OLD
BALDY

Shields I

Kano
In

Von
Inlet

Cartwright

Marble I

Sound

Chaatl
Chaatl Island

Skidegate

Boat

Kaisun

Lihou I

Englefield
Bay

Hibben I

Moore
Chan

MT
NEEDHAM

Dawson
In

Skidegate   Chan

TURNER
PK

Yakoun

Honna

Lina I

Kagan
B

Lonq
In

Security
In

Inskip Chan

Douglas
In

Queen
Charlotte

Haina
Maude I

Sandilands I

Moresby
Camp

NEWCOMBE
PK
1050

MORESBY

3

ISLANDS

OCEAN

53°

Kootenay
In

Newcombe

Tasu Sd

Tasu

Fairfax

4

A   B   133°   C   D

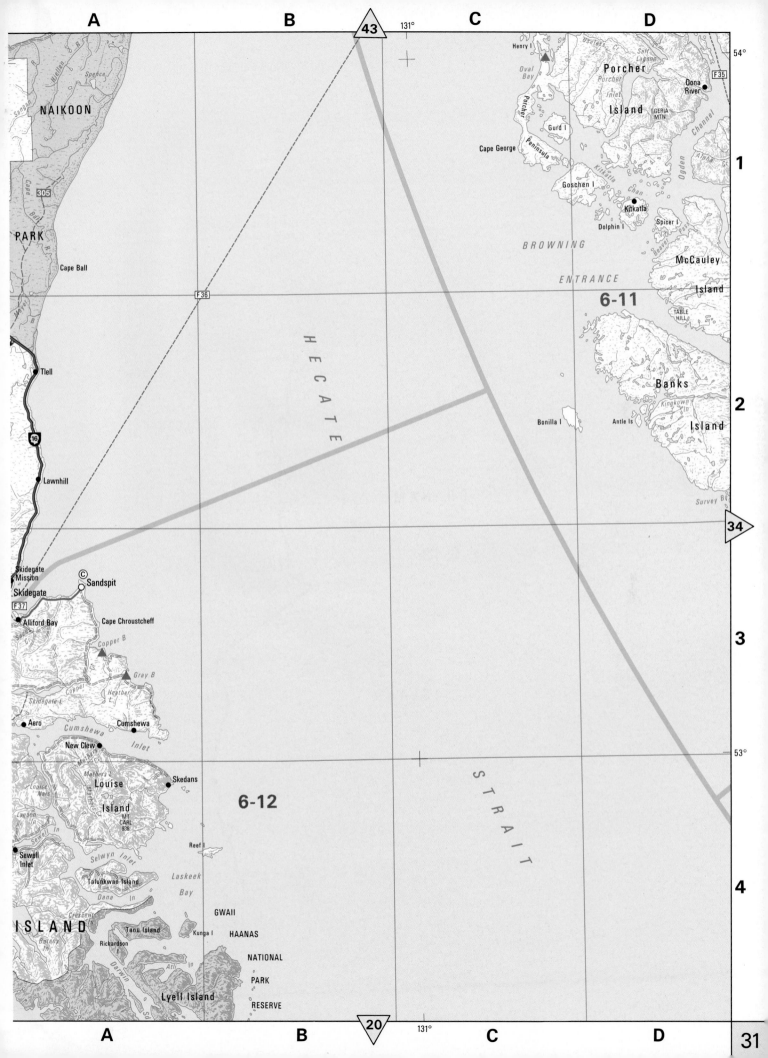

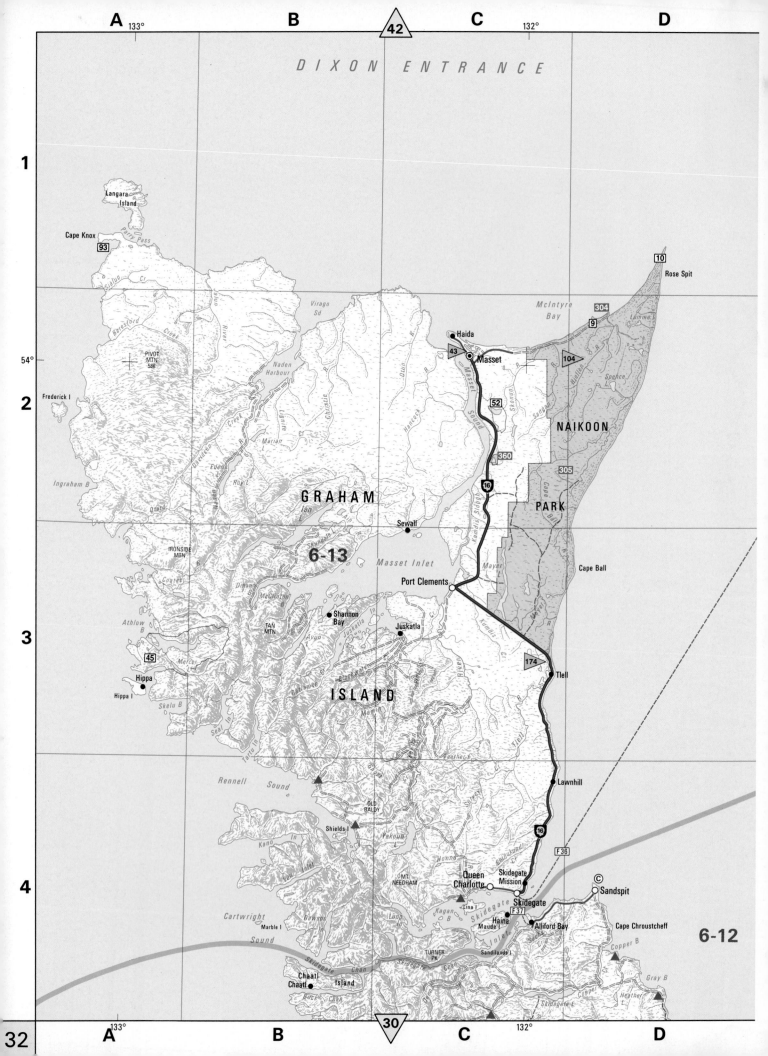

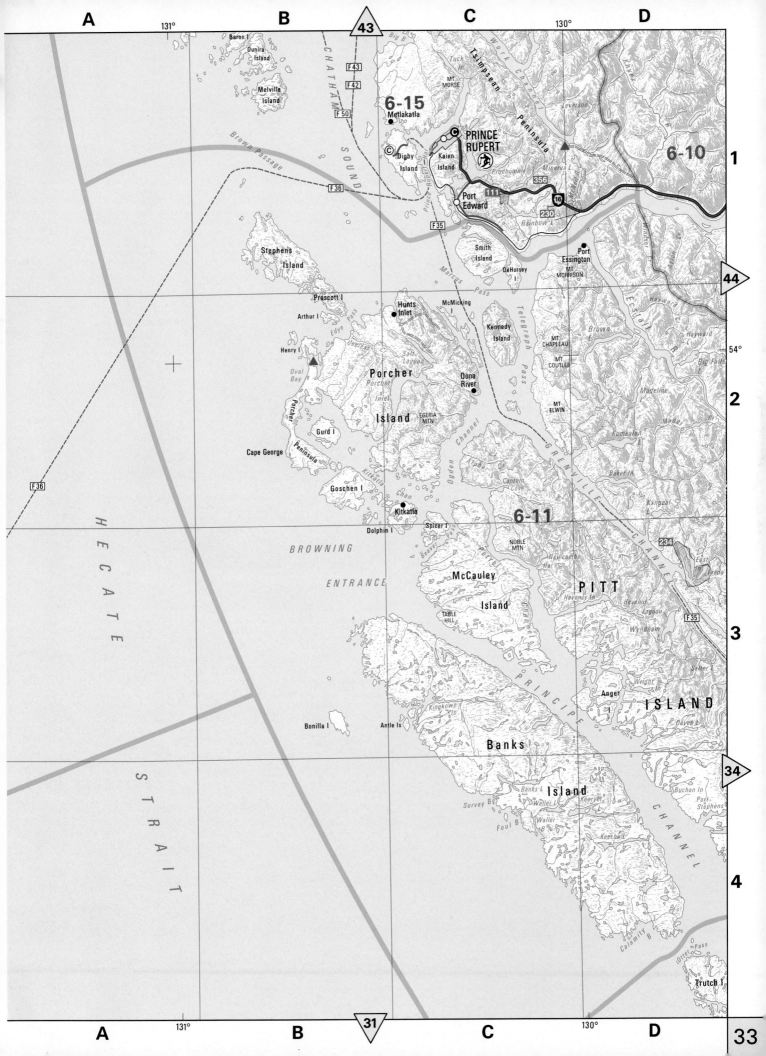

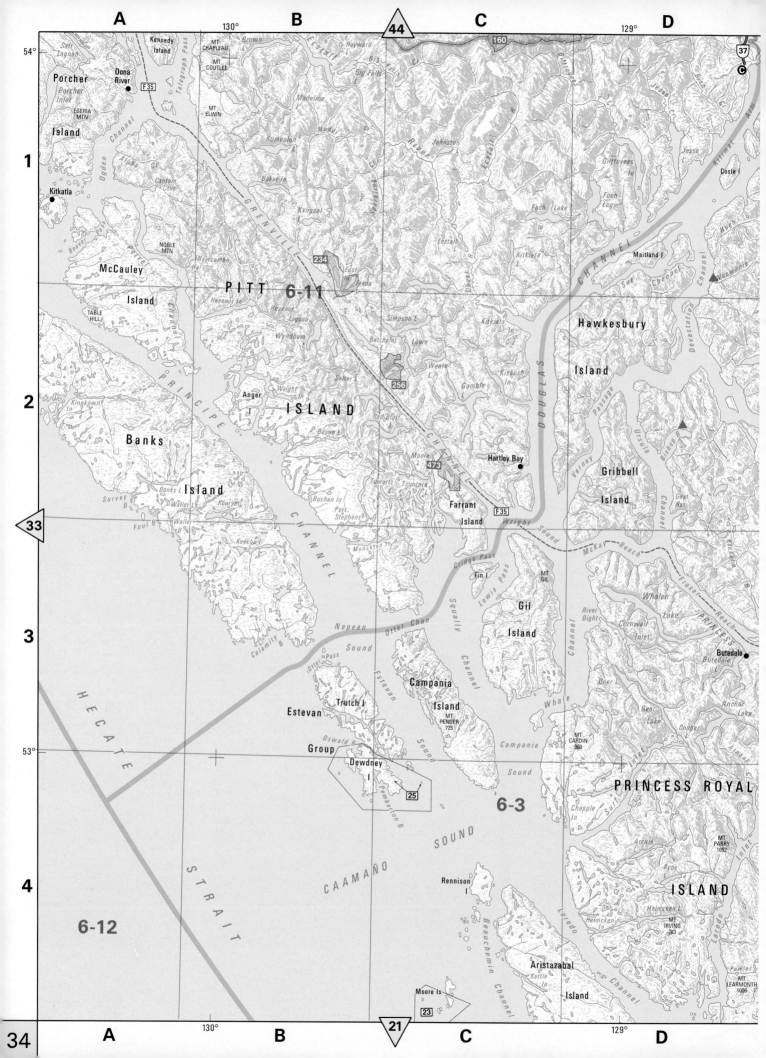

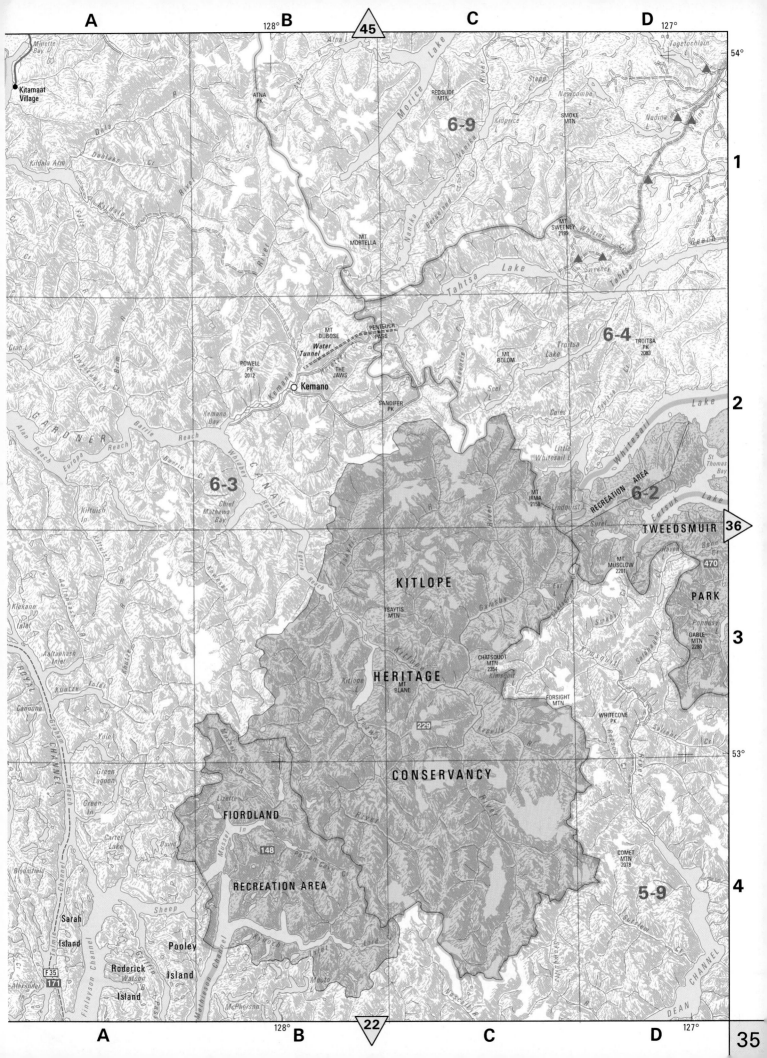

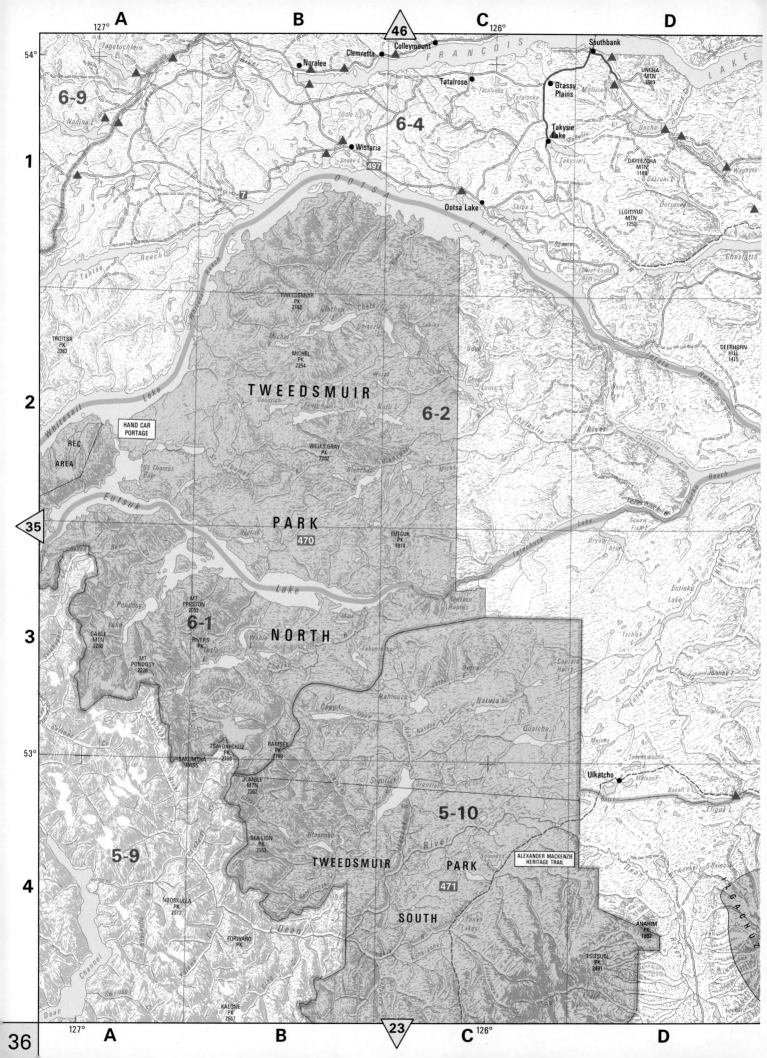

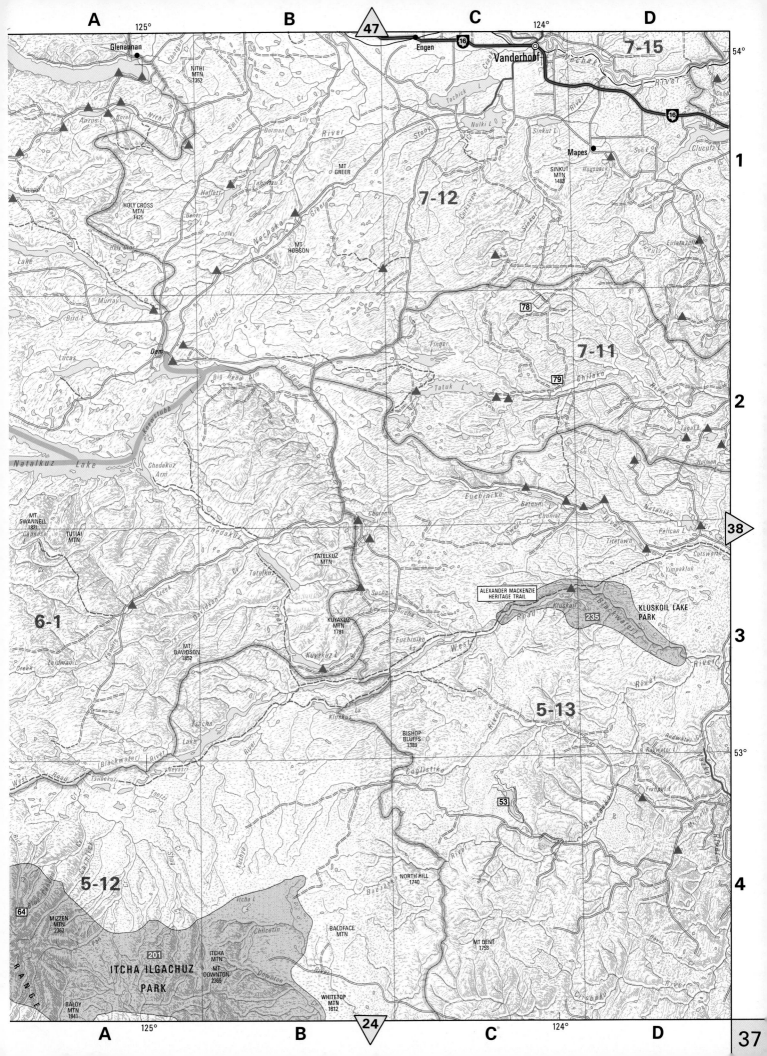

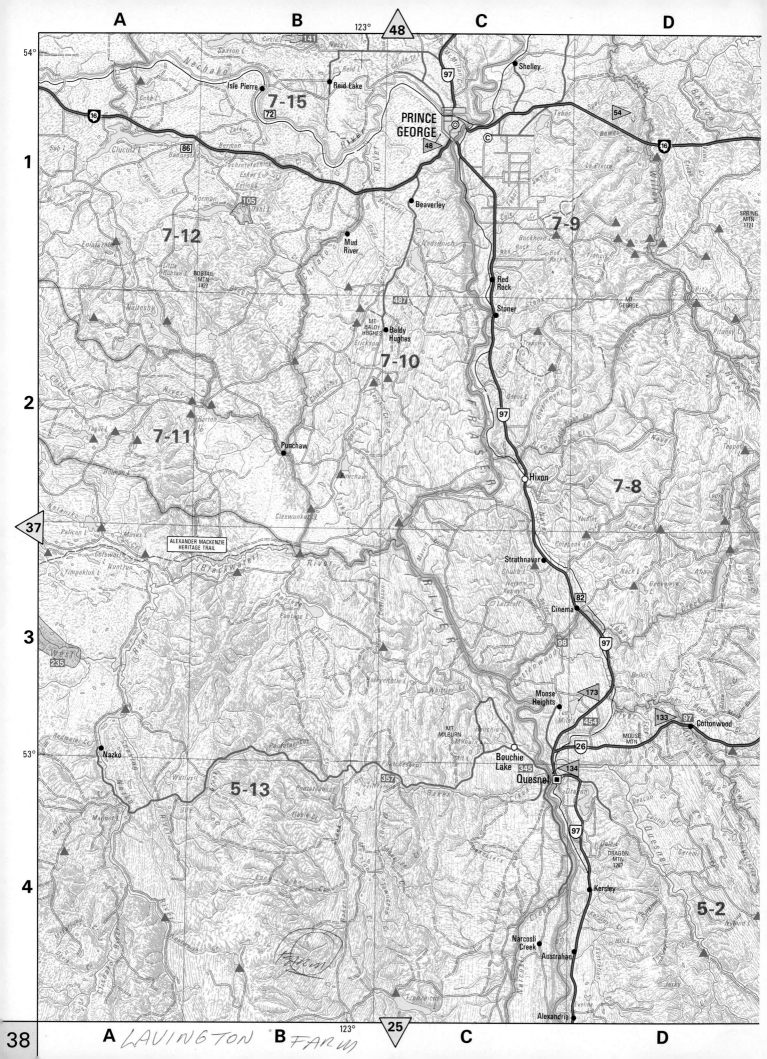

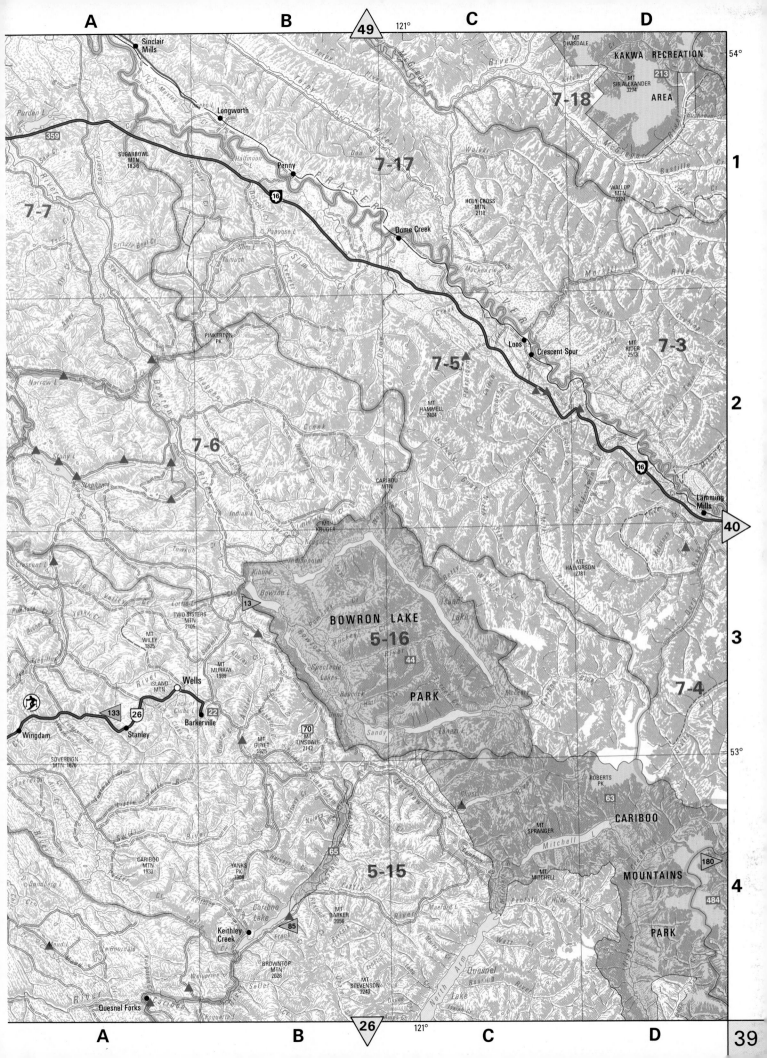

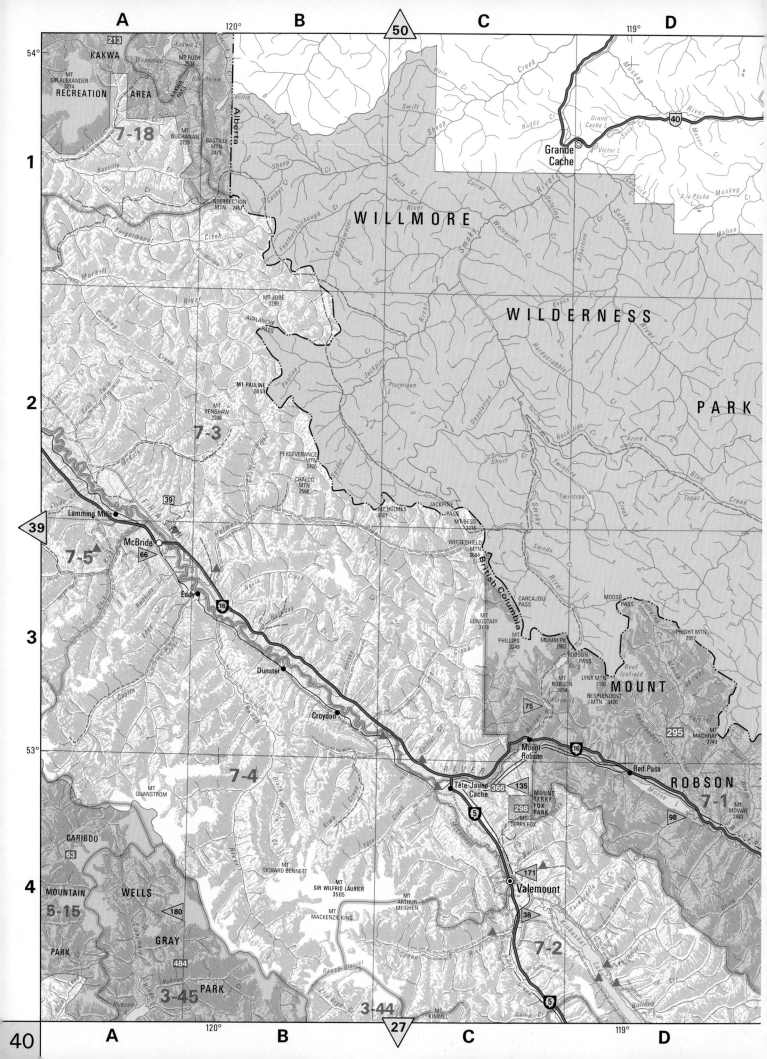

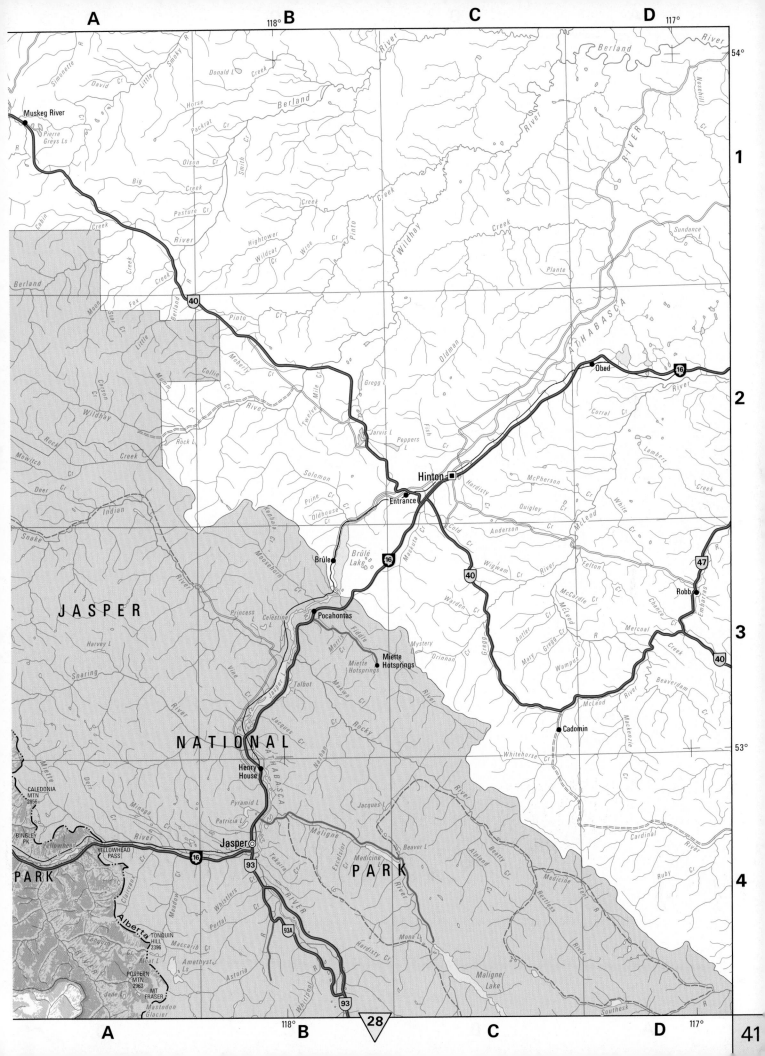

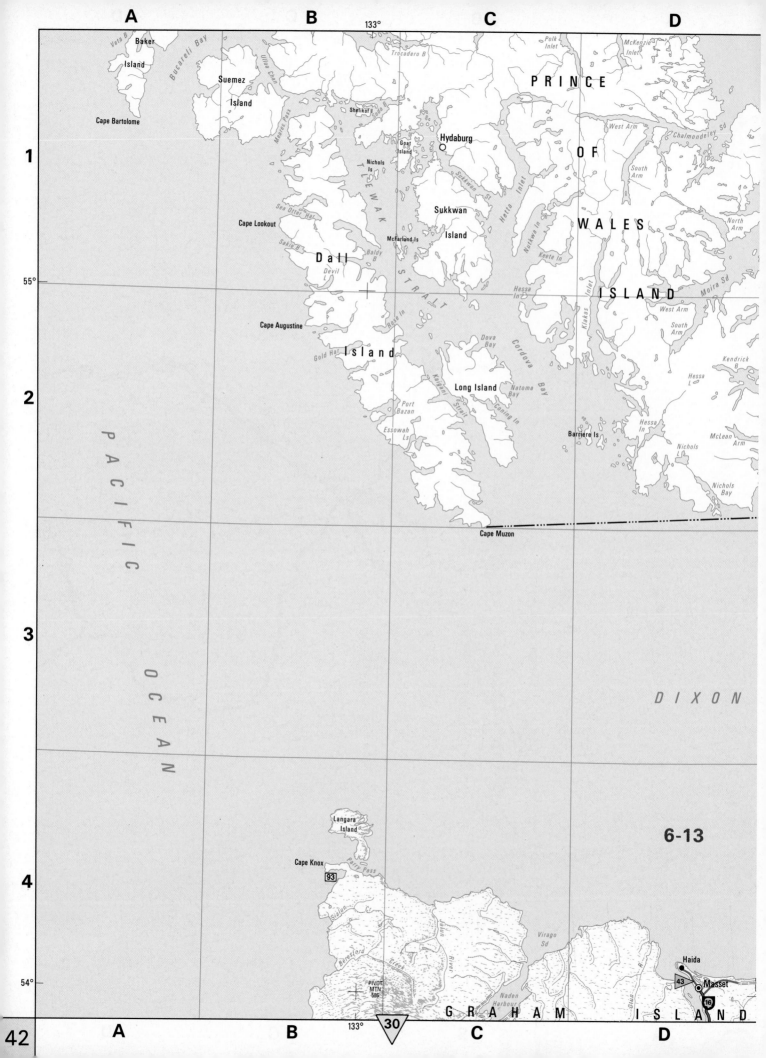

Veta B
Baker
Island
Bucareli Bay
Ulloa Chan
Polk Inlet
Trocadero B
McKenzie Inlet

Cape Bartolome
Suemez
Island

P R I N C E

Shelikof I
Soda B

Cape Lookout

West Arm
Chalmondeley Sd

O F

Goat
Island
Hydaburg

Nichols
Is

W A L E S

Sea Otter Har

Sukkwan
Island

South
Arm

T L E W A K

Sukkwan St

Hetta Inlet

Dall

McFarland Is

Nutkwa In

North
Arm

Sakie B

Baldy
B

Keete In

I S L A N D

Moira Sd

Devil
L

Cape Augustine

Rose In

S T R A I T

Hessa
In

Klakas Inlet

West Arm

South
Arm

Kendrick
B

Island

Gold Har

Dova
Bay

Hessa
L

Long Island

Natoma
Bay

Cordova Bay

Hessa
In

McLean
Arm

Port
Bazan

Kaigani Strait

Coning In

Barriere Is

Nichols
L

Essowah
Ls

Nichols
Bay

Cape Muzon

P A C I F I C

D I X O N

O C E A N

Langara
Island

6-13

Cape Knox

93

Patty Pass

Virago
Sd

Haida

Sialun Cr

Kalun River

Naden R

43

Masset

Beresford

 Datlar Creek

Naden Harbour

16

PIVOT
MTN
586

G R A H A M   I S L A N D

55°
54°
1
2
3
4

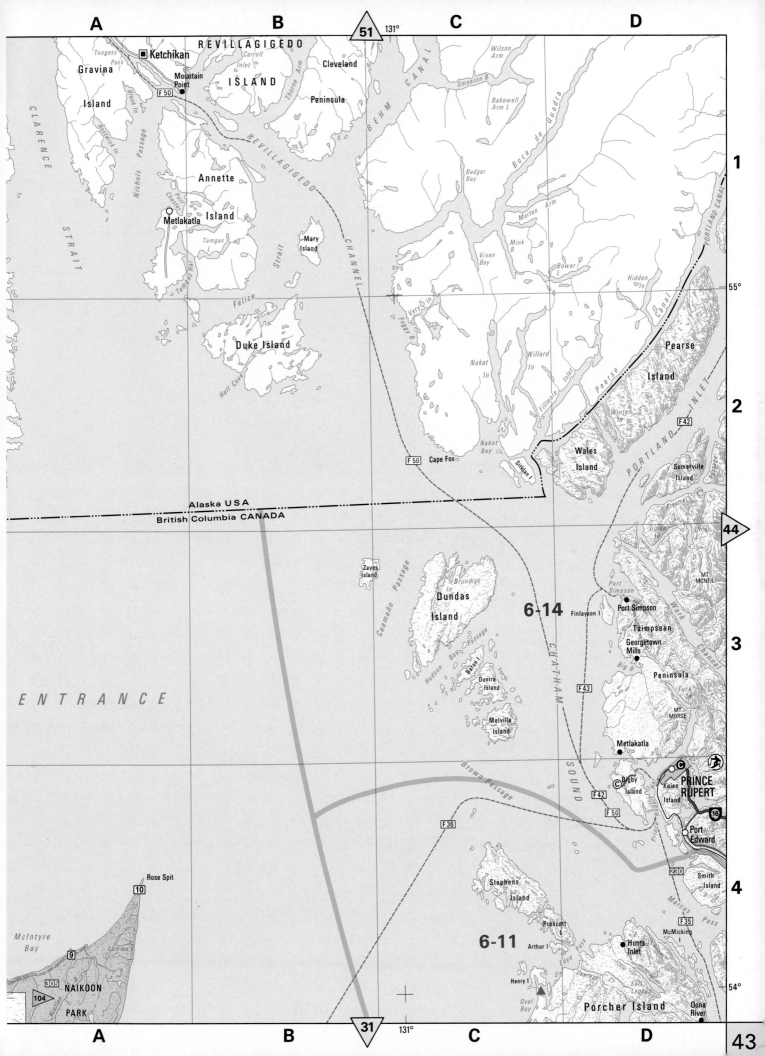

CLARENCE STRAIT

Tongass Pass
Bostwick In
Gravina Island
■ Ketchikan
Mountain Point
F 50
Blank In

REVILLAGIGEDO
Carroll Inlet
Cleveland
ISLAND
Peninsula
Thorne Arm

BEHM CANAL

Wilson Arm
Smeaton B
Bakewell Arm L
Badger Bay

Boca de Quadra

Annette
Nichols Passage
Portland Channel
Metlakatla

REVILLAGIGEDO CHANNEL

Felice Strait
Tamgas Har
Tamgas
Mary Island

Marten Arm
Vixen Bay
Mink B
Bower L
Hidden In

Pearse Island

55°

Duke Island

Very In
Foggy B
Nakat In
Willard In
Fillmore Inlet
Pearse Canal

Winter In
F 42

Hall Cove

Nakat Bay
F 50
Cape Fox
Sitklan I

Wales Island

Somerville Island

PORTLAND INLET

Steamer

Alaska USA
British Columbia CANADA

44

Union In
Union

MT MCNEIL

ENTRANCE

Zayas Island
Caamaño Passage
Brundige In
Dundas Island

6-14

Port Simpson
Finlayson I
Port Simpson

Tsimpsean
Georgetown Mills

Work Channel

3

Hudson Bay
Baron I.
Dunira Island

Passage

Big B
Peninsula
Tuck In
MT MORSE

CHATHAM

Metlakatla

F 43

Brown Passage

Melville Island

SOUND

Digby Island
Kaien Island
PRINCE RUPERT

Rose Spit
10

F 36

F 42
F 50

16

Stephens Island

Port Edward
230

McIntyre Bay
9

Prescott
Arthur I

Smith Island

4

Marcus Pass

305
NAIKOON
104
Hallen

6-11

Edye Pass
Henry I

Hunts Inlet
McMicking
F 35

PARK

Oval Bay
Porcher Island
Salt Lagoon
Oona River

54°

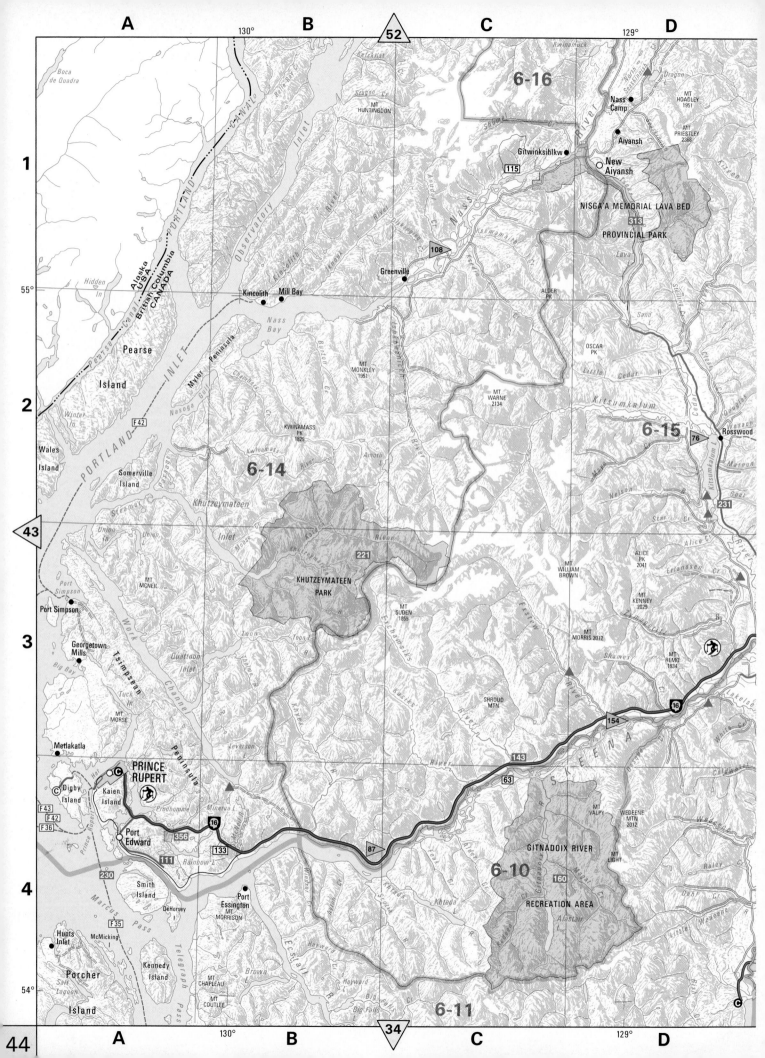

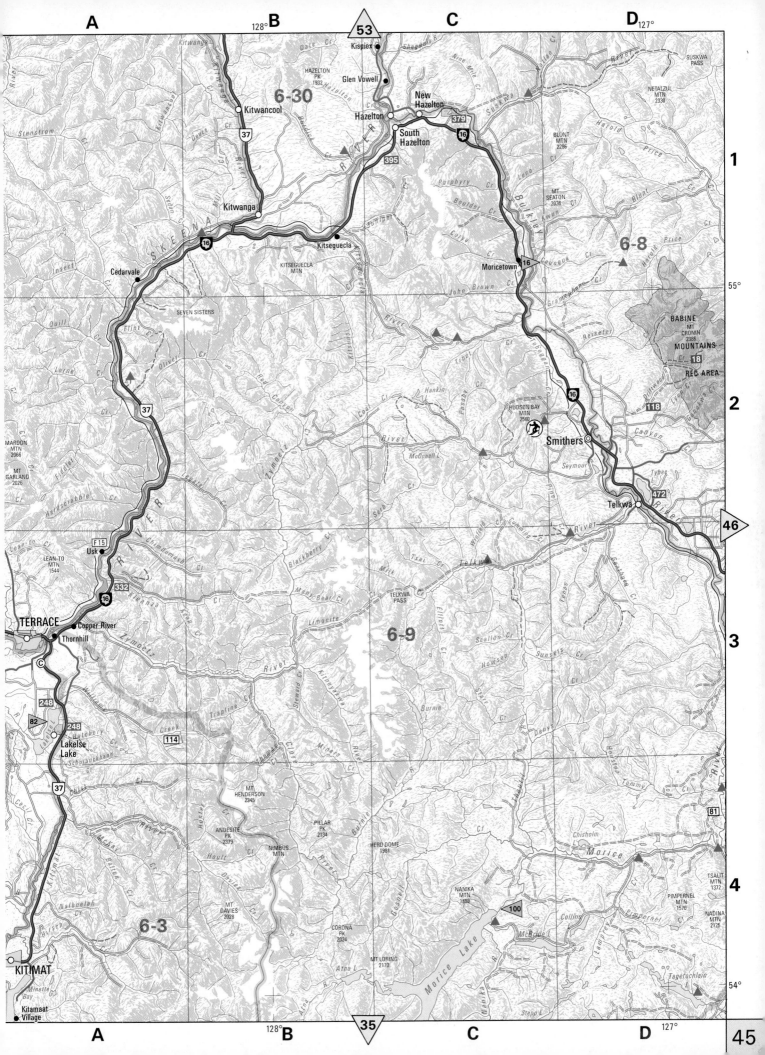

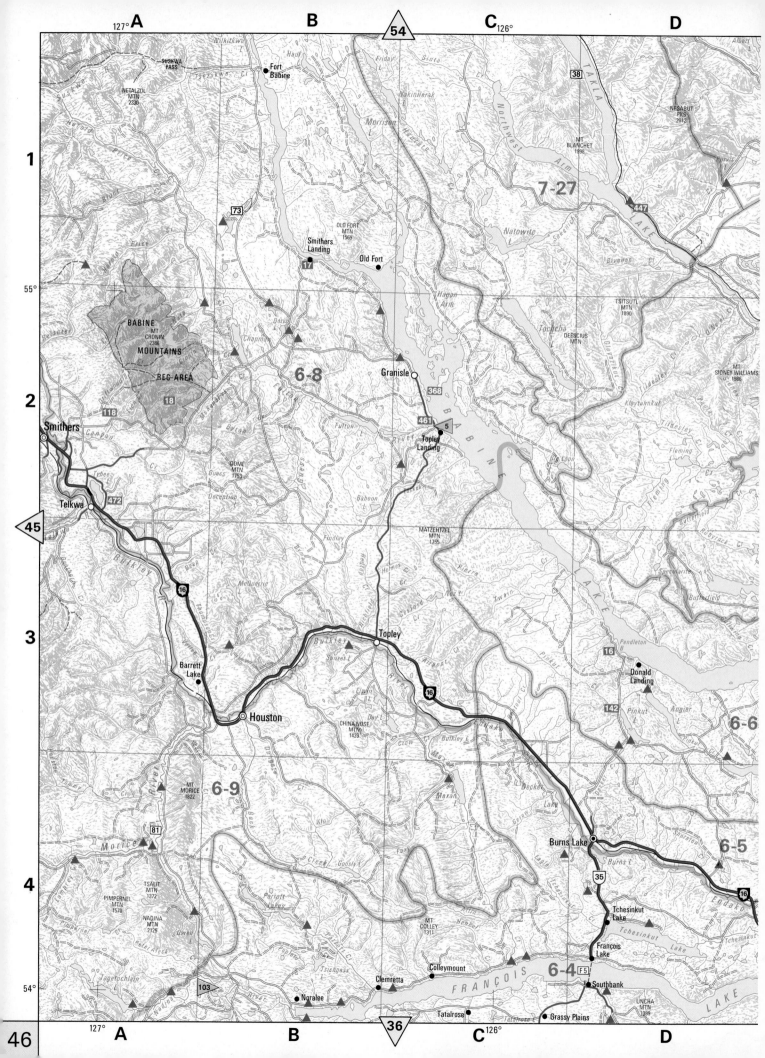

NETALZOL
MTN
2330

SUSKWA
PASS

Ndikitkwa

Fort
Babine

Haut

Friday
L.

Sinta

Nakinilerak

TAKLA

38

NESABUT
PKS
2012

Albert

MT
BLANCHET
1998

7-27

447

1

73

Smithers
Landing

17

OLD FORT
MTN
1569

Old Fort

Natowite

Sakenich

Bivouac

TSITSUTL
MTN
1890

DEESCIUS
MTN

MT
SIDNEY WILLIAMS
1986

55°

BABINE

MT
CRONIN
2386

MOUNTAINS

REC AREA

18

Dorn

Chapman

Hagan
Arm

Granisle

Topicha

Kloytahnkut

Tildesley

2

118

Smithers

Canyon

Tyhee

472

Telkwa

DOME
MTN
1753

Guess

Fulton
L.

368

461

5

Topley
Landing

Big Loon

Baboon

Fleming

MATZEHTZEL
MTN
1755

45

BULKLEY

16

Deep

McQuarrie
L.

Bryan
Cr.

Redtop

Holmes

Pierre

Twain

Decker

Pendleton
B.

16

Donald
Landing

142

Pinkut

Angler

6-6

3

Barrett
Lake

Houston

Bulkley

Sunset L.

Topley

16

Crow

Bulkley L.

Maxan
Lake

Goren

6-9

MT
MORICE
1822

CHINA NOSE
MTN
1439

Day L.

Klo

Maxan

Burns Lake

Burns L.

6-5

81

Morice

TSALIT
MTN
1372

Parrott
Lakes

Goosly L.

Henkel

35

Tchesinkut
Lake

16

Endako

4

NADINA
MTN
2125

O'Neil

Owen

Paririt
Lakes

MT
COLLEY
1311

François
Lake

Tchesinkut Lake

UNCHA
MTN
1399

PIMPERNEL
MTN
1570

Tsichgass

Colleymount

6-4

F5

Southbank

LAKE

Tagetochlain

103

Clemretta

Noralee

Tatalrose

Grassy Plains

FRANÇOIS

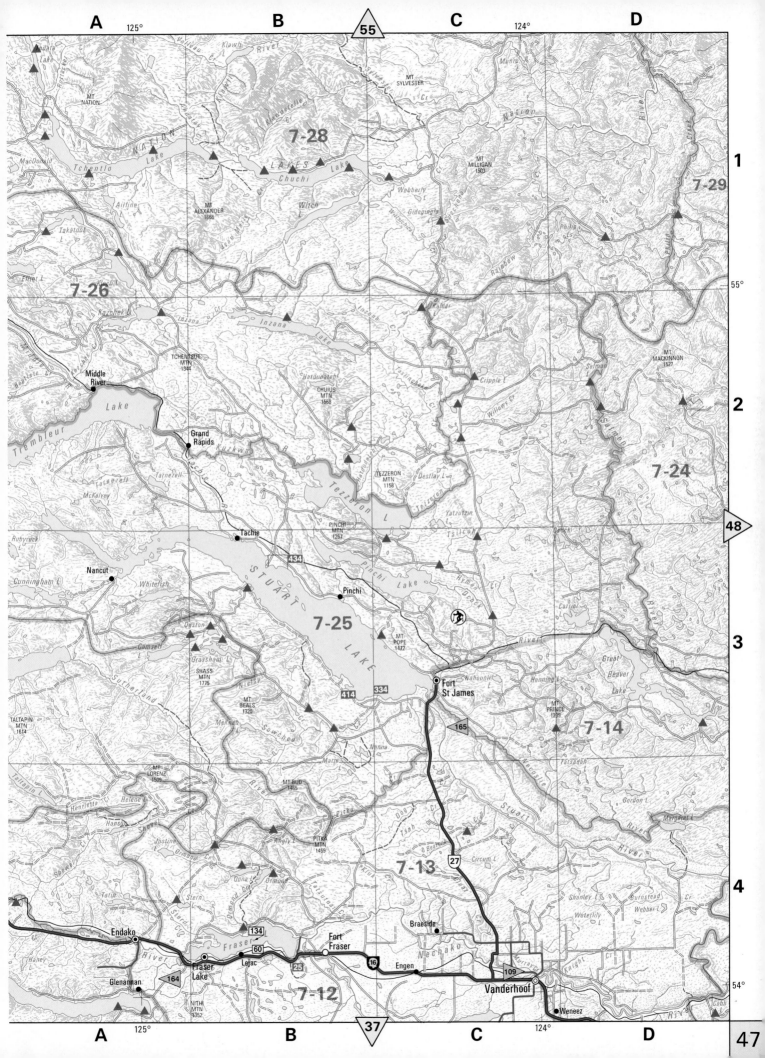

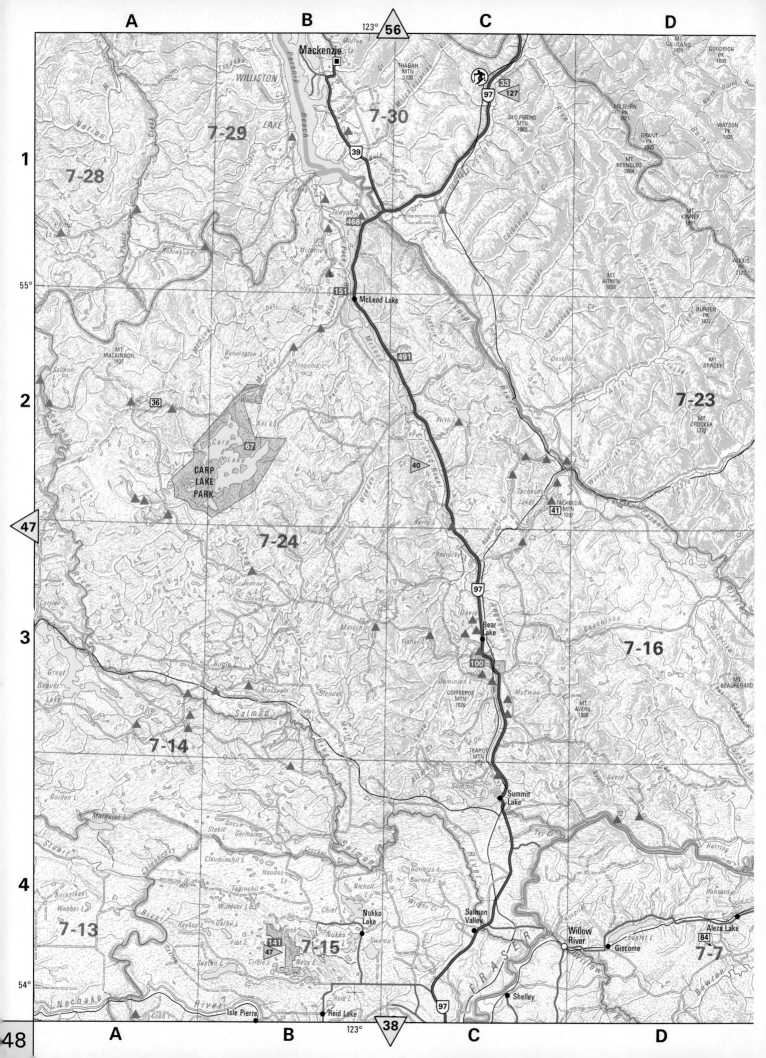

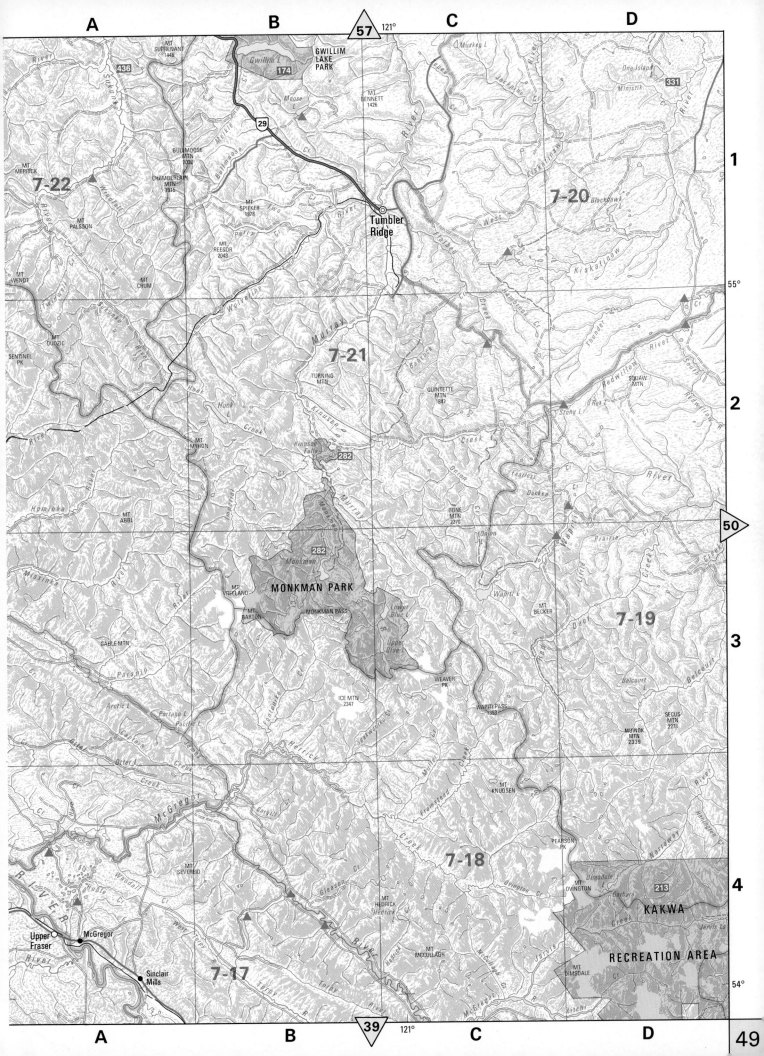

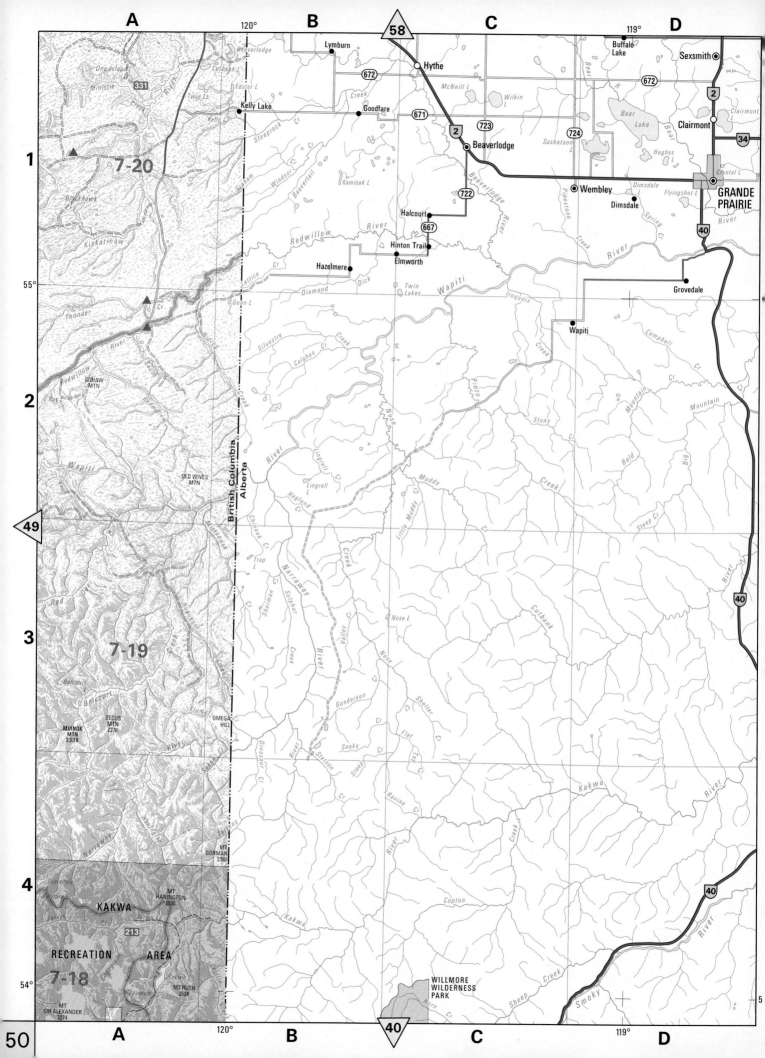

GITNADOIX RIVER REC AREA

SEELEY LAKE PARK

PHOTO: BC PARKS/SKEENA DISTRICT

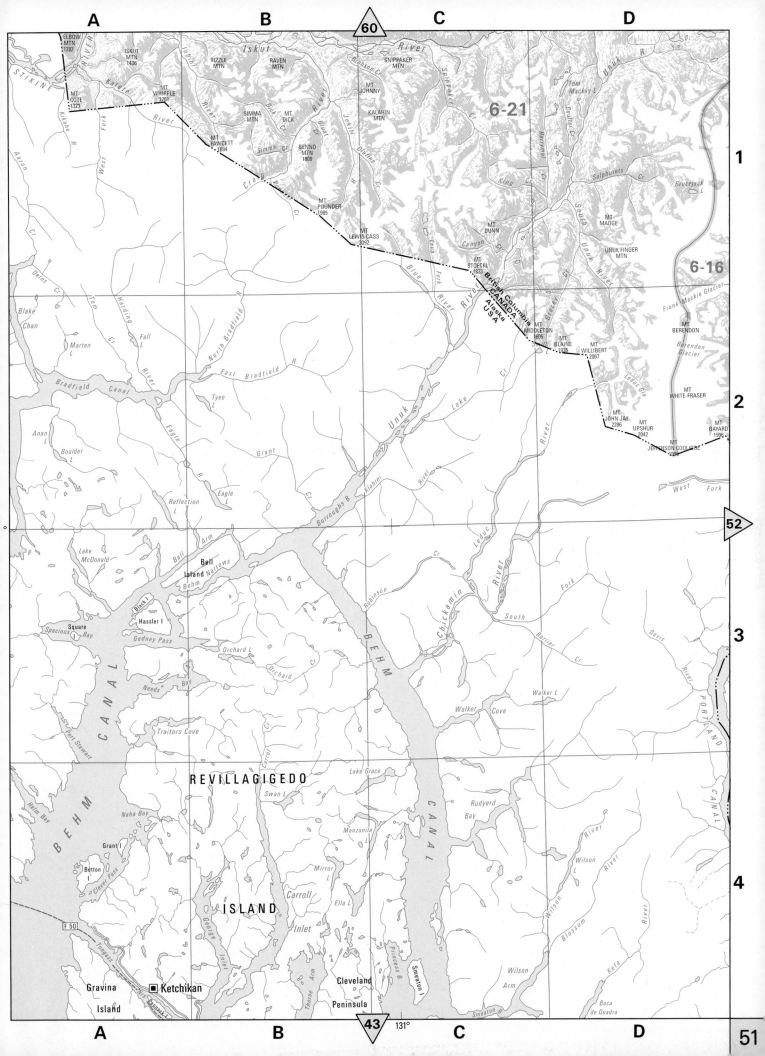

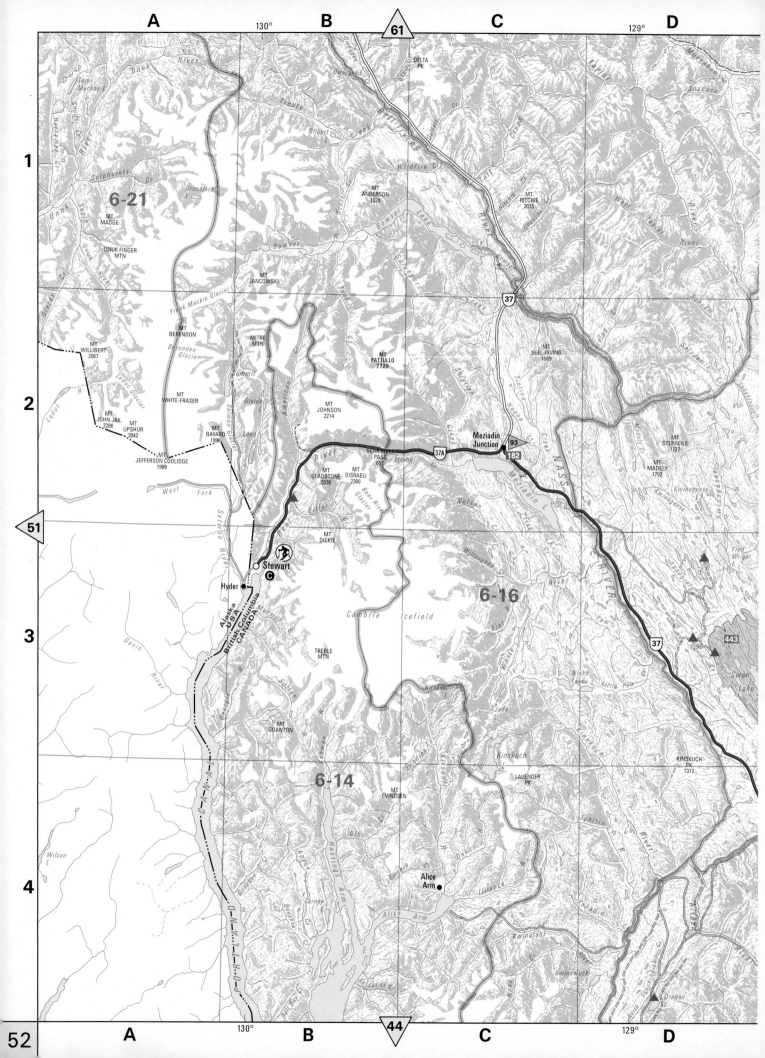

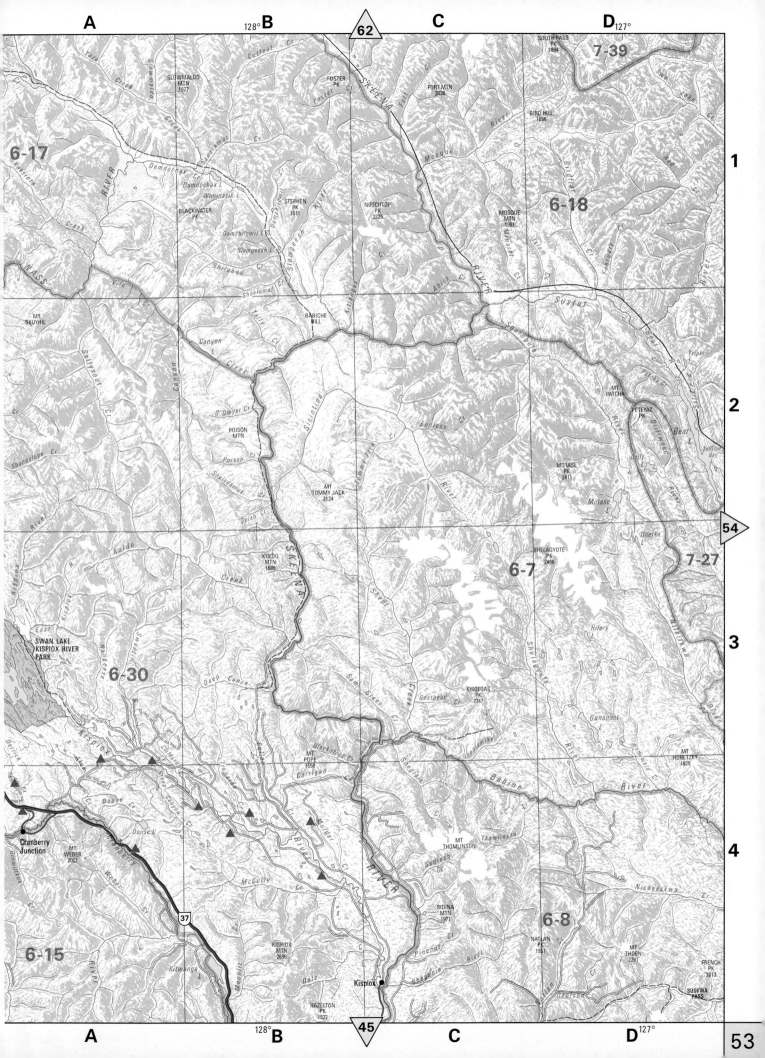

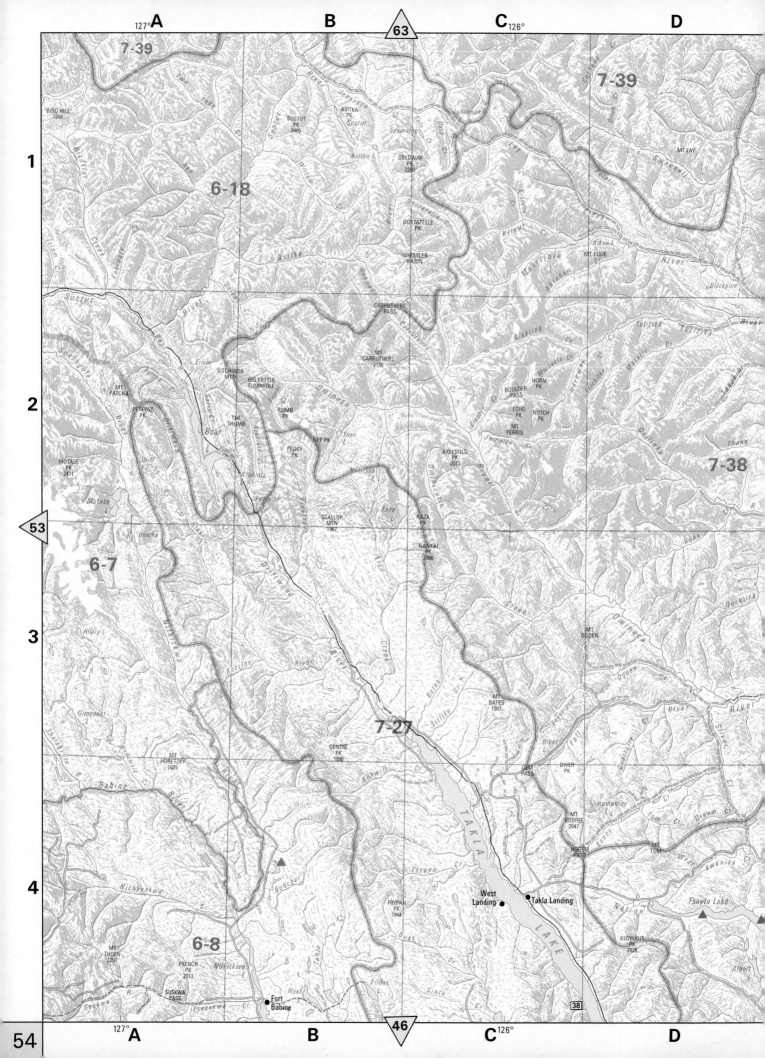

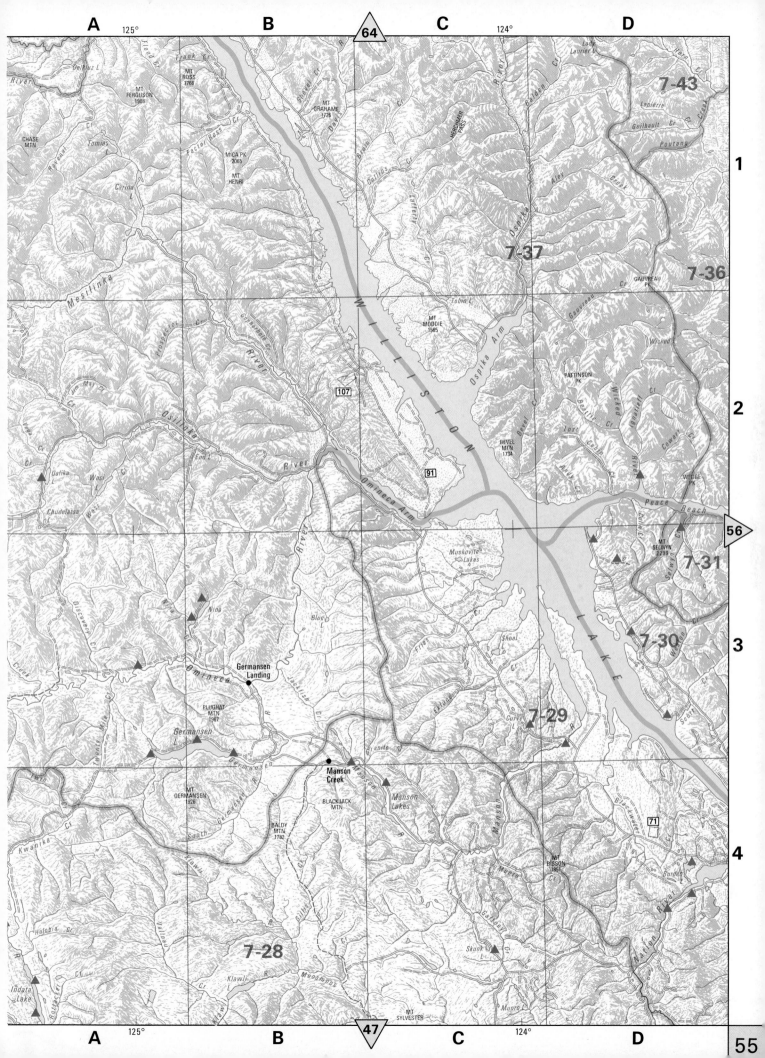

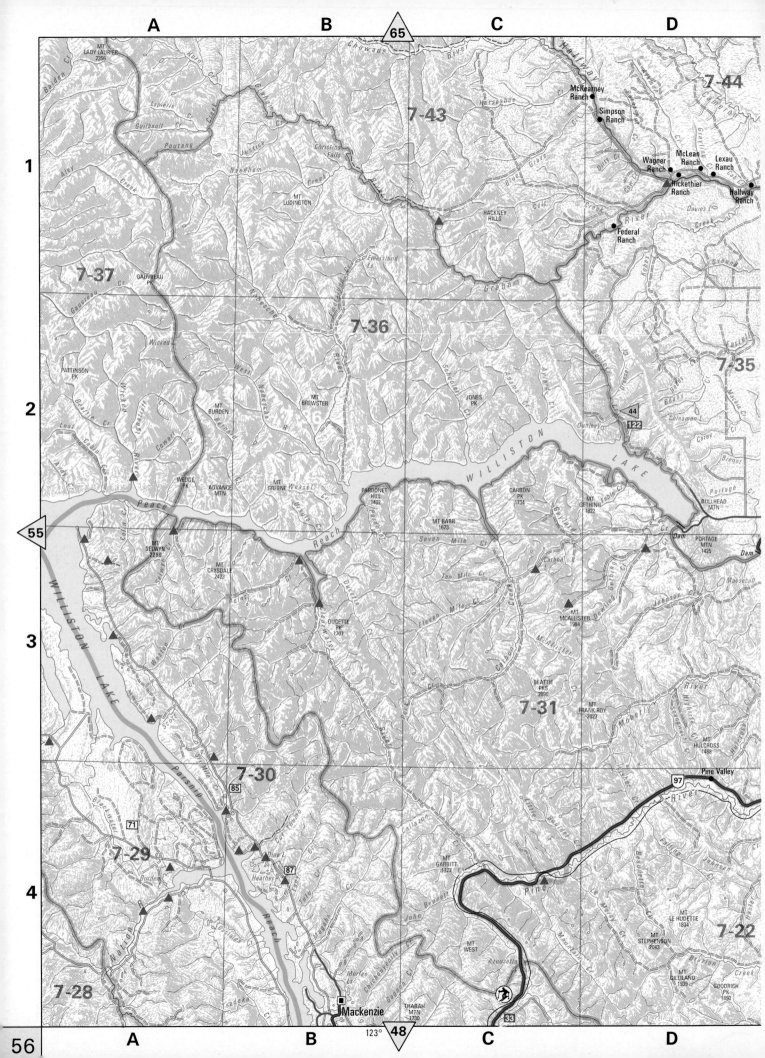

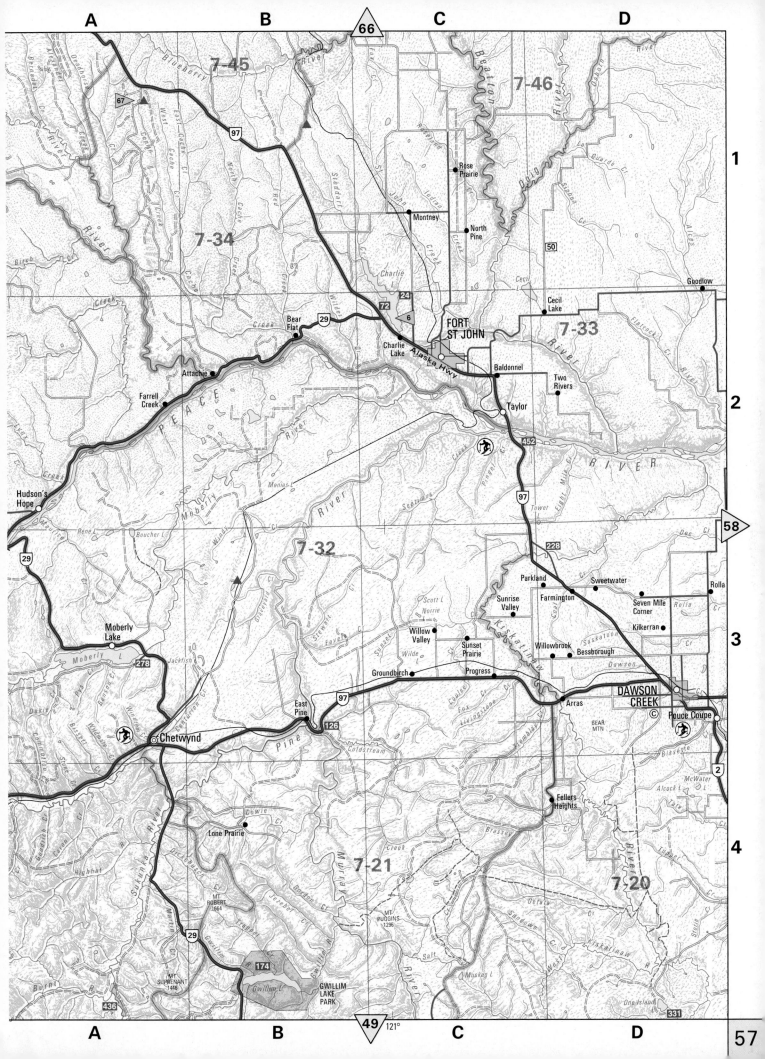

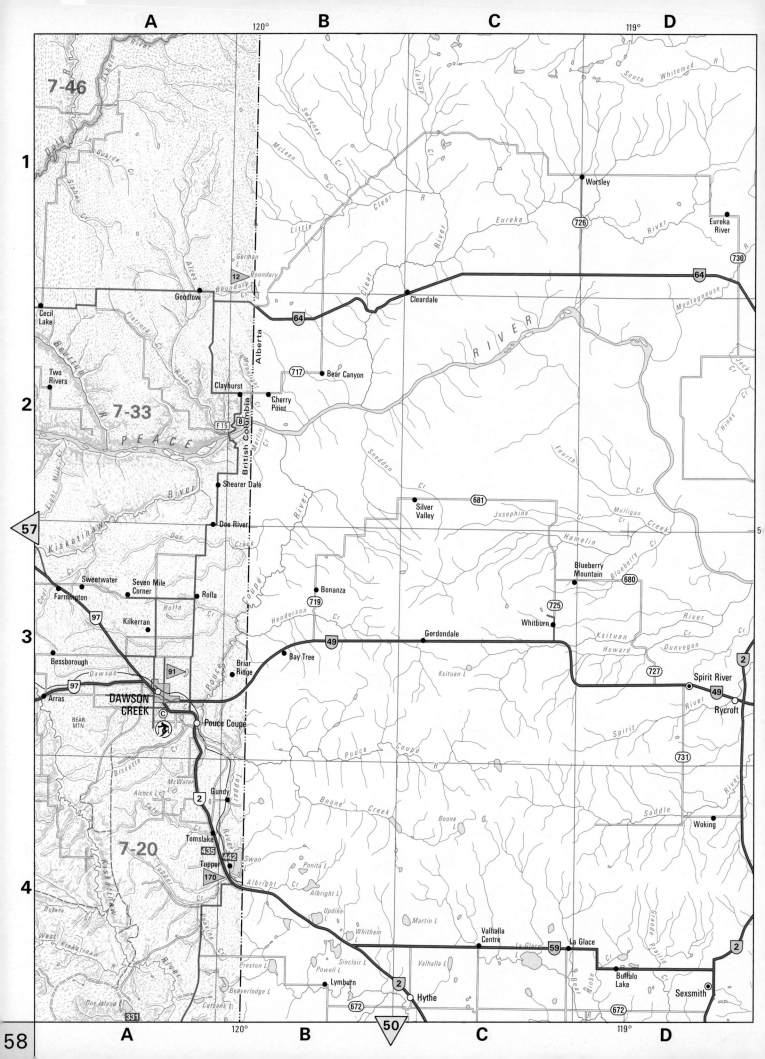

PIGEON SPIRE/BUGABOO ALPINE REC AREA

PHOTO: BC PARKS/EAST KOOTENAY DISTRICT

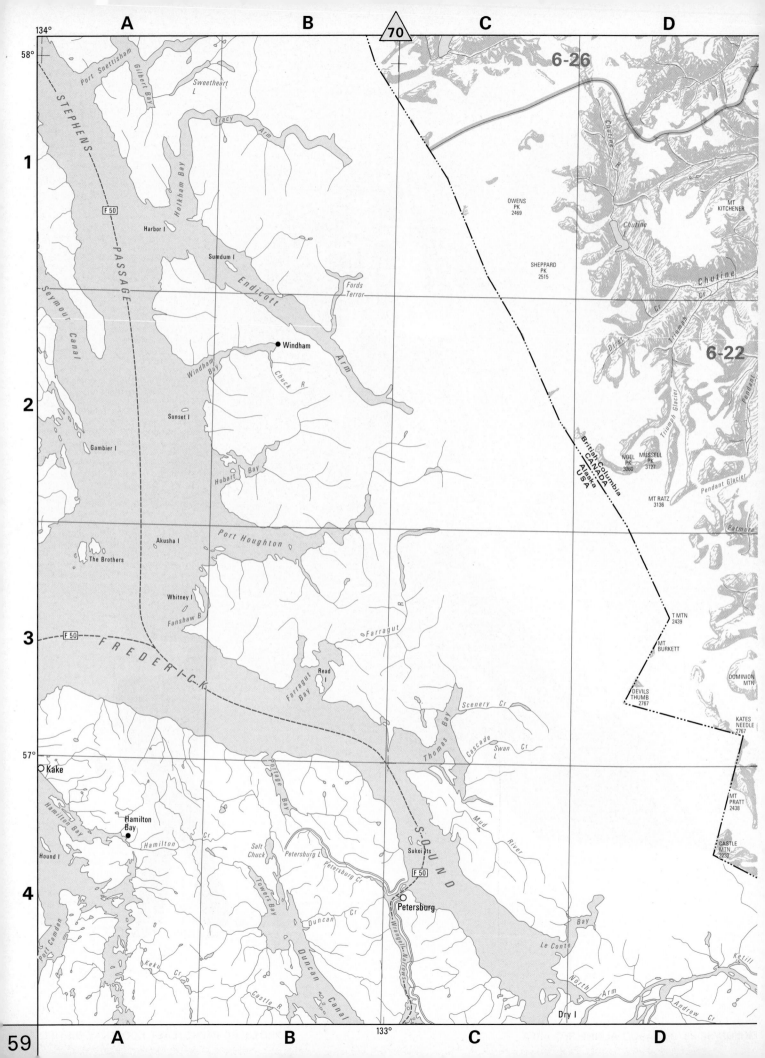

A B C D

58°

134°

STEPHENS

Port Snettisham

Gilbert Bay

Sweetheart L

F 50

Tracy Arm

Holkham Bay

Harbor I

Sumdum I

Endicott

Fords Terror

6-26

OWENS PK 2469

Chutine R

MT KITCHENER

SHEPPARD PK 2515

Chutine

Cr

1

PASSAGE

Seymour Canal

Windham Bay

Windham

Chuck R

Arm

Birst Cr

Triumph

6-22

2

Sunset I

Gambier I

Hobart

Bay

British Columbia
CANADA
Alaska
USA

NOEL PK 3060

MUSSELL PK 3127

Triumph Glacier

Pendant Glacier

Pendant

The Brothers

Akusha I

Port Houghton

MT RATZ 3136

Patmore

Whitney I

Fanshaw B

Farragut

R

T MTN 2439

3

FREDERICK

F 50

Farragut Bay

Read I

Scenery Cr

Thomas Bay

MT BURKETT

DEVILS THUMB 2767

DOMINION MTN

KATES NEEDLE 2767

57°

Kake

Portage Bay

Cascade

Swan Cr

Swan L

MT PRATT 2438

Hamilton Bay

Hamilton Bay

Hamilton

Salt Chuck

Cr

Petersburg L

Petersburg Cr

SOUND

Mud

River

CASTLE MTN 2232

Hound I

Sukoi Its

F 50

Bay

Le Conte

4

Port Camden

Keku Cr

Towers Bay

Duncan Cr

Petersburg

Wrangell Narrows

North Arm

Ketili

Castle R

Duncan Canal

Dry I

Andrew Cr

A B 133° C D

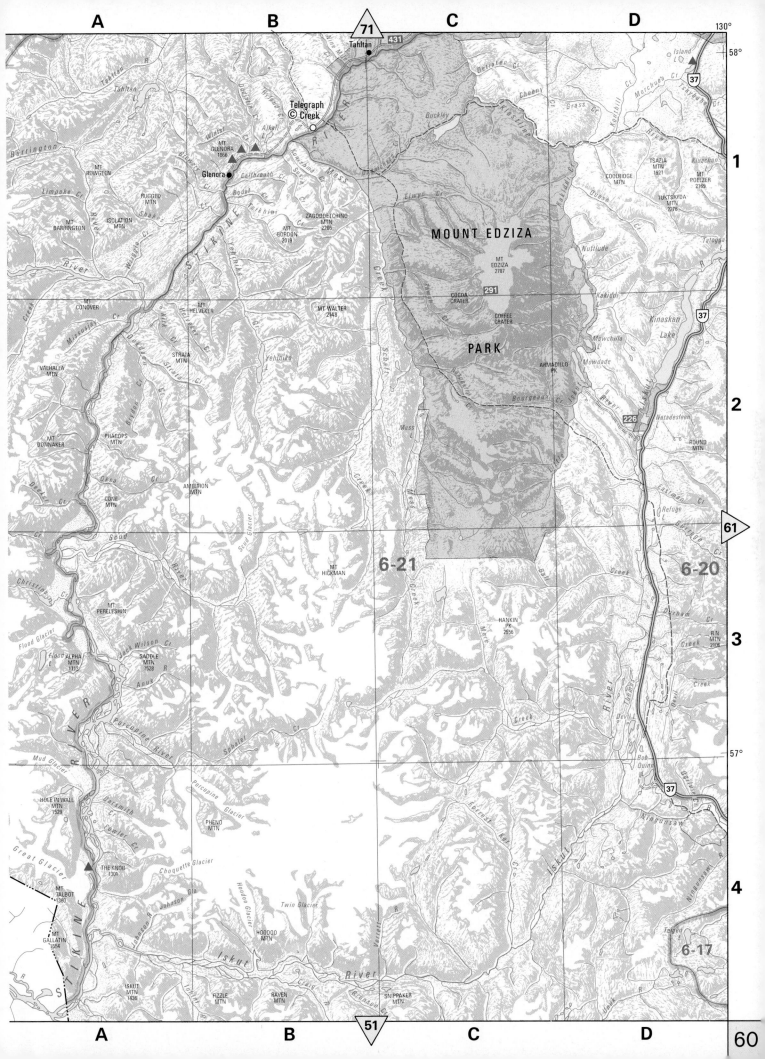

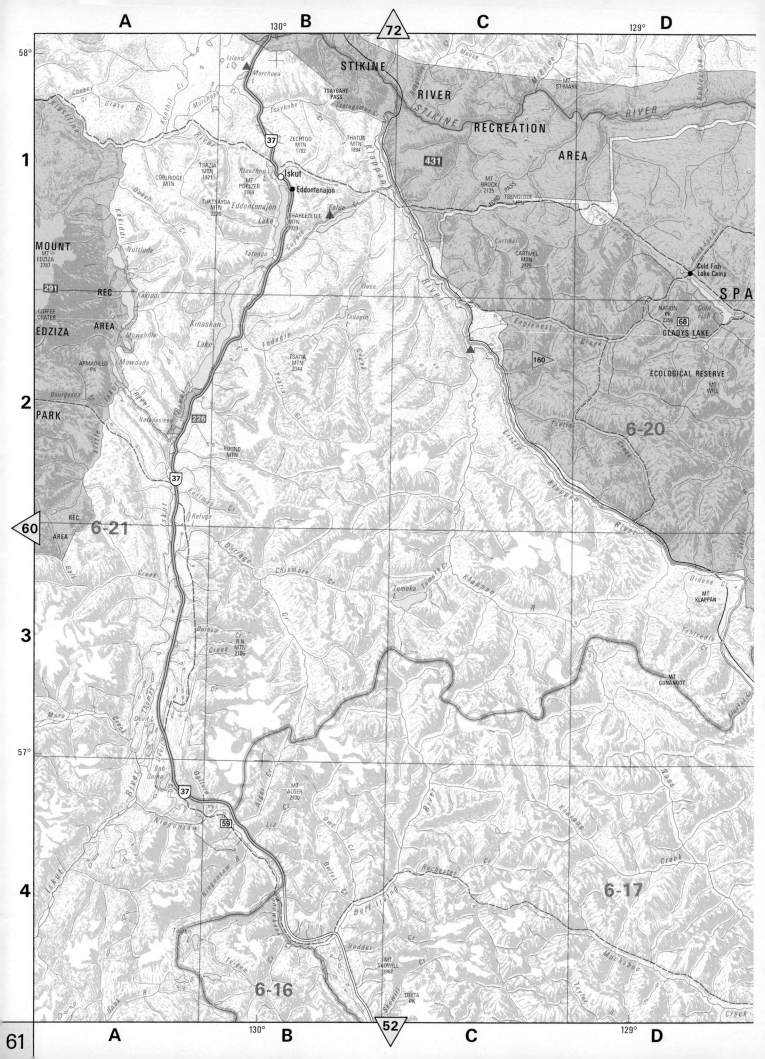

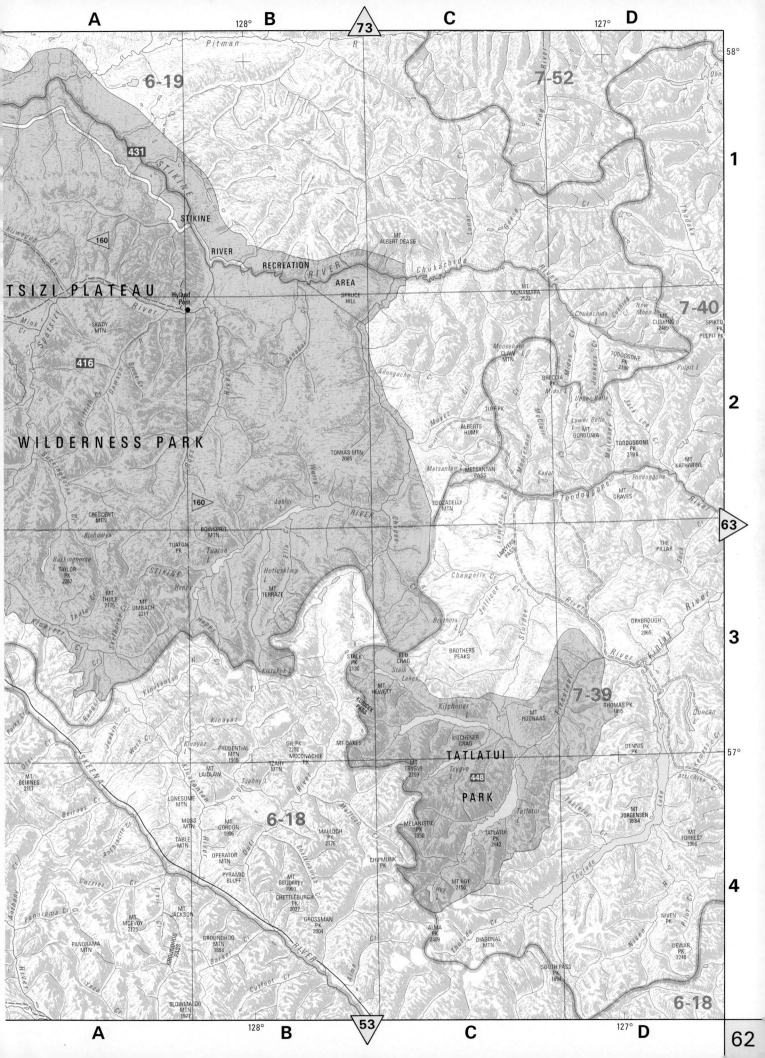

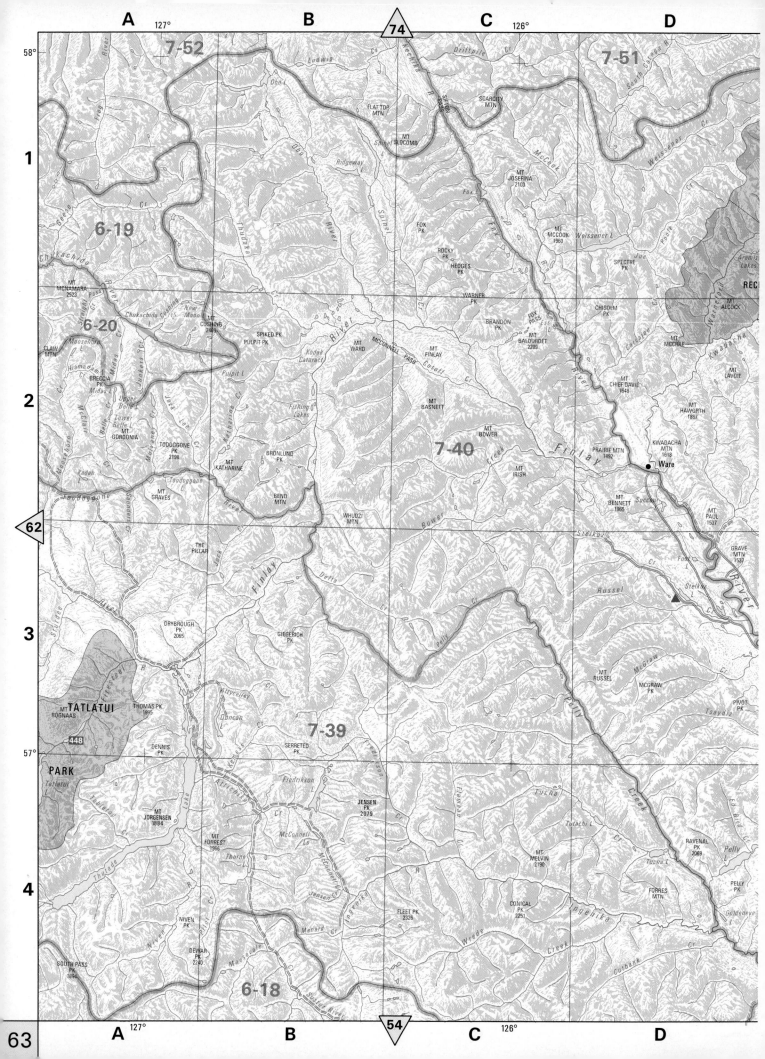

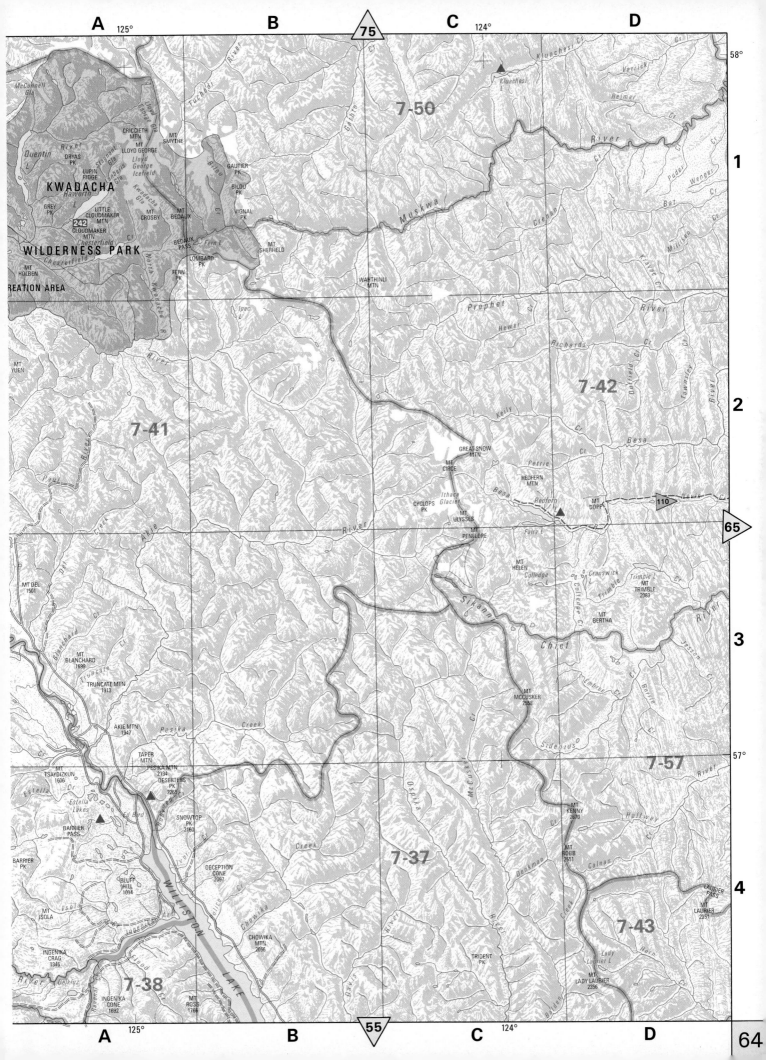

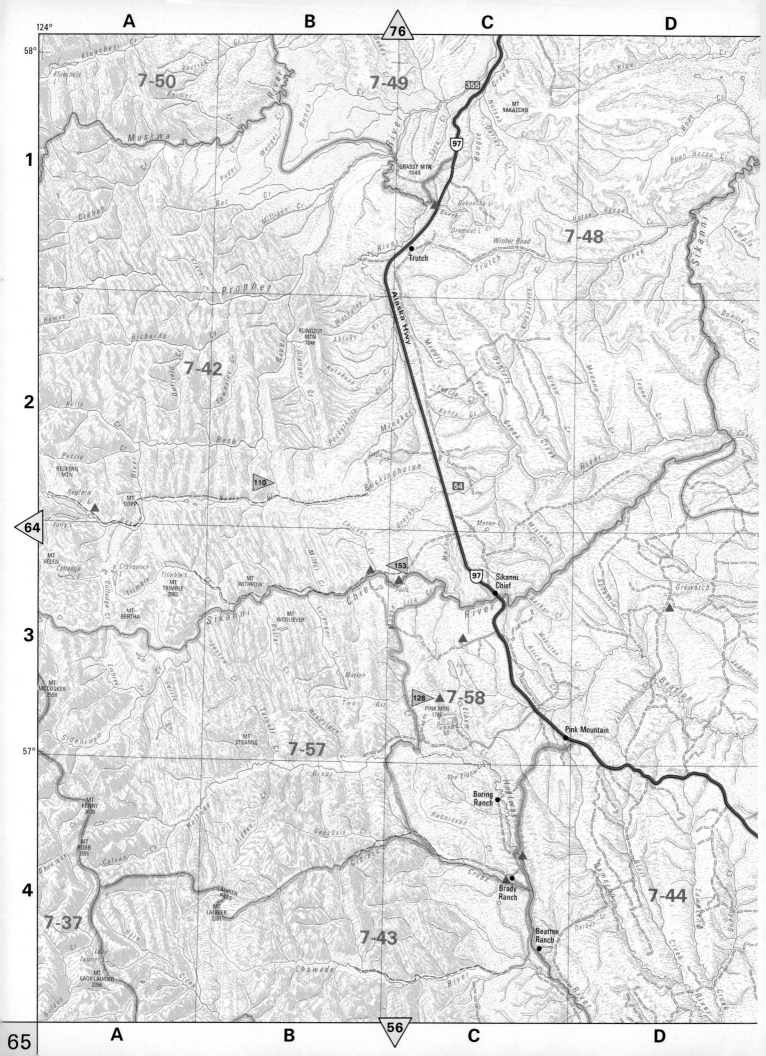

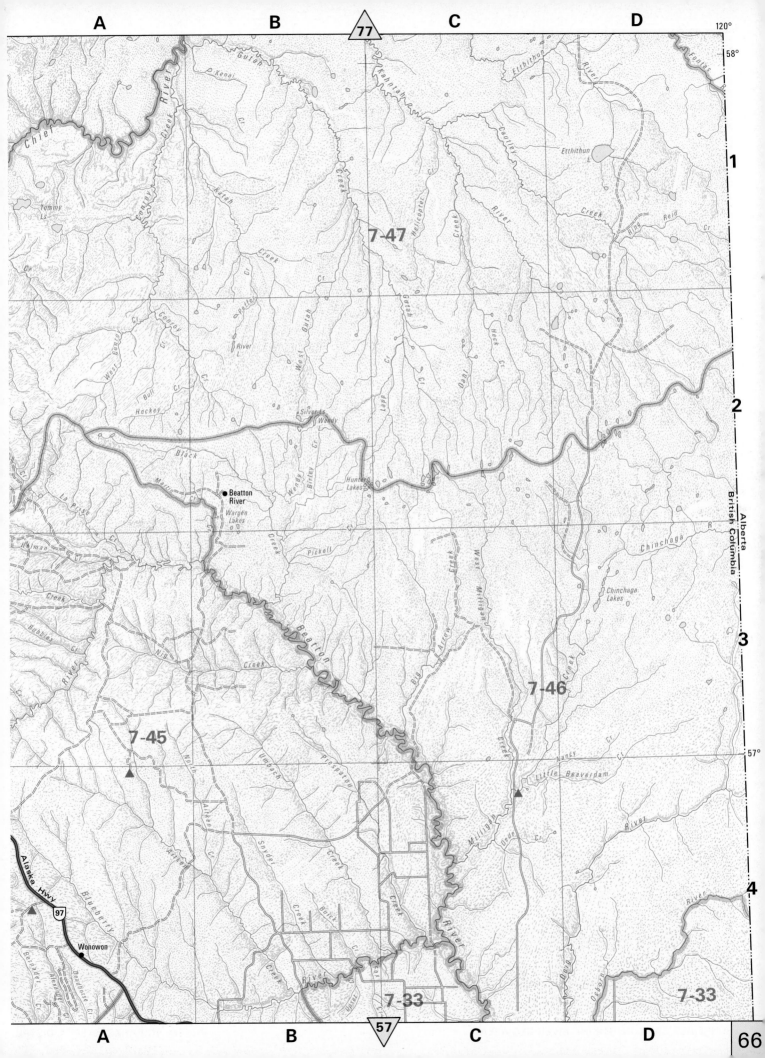

SCHREIBER CANYON/STIKINE RIVER REC AREA

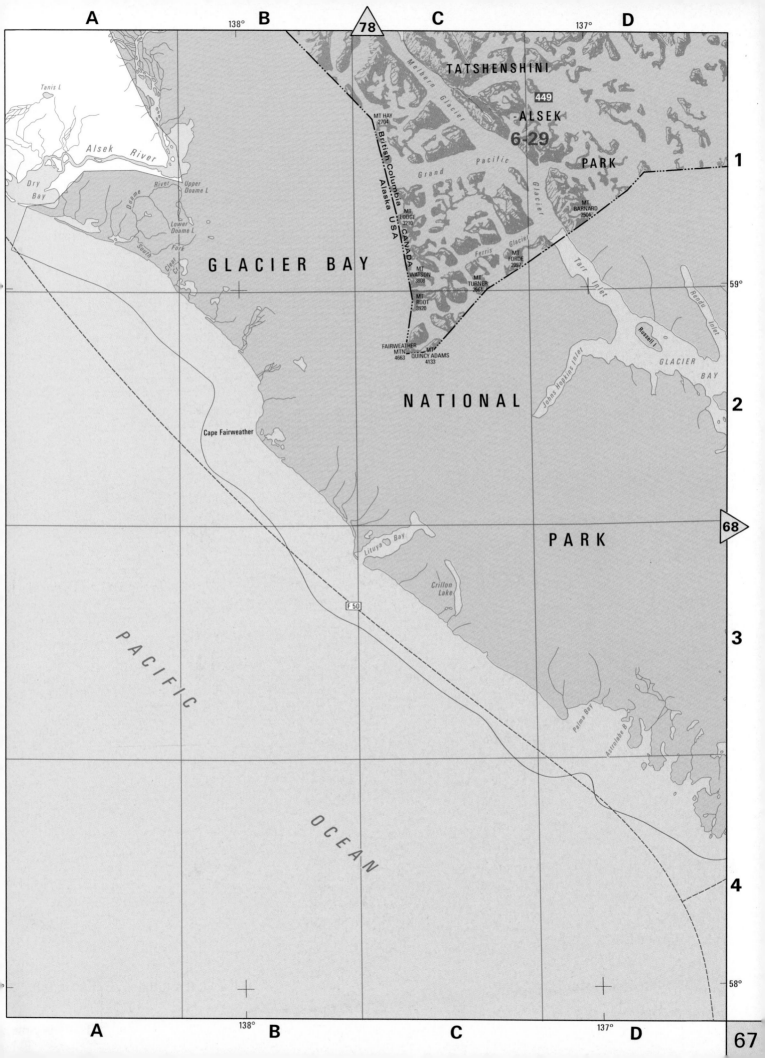

138°

137°

△78▽

Tanis L

Alsek River

Dry Bay

Doame River

Upper Doame L

Lower Doame L

South Fork

Clear Cr.

GLACIER BAY

TATSHENSHINI

449

-ALSEK

6-29

Melbern Glacier

PARK

Grand Pacific Glacier

MT HAY
2704

British Columbia

Alaska   USA

CANADA

MT LODGE
3210

MT WATSON
3808

MT ROOT
3920

MT TURNER
2661

Ferris Glacier

MT FORDE
2097

MT BARNARD
2504

1

Tarr Inlet

Rendu Inlet

59°

Russell I

GLACIER BAY

FAIRWEATHER MTN
4663

MT QUINCY ADAMS
4133

N A T I O N A L

Johns Hopkins Inlet

2

Cape Fairweather

Lituya Bay

P A R K

△68▷

Crillon Lake

3

P A C I F I C

F 50

Palma Bay

Astrolabe B

O C E A N

4

58°

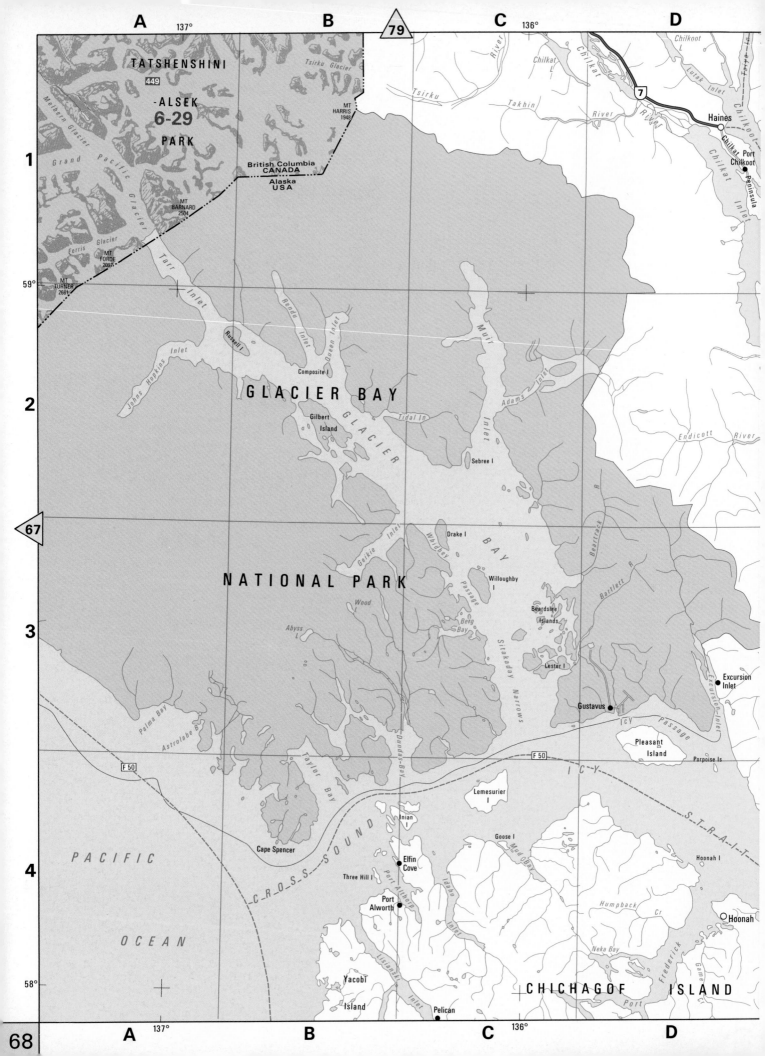

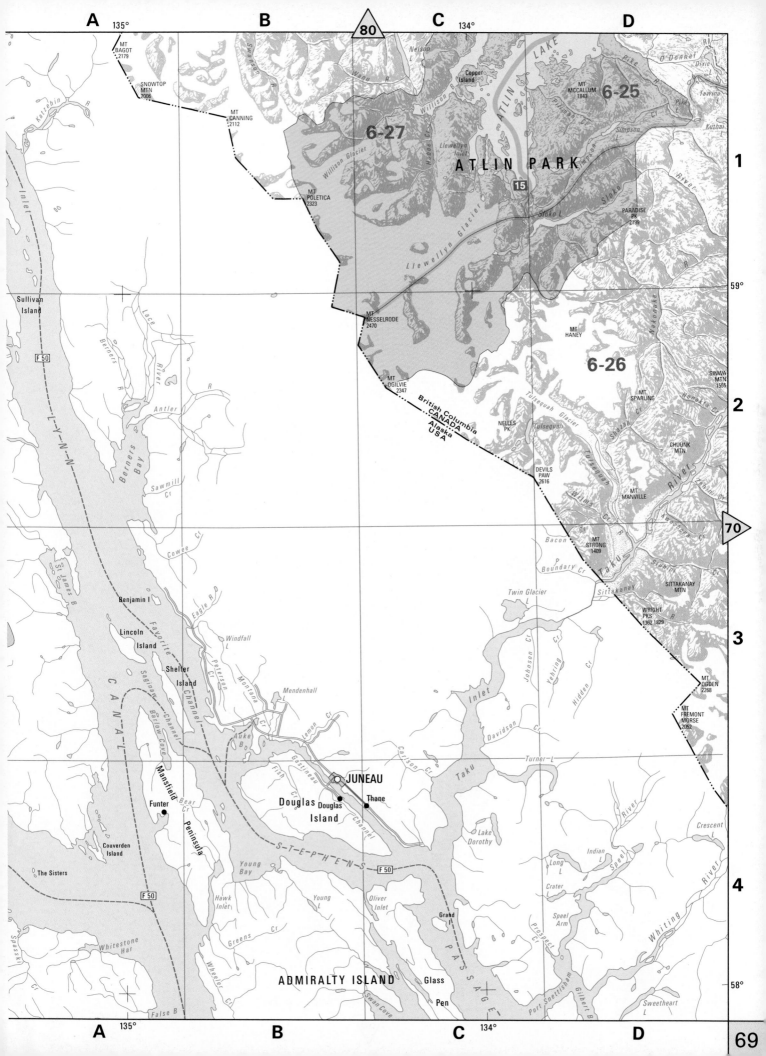

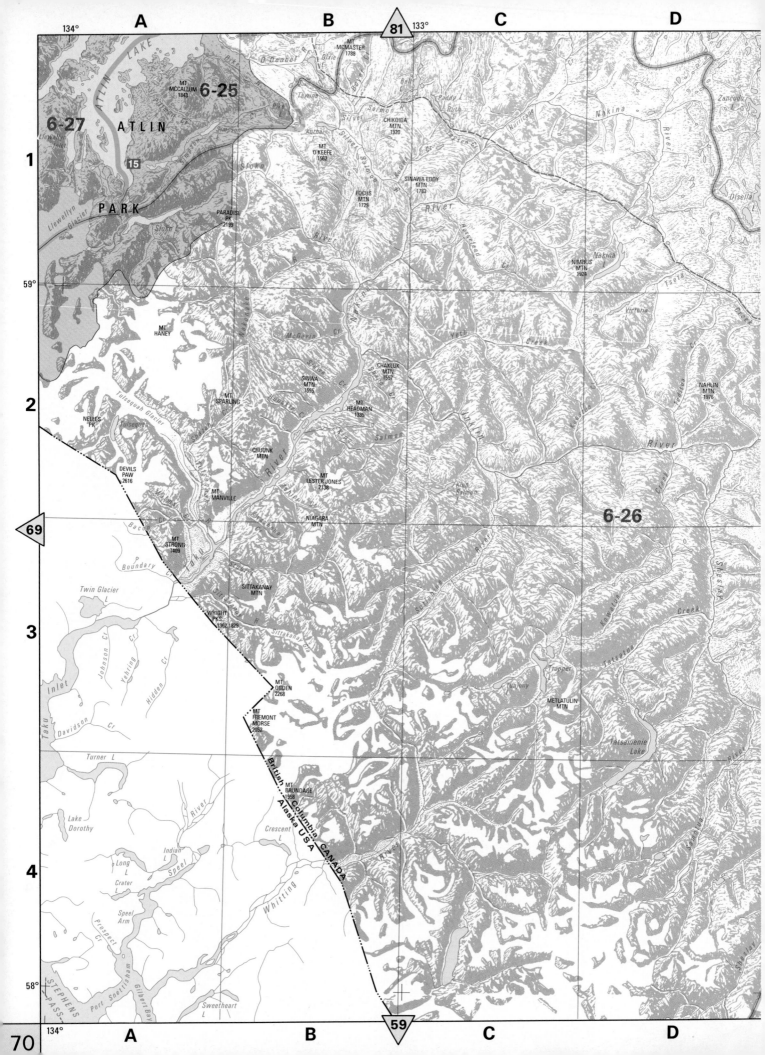

6-27   6-25

ATLIN

15

PARK

ATLIN LAKE

MT McCALLUM 1843

MT McMASTER 1788

CHIKOIDA MTN 1920

MT O'KEEFE 1562

SINAWA EDDY MTN 1783

FOCUS MTN 1729

NIMBUS MTN 1974

PARADISE PK 2199

MT HANEY

McGavin

CHAKLUK MTN 1557

NAHLIN MTN 1976

SINWA MTN 1555

MT SPARLING

MT HEADMAN 1335

NELLES PK

CHUUNK MTN

MT LESTER JONES 2138

DEVILS PAW 2616

MT MANVILLE

NIAGARA MTN

6-26

MT STRONG 1409

SITTAKANAY MTN

Twin Glacier L

WRIGHT PKS 1362 1829

METLATULIN MTN

Trapper

MT OGDEN 2268

Taku Inlet

MT FREMONT MORSE 2052

Tatsamenie Lake

Turner L

Lake Dorothy

MT BRUNDAGE 1958

British Columbia CANADA
Alaska U S A

Crescent L

Long L

Crater L

Indian L

Speel

Speel Arm

Whitting

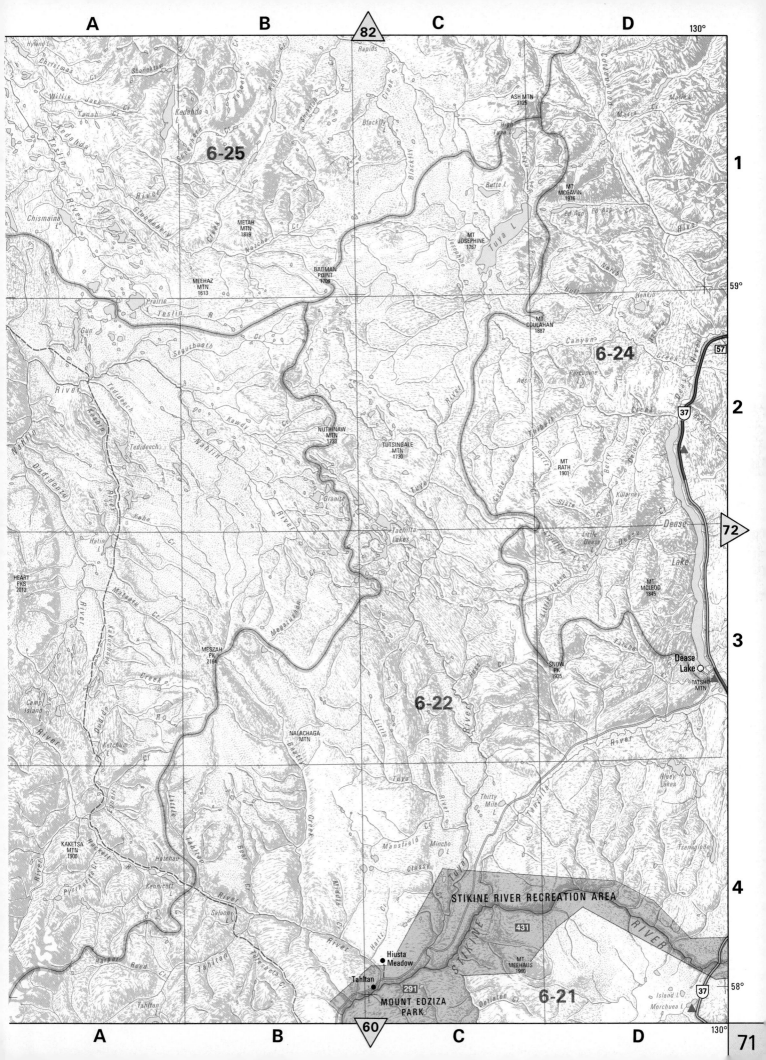

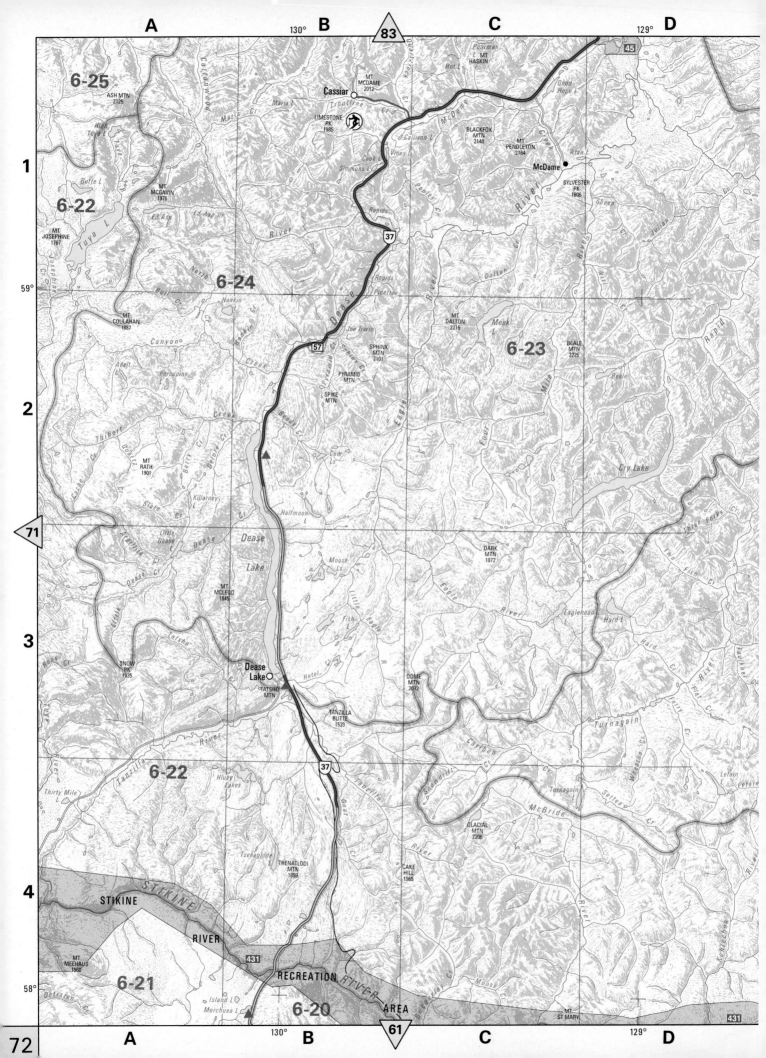

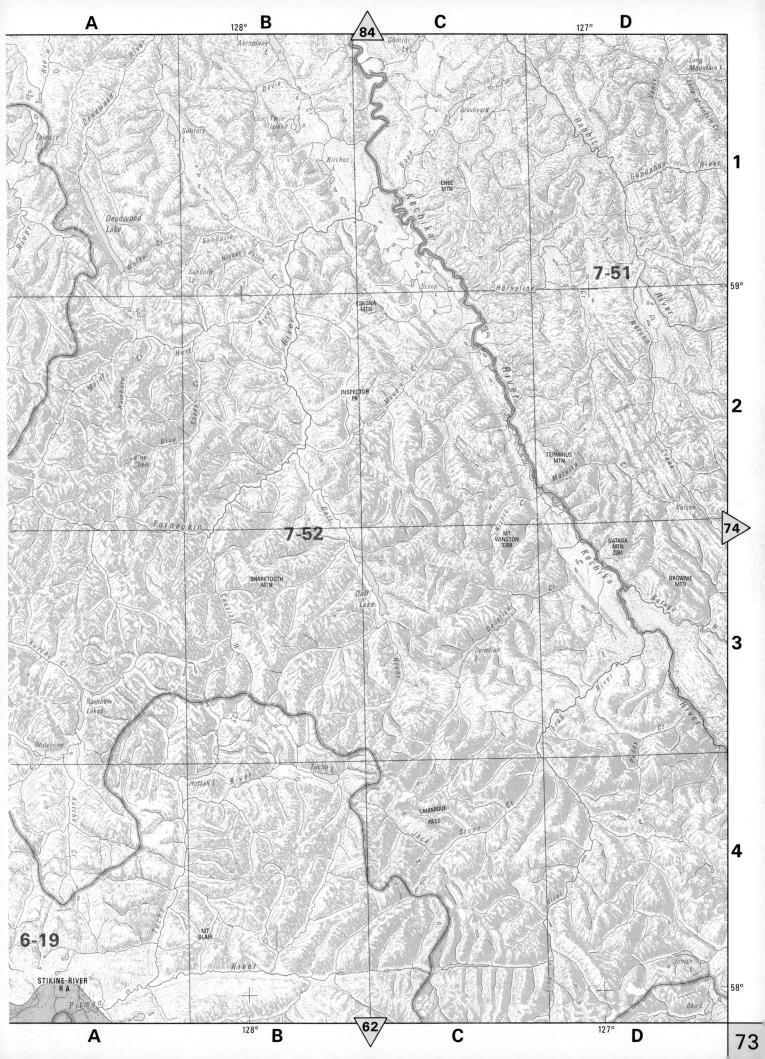

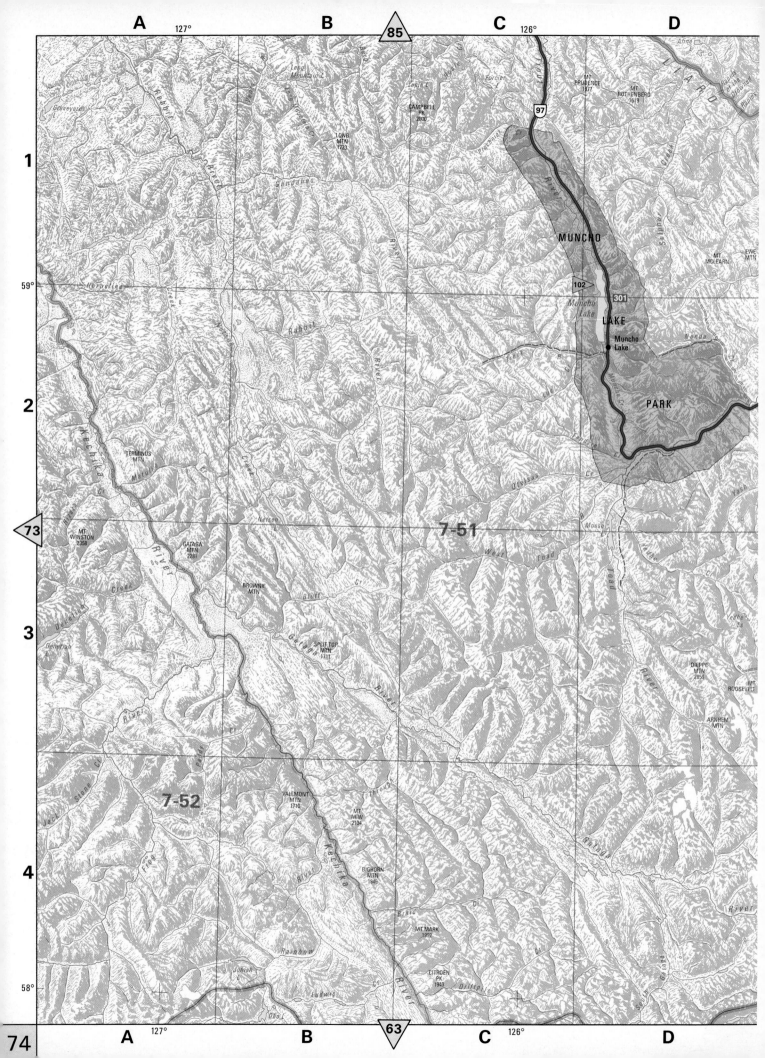

MUNCHO

LAKE

PARK

7-51

7-52

Graveyard L.

CAMPBELL PK 2000

LONG MTN 1723

MT PRUDENCE 1977

MT ROTHENBERG 1619

MT McLEARN

EWE MTN

97

102

301

Muncho Lake

Muncho Lake

TERMINUS MTN

MT WINSTON 2358

GATAGA MTN 2281

BROWNIE MTN

SPLIT TOP MTN 1711

DIEPPE MTN 2859

MT ROOSEVELT

ARNHEM MTN

VALEMONT MTN 1710

MT NEW 2134

BIGHORN MTN 1946

MT MARK 1992

CITRDEN PK 1943

Rabbit River

Kechika River

Gundahoo

Rabbit River

Trout R.

Kechika River

Gataga River

59°

58°

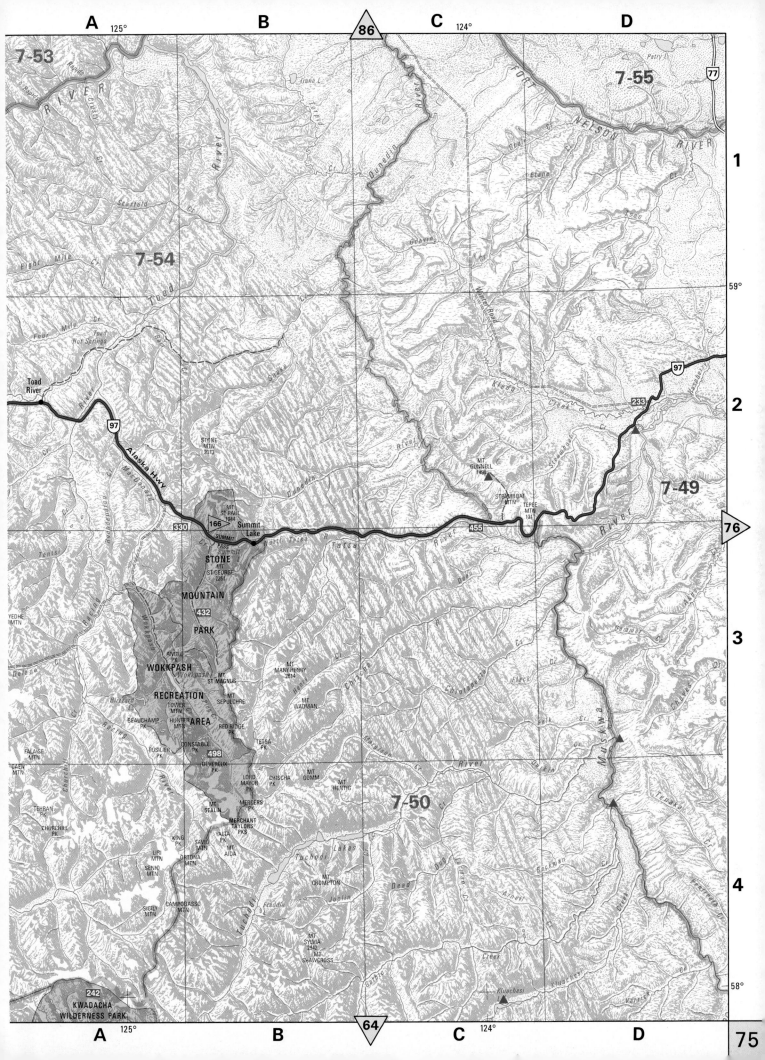

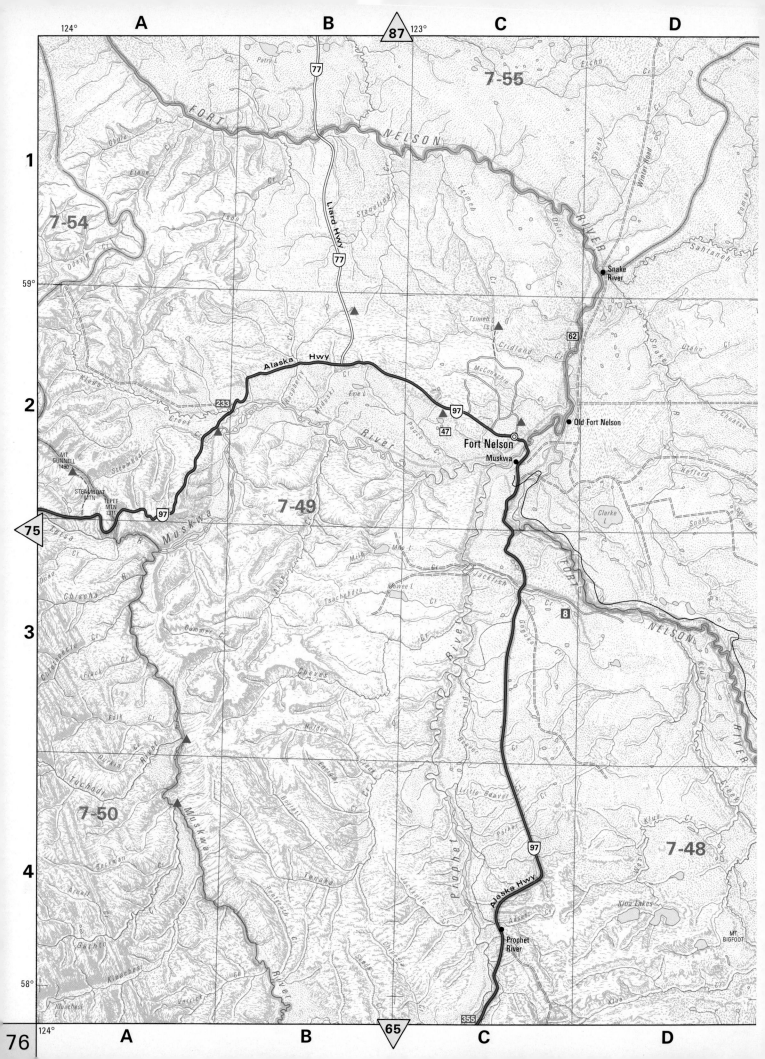

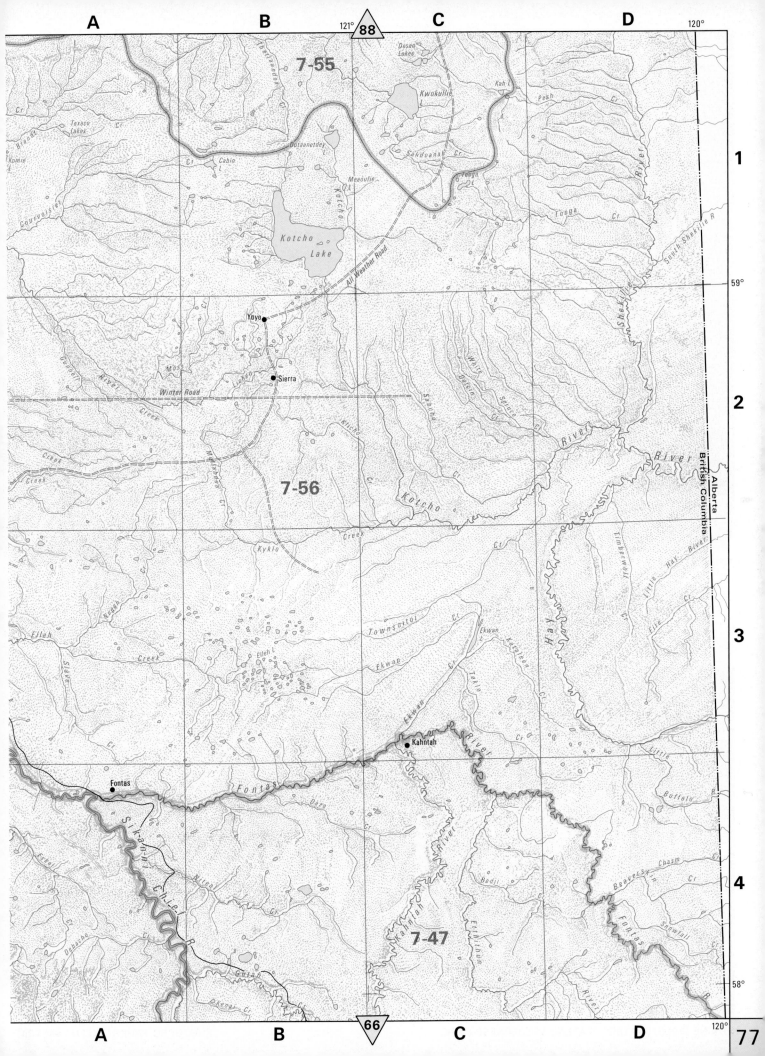

STIKINE RIVER/SPATSIZI PLATEAU WILDERNESS PARK

PHOTO: BC PARKS/SKEENA DISTRICT

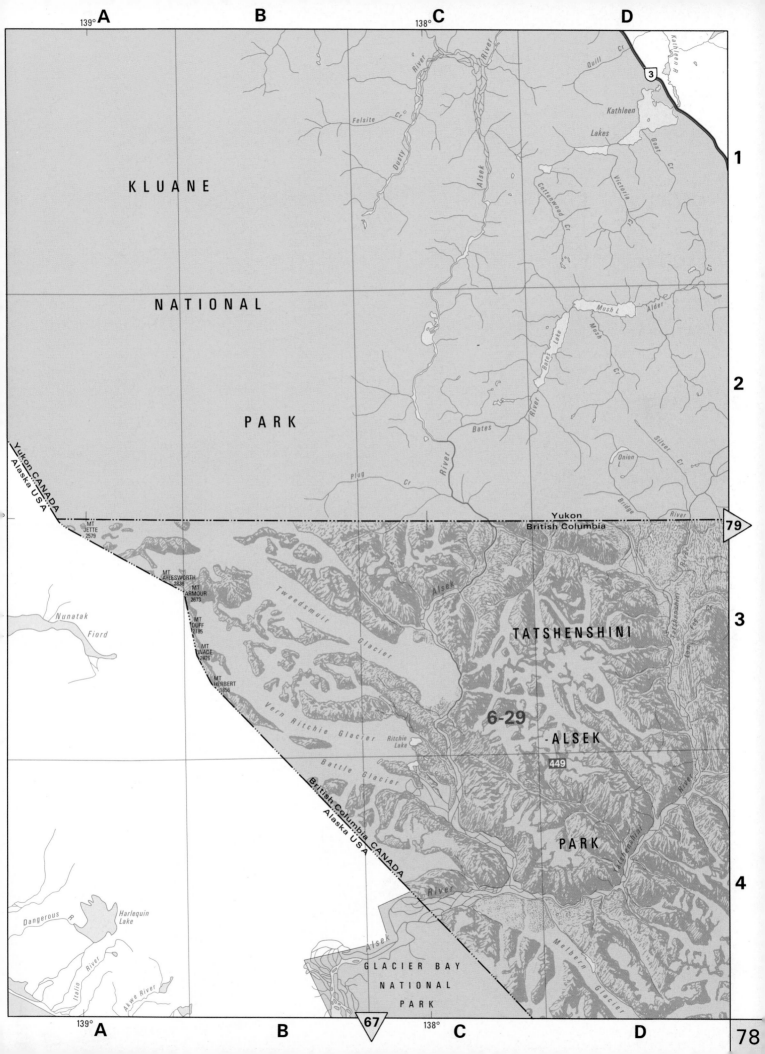

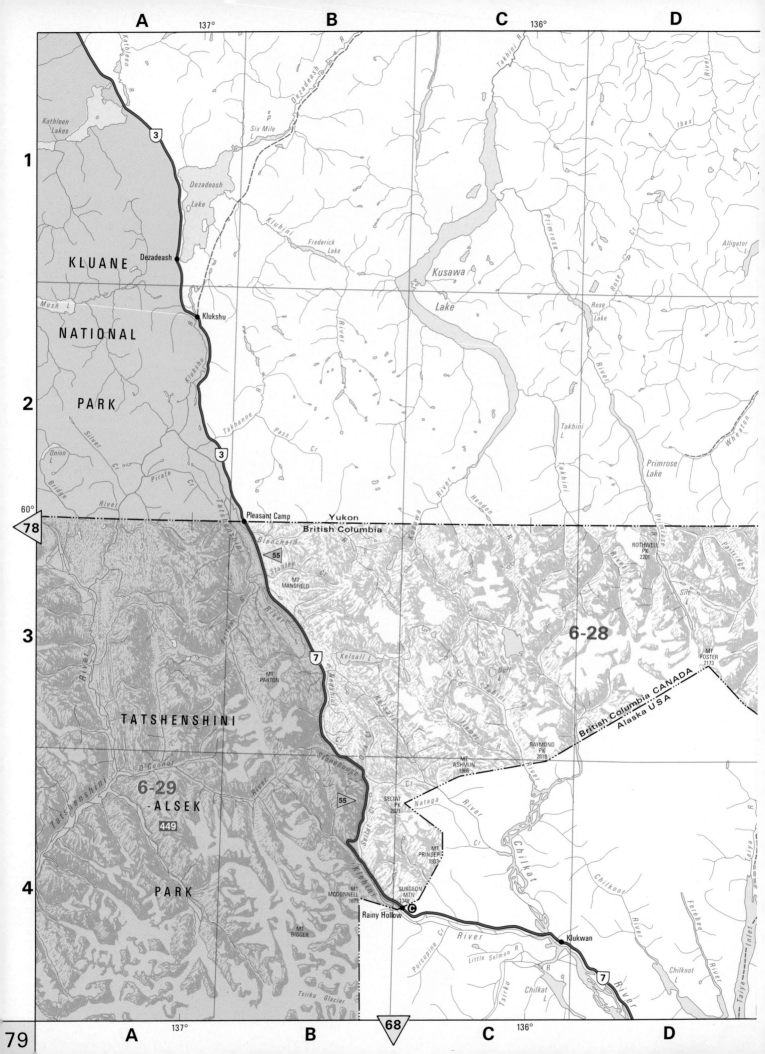

1

2

3

4

KLUANE

NATIONAL

PARK

Kathleen Lakes

Kathleen R.

Dezadeash

Klukshu

Mush L.

Onion L.

Silver Cr.

Pirate Cr.

Bridge River

Dezadeash R.

Dezadeash Lake

Six Mile L.

Kluhini

Frederick Lake

Takhanne R.

Takhanne R.

Pass Cr.

Tatshenshini R.

Pleasant Camp

Blanchard

Stanley Cr.

MT MANSFIELD

MT PARTON

Naashini R.

Kelsall L.

Kelsall R.

Kelsall Cr.

Stonehouse Cr.

Seltat Cr.

Klehini R.

MT McDONNELL 1679

Rainy Hollow

SELTAT PK 2021

MT PRINSEP 1933

SURGEON MTN 1348

Nataga Cr.

MT ASHMUN 1966

RAYMOND PK 2018

Kusawa Lake

Kusawa River

Hendon R.

Takhini L.

Takhini R.

Duff L.

Tahini R.

Takhini R.

Takhini R.

Rose Cr.

Rose Lake

Primrose R.

Primrose Lake

Wheaton R.

Partridge

Silt

ROTHWELL PK 2201

MT FOSTER 2173

Ibex

Alligator L.

6-28

British Columbia CANADA
Alaska USA

TATSHENSHINI

6-29
- ALSEK

449

PARK

O'Connor River

Tatshenshini River

MT BIGGER

Tsirku Glacier

Chilkat River

Chilkat R.

Porcupine Cr.

Little Salmon R.

River

Klukwan

Tsirku L.

Chilkat L.

Chilkoot River

Ferebee River

Taiya R.

Taiya Inlet

Chilkoot L.

60°   Yukon   British Columbia

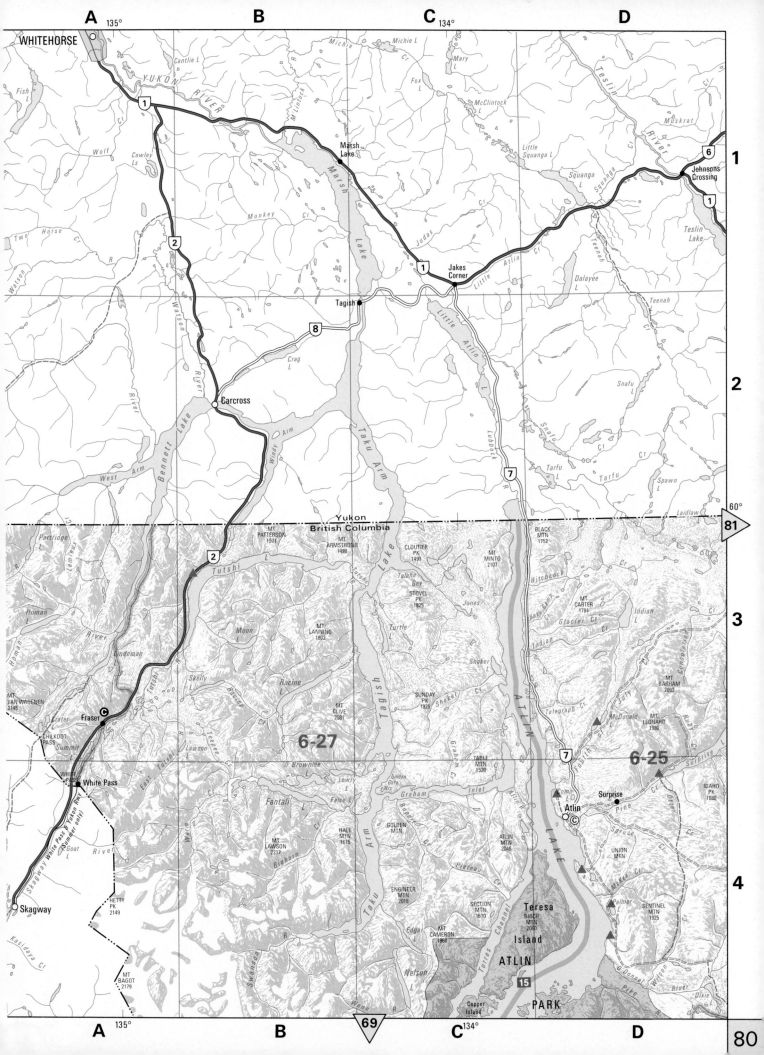

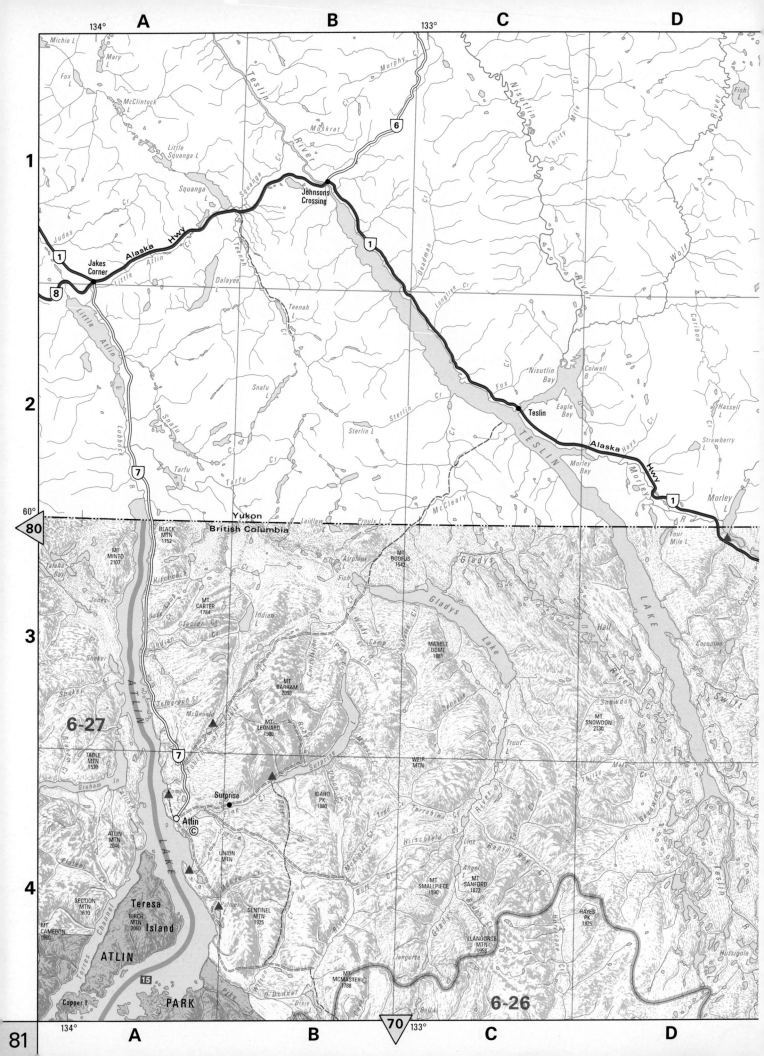

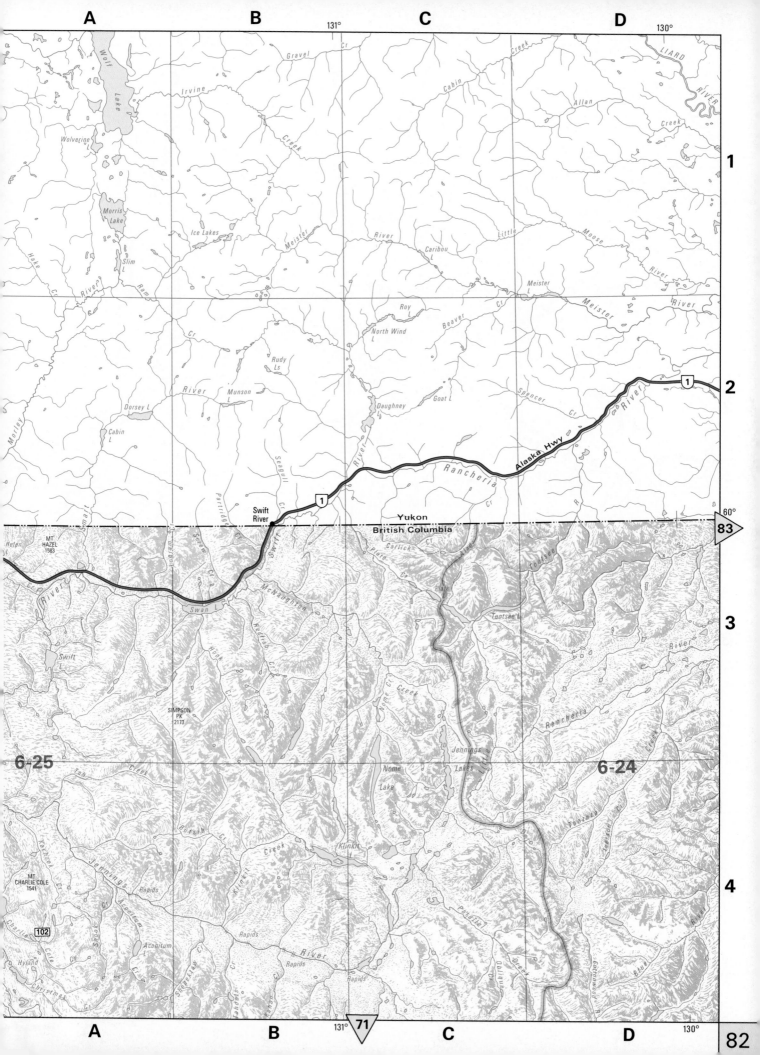

1

2

83

Wolf Lake

Wolverine L

Morris Lake

Ice Lakes

Slim L

Hoke Cr

River

Ram

Cr

Irvine

Creek

Gravel

Cr

Creek

Cabin

Creek

LIARD RIVER

Allan Creek

Meister

River

Caribou L

Little

Moose River

River

Meister L

Meister River

Morley

River

Dorsey L

Cabin L

Munson L

River

Rudy Ls

Daughney

Roy L

North Wind L

Beaver

Goat L

Cr

Spencer Cr

River

Alaska Hwy

Rancheria

Seagull Cr

Partridge Cr

River

Cr

R

1

Swift River

Yukon
British Columbia

60°

Helen

MT HAZEL 1583

River

Swift

Swan L

Screw Cr

Cunningham Cr

McNaughton

Redfish Cr

Plate

Carlick

Cr

Cr

Plate

Blind Cr

Tootser

Cr

Tootsee L

River

Rancheria

Creek

3

Swift L

Hook Cr

SIMPSON PK 2173

Nome Cr

Creek

Jennings

Lakes

Little

6-25

Fall

Creek

Nome Lake

Klinkit L

Ranch

6-24

Thozzza Cr

Greenwood Cr

MT CHARLIE COLE 1541

Jennings

Cr

Aconitum Cr

Rapids

Klinkit Creek

Burfish Cr

Klinkit L

Parallel Creek

Dahti Creek

Blue River

4

102

Charlie Cole Cr

Hyland

Christmas Cr

Aconitum L

Shepaxiaw Cr

Jakobis Cr

Rapids

River

Rapids

Rapids

Rapids

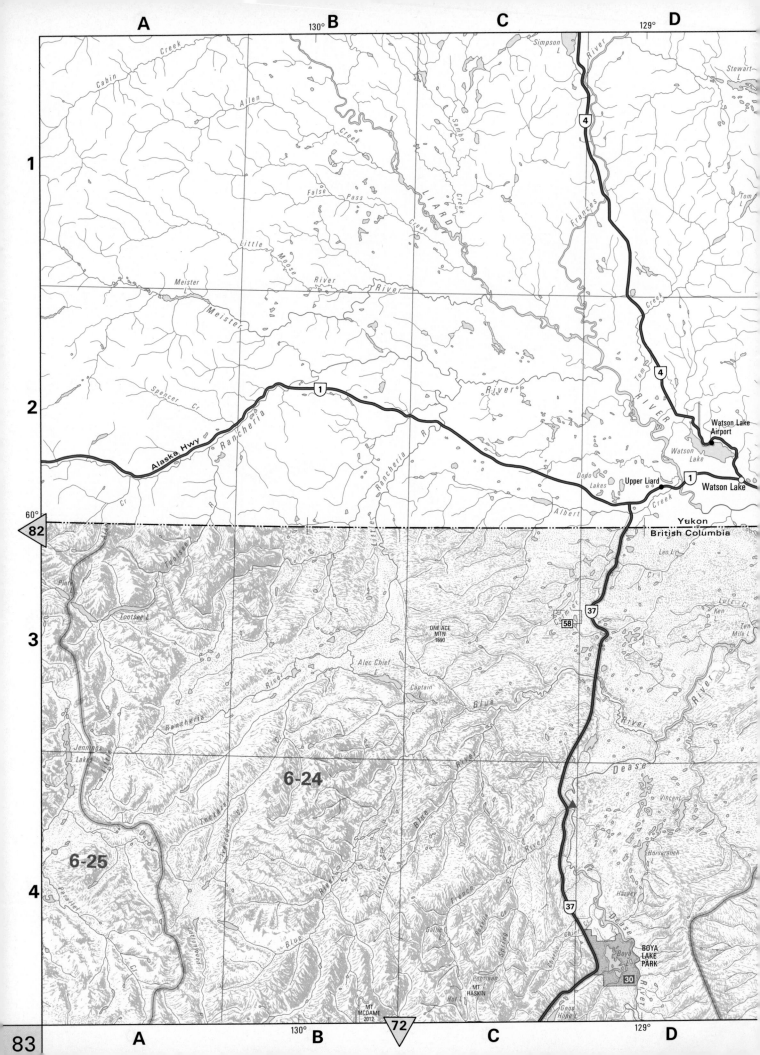

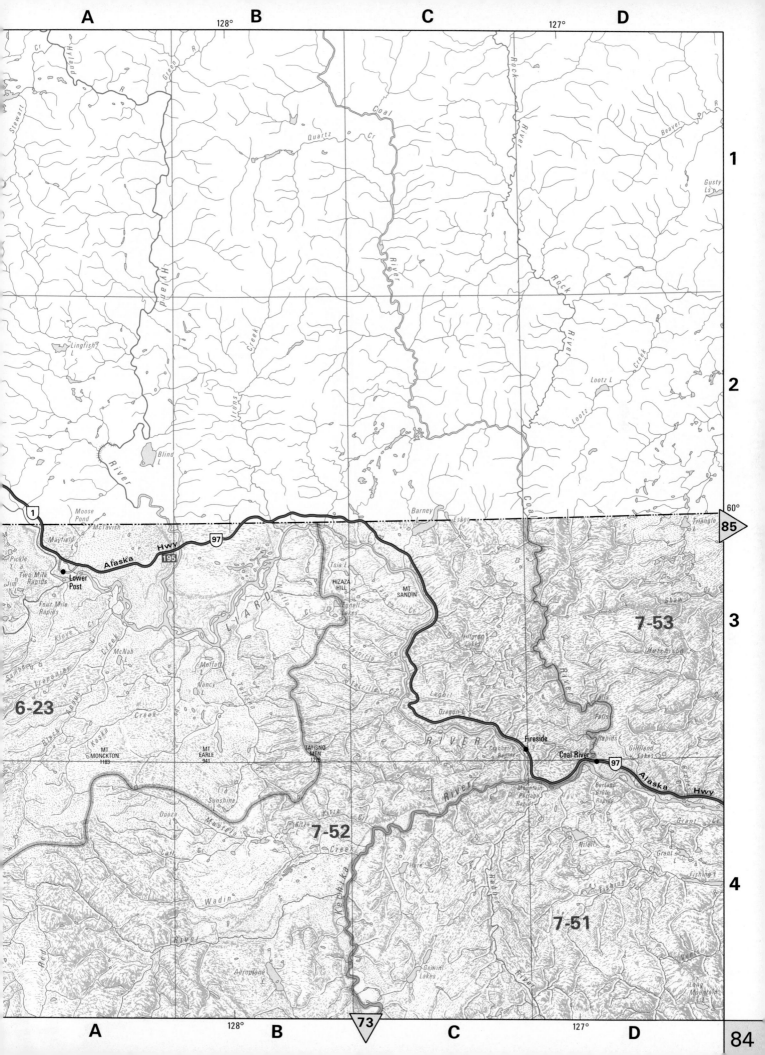

1

2

3

4

85

73

84

6-23

7-52

7-53

7-51

Hyland R

Green R

Stewart Cr

Cr

Gusty Ls

Beaver R

Lootz L

Lingfish L

Irons Creek

Quartz Cr

Coal Cr

Coal River

Rock River

Rock River

Lootz Creek

Blind L

River

Moose Pond

McTavish L

Mayfield L

Triangle

Esker R

Barney

60°

Alaska Hwy

97

195

Pickle Jim

Two Mile Rapids

Lower Post

Four Mile Rapids

LIARD

Kloye Cr

Sambaa Creek

Kaska Creek

Black Fogus

Trevanian Cr

McNab L

Moffatt L

Nancy L

Nelita Cr

Tsia L

HIZAZA HILL

Tsinita Cr

Egnell Lakes

MT SANDIN

Dall Cr

Hilltop Lakes

Shaw Cr

Hutchison

7-53

Pacific Cr

Legait Cr

Oregon L

RIVER

Stablford Rapids

Fireside

Coal River

97

Falls

Rapids

Gilliland Lakes

Alaska Hwy

MT MONCKTON 1183

MT EARLE 941

TATISNO MTN 1278

Old Sunshine

Dooza L

Mustela Cr

Kitla L

Kitla Cr

Tait Cr

Cell Cr

Wadin

Red R

Kechika

River

Aeroplane L

Hare L

Gemini Lakes

Mountain Portage Rapids

Rabbit River

Portland Knife Rapids

Niloit L

Grant Cr

Fishing

Grant L

Fishing L

Long Mountain Lk

Vance Cr

River

1

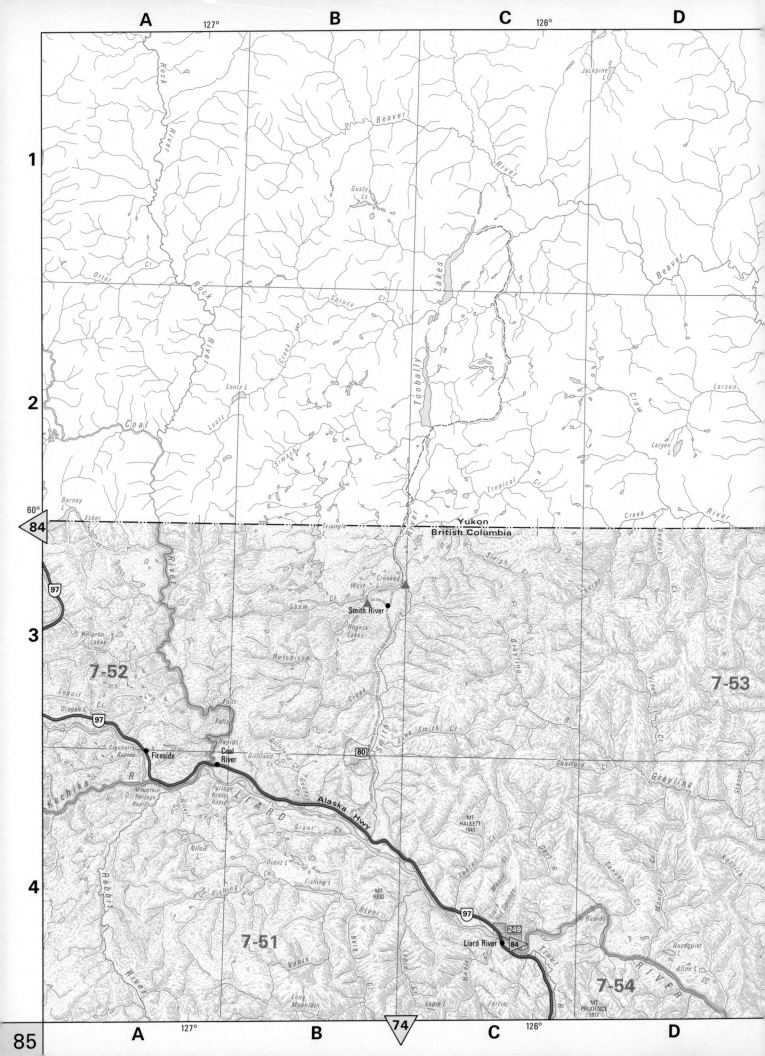

1

Jackpine L

Beaver

River

Gusty Ls

Rock

River

Otter Cr

Rock River

Lootz L

Lootz

Coal

Siwash Creek

Spruce Cr

Toobally

Lakes

Larsen

Crow

Larsen L

Tropical Cr

2

Barney L

Esker

Triangle L

Creek

River

Yukon
British Columbia

97

River

West Cr

Cronked

Smith River

Shaw Cr

Sleigh Cr

Thorpe

Cr

Hilgron Lakes

Rogers Lakes

Hutchison

Grayling

7-52

7-53

Leguil

Oregon L

Cr

Falls

Creek

Smith

Jane Smith Cr

R

97

Falls

Rapids

Cranberry Rapids

Fireside

Coal River

Gilliland Ls

Gilliland Cr

Geddes Cr

80

Chalford Cr

Grayling

Stane Cr

Kechika

R

Mountain Portage Rapids

Portage Brulé Rapids

LIARD

Alaska Hwy

MT HALKETT 1541

Devil R

Grayling

4

Rabbit

Niloil L

Grant Cr

Grant L

Fishing Cr

Fishing L

River

MT REID

Tresfre Cr

Moult Cr

Liard Hot Springs

97

Rapids

Kosick

Canyon Cr

Maula Cr

Nordquist L

7-51

Vents

Long Mountain

Beth

R

Hooler Cr

249

Liard River ●**84** →

Trout

R

RIVER

Alline L

7-54

Lapie L

Forcier L

MT PRUDENCE 1977

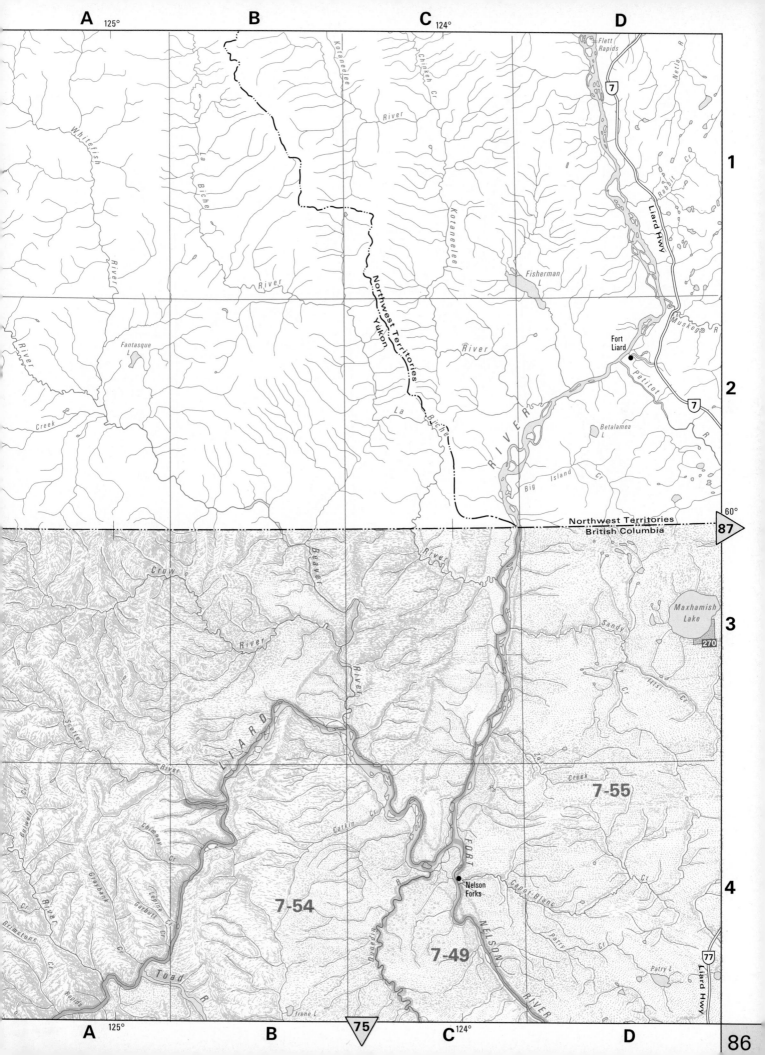

1

2

Flett Rapids

7

Liard Hwy

Netla R

Rabbit Cr

Whitefish

River

La Biche

Kotaneelee

Chinkeh Cr

River

Kotaneelee

River

Fisherman L

Muskeg R

Fantasque L

River

Northwest Territories

Yukon

River

Fort Liard

Petitot

7

Creek

La Biche

R I V E R

Betalamea L

Big Island Cr

Northwest Territories
British Columbia

60°

87

3

Crow

Beaver

River

Sandy

Maxhamish Lake

270

River

River

River

Itsi Cr

LIARD

River

Las

Creek

7-55

Sooter Cr

Bulwell Cr

Chimney Cr

Catkin Cr

FORT

7-54

Nelson Forks

Cabot Blanc Cr

Patry Cr

Greybank

Lenin Cr

Garbutt Cr

NELSON

7-49

Patry L

4

Brimstone Cr

Toad R

77

Liard Hwy

Rapids

Irene L

RIVER

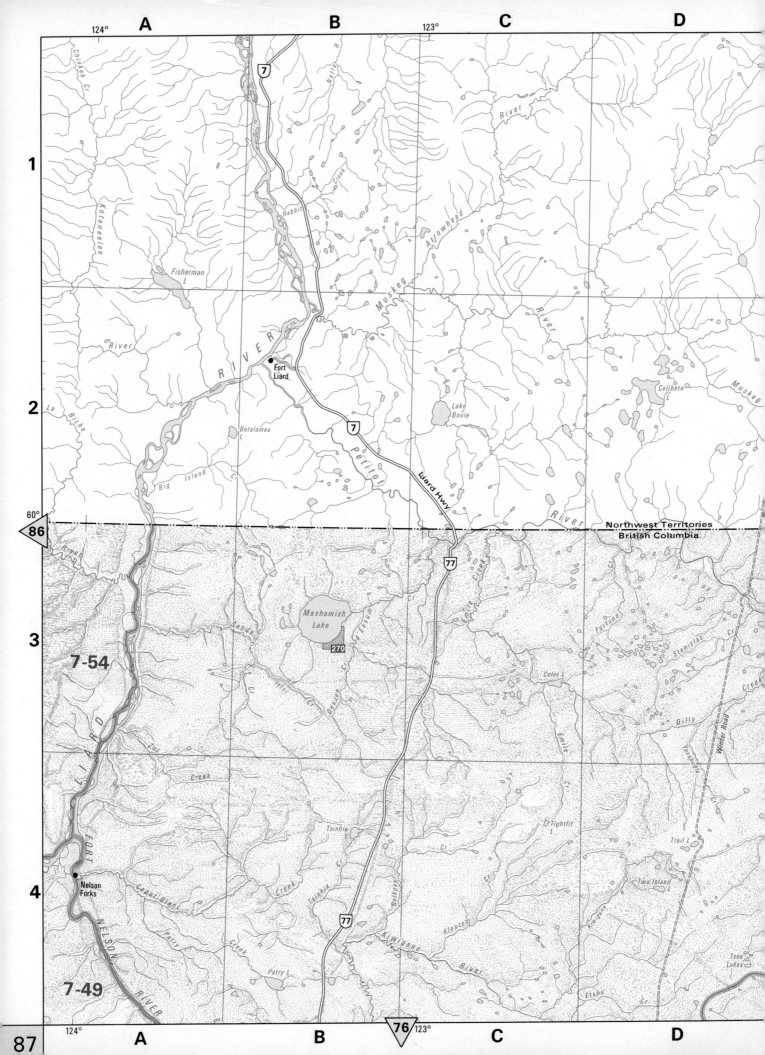

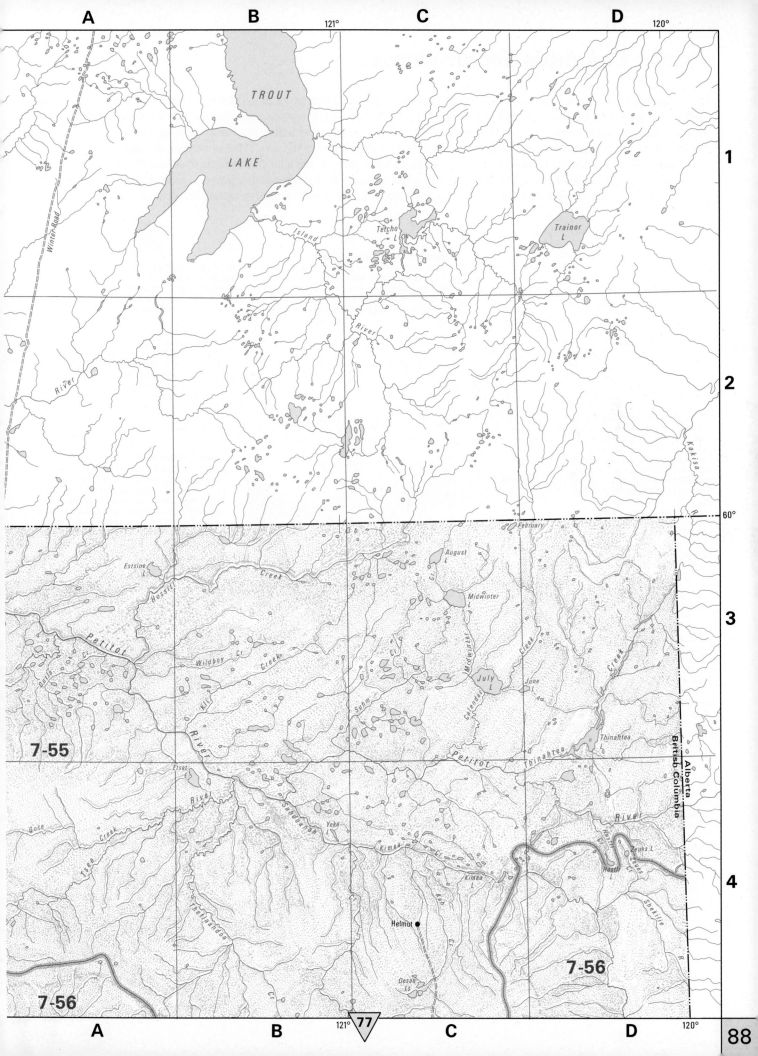

TROUT LAKE

Trainor L

Tetcho L

Winter-Road

River

River

Kakisa R

February L

Estsine L

August L

Hossit

Midwinter L

Petitot

Wildboy Cr.

Creek

Creek

Ci

Midwinter

Creek

Thinahtea Creek

July L

June L

Suhm

Calendaci

7-55

Petitot

Thinahtea

Thinahtea L

Etset L

River

Gote Creek

Tsea

Sandialah Creek

Yeka L

Kimea

Koh Cr.

River

Hay

Zeues L

Hosti L

Feutes

British Columbia

Alberta

Kimea L

Thelaahdoa

Cr.

Helmut

Desan Ls

7-56

Shekilie R

7-56

88

British Columbia Ecoprovinces

British Columbia has many ecosystems due to its varied physiography and climates. Its varied geological history has resulted in a complex topography. In addition, the Province has had a complex climatic history. Current climatic patterns are varied but, most typically, the Province is dominated by moist, cool to cold, temperate climates in a mountainous setting, most of which is higher than 1000 metres above sea level. An Ecoregion classification was developed in order to provide a systematic view of the small scale ecological relationships in the Province. This classification is based on climatic processes and landforms, and it brings into focus the extent of critical habitats and their relationship with adjacent areas. The Wildlife Viewing information on the following pages gives an Ecoprovince designation to each viewing site to give people a sense of species distribution through the diverse ecological area we call British Columbia.

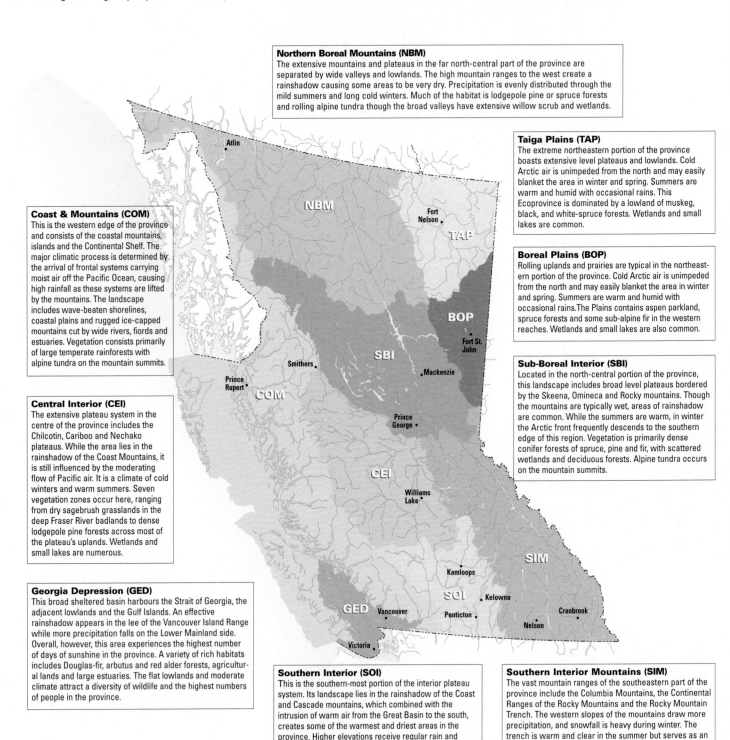

Northern Boreal Mountains (NBM)
The extensive mountains and plateaus in the far north-central part of the province are separated by wide valleys and lowlands. The high mountain ranges to the west create a rainshadow causing some areas to be very dry. Precipitation is evenly distributed through the mild summers and long cold winters. Much of the habitat is lodgepole pine or spruce forests and rolling alpine tundra though the broad valleys have extensive willow scrub and wetlands.

Taiga Plains (TAP)
The extreme northeastern portion of the province boasts extensive level plateaus and lowlands. Cold Arctic air is unimpeded from the north and may easily blanket the area in winter and spring. Summers are warm and humid with occasional rains. This Ecoprovince is dominated by a lowland of muskeg, black, and white-spruce forests. Wetlands and small lakes are common.

Boreal Plains (BOP)
Rolling uplands and prairies are typical in the northeastern portion of the province. Cold Arctic air is unimpeded from the north and may easily blanket the area in winter and spring. Summers are warm and humid with occasional rains.The Plains contains aspen parkland, spruce forests and some sub-alpine fir in the western reaches. Wetlands and small lakes are also common.

Coast & Mountains (COM)
This is the western edge of the province and consists of the coastal mountains, islands and the Continental Shelf. The major climatic process is determined by the arrival of frontal systems carrying moist air off the Pacific Ocean, causing high rainfall as these systems are lifted by the mountains. The landscape includes wave-beaten shorelines, coastal plains and rugged ice-capped mountains cut by wide rivers, fiords and estuaries. Vegetation consists primarily of large temperate rainforests with alpine tundra on the mountain summits.

Sub-Boreal Interior (SBI)
Located in the north-central portion of the province, this landscape includes broad level plateaus bordered by the Skeena, Omineca and Rocky mountains. Though the mountains are typically wet, areas of rainshadow are common. While the summers are warm, in winter the Arctic front frequently descends to the southern edge of this region. Vegetation is primarily dense conifer forests of spruce, pine and fir, with scattered wetlands and deciduous forests. Alpine tundra occurs on the mountain summits.

Central Interior (CEI)
The extensive plateau system in the centre of the province includes the Chilcotin, Cariboo and Nechako plateaus. While the area lies in the rainshadow of the Coast Mountains, it is still influenced by the moderating flow of Pacific air. It is a climate of cold winters and warm summers. Seven vegetation zones occur here, ranging from dry sagebrush grasslands in the deep Fraser River badlands to dense lodgepole pine forests across most of the plateau's uplands. Wetlands and small lakes are numerous.

Georgia Depression (GED)
This broad sheltered basin harbours the Strait of Georgia, the adjacent lowlands and the Gulf Islands. An effective rainshadow appears in the lee of the Vancouver Island Range while more precipitation falls on the Lower Mainland side. Overall, however, this area experiences the highest number of days of sunshine in the province. A variety of rich habitats includes Douglas-fir, arbutus and red alder forests, agricultural lands and large estuaries. The flat lowlands and moderate climate attract a diversity of wildlife and the highest numbers of people in the province.

Southern Interior (SOI)
This is the southern-most portion of the interior plateau system. Its landscape lies in the rainshadow of the Coast and Cascade mountains, which combined with the intrusion of warm air from the Great Basin to the south, creates some of the warmest and driest areas in the province. Higher elevations receive regular rain and snowfall in the winter, but this is the mildest area in the interior. Habitats include dry grasslands in the major valleys, ponderosa pine and Douglas-fir forests, large deep lakes and numerous small wetlands and rivers.

Southern Interior Mountains (SIM)
The vast mountain ranges of the southeastern part of the province include the Columbia Mountains, the Continental Ranges of the Rocky Mountains and the Rocky Mountain Trench. The western slopes of the mountains draw more precipitation, and snowfall is heavy during winter. The trench is warm and clear in the summer but serves as an access route for outbreaks of cold Arctic air in winter. Dense conifer forests are common here, though dry forests occupy the southern valleys, and alpine tundra and barren rock etch the mountain summits.

British Columbia Wildlife Watch is a wildlife viewing program designed to provide opportunities for viewing wildlife and encourage public understanding and appreciation of wildlife species and their habitats. Led by the Ministry of Environment, Lands and Parks, it involves many other agencies and ministries, public conservation groups and local communities. Look for the program's blue and white binoculars logo on highway directional signs throughout British Columbia. It indicates a wildlife viewing site.

Some wildlife viewing areas shown on the Atlas maps and listed on the following pages have no directional signs, viewing facilities, interpretive information or developed access. Developed viewing areas are most likely to be found near population centres, along highways, or within wildlife reserves or parks.

For further information on British Columbia Wildlife Watch, contact:

Wildlife Branch
Ministry of Environment, Lands and Parks
780 Blanshard Street
Victoria, BC V8V 1X4
Attention: Wildlife Watch Coordinator

Tips for Wildlife Viewers

These tips will improve your chances to see wildlife in their natural habitats. Remember, wildlife are wild and they may choose not to be seen.

Choose the right season and time of day
Most sites offer wildlife viewing opportunities only at certain times of the year. Before heading to a site, make sure it is the right season. Many species, other than fish, are most active during the cooler morning and early evening hours. A hot, dry sunny afternoon is usually not the best time to look.

Be quiet and be patient
Noise frightens wildlife away. Sit quietly in one place for a while. Successful wildlife viewing often requires longer waits and searches than you might expect.

Use binoculars or a spotting scope
Visual aids can let you scan wide areas and will increase your chances to observe wildlife without disturbing them.

Move slowly and reduce visibility
Wildlife will usually sense your presence long before you have sensed their. Hiding behind natural or artificial blinds (even your vehicle) will help you see more wildlife.

Use field guides
Field guides will help you identify and locate species and their habitats.

Viewing Ethics for Conservation

British Columbia offers many opportunities to see wildlife in a natural setting. Just looking can be a fascinating experience, but remember that these are wild animals. Wildlife viewing demands courtesy and common sense. For the well being of the wildlife and habitats, please follow these guidelines:

Be considerate of wildlife
Use binoculars and cameras with long lenses for that really close look. Use caution, especially when viewing or photographing large animals such as moose, elk and bears. Do not try to feed them. Wild animals that adapt to regular handouts may lose much of their ability to fend for themselves and may suffer in the lean months when their human benefactors are not around. They may also lose their fear of humans and could endanger both themselves and people they encounter.

Be considerate of habitat
Plants and the landscape are important parts of wildlife habitat. Leave flowers, plants, rocks, fossils, artifacts, shells and wood as you find them. Stay on designated trails or roads to protect plant life and assist animals in adapting to human movement.

Be considerate of other people
Respect private property and the wildlife viewing activities of others.

Control pets
Pets can harm wildlife and hinder viewing opportunities.

Do not approach young wildlife
Young wildlife are rarely abandoned or lost. An adult is usually a safe distance away waiting for you to leave. Always respect animal nests and dens.

Site Number	Map Reference	Viewing Site	Ecoprovince	Wildlife Viewing Highlights	Jan	Feb	Mar	Apr	May	Jun	Jul	Aug	Sep	Oct	Nov	Dec	Brochure	Interpretive Displays	Trails	Viewing Structure	Day Use	Campsites	Toilets	Nearest Hwy/Road	Nearest City/Town	Access
1	3 D2	**Active Pass/Bellhouse Provincial Park**	GED	Bald Eagle	•	•	•	•	•	•	•	•	•	•	•	•					•			17	Sidney, Tsawwassen Galiano & Mayne	BC Ferries, boat
				Bonaparte's Gull							•	•	•													
				Pacific Loon				•	•	•																
				Other seabirds	•	•	•	•	•	•	•	•	•	•	•	•										
				Sea Lion							•	•	•	•												
2	16 B2	**Adams River/ R. Haig-Brown Provincial Park**	SOI	Spawning Sockeye Salmon (largest run in North America, every 4 years - 1994...)								•	•				•	•	•	•	•	•	•	1	Chase	car
				American Dipper, Bald Eagle	•							•	•	•												
				Other spawning salmon									•													
				Spawning Rainbow Trout				•	•																	
3	25 D3	**Alkali Lake - Reidemann Wildlife Sanctuary**	CEI	Migrating waterfowl				•	•			•							•		•			20 to Dog Creek	Williams Lake, Alkali Lake	car, gravel road
				American White Pelican				•	•	•																
				Long-billed Curlew				•	•	•																
				Tundra Swan				•	•																	
4	23 C1	**Atnarko River (Tweedsmuir Prov. Park)**	COM	Bears, raptors				•	•	•	•	•	•	•				•	•		•	•	•	20	Bella Coola	car, gravel road
5	46 C2	**Babine Lake (Fulton River at Topley Landing)**	SBI	Spawning Sockeye Salmon								•	•						•		•			16	Granisle, Topley	car
6	57 C2	**Beatton Provincial Park/Charlie Lake**	BOP	Waterfowl, raptors, songbirds, shorebirds				•	•	•	•	•	•	•	•				•		•	•	•	97	Fort St. John	car
				Moose, deer, fox				•	•	•	•	•	•													
				Furbearers	•	•								•	•	•										
				Walleye					•	•	•	•	•													
				Burbot, perch, Northern Pike				•	•	•	•	•	•	•												
7	14 C3	**Birkenhead Lake Provincial Park**	COM	Ruffed Grouse				•	•	•				•	•		•	•	•		•	•	•	99	Pemberton	car
				Forest birds				•	•	•	•	•														
				Spawning Kokanee								•	•													
				Great Blue Heron							•	•	•													
				Osprey							•	•	•													
				Mountain Goat					•	•	•															
8	12 A3	**Blackfish Sound/ Johnstone Strait**	COM	Bald Eagle					•	•	•	•	•												Telegraph Cove, Port McNeill	Boat, charters
				Orca							•	•	•													
				Dall's Porpoise	•	•	•	•	•	•	•	•	•	•	•	•										
				Harbor Seal	•	•	•	•	•	•	•	•	•	•	•	•										
9	15 B2	**Bonaparte River**	SOI	Fish ladder (Dept. of Fisheries & Oceans)								•	•											97C	Ashcroft	car (very narrow road)
10	3 B3	**Botanical Beach Provincial Park**	GED	Tidepools / Intertidal Area (best at 0.6 m or lower tide)	•	•	•	•	•	•	•	•	•	•	•	•		•	•					14	Port Renfrew	car
				Gray Whale					•	•																
				Orca					•	•	•															
11	5 B3	**Boundary Bay**	GED	Excellent opportunities during spring & fall migrations for waterfowl & shorebirds				•	•			•	•	•			•	•		•	•	•	•	10, 17, 91 & 99	Delta, Tsawwassen, White Rock	car, hiking
				Overwintering shorebirds & waterfowls	•	•	•							•	•	•										
				Wintering raptors	•	•	•						•	•	•	•										
12	58 A-B1	**Boundary Lake**	BOP	Migrating Snow Goose, Tundra & Trumpeter Swans				•	•			•	•											97, then rural gravel road	Fort St. John	car
				Waterfowl				•	•			•	•													
				Shorebirds				•	•			•	•													
				Eastern songbirds				•	•			•	•													
				Moose, deer	•	•	•	•	•	•	•	•	•	•												
13	39 B3	**Bowron Lake Provincial Park**	SIM	Moose	•	•	•	•	•	•	•	•	•											26	Wells, Quesnel	Boat access only
				Bears, Hoary Marmots					•	•	•	•	•													
				Woodland Caribou						•	•	•														
14	17 B2	**Bridge Creek**	SIM	Spawning Rainbow Trout						•									•		•			1	Revelstoke	car
				Spawning Kokanee								•	•													
15	26 C4	**Bridge Lake & Creek**	CEI	Herring Gull, Black Swift				•	•	•	•	•	•	•					•		•			24	100 Mile House	car
				Spawning Kokanee								•	•													
16	45 C1	**Bulkley River/ Moricetown Falls**	COM	Migrating salmon (People have been catching salmon here for over 5000 years)								•												16	Smithers	car
17	4 A1	**Burnaby Lake Regional Park**	GED	Beaver, Muskrat			•	•	•	•	•	•	•				•	•	•		•		•	1 & 7	Burnaby	car
				Osprey					•	•	•	•														
				Waterfowl	•	•	•	•	•	•	•	•	•													
				Nature House							•	•	•													
18	2 D3	**Buttertubs Marsh**	GED	Waterfowl	•	•	•	•	•	•	•	•	•	•	•	•				•	•			19	within Nanaimo city limits	car
				Great Blue Heron	•	•	•	•	•	•	•	•	•	•	•	•										

Site Number	Map Reference	Viewing Site	Ecoprovince	Wildlife Viewing Highlights	Jan	Feb	Mar	Apr	May	Jun	Jul	Aug	Sep	Oct	Nov	Dec	Brochure	Interpretive Displays	Trails	Viewing Structure	Day Use	Campsites	Toilets	Nearest Hwy/Road	Nearest City/Town	Access
		Buttertubs Marsh (cont.)		Beaver			•	•	•	•	•	•	•													
				Painted Turtle				•	•	•	•	•														
19	4 C1	Camp and Hope Sloughs	GED	Great Blue Heron	•	•	•	•	•	•	•	•	•	•	•									1	Chilliwack	car
				Waterfowl	•	•	•	•	•	•	•	•	•	•	•											
				Woodpeckers				•	•	•	•	•	•													
				Riparian Habitat	•	•	•	•	•	•	•	•	•	•	•	•										
20	26 C-D3	Canim Lake	CEI	Bald Eagle	•	•	•	•	•						•	•					•	•		97	100 Mile House	car
				Bobolink, American Bittern					•	•	•	•														
21	25 D2	Cariboo Educational Woodlot (Bull Mountain)	CEI	Moose, Mule Deer	•	•	•	•	•	•	•	•	•	•	•				•	•	•			97, Bull Mtn. Rd.	Williams Lake	car
22	7 A3	Cathedral Lake Provincial Park/ Ashnola River Wildlife Reserve	SOI	Hoary Marmot, pika						•	•	•	•											3	Hedley, Keremeos	car, foot, horseback
				Mountain Goat						•	•	•	•													
				California Bighorn Sheep (can be seen on the road into the park)						•	•	•	•													
				Golden Eagle				•	•	•	•		•	•	•											
23	16 C2	Cedar Creek	SOI	Spawning Rainbow Trout					•										•	•				1	Salmon Arm	car
24	3 C1	Chapman Creek	GED	Spawning Chum Salmon										•	•	•			•	•				101	Sechelt	car
25	16 A4	Chapperon Lake	SOI	Grassland species (e.g., Long-billed Curlew, Badger)	•	•	•	•	•	•	•	•	•	•	•									5A to Douglas Lake Rd	Merritt	car
				Migrating Sandhill Crane				•	•				•	•												
26	5 B1	Cheakamus River	COM	Bald Eagle	•										•	•								99	Squamish	car
27	4 D1	Cheam Lake Wetlands Regional Park	GED	Waterfowl, raptors, songbirds	•	•	•	•	•	•	•	•	•	•	•	•		•	•	•	•		•	1 & 9	Chilliwack, Popkum	car
28	24 C2	Chilanko Marsh Wildlife Management Area	CEI	Migratory waterfowl, Beaver, Muskrat				•	•	•	•	•	•							•	•			20	Williams Lake	car, gravel road
29	24 C3	Chilko River (spawning channel)	CEI	Spawning Sockeye Salmon							•	•												20	Williams Lake	car, gravel road
				Spawning Chinook Salmon								•														
				Spawning Steelhead					•																	
30	8 A3	Christina Lake - Hwy. 3	SIM	Mule Deer, White-tailed Deer	•	•	•	•	•	•	•	•	•	•	•									3	Christina Lake	car
				Eagles					•	•	•	•	•	•	•											
31	16 C4	Coldstream Creek	SOI	Spawning Kokanee									•	•						•			•	6	Vernon	car
32	5 C3	Colony Farm Regional Park	GED	Raptors, Great Blue Heron, waterfowl	•	•	•	•	•	•	•	•	•	•	•				•		•			1 & 7	Port Coquitlam, Coquitlam	car
				Songbirds				•	•	•	•	•														
				Beaver, Muskrat				•	•	•	•	•														
33	18 C4	Columbia Lake Provincial Park/Columbia Lake Wildlife Reserves	SIM	Winter range for Rocky Mountain Bighorn Sheep, Elk, deer	•	•	•	•						•	•	•			•	•	•	•	•	93/95	Canal Flats, Fairmont Hot Springs	car
34	18 A1	Columbia Wetlands (26,000 - ha)	SIM	Elk, Moose, Gray Wolf, deer, raptors	•	•	•	•	•	•	•	•	•	•						•				95	Golden to Canal Flats	car
35	6 B2	Coquihalla Canyon Provincial Park	COM	Spawning Steelhead Trout (Short walk along old Kettle Valley railway grade)							•	•							•	•	•		•	5	Hope	car
36	2 A1	Courtenay River Estuary	GED	Major estuary on the Pacific Flyway;															•		•			19	Courtenay, Comox	car
				Trumpeter Swan (highest wintering concentration in North America)	•	•	•	•							•	•										
				Shorebirds					•	•																
				Waterfowl	•	•	•	•	•	•	•	•		•	•	•										
37	3 D3	Cowichan River Estuary	GED	Major waterfowl wintering area	•	•	•							•	•	•								1	Duncan	car
38	40 C4	Cranberry Marsh	SIM	Waterfowl, raptors					•	•	•	•	•						•	•	•			5	Valemount	car
				Muskrat, Moose					•	•	•	•	•													
39	9 A3	Creston Valley Wildlife Management Area	SIM	Ramsar site - internationally recognized staging and nesting area for migratory birds on the Pacific Flyway	•	•	•	•	•	•	•	•	•	•	•	•		•	•	•	•	•	•	3	Creston	car, canoe
40	48 C2	Crooked River	SBI	Wintering populations of Trumpeter Swan	•	•	•	•						•	•	•					•			5	Prince George, McLeod Lake	car
				Barrow's Goldeneye, Belted Kingfisher, American Dipper	•	•	•							•	•	•										
				Moose	•	•	•	•	•	•	•	•	•	•	•											
41	5 B3	Deas Island Regional Park	GED	Several gull species	•	•	•	•	•	•	•	•	•	•	•	•		•	•	•	•		•	17 & 99	Ladner	car
				Marsh Wren, Red-winged Blackbird				•	•	•	•	•														
				Grebes, shorebirds								•	•	•												

Site Number	Map Reference	Viewing Site	Ecoprovince	Wildlife Viewing Highlights	Time of Year												Facilities							Nearest Hwy/Road	Nearest City/Town	Access
					Jan	Feb	Mar	Apr	May	Jun	Jul	Aug	Sep	Oct	Nov	Dec	Brochure	Interpretive Displays	Trails	Viewing Structure	Day Use	Campsites	Toilets			
42	5 C3	DeBouville Slough	GED	Great Blue Heron colonies			•	•	•	•	•	•					•		•					7	Port Coquitlam	car
				Green Heron				•	•	•	•	•														
				Beaver, Muskrat			•	•	•	•	•	•	•	•													
43	32 C2	Delkatla Wildlife Sanctuary	COM	Sandhill Crane, Bald Eagle, shorebirds, waterfowl	•	•	•	•	•	•	•	•	•	•	•	•	•	•	•	•	•			16	Masset	car
44	56 D2	Dunlevy Creek	SBI	Stone Sheep, Elk, Mule Deer	•	•	•	•					•	•	•	•				•				29 -190 rd, gravel	Hudson's Hope	car
				Bald Eagle	•	•	•	•	•	•	•	•	•	•	•	•										
45	10 A3	Elko	SIM	Rocky Mountain Bighorn Sheep, Mountain Goat, deer	•	•	•	•						•	•	•		•	•					3	Elko, Fernie	car
46	2 C3	Englishman River	GED	Spawning Steelhead Trout					•										•					4	Parksville, Errington	car
47	48 B4	Eskers Provincial Park	SBI	Snowshoe Hare, Mule Deer	•	•	•	•	•	•	•	•	•	•	•	•	•	•	•		•		•	97	Prince George	car
				Beaver, Muskrat					•	•	•	•	•													
				Moose	•	•	•								•	•										
				Waterfowl, raptors, songbirds				•	•	•	•	•	•													
48	38 C1	Forests for the World (interpretive forest)	SBI	Moose	•	•	•	•	•	•	•				•	•	•	•	•					16, 97 to Foothills Drive	Prince George city limits	car
				Grouse	•	•	•	•	•	•	•				•	•										
				Songbirds				•	•	•	•	•														
				Frogs, aquatic insects				•	•	•	•	•														
				Forest successional stages & a variety of wildlife habitat																						
49	3 C4	French Beach Provincial Park	COM	Gray Whale			•	•					•	•			•	•	•		•	•	•	14	Sooke, Jordan River	car
				Seabirds	•	•	•	•	•	•	•	•	•	•	•	•										
				Intertidal fauna	•	•	•	•	•	•	•	•	•	•	•	•										
50	17 D3	Gerrard	SIM	Spawning Kokanee									•							•				31	Kaslo	car
				Spawning Rainbow Trout (1000 of the largest Rainbow Trout in the world - up to 16 kg)				•	•																	
51	5 C3	Golden Ears Provincial Park	COM	Songbirds				•	•	•	•	•					•	•	•	•	•	•	•	7	Maple Ridge	car
				Mountain Goat (Gold Creek area)					•	•	•															
52	3 D3	Goldstream River Provincial Park	GED	Spawning Chum and Coho Salmon										•	•	•	•	•	•		•	•	•	1	Victoria	car
				Bald Eagle, Great Blue Heron, gulls	•	•	•	•	•	•	•	•	•	•	•	•										
				Tidal estuary, mature western red cedar - black cottonwood forest, riparian habitat																						
53	26 B-C4	Green Lake/Watch Creek	CEI	Spawning Rainbow Trout					•	•	•													24, 97	100 Mile House	car, gravel road
54	38 D1	Grove Burn/ Tabor Mountain	SBI	Moose	•	•	•							•	•		•	•						16	Prince George	car
				Black Bear				•	•	•	•	•														
				Songbirds				•	•	•	•	•														
55	79 B2-3	Haines Road	COM/NBM	Moose, Stone Sheep, caribou, bear, many bird species				•	•	•	•	•												7	north of Pleasant Camp	car
56	6 A3	Harrison River/Kilby Provincial Park	GED	Bald Eagle (Bald Eagle Festival, early Dec.)	•	•								•	•	•		•	•		•	•	•	7	Harrison Hot Springs, Mission	car
				Trumpeter Swan	•	•								•	•	•										
				Spawning salmon	•									•	•	•										
				Waterfowl	•	•	•						•	•	•	•										
57	7 C3	Haynes Point Prov. Park	SOI	Waterfowl, songbirds				•	•	•	•	•	•	•							•	•	•	3	Osoyoos	car
58	5 D3	Hayward Lake Reservoir Rec. Area	GED	Waterfowl, woodpeckers, Beaver	•	•	•	•	•	•	•	•	•	•	•	•	•	•	•		•		•	7	Mission, Maple Ridge	car
				Songbirds				•	•	•	•	•	•													
59	7 A3	Hedley-Keremeos cliffs along Hwy. 3	SOI	Mountain Goat	•	•	•	•	•	•			•	•	•			•		•				3	Hedley, Keremeos	car
60	19 A3	Height of the Rockies	SIM	Moose, Rocky Mountain Bighorn Sheep, Elk, Mountain Goat, deer						•	•	•	•	•										43	Elkford	Gravel & back road access only
61	2 B2	Helliwell Provincial Park	GED	Pelagic Cormorant, Harlequin Duck	•	•	•	•	•	•	•	•	•	•	•	•			•	•				19	Courtenay, Hornby Island	car, walking
				Pigeon Guillemot, scoters, murrelets	•	•	•																			
62	14 D1	High Bar	CEI	California Bighorn Sheep	•	•	•	•	•	•	•	•	•	•	•	•								99	Lillooet	car June - Sept; 4X4 other times
				Mule Deer			•	•	•	•	•															
				Chukar	•	•	•	•	•	•	•	•	•	•	•	•										
63	17 B2	Hill Creek	SIM	Spawning Kokanee, Bull Trout									•	•			•	•	•	•	•		•	23, 31	Nakusp	car
				Spawning Rainbow Trout					•																	
				Osprey, eagles									•	•												
64	26 B1	Horsefly Lake/ Quesnel Lake & Area	SIM	Moose, Mule Deer	•	•	•	•	•	•	•	•	•	•			•							97 to Horsefly Road	Horsefly	car
				Spawning Kokanee									•	•												
				Black Bear				•	•	•	•	•	•													

Site Number	Map Reference	Viewing Site	Ecoprovince	Wildlife Viewing Highlights	Jan	Feb	Mar	Apr	May	Jun	Jul	Aug	Sep	Oct	Nov	Dec	Brochure	Interpretive Displays	Trails	Viewing Structure	Day Use	Campsites	Toilets	Nearest Hwy/Road	Nearest City/Town	Access
65	26 B1	Horsefly River	CEI	Spawning Sockeye Salmon								•	•					•		•				97	Horsefly	car
66	40 A3	Horseshoe Lake	SIM	Waterfowl				•	•	•	•							•		•				16	McBride	car
				Muskrat				•	•	•	•															
67	57 A1	Inga Lake	BOP	Rainbow Trout					•	•										•				29	Fort St. John	car
				Brook Trout							•															
				Waterfowl, Moose				•	•	•	•	•														
68	7 C3	Inkaneep Provincial Park	SOI	Lewis' Woodpecker, Bald Eagle, Orioles,				•	•	•	•	•						•				•	•	97	Oliver	car
				warblers, grosbeaks, songbirds, quail				•	•	•																
				Kokanee									•													
69	5 B3	Iona Island Regional Park	GED	Shorebirds, waterfowl	•	•	•	•	•	•	•	•	•	•	•	•		•	•				•	17, 99	Richmond	car
				Excellent area for rarities during spring and fall migrations				•	•																	
70	2 D2	John Daly Regional Park	GED	Spawning Coho and Chum Salmon									•	•				•	•	•	•			101	Pender Harbour	car
71	25 C3	Junction Sheep Range Provincial Park	CEI	California Bighorn Sheep				•	•	•	•	•					•	•					20	Williams Lake, Riske Creek	rough gravel road
				Long-billed Curlew					•	•																
				Grouse						•	•	•														
72	16 C4	Kalamalka Provincial Park	SOI	Grassland birds				•	•	•	•	•					•	•		•		•	97	Vernon	car
				Marmots					•	•	•	•														
				Mule Deer, White-tailed Deer	•	•	•	•	•	•	•	•	•	•	•	•										
73	5 C3	Kanaka Creek Regional Park	GED	Chum and Coho Salmon									•	•	•			•	•		•		•	7	Maple Ridge	car
74	10 A3	Kikomun Creek Provincial Park	SIM	Spawning Kokanee									•					•	•	•	•	•	•	93	Jaffray	car
				Painted Turtle					•	•	•															
				Osprey				•	•	•	•															
75	40 D3	Kinney Lake (Mount Robson Provincial Park)	SIM	Songbirds					•	•	•									•	•	•	•	16	Tete Jaune Cache	hiking
				Beaver, pika					•	•	•															
				Moose	•	•	•	•						•	•	•										
				Mountain Goat									•	•												
76	44 D2	Kitsumkalum Lake	COM	Spawning Steelhead								•	•	•										16	Terrace, Rosswood	car
77	16 A3	Knutsford Corridor	SOI	Raptors	•	•	•	•	•	•	•	•	•	•	•	•								5A	Kamloops	car
				Sandhill Crane					•																	
				Short-eared Owl	•	•	•	•	•	•	•	•	•	•												
78	18 C2	Kootenay National Park	SIM	Rocky Mountain Bighorn Sheep, Elk	•	•	•	•	•	•	•	•	•	•	•	•	•	•	•	•	•	•	•	93	Radium Hot Springs	car
				Mule Deer, Mountain Goat	•	•	•	•	•	•	•	•	•	•	•	•										
				Songbirds					•	•	•															
				Wildflowers						•	•															
79	15 D2	Lac du Bois	SOI	Waterfowl				•	•	•										•				5	Kamloops	car
				Flammulated Owl					•	•																
				Grassland birds				•	•	•																
				Mountain Bluebird				•	•																	
80	26 A3	Lac La Hache & Area - facilities at provincial park	CEI	Bald Eagle, Marten, Red Crossbill	•	•	•	•	•	•	•	•	•	•	•	•	•	•	•	•	•	•	•	97	Lac La Hache	car
				Sandhill Crane, Pileated Woodpecker					•	•																
81	15 D3	Lac Le Jeune	SOI	Spawning Rainbow Trout					•										•	•	•	•	•	5	Kamloops	car
82	45 A3	Lakelse Lake Provincial Park/Lakelse Lake Wildlife Reserve	COM	Spawning Salmon									•	•			•	•	•	•	•	•	•	3	Terrace	car
				Trumpeter Swan	•	•	•								•	•										
				Moose	•	•	•	•	•	•	•	•	•	•	•	•										
83	2 C1	Lang Creek Spawning Channel	GED	Spawning Coho Salmon									•	•	•				•	•	•			101	Powell River	car
84	85 C4	Liard River Hotsprings Provincial Park	NBM	Moose	•	•	•	•	•	•	•	•	•	•	•	•	•	•	•	•	•	•		97	Liard River	car
				Lake Chub	•	•	•	•	•	•	•	•	•	•	•	•										
				Elk, wolf, furbearers	•	•	•	•	•	•	•	•	•	•	•	•										
				Several species of bats						•	•	•	•													
				Large hotspring system with more than 250 species of boreal plants including 14 species of orchids and some species of carnivorous plants																						
85	39 B4	Likely/Cariboo River & Lake	SIM	Moose, Mule Deer	•	•	•	•	•	•	•	•	•	•	•	•								97	Williams Lake, Likely	backroads

Site Number	Map Reference	Viewing Site	Ecoprovince	Wildlife Viewing Highlights	Jan	Feb	Mar	Apr	May	Jun	Jul	Aug	Sep	Oct	Nov	Dec	Brochure	Interpretive Displays	Trails	Viewing Structure	Day Use	Campsites	Toilets	Nearest Hwy/Road	Nearest City/Town	Access
86	8 B2	Lower Arrow Lake/ Syringa Creek Prov. Park	SIM	Rocky Mountain Bighorn Sheep	●	●	●	●	●	●	●	●	●	●	●	●	●		●		●			3A	Castlegar	car
				Elk, deer				●					●	●	●											
				Mountain Goat	●	●	●	●						●	●											
				Spawning Kokanee								●	●													
				Wintering waterfowl	●	●	●									●										
87	44 C4	Lower Skeena River	COM	Spawning Eulachon, Bald Eagle, sea lions, seals				●	●												●		●	16	Prince Rupert	car
88	6 C3	E.C. Manning Provincial Park	COM	Marmots						●	●	●	●				●	●	●	●	●			3	Hope, Princeton	car, hiking
				Songbirds					●	●	●	●														
				Ground squirrels					●	●	●	●														
				Wildflowers							●	●														
89	5 B3	Maplewood Flats	GED	Songbirds				●	●	●			●				●		●					1 to Dollarton Hwy	North Vancouver	car
				Waterfowl	●	●	●	●	●			●	●	●	●	●										
				Harbour Seal	●	●	●	●	●			●	●	●	●	●										
90	25 D1	McLeese Lake/ Sheridan Creek	CEI	Spawning Kokanee								●	●					●			●	●		97	100 Mile House	car
91	58 A3	McQueen's Slough	BOP	Waterfowl, shorebirds, songbirds					●	●	●	●	●	●			●	●	●	●				97, to gravel rd	Dawson Creek	car
92	18 A4	Meadow Creek	SIM	Spawning Kokanee								●	●						●	●	●			31	Kaslo	car
93	52 C2	Meziadin Lake Provincial Park	COM	Spawning Sockeye Salmon								●							●	●	●	●	●	37	Meziadin Junction	car
94	5 C3	Minnekhada Regional Park	GED	Waterfowl				●	●	●	●	●	●	●	●	●	●						●	7	Port Coquitlam	car, hiking
				Woodpeckers, raptors	●	●	●	●	●	●			●	●	●	●										
				Bald Eagle	●	●									●	●										
95	7 C1	Mission Creek Regional Park	SOI	Spawning Kokanee									●	●			●	●	●					97	Kelowna	car
				Wildflowers					●	●	●															
96	2 A1	Mitlenatch Island Provincial Park	GED	Seabird nesting colony (sensitive site when seabirds are nesting; visitors must keep to trails)						●	●	●					●	●	●					19	Courtenay, Campbell River	Boat only
97	28 D4	Moberly Marsh/Bergenham Wildlife Reserve	SIM	Waterfowl	●	●	●	●	●	●	●	●	●	●	●									1	Golden	car
98	40 D4	Moose Lake & Marsh (Mount Robson Provincial Park)	SIM	Moose	●	●	●	●	●	●	●	●	●	●	●	●	●	●	●	●	●	●	●	16	Tete Jaune Cache	car
				Elk					●	●	●	●	●													
				Loons, grebes, waterfowl					●	●	●	●														
99	2 D3	Morell Nature Sanctuary	GED	Mixed Douglas-fir forest with beaver pond & small lake	●	●	●	●	●	●	●	●	●	●	●	●	●	●	●					1	Nanaimo	car
100	45 C4	Morice Lake	COM	Spawning Chinook Salmon								●												16 to gravel road	Houston	car
101	17 B1	Mt. Revelstoke National Park	SIM	Wide range of mountain & other bird species	●	●	●	●	●	●	●	●	●	●	●	●	●	●	●					1	Revelstoke	car
102	74 C-D1	Muncho Lake Provincial Park	NBM	Deer, Moose	●	●	●	●	●	●	●	●	●	●	●	●	●	●	●		●	●	●	97	Toad River, Muncho Lake	car
				Stone Sheep					●	●	●	●	●													
				Caribou					●	●																
				Many bird species					●	●	●	●														
				Trumpeter Swan									●	●	●											
				Wolves	●	●								●	●											
				Wildflowers							●															
103	46 B4	Nadina River	CEI	Moose winter range	●	●	●								●	●								16 to gravel road	Houston, Burns Lake	car
104	32 C-D2	Naikoon Provincial Park	COM	Waterfowl, seabirds along shoreline	●	●	●	●	●				●	●	●	●			●	●	●	●	●	16	Masset	car
105	3 C1	Nanaimo Harbour Nanaimo River Estuary Wildlife Reserve	GED	Bald Eagle	●	●										●								1	Nanaimo	car, boat, charters
				Seabirds	●	●	●	●								●										
				Sea lions (Sea Lion Festival in late Jan.)	●	●										●										
106	8 B3	Nancy Greene Provincial Park	SIM	Moose	●	●	●	●	●	●	●	●	●					●	●		●	●		3	Rossland	car
				Mule Deer, White-tailed Deer					●	●	●	●	●													
				Ground squirrels						●	●	●	●													
107	7 B2	Naramata Creek	SOI	Spawning Kokanee									●	●							●			97	Penticton, Naramata	car
				Elk, Mule Deer	●	●	●								●	●										
				Sea mammals							●	●														

Site Number	Map Reference	Viewing Site	Ecoprovince	Wildlife Viewing Highlights	Jan	Feb	Mar	Apr	May	Jun	Jul	Aug	Sep	Oct	Nov	Dec	Brochure	Interpretive Displays	Trails	Viewing Structure	Day Use	Campsites	Toilets	Nearest Hwy/Road	Nearest City/Town	Access
108	44 C1	**Nass River**	COM	Spawning Sockeye Salmon								•	•											16 to gravel road	New Aiyanish	car, boat
				Bald Eagle				•	•	•	•	•														
				Waterfowl									•	•	•											
109	47 C4	**Nechako River Migratory Bird Sanctuary**	SBI	Coyote	•	•	•	•	•	•	•	•	•	•	•	•	•				•			16	Vanderhoof	car
				Caribou	•	•	•																			
				Moose	•	•	•	•	•	•	•	•	•	•	•	•										
110	65 B2	**Nevis Creek**	NBM	Stone Sheep	•	•	•	•	•	•	•	•	•	•	•	•								97 to Mile 178	Pink Mountain	4x4s, ATVs, horse
				Coyote	•	•	•	•	•	•	•	•	•	•	•	•										
				Wolves	•	•																				
				Ptarmigan	•	•	•	•	•	•	•	•	•	•	•	•										
111	15 D3-4	**Nicola Valley Corridor**	SOI	Sandhill Crane migration				•	•				•	•						•				5A	Kamloops, Merritt	car
				Raptors				•	•				•	•												
				Golden Eagle				•	•				•	•												
				Coyote, Badger, Mule Deer	•	•	•	•	•	•	•	•	•	•	•											
				Sharp-tailed Grouse				•	•																	
112	5 D3	**Nicomen Slough**	GED	Wintering ducks and geese	•	•	•							•	•	•								7	Mission	car
				Swans, Bald Eagle	•	•									•	•										
113	12 A4	**Nimpkish River (Woss Branch)**	COM	Spawning Sockeye Salmon								•												19	Woss	car
114	7 B3	**Okanagan Falls Provincial Park**	SOI	Bats, Common Nighthawk					•	•	•	•	•				•	•	•		•	•	•	97	Okanagan Falls	car
				Waterfowl	•	•	•	•							•	•										
				Swallows				•	•	•	•	•	•													
115	7 B-C3	**Okanagan River @ Oliver**	SOI	Spawning Kokanee										•						•				97	Penticton	car
116	7 B2	**Okanagan River @ Penticton**	SOI	Spawning Kokanee										•						•				97	Oliver	car
117	26 B4	**100 Mile Marsh Wildlife Sanctuary**	CEI	Beaver, Muskrat					•	•	•	•	•				•	•	•		•		•	97	100 Mile House	car
				Tundra Swan					•	•				•	•											
				Waterfowl					•	•	•															
118	26 B3	**108-Mile & Area**	CEI	Mule Deer	•	•	•	•	•	•	•	•	•	•	•					•				97	100 Mile House, Lac La Hache	car
				Yellow-bellied Marmot					•	•	•	•	•													
119	7 B-C3	**Osoyoos Oxbows Fish & Wildlife Management Reserve**	SOI	Bobolink					•	•	•							•	•		•		•	97	Osoyoos	car
				Great Blue Heron				•	•	•	•	•	•	•	•											
				Shorebirds, Osprey				•	•	•	•	•	•	•	•											
				Bats					•	•	•	•	•													
				Raptors, waterfowl	•	•	•	•	•	•	•	•	•	•	•											
				Sockeye Salmon, Kokanee										•	•											
120	1 D4	**Pacific Rim National Park - Barkley Sound**	COM	Whales, sea lions			•	•	•	•	•	•	•	•										4	Ucluelet	Boat only
				Bald Eagle	•	•	•	•	•	•	•	•	•	•	•	•										
121	1 D3-4	**Pacific Rim National Park - Long Beach**	COM	Gray Whale			•	•	•	•	•	•	•	•	•			•	•	•	•	•	•	4	Tofino, Ucluelet	car
				Other marine mammals				•	•	•	•	•	•	•												
				Shorebirds				•	•	•	•	•	•	•												
				Intertidal life	•	•	•	•	•	•	•	•	•	•	•	•										
				Old-growth forests and bog habitats																						
122	3 B1	**Parksville/Qualicum Beach Wildlife Management Area**	GED	Brant (Brant Festival in mid-April)			•	•									•	•	•	•	•	•	•	19	Parksville, Qualicum Beach	car
				Waterfowl	•	•	•	•							•	•										
123	7 B1	**Peachland Creek**	SOI	Spawning Kokanee									•	•			•	•	•	•	•		•	97	Peachland	car
				American Dipper	•	•	•	•	•	•	•	•	•	•	•	•										
124	8 C3	**Pend d'Oreille**	SIM	Praying Mantis								•	•				•			•				3B, 6	Trail, Salmo	car in summer only
				White-tailed Deer	•	•	•	•							•											
				Marmots					•	•	•	•														
				Osprey, Turkey Vultures				•	•	•	•	•	•													
				Eagles	•	•	•	•	•	•	•	•	•													
				Western Bluebird				•	•	•	•	•														
125	7 A1	**Pennask Lake**	SOI	Loons, Osprey						•	•	•	•									•	•	5A	Merritt	4 x 4 only
				Spawning Rainbow Trout						•																
126	7 B-C2	**Penticton Creek**	SOI	Spawning Kokanee									•	•						•				97	Penticton	car
127	48 C1	**Pine Pass**	SBI	Moose	•	•	•	•	•	•	•	•	•	•	•	•								97	McLeod Lake	car
				Woodland Caribou	•	•	•								•	•										
128	65 C3	**Pink Mountain**	NBM	Caribou, Moose, Plains Bison						•	•	•	•	•										97 to Road 192	Pink Mountain	4x4s, ATVs, horse, hiking
				Wolves, Coyote						•	•	•	•	•												
				Bears					•	•	•	•	•													

Site Number	Map Reference	Viewing Site	Ecoprovince	Wildlife Viewing Highlights	Jan	Feb	Mar	Apr	May	Jun	Jul	Aug	Sep	Oct	Nov	Dec	Brochure	Interpretive Displays	Trails	Viewing Structure	Day Use	Campsites	Toilets	Nearest Hwy/Road	Nearest City/Town	Access
		Pink Mountain (cont.)		Ptarmigan					●	●	●	●	●	●												
				Raptors					●	●	●	●	●	●												
				Arctic butterflies							●	●														
				Wildflowers							●	●														
129 B1	4	**Pitt-Addington Marsh Wildlife Management Area**	GED	Tundra & Trumpeter Swans	●	●	●						●	●	●	●	●		●	●	●		●	7	Port Coquitlam, Pitt Meadows	car
				Osprey				●	●	●	●	●	●													
				Waterfowl	●	●	●	●						●	●	●										
				Important area on the Pacific Flyway																						
130 D2	2	**Porpoise Bay Provincial Park/Porpoise Bay Wildlife Reserve**	GED	Waterfowl	●	●	●						●	●	●	●	●	●			●	●	●	101	Sechelt	car
				Shorebirds, Harbour Seal	●	●	●	●	●	●	●	●	●													
				Spawning Chum Salmon										●	●											
131 B1	7	**Powers Creek**	SOI	Spawning Kokanee								●	●						●					97	Kelowna	car
132 D2	9	**Premier Lake Provincial Park/Premier Ridge Wildlife Reserve**	SIM	Spawning Rainbow Trout					●	●							●	●	●	●	●	●	●	93/95	Skookumchuck	car
				Osprey, eagles					●	●																
				Winter range for Rocky Mountain Bighorn Sheep & Elk, deer	●	●	●								●	●										
133 D3	38	**Quesnel/Wells (Hwy. 26)**	SBI/SIM	Moose	●	●	●	●	●	●	●	●	●	●					●					26	Quesnel - Wells	car
				Migrating Woodland Caribou						●	●	●														
				Beaver						●	●															
134 C-D4	38	**Quesnel River Waterfront Trail**	SBI	Ring-billed Gulls					●	●	●	●	●				●	●	●					97	Quesnel	car
135 C4	40	**Rearguard Falls Provincial Park**	SIM	Spawning Chinook Salmon - falls are final barrier in the 1200 km journey up the Fraser River.								●	●				●	●	●				●	16	Tete Jaune Cache	car
136 B3	5	**George C. Reifel Migratory Bird Sanctuary**	GED	Snow Goose (as many as 30,000)	●	●							●	●	●	●	●	●	●	●			●	10, 17	Ladner	car
				Snow Goose Festival											●											
				More than 230 other bird species observed	●	●	●	●	●	●	●	●	●	●	●	●										
137 B3	5	**Roberts Bank (inc. ferry terminal, coal port, Brunswick Point & Canoe Pass)**	GED	Spring and fall migration of waterfowl and shorebirds				●	●			●	●											17	Ladner	car
				Harbour Seal	●	●	●	●	●	●	●	●	●	●	●	●										
138 D3	5	**Rolley Lake Provincial Park**	GED	Warblers, waxwings, flycatchers, swifts, swallows				●	●	●	●	●	●				●	●	●		●	●	●	7	Mission, Maple Ridge	car
				Spawning Rainbow Trout					●	●																
139 A4	27	**Roundtop/ Mosquito Flats**	SOI	Mule Deer						●	●									●				5	Little Fort, Clearwater	car
				Woodpeckers	●	●	●	●						●												
				Beaver	●	●	●	●	●	●	●	●														
				Waterfowl				●	●	●	●	●	●	●												
				Warbler migration						●		●	●													
140 D1	2	**Ruby Lake**	GED	River outlet spawning channel for Cutthroat Trout									●	●	●		●							101	Sechelt	car
141 C-D3	5	**Ruskin Recreation Site**	GED	Spawning Chum Salmon									●	●			●	●	●				●	7	Mission	car
142 C2	16	**Salmon Arm Bay**	SOI	Western Grebe					●	●	●	●					●	●	●	●			●	1	Salmon Arm	car
				Fall migration of shorebirds								●	●	●												
				Migrating & nesting waterfowl				●	●	●		●	●	●												
143 A3	26	**San Jose River (along Hwy. 97)**	CEI	Muskrat, Beaver				●	●	●	●	●	●							●				97	Lac La Hache, Enterprise	car
144 A3	8	**Sandner Creek**	SIM	Spawning Kokanee								●	●	●			●							3	Christina Lake	car
145 D2	2	**Sargeant Bay Provincial Park**	GED	Waterfowl	●	●	●	●	●	●	●	●	●	●	●	●	●	●	●		●		●	101	Sechelt	car
				Songbirds				●	●	●	●	●	●													
146 A2	6	**Sasquatch Provincial Park**	GED	Beaver					●	●	●	●	●				●	●	●		●	●	●	7	Harrison Hot Springs	car
				Waterfowl					●	●	●	●	●													
				Woodpeckers					●	●	●	●	●													
				Warblers					●	●	●	●	●													
147 D2	25	**Scout Island Nature Centre (Williams Lake)**	CEI	Red Fox	●	●	●	●	●	●	●	●	●	●	●	●	●	●	●	●	●		●	97	Williams Lake	car
				Muskrat, River Otter, Beaver, Milbert's Tortoiseshell Butterfly, Great Blue Heron					●	●	●	●														
148 C3	5	**Serpentine Wildlife Area**	GED	Waterfowl	●	●	●	●	●	●	●	●	●	●	●	●	●	●	●	●				99, 99A	White Rock	car
				Northern Harrier	●	●	●							●												
				Shorebirds				●	●			●	●													
				Muskrat				●	●	●	●	●	●													
149 D2	14	**Seton Lake**	CEI	Mountain Goat	●	●	●	●	●	●	●	●	●	●	●						●	●		99	Lillooet	car

Site #	Map Ref	Viewing Site	Eco	Wildlife Viewing Highlights	Jan	Feb	Mar	Apr	May	Jun	Jul	Aug	Sep	Oct	Nov	Dec	Brochure	Interpretive Displays	Trails	Viewing Structure	Day Use	Campsites	Toilets	Nearest Hwy/Road	Nearest City/Town	Access
150	26 C4	Sheridan Lake (spawning channel)	CEI	Spawning Pink Salmon									•	•						•				24	100 Mile House	car
				Spawning Rainbow Trout					•	•																
151	5 C3	Shoreline Park	GED	Spawning salmon (Noons Creek)										•	•		•	•	•	•	•		•	7	Port Moody	car, boat
				Songbirds	•	•	•	•	•	•	•	•	•	•	•	•										
				Waterfowl	•	•	•	•	•					•	•	•										
152	3 D3	Sidney Spit Provincial Marine Park	GED	Large Fallow Deer population	•	•	•	•	•	•	•	•	•	•	•	•		•	•	•	•	•	•	17	Sidney	boat only - small ferry runs mid-May to early October
				Great Blue Heron	•	•	•	•	•	•	•	•	•	•	•	•										
				Bald Eagle	•	•	•	•	•	•	•	•	•	•	•	•										
				Cormorants, Pigeon Guillemot, Black Oystercatcher	•	•	•	•	•	•	•	•	•	•	•	•										
				Grebes, waterfowl	•	•	•	•						•	•	•										
				Large tidal marsh and mud flat that attracts many pelagic & shore birds; long sand spits																						
153	65 B3	Sikanni Chief River	NBM /BOP	Plains Bison, Moose	•	•	•	•	•	•	•	•	•	•	•	•								97 between Mile 150 & 171	Pink Mountain	car for 5 km then ATVs or 4x4s
				Caribou	•	•	•	•						•	•	•										
				Elk	•	•	•	•	•	•	•	•	•	•	•	•										
				Wolves, Coyote	•	•	•	•	•	•	•	•	•	•	•	•										
				Grouse, Ptarmigan, raptors	•				•	•	•	•	•	•												
154	44 D3	Skeena Islands	COM	Moose	•	•	•	•	•	•	•	•	•	•	•									16	Terrace	car
155	2 D4	Skutz Falls	GED	Spawning Rainbow Trout				•	•	•														18	Duncan, Lake Cowichan	car
				Spawning Steelhead			•	•	•																	
				Spawning Brown Trout							•	•														
156	2 B1	Sliammon Creek	GED	Spawning Coho and Chum Salmon										•	•	•			•					101	Powell River	car
157	2 D4	Somenos Marsh	GED	Wildlife Reserve for waterfowl (major freshwater wintering area).	•	•	•							•	•	•	•	•	•	•				1	Duncan	car
158	5 B3	South Arm Marshes WMA (includes Ladner Marsh and islands in the South Arm of the Fraser R.)	GED	Waterfowl	•	•	•	•	•	•	•	•	•	•	•	•		•	•	•				10, 17, 99	Ladner	car, boat
				Raptors	•	•	•	•	•	•	•	•	•	•												
159	16 A2	South Thompson River	SOI	Trumpeter & Tundra Swans	•	•	•							•	•					•				1	Chase to Kamloops	car
				Osprey					•	•	•															
				Waterfowl staging area				•		•																
				California Bighorn Sheep	•	•	•	•	•	•	•	•	•	•	•	•										
160	62 A1	Spatsizi Plateau Wilderness Park	NBM	Mountain Goat, Stone Sheep, Caribou, many bird species	•	•	•	•	•	•	•	•	•											37	Iskut	trail only
161	15 B3	Spences Bridge	SOI	Rocky Mountain Bighorn Sheep, Chukar	•	•	•	•	•	•	•	•	•	•	•	•				•				1	Spences Bridge	car
				Sockeye Salmon								•	•													
162	5 B1	Squamish Estuary	COM	Bald Eagle, Swans	•	•									•	•			•					99	Squamish	car
				Waterfowl	•	•	•	•							•	•										
				Shorebirds					•	•	•															
163	2 A2-3	Stamp Falls Provincial Park	GED	A very large (>100,000) Sockeye Salmon run								•	•	•	•		•	•	•	•	•	•	•	4	Port Alberni	car
				Spawning Chinook Salmon										•	•	•										
				Spawning Coho Salmon	•									•	•	•										
164	47 A4	Stellako River @ Francois Lake	CEI	Spawning Rainbow Trout					•	•	•							•	•	•				16	Fraser Lake	car
				Spawning Sockeye Salmon									•	•												
				Trumpeter Swan	•	•	•								•	•										
				Bald Eagle						•	•	•	•	•												
				Mule Deer	•	•	•	•	•	•	•	•	•	•	•	•										
165	47 A4	Stuart River	SBI	Trumpeter Swan	•	•	•								•	•								27	Fort St. James	car
				Spawning Chinook Salmon								•	•													
				Spawning Sockeye Salmon								•	•													
166	75 B2-3	Stone Mountain Provincial Park	NBM	Moose	•	•	•	•	•	•	•	•	•	•	•	•		•	•	•	•	•	•	97	Summit Lake	car
				Stone Sheep							•	•	•													
				Caribou							•	•	•													
				Ptarmigan, grouse, songbirds							•	•	•													
				Wildflowers							•															
167	1 C1	Strathcona Provincial Park/Elk River	GED	Roosevelt Elk	•	•	•								•	•	•	•	•	•	•	•	•	28	Campbell River	car
				Trumpeter Swan	•	•	•								•											
168	8 B3	Sutherland Creek	SIM	Spawning Kokanee								•	•	•										3	Christina Lake	car

Site Number	Map Reference	Viewing Site	Ecoprovince	Wildlife Viewing Highlights	Jan	Feb	Mar	Apr	May	Jun	Jul	Aug	Sep	Oct	Nov	Dec	Brochure	Interpretive Displays	Trails	Viewing Structure	Day Use	Campsites	Toilets	Nearest Hwy/Road	Nearest City/Town	Access
169	3 D4	Swan Lake/Christmas Hill Nature Sanctuary	GED	Close to downtown Victoria, this is an excellent area for birdwatching year-round but especially in winter.	●	●	●	●	●	●	●	●	●	●	●	●	●	●	●	●			●	17	Victoria	car
170	58 A4	Swan Lake Provincial Park	BOP	Eastern songbirds				●	●	●	●		●								●	●	●	2	Dawson Creek	car
				Waterfowl			●	●	●			●	●													
				Shorebirds			●	●	●																	
171	40 C4	Swift Creek	SIM	Spawning Chinook Salmon								●	●					●	●	●	●			5	Valemount	car
172	2 A3	Taylor River	GED	Spawning Coastal Cutthroat Trout	●	●	●												●					4	Port Alberni	car
				Rainbow Trout				●	●	●															
173	38 D3	Ten-Mile Lake Provincial Park	SBI	Beaver (lodge, dams / slides)				●	●	●	●	●	●	●				●	●	●	●	●	●	97	Quesnel	car
174	32 C3	Tlell River	COM	Spawning Steelhead	●										●									16	Tlell	car
				Spawning Coho Salmon									●	●											
175	15 D2	Tranquille Wildlife Management Area/ Dewdrop - Rosseau Wildlife Management Area	SOI	Waterfowl migrations			●	●	●	●			●	●						●				1, 5	Kamloops	car
				Small songbirds			●	●	●	●															
				Mule Deer	●	●	●	●							●	●									
				California Bighorn Sheep	●	●	●								●	●									
176	15 C3	Tunkwa Lake/ Jacks Creek	SOI	Spawning Rainbow Trout							●							●			●	●		97C	Savona, Logan Lake	car
				Sandhill Crane					●																
				Canada Goose					●	●	●														
177	7 B3	Vaseux Lake	SOI	California Bighorn Sheep	●	●	●	●	●	●	●	●	●	●	●	●	●	●	●	●	●		●	97	Okanagan Falls, Oliver	car
				Bats						●	●	●													
				Beaver						●	●	●													
				Waterfowl, Canyon Wren	●	●	●	●	●	●	●	●													
				Songbirds					●	●	●	●													
				Swans	●	●	●							●	●	●									
178	3 D4	Victoria Foreshore including Esquimalt Lagoon	GED	Federal Migratory Bird Sanctuary; marine birds and mammals	●	●	●	●	●	●	●	●	●	●	●	●	●							Marine drive around waterfront	Victoria	car
				Wildflowers				●	●																
				Garry oak meadows (one of the most endangered ecosystems in Canada)																					
179	6 A2	Weaver Creek Spawning Channel	COM	Spawning Sockeye Salmon									●	●				●	●	●				7	Harrison Bay	car
180	27 A1-3	Wells Gray Park	SIM	Mule Deer, Moose, caribou	●	●	●	●	●	●	●	●	●	●	●	●	●	●	●	●	●	●	●	5	Clearwater	car
				Loons (Murtle Lake)						●	●	●	●												
				Spawning Chinook Salmon (Horseshoe, Bailey's Chute)								●	●	●											
				Bald Eagle								●	●												
				Osprey						●	●	●	●												
181	8 D2	West Arm Kootenay Lake - Kokanee Creek Provincial Park	SIM	Spawning Kokanee								●	●					●		●	●	●	●	3A	Nelson, Balfour	car
182	8 D2	West Arm Kootenay Lake - Highway 3A (between Nelson & Balfour)	SIM	Osprey						●	●	●												3A	Nelson, Balfour	
183	8 D2	West Arm Kootenay Lake - Kokanee Glacier Provincial Park	SIM	Marmots, pikas							●	●	●											3A	Nelson, Balfour	
				Wildflowers							●	●													
				Cutthroat Trout							●	●													
184	8 D2	West Arm Kootenay Lake - Kokanee Ck. Road	SIM	Deer, grouse							●	●	●											3A	Nelson, Balfour	Gravel - open June to Oct
				Avalanche chutes							●														
185	8 D2	West Arm Kootenay Lake - Nelson waterfront	SIM	Waterfowl	●	●	●							●	●									3A	Nelson	
				Osprey							●	●	●												
186	8 D2	West Arm Kootenay Lake - Redfish Ck.	SIM	Spawning Kokanee								●	●											3A	Nelson, Balfour	
187	18 D4	Whiteswan Lake Provincial Park	SIM	Spawning Rainbow Trout					●									●			●	●		93/95	Canal Flats	car
				Moose					●	●															
188	18 C3	Windermere Lake	SIM	Spawning Kokanee									●	●										93/95	Invermere	
189	2 A1	Woodhus Slough	GED	Waterfowl	●	●	●							●	●	●				●				19	Campbell River, Courtenay	car
				Raptors	●	●	●	●	●	●	●	●	●	●											
				Shorebirds			●	●			●														
				Songbirds					●	●	●														

British Columbia Ecological Reserves

British Columbia was the first province in Canada to establish legislation dedicated exclusively to ecological reserves. The ecological reserves system has grown considerably since the establishment of the first ecological reserves in 1971. Today, 139 ecological reserves, encompassing over 159,477 hectares, protect some of the most distinctive and outstanding examples of our natural heritage.

Ecological reserves are permanent sanctuaries established to:

- preserve representative examples of plant and animal communities;
- protect rare and endangered plants and animals in their natural habitat;
- preserve unique or rare zoological, botanical or geological phenomena;
- serve as benchmarks for long-term scientific research and educational use;
- serve as examples of habitats recovering from modifications caused by human activity.

Most ecological reserves are open to the public for non-destructive, observational uses (eg. hiking, photography, wildlife viewing), but in some ecological reserves, where resources are easily impacted by human presence, access is not permitted without a ministerial permit (these ecological reserves are indicated in the following table). Further, all consumptive resource uses such as timber harvesting, mining, hunting, trapping, grazing, camping, lighting fires, road and trail building, removal of materials, plants and animals, and the operation of motorized vehicles, are prohibited.

The following table provides general information on the individual ecological reserves in British Columbia. Before entering an ecological reserve or for further information on ecological reserves, please contact a BC Parks office (listed on page 109). The Ecological Reserve number in the first column is shown on the map pages in a white box (see Atlas map legend on page I).

ECOLOGICAL RESERVE MAP NUMBER	MAP REFERENCE	Ecological Reserve Area	Main Features
1	1C3	Cleland and Vargas Islands*	Seabird colony
2	13B4	East Redonda Island	Representative forest with three biogeoclimatic zones
3	15B3	Soap Lake	Saline lake, Douglas-fir forest and grassland
4	3B1	Lasqueti Island	Shoreline forest with Rocky Mountain juniper
5	16D4	Lily Pad Lake	Undisturbed highland lake
6	16D4	Buck Hills Road	Small stand of old western larch
7	7B2	Trout Creek	Ponderosa pine parkland
8	58B2	Clayhurst	Eroding bluffs within Peace River parklands
9	32D2	Tow Hill	Forested sand dunes, swamp and peat bogs
10	32D1	Rose Spit	Sand spit, open dunes and shoreline meadows
11	11A4	Sartine Island*	Seabird colony
12	11A4	Beresford Island*	Seabird colony
13	11A4	Anne Vallee (Triangle Island)*	Largest seabird and sea lion colonies in province
14	11B4	Solander Island*	Seabird colony
15	4A3	Saturna Island	Young Douglas-fir forest
16	3D3	Mount Tuam	Arbutus/Douglas-fir forest
17	3D2	Canoe Islets*	Seabird colony
18	3C-D2	Rose Islets*	Seabird colony
19	18C4	Mount Sabine	Mixed conifer forest
20	18C4	Columbia Lake	Limestone flora
21	6C3	Skagit River Forest	Douglas-fir forest
22	6C3	Ross Lake	Ponderosa pine in coastal Douglas-fir forest
23	21C1	Moore/McKenney/Whitmore Islands*	Seabird colony
24	2A4	Baeria Rocks*	Seabird colony and subtidal marine life
25	34C4	Dewdney and Glide Islands*	Variety of maritime bog, pond and scrub forest communities, seabirds
26	18D4	Ram Creek	Hotsprings and burnt forest
27	6D2	Whipsaw Creek	Ponderosa pine stands
28	2D1	Ambrose Lake	Coastal bog lake
29	15D2	Tranquille	Ponderosa pine and sagebrush plant communities
30	16D3	Vance Creek	Highly diverse mixed conifer forest

ECOLOGICAL RESERVE MAP NUMBER	MAP REFERENCE	Ecological Reserve Area	Main Features
31	17C3	Lew Creek	Three biogeoclimatic zones in one drainage basin
32	8C1	Evans Lake	Subalpine forests including a stand of rare yellow cedar
33	7B3	Field's Lease	Semi-arid shrub steppe communities
34	7D1	Big White Mountain	Subalpine and alpine plant communities
35	25D3	Westwick Lake	Shoreline and area surrounding an interior saline lake
36	48A2	Mackinnon Esker	Long compound esker, well-developed lichen communities
37	3D2	Mount Maxwell	Garry oak stand
38	46C-D1	Takla Lake	Most northerly known occurrence of Douglas-fir
39	40A2	Sunbeam Creek	Representative subalpine plant communities
40	12C1	Kingcome River/Atlatzi River	Rich alluvial swamps, bogs and forest
41	48C2	Tacheeda Lakes	Representative forest communities on the McGregor plateau
42	16C-D2	Mara Meadows*	Unique calcareous fen; rare orchids
43	17A2	Mount Griffin	Secondary and climax interior western hemlock forests
44	3B3	San Juan River Estuary	The only existing ecological reserve containing an alluvial forest community, archaelogical sites
45	32A3	Vladimir J. Krajina (Port Chanal)	Virgin marine shoreline, forest, muskeg and alpine communities, rare mosses, seabird colony
46	64C3	Sikanni Chief	Engelmann spruce at northern extremity of range; subalpine lichens
47	76C2	Parker Lake	Extensive bog habitat with Sarracenia purpurea (pitcher plant)
48	3D1	Bowen Island	Forest of Douglas-fir and red cedar; dry subzone of western hemlock zone
49	16D2	Kingfisher Creek	Representative flora of northern Monashee Mountains
50	57D1	Cecil Lake	Sphagnum bog community with black spruce
51	7C1	Browne Lake	Marsh and forest, rich in wild flowers
52	32C2	Drizzle Lake	Lake and surrounding bogs; unique species of stickleback
53	37C4	Narcosli Lake	Protection of waterfowl breeding grounds; well-developed aquatic communities
54	2B4	Nitinat Lake	Steep west coast forest; maritime population of Douglas-fir
55	24D4	Cardiff Mountain	Example of lava plateau, basalt columns and crater lake
56	28A2	Goosegrass Creek	A cross-section of three biogeoclimatic zones; forests including mountain hemlock
57	72B2	Chickens Neck Mountain	Climax stand of white spruce and subalpine fir
58	83C3	Blue/Dease Rivers	Terrestrial and aquatic communities associated with the boreal black and white spruce zone
59	61B4	Ningunsaw River	Coastal western hemlock zone near its northern limit and associated Englemann spruce-subalpine fir and alpine tundra zones
60	47B4	Drywilliam Lake	Excellent old growth stand of Douglas-fir
61	17A2-3	Upper Shuswap River	Western red cedar in interior western hemlock zone
62	76C2	Fort Nelson River	White spruce within alluvial stands of black cottonwood
63	44C4	Skeena River	Mature cottonwood on alluvial floodplain
64	37D1	Ilgachuz Range	Subalpine/alpine vegetation on the dry east side of the Coast Mountains
65	15B1	Chasm	Ponderosa pine at its northern limit
66	3D4	Ten Mile Point	Inter-and subtidal marine life
67	3D3	Satellite Channel	Subtidal marine life
68	61D2	Gladys Lake	Stone sheep, mountain goats, caribou and their environment
69	5B1	Baynes Island	Undisturbed alluvial black cottonwood forest
70	39B3	Mount Tinsdale	Representative alpine and subalpine communities
71	56A4	Blackwater Creek	Boreal forest and portion of extensive low moor area
72	38B1	Nechako River	Southern occurrence of tamarack
73	46B1	Torkelsen Lake	Low moor wetlands with cloudberry
74	3D1	UBC Endowment Lands	Second-growth Puget Sound lowland forest
75	11C4	Clanninick Creek	Alluvial Sitka spruce
76	4C1	Fraser River	Seral alluvial cottonwood and willow forest
77	16C4	Campbell-Brown (Kalamalka Lake)	Ponderosa pine-bunchgrass site; rattlesnake den
78	37C2	Meridian Road (Vanderhoof)	Engelmann spruce-subalpine fir-lodgepole pine forest
79	37C2	Chilako River	Tamarack at its southern limit in BC, swamp, fen, bog ecosystem mosaic
80	85B3	Smith River	Representative boreal black and white spruce forest
81	46A4	Morice River	Burnt sub-boreal spruce forest
82	38D3	Cinema Bog	Lowland black spruce sphagnum bog
83	3B3	San Juan Ridge	Protection of rare white avalanche lily (Erythronium montanum)
84	48D4	Aleza Lake	Representative sub-boreal spruce forest, lakes and wetland ecosystems
85	56B4	Patsuk Creek	Paper birch and other seral forest
86	38A1	Bednesti Lake	Kettle lake wetland succession

ECOLOGICAL RESERVE MAP NUMBER	MAP REFERENCE	Ecological Reserve Area	Main Features
87	56B4	Heather Lake	Excellent aspen stands
88	15B3	Skwaha Lake	Subalpine forest and superb flower meadows
89	6C3	Skagit River Cottonwoods	Excellent cottonwood stands reserved for gene pool purposes
90	1D3	Sutton Pass	Rare Adder's tongue fern (*Ophioglossum vulgatum*)
91	55C2	Raspberry Harbour	High-quality lodgepole pines for use in forest research
92	15B4	Skihist	Ungrazed Ponderosa pine-bunchgrass site
93	32A1	Lepas Bay	Seabird colony
94	3D4	Oak Bay Islands	Spring flowers, rare plants, seabirds and marine life
95	3A1	Bowser	Conservation of rare plant species and communities, transitional old growth, rare and diverse dragonfly species
96	3C2	Woodley Range	Conservation of rare meadow plant species and unique communities
97	3D4	Race Rocks	Outstanding marine community, sea-lion haul-out, seabirds
98	6B3	Chilliwack River	Mature alluvial forest with large western red cedars; hybrid spruces
99	5C3	Pitt Polder	Two forested hills surrounded by swamp, fen and bog communities
100	7C3	Haynes' Lease	Representative semi-arid land with elements of "pocket desert" vegetation
101	25D3	Dog English Bluff	Limestone cliff with 10 species of rare plants; colony of white-throated swifts
102	82A4	Charlie Cole Creek	Unique cone-shaped cold-water mineral springs used by ungulates as salt licks
103	21C1	Byers/Conroy/Harvey/Sinnett Islands	Important seabird and marine mammal breeding areas
104	9D3	Gilnockie Creek	Mature western larch, seral lodgepole pine, small wetland
105	1C2	Megin River	Typical west coast alluvial and upland forests
106	6B3	Skagit River Rhododendrons	Two stands of California rhododendrons, fire-induced seral forest
107	55B2	Chunamon Creek	Two small drainages; Engelmann and white spruce forest
108	16C4	Cougar Canyon	Mosaic of plant communities including wetlands in canyon setting
109	11C4	Checleset Bay	Extensive area of marine shoreline, reefs and islets providing habitat for B.C.'s prime sea otter population, seabirds, marine life
110	16A2	McQueen Creek	Native grasses and flowers on small hill
111	12B3	Robson Bight (Michael Bigg)*	Killer whales and a crucial part of their habitat; pristine estuary and forested slopes
112	3D2-3	Mount Tzuhalem	Garry oak woods with profusion of spring wildflowers, rare plants
113	3B2	Honeymoon Bay	Outstanding population of pink fawn-lily (*Erythronium revolutum*)
114	45A3	Williams Creek	Representative coastal western hemlock forest and outstanding terraced bogs
115	44C1	Gingietl Creek	Undisturbed watershed in virgin coastal western hemlock forest
116	6A3	Katherine Tye (Vedder Crossing)	Rare white phantom orchid (*Cephalanthera austinae*) and its habitat
117	2C3	Haley Lake	Population of endangered Vancouver Island marmot
118	12B4	Nimpkish River	Sample of Canada's tallest Douglas-firs
119	11D4	Tahsish River	Pristine westcoast estuary
120	11C2	Duke of Edinburgh (Pine/Storm/Tree Is.)	Largest seabird nesting colony in Queen Charlotte Strait
121	3D3	Brackman Island	Pristine, ungrazed Gulf Island vegetation and marine buffer
122	12A-B3	Tsitika Mountain	Alpine communities, wet subalpine forest, unusual terraced fen, and small lake
123	12B3	Mount Derby	Alpine peak and precipitous, partly forested slopes
124	12B4	Tsitika River	Low-elevation swamp/fen/bog complex
125	12B4	Mount Elliott	Representative subalpine subdrainage surrounding Cirque Lake
126	12B4	Claud Elliott Creek	Representative hemlock, amabilis fir and red cedar forest
127	25C3	Big Creek	Representative grasslands of Chilcotins, in Ponderosa pine bunchgrass zone
128	3D2	Galiano Island	Rare undisturbed peat bog ecosystem in dry coastal Douglas-fir zone
129	11C4	Klaskish River	Estuary and alluvial forest in coastal western hemlock zone; native oysters
130	7B3	Mahoney Lake	Southern interior saline lake with unique limnological features of international scientific recognition
131	6B1	Stoyoma Creek	Meeting of three biogeoclimatic zones, with seven coniferous tree species; to conserve special seed provenances
132	3D4	Trial Islands	The most outstanding assemblage of rare and endangered plant species in B.C.
133	44B4	Gamble Creek	North coastal forest/bog complex and occurrence of pacific silver fir near the northern limit of its range
134	47B4	Ellis Island	Inland breeding colony of herring and ring-billed gulls
135	2A2	Comox Lake Bluffs	Unique botanical phenomena, rare plants
136	2D3	Hudson Rocks	Nationally significant breeding colony of endangered Pelagic Cormorant
137	2A4	Klanawa River	Marbled Murrelet, Oxalis and other rare plants
138	2D3	Ladysmith Bog	Unique botanical association - bog plants, sphagnum mosses, bladderwort, sundew, etc.
139	11D3	Misty Lake	One of only three lakes in the world with the endangered Giant Black Stickleback fish

* These ecological reserves are closed to the public due to the sensitive nature of the area. The closure at Robson Bight (Michael Bigg) Ecological Reserve covers the land base of the ecological reserve only.

Provincial and National Parks

It's little wonder British Columbia's 6 National and over 500 Provincial Parks are admired by people from around the world. They comprise nearly 8,900,000 hectares, more than 9 percent of B.C.'s total land area, and vary from little known beaches to vast tracts of mountains, forests and waterways.

Caves and alpine meadows, mountain peaks, virgin rain forests, extinct volcanoes, paddling and portage routes, historic towns, Pacific islands and the nation's highest waterfall are park features which make up more than half of the "representative landscapes" of B.C.

BC PARKS FACILITIES GUIDE

The matrix on the following pages lists all the available facilities in BC Parks. The information below lists the columns in order and gives a brief description of how to read the codes.

PARK / MAP NUMBER ....This number corresponds with the boxed number on the Atlas maps indicating Park location (see Atlas map legend on page I-II).

MAP REFERENCE ....The number refers to the page in the Atlas and the letter identifies the location on that page (see Atlas map legend on page I-II).

PARK ....Park area is shown in hectares. RA indicates recreational area classification.

NEAREST HIGHWAY ....Indicates the route number of the highway nearest the main entry of the park.

ROAD ACCESS ....The number indicates distance from nearest highway in kilometres and the letter indicates road surface . P = paved, G = gravel, R = rough, NO = roads do not enter park, F = vehicle ferry.

OPERATING DATES ....Time of year that the park is open to the public, although paid staying times are generally between April 1 and October 31.

FEE (Y,N) RESERVATIONS ....Y = fee charged for vehicle/tent overnight camping, R = Reservations are accepted in this campground.
Campground Reservations: call Discover Camping at 1-800-689-9025 (in Vancouver (604) 689-9025) March 1-Sept. 15 Reservations may be made up to 3 months in advance, and carry an additional non-refundable fee.
Note: Not all provincial Parks accept reservations. Listings in this guide which accept reservations at time of publishing may be subject to change. **For further information:** call headquarters office at (250) 387-4550 or Discover Camping.

VEHICLE / TENT CAMPSITES ..A number indicates how many campsites are available on site, * = group camping is available.

WILDERNESS / WALK-IN .....Sites which cannot be accessed by vehicle, number indicates campsites available, X = camping is permitted.

PICNICKING / DAY USE ......A number indicates parking spaces for cars, X = facilities available.

BOAT LAUNCH / CANOEING ..R = one or more boat launching ramps available, C = canoeing/kayaking is an on-site activity.

FIREWOOD / WATER ....F = firewood available on site during fee collection period, W = certified drinking water source is available on-site.

SANI-STATION ....X = effluent dumping and water replenishment facility for Recreational Vehicles is available on-site.

TOILETS / SHOWERS ....F = flush toilets on site, P = toilets other than flush type, S = showers available.

SWIMMING ....X = indicates that swimming is a principal on-site activity.

FISHING ....X = indicates that freshwater fishing is available on-site or nearby. You will need a BC angling licence to fish in a Provincial Park.

HIKING / WALKING TRAILS ...H = hiking trails with total lengths given in kilometres, W = indicates short, generally easy trails often leading to special features. Local knowledge may be required to locate starting points of many trails.

BC PARKS – DISTRICT OFFICES

BC Parks staff can provide you with **detailed information** about interpretation programs, conservation, facilities, services, and recreational opportunities within the parks of their district.

BC Parks
Box 220
BRACKENDALE, B.C.
V0N 1H0
(604) 898-3678

BC Parks
10003 - 110th Ave.
FORT ST. JOHN, B.C.
V1J 6M7
(250) 787-3407

BC Parks
Site 8, Comp. 5, RR #3
NELSON, B.C.
V1L 5P6
(250) 825-3500

BC Parks
Box 1479
PARKSVILLE, B.C.
V9P 2H4
(250) 954-4600

BC Parks
Bag 5000
SMITHERS, B .C.
V0J 2N0
(250) 847-7320

BC Parks
2930 Trans-Canada Hwy
RR #6
VICTORIA, B.C.
V9B 5T9
(250) 391-2300

BC Parks
181-1st Ave. N.
WILLIAMS LAKE, B.C.
V2G 1R8
(250) 398-4414

BC Parks
Box 3010
CULTUS LAKE, B.C.
V2R 5H6
(250) 824-2300

BC Parks
1210 McGill Rd.
KAMLOOPS, B.C.
V2C 6N6
(250) 851-3000

BC Parks
1610 Mt. Seymour Rd.
NORTH VANCOUVER, B.C.
V7G 1L3
(604) 924-2200

BC Parks
Box 2045
PRINCE GEORGE, B.C.
V2N 2J6
(250)565-6340

BC Parks
Box 399
SUMMERLAND, B.C.
V0H 1Z0
(250) 494-6500

BC Parks
Box 118
WASA, B.C.
V0B 2K0
(250) 422-3212

For **general information** on all aspects of BC Parks, contact the headquarters office at: BC Parks, 2-800 Johnson St., Victoria, B.C. V8V 1X4 (250) 387-4550

Note: Parks information is correct at time of publishing, and may be subject to change. Check with administrative offices for up-to-date information. Parks information is also available on the Ministry of Environment, Lands and Parks web site at http://www.env.gov.bc.ca

PARK / MAP NUMBER	MAP REFERENCE	Park	NEAREST HIGHWAY	ROAD ACCESS	OPERATING DATES	FEE (Y) RESERVATIONS (R)	VEHICLE / TENT CAMPSITES GROUP CAMPING (*)	WILDERNESS / WALK-IN CAMPSITES	PICNICKING / DAY USE (Car Spaces)	BOAT LAUNCHING RAMP (R) CANOEING / KAYAKING (C)	FIREWOOD (F) DRINKING WATER (W)	SANI-STATION	FLUSH TOILETS (F) PIT TOILETS (P) SHOWERS (S)	SWIMMING	FISHING	HIKING TRAILS (Km H) WALKING TRAILS (W)
1 · 16 B2		ADAMS LAKE RA 56 ha	1	15P G	Apr-Oct	Y	32			C	F W		4P	X	X	
2 · 16 C1		ADAMS LAKE Poplar Point														
3 · 10 C3		AKAMINA-KISHINENA RA 10,922 ha	3	NO	Jun-Sept	Y		18					3P		X	52H
4 · 6 B1		ALEXANDRA BRIDGE 55 ha	1	P	All Year				35		W		4P			W
5 · 5 B1		ALICE LAKE 396 ha	99	1P	All Year	Y R	88*		312	C	F W	X	10F S 12P	X	X	7H W
6 · 6 D1		ALLISON LAKE 23 ha	5A	P	May-Oct	Y	24		40	R	F W	X	8P	X	X	
7 · 36 B1		ANDREWS BAY 45 ha	35	60G	May-Nov			X	X	R			2P			
8 · 76 C3		ANDY BAILEY RA 174 ha	97	11G	May-Oct		12	X	6	R C	F W		5P	X	X	
9 · 7 B2		APEX MOUNTAIN RA 575 ha	97	30P	All Year											H
10 · 5 A2		APODACA 8 ha	99	NO	All Year											
11 · 2 C3		ARBUTUS GROVE 22 ha	19	NO	All Year											
12 · 8 B1		ARROW LAKES Shelter Bay 93 ha	23	P	Apr-Oct	Y	23		X	R	F W		4P	X	X	
13 · 15 B2		ARROWSTONE														
14 · 12 A4		ARTLISH CAVES 234 ha	19	40R												
15 · 69 C1		ATLIN 271,140 ha	7	NO	All Year			X							X	2H
16 · 46 D3		BABINE BAY MARINE Pendleton Bay 37 ha	16	35G	May-Oct	Y	12		10	R	F W		2P	X	X	
17 · 46 B1		BABINE BAY MARINE Smithers Landing 120 ha	16	35G	May-Sept	Y	10			R	F W		2P	X	X	
18 · 46 A2		BABINE MOUNTAINS RA 32,400 ha	16	14G	All Year			X								60H
19 · 5 A4		BALLINGALL ISLETS 1 ha	17	NO	All Year											
20 · 3 D3		BAMBERTON 28 ha	1	1P	All Year	Y R	47		41		F W		8F 18P	X	X	6H
21 · 16 B2		BANANA ISLAND														
22 · 39 B3		BARKERVILLE 55 ha	26	P	May-Oct	Y R	168*		420		F W	X	16F S 26P			W
23 · 7 C1		BEAR CREEK 178 ha	97	8P	Mar-Nov	Y R	80		184	C	F W	X	22F S 7P	X	X	10H
24 · 57 C2		BEATTON 312 ha	97	10G	May-Oct	Y R	37		100	R C	F W		12P	X	X	W
25 · 47 B4		BEAUMONT 191 ha	16	P	Apr-Sept	Y R	49		224	R C	F W	X	2F 8P	X	X	H W
26 · 5 B4		BEAUMONT MARINE 58 ha	17	NO	All Year	Y		11	X	C	W		4P	X	X	3H W
27 · 8 C3		BEAVER CREEK 44 ha	22A	P	Apr-Oct				24	7R	F W		4P		X	W
28 · 15 B2		BEDARD ASPEN														
29 · 5 A4		BELLHOUSE 2 ha	17	9P	All Year				4						X	1H W
30 · 15 A1		BIG BAR LAKE 332 ha	97	33G	May-Oct	Y	33		90	R C	F W		8P	X	X	4H W
31 · 11 B4		BIG BUNSBY 639 ha		NO						C					X	
32 · 14 B1		BIG CREEK 65,982 ha	20	G				X								H
33 · 48 C1		BIJOUX FALLS 41 ha	97	P	May-Oct				50				6P			
34 · 14 C3		BIRKENHEAD LAKE 3,642 ha	99	17G	Apr-Nov	Y	85	6	X	R C	F W	X	19P	X	X	3H W
35 · 14 B4		BLACKCOMB GLACIER 250 ha	99	NO												
36 · 17 B2		BLANKET CREEK 316 ha	23	2P	Apr-Oct	Y	64		185		F W		16P	X	X	1H
37 · 28 B2		BLIGH ISLAND 4,456 ha	28	NO						C					X	
38 · 15 B3		BLUE EARTH LAKE														
39 · 27 C2		BLUE RIVER Black Spruce														
40 · 27 C2		BLUE RIVER PINE														
41 · 15 D1		BONAPARTE														
42 · 3 B3		BOTANICAL BEACH 351 ha	14	3G	All Year											H W
43 · 7 D3		BOUNDARY CREEK 2 ha	3	P	Apr-Oct	Y	18				F W		2F 2P	X		
44 · 39 C3		BOWRON LAKE 123,117 ha	26	28G	May-Oct	Y	25	103	60	80R C	F W		65P	X	X	14H W
45 · 83 D4		BOYA LAKE 4,597 ha	37	P	May-Oct	Y	45	X	17	10R C	F W		10P	X	X	
46 · 2 B2		BOYLE POINT 125 ha	19	F 10P	All Year											W
47 · 5 B1		BRANDYWINE FALLS 143 ha	99	P	Apr-Nov	Y	15		35		F W		4P		X	1H W
48 · 6 A3		BRIDAL VEIL FALLS 32 ha	1	P	May-Oct				60		W		4F 2P			2H
49 · 26 D4		BRIDGE LAKE 6 ha	24	P	Apr-Oct	Y	20	7	X	R C	F W		4P	X	X	2H
50 · 7 B2		BROMLEY ROCK 149 ha	3	P	All Year	Y	17		30		F W		6P	X	X	
51 · 11 B4		BROOKS PENINSULA 51,632 ha		NO	All Year					C					X	X
52 · 12 A2		BROUGHTON ARCHIPELAGO MARINE 11,679 ha	19	NO	All Year					C					X	
53 · 2 D2		BUCCANEER BAY 1 ha	101	NO	All Year			X	X				1P	X	X	
54 · 65 C2		BUCKINGHORSE RIVER WAY 55 ha	97	G	May-Oct	Y	33			C	F W		6P		X	
55 · 18 A2		BUGABOO 13,647 ha	95	45G	June-Sept	Y	50	20	30		W		4P			13H
56 · 25 A2		BULL CANYON 369 ha	20	G	May-Oct	Y	20		5		F W		4P		X	W
57 · 28 D4		BURGES & JAMES GADSDEN 352 ha	1	P	All Year											10W
58 · 5 B4		CABBAGE ISLAND MARINE 4 ha	17	NO	All Year	Y		6	X	C			2P	X	X	
59 · 27 B2		CALIGATA LAKE														
60 · 18 C4		CANAL FLATS 6 ha	93	3P	Apr-Oct				64	R	W		2P	X	X	
61 · 26 C3		CANIM BEACH 6 ha	97	43P	May-Oct	Y	7	9	15		W		4P	X	X	
62 · 11 A2		CAPE SCOTT 21,849 ha	19	63G	All Year				19	C			3P	X	X	40H
63 · 39 D4		CARIBOO MOUNTAINS 113,470 ha	97	NO				X							X	
64 · 26 A3		CARIBOO NATURE 98 ha	97	NO												
65 · 39 D4		CARIBOO RIVER 3,212 ha	97	NO												
66 · 2 B4		CARMANAH WALBRAN 16,450 ha	18	70G	All Year			X	X		W		13P			H W

PARK / MAP NUMBER	MAP REFERENCE	Park	NEAREST HIGHWAY	ROAD ACCESS	OPERATING DATES	FEE (Y) RESERVATIONS (R)	VEHICLE / TENT CAMPSITES GROUP CAMPING (*)	WILDERNESS / WALK-IN CAMPSITES	PICNICKING / DAY USE (Car Spaces)	BOAT LAUNCHING RAMP (R) CANOEING / KAYAKING (C)	FIREWOOD (F) DRINKING WATER (W)	SANI-STATION	FLUSH TOILETS (F) PIT TOILETS (P) SHOWERS (S)	SWIMMING	FISHING	HIKING TRAILS (Km H) WALKING TRAILS (W)
67	48 A2	CARP LAKE 19,344 ha	97	32G	May-Oct	Y	102		X	R C	F W	X	13P	X	X	3H W
68	6 C3	CASCADE RA 16,680 ha	3	P	All Year			X					2P		X	75H
69	1 B4	CATALA ISLAND MARINE 851 ha	19	NO					C							
70	7 A3	CATHEDRAL 33,272 ha	3	25G	Apr-Oct	Y	16	62	30				13P	X	X	85H
71	8 C3	CHAMPION LAKES 1,425 ha	3B	10P	May-Oct	Y	95		180	R C	F W	X	28F 16P	X	X	6H W
72	57 C2	CHARLIE LAKE 92 ha	97	P	May-Oct	Y R	58		40	R	F W	X	14P	X	X	1H W
73	15 B1	CHASM 3,068 ha	97	3P	June-Sept		8		15				2P			W
74	2 D4	CHEMAINUS RIVER 86 ha	1	11G	All Year								2P	X	X	
75	6 B3	CHILLIWACK LAKE 162 ha	1	52P 7G	May-Oct	Y	100		15	R	F W		24P	X	X	H
76	6 A3	CHILLIWACK RIVER 23 ha	1	11G	All Year				16				2P			
77	3 B4	CHINA BEACH 61 ha	14	P	All Year				60				4P	X		1H
78	7 B2	CHRISTIE MEMORIAL 3 ha	97	P	Apr-Oct				27	C	W		7F	X	X	
79	8 A-B3	CHRISTINA LAKE 6 ha	3	P	May-Sept				220		W		10F 6P	X	X	
80	27 A4	CHU CHUA COTTONWOOD														
81	25 D4	CHURN CREEK														
82	16 D2	CINNEMOUSUN NARROWS 533 ha	1	NO	All Year	Y		28	X	C	W	X	8P	X	X	4H
83	12 B3	CLAUD ELLIOT LAKE 289 ha	19	NO												
84	1 D3	CLAYOQUOT ARM 3,491 ha	4	NO												
85	1 D3	CLAYOQUOT PLATEAU 3,156 ha	4	NO												
86	22 B2	CODVILLE LAGOON MARINE 755 ha	20	NO					C					X		H
87	9 A1	CODY CAVES 63 ha	31	13R	June-Sept				4				1P			1H
88	6 C1	COLDWATER RIVER 76 ha	5	P	May-Oct				66				4P	X		
89	18 C4	COLUMBIA LAKE 260 ha	93	5P G	All Year											
90	7 C3	CONKLE LAKE 587 ha	33	24G	May-Oct	Y	34	2	24	R C	F W		8P	X	X	4H
91	2 B1	COPELAND ISLANDS MARINE 423 ha	101	NO	All Year			X		C			2P	X	X	
92	6 B2	COQUIHALLA CANYON RA 150 ha	5	4P G	May-Oct				20				2P		X	2W
93	6 B2	COQUIHALLA RIVER RA 100 ha	5	P					34				2P		X	
94	6 C2	COQUIHALLA SUMMIT RA 5,750 ha	5	P	All Year				103				12F 6P			
95	12 A3	CORMORANT CHANNEL MARINE 744 ha	19	NO	All Year			X		C				X		
96	15 B2	CORNWALL HILLS														
97	38 D3	COTTONWOOD HOUSE HISTORIC 11 ha	26	23P												
98	38 C3	COTTONWOOD RIVER 68 ha	26	NO												
99	3 C3	COWICHAN RIVER 1,156 ha	18	G	All Year	Y	20		2	R C			P	X	X	W
100	48 C3	CROOKED RIVER 873 ha	97	P	May-Oct	Y R	90		530	C	F W	X	15F 14P	X	X	9H W
101	10 B2	CROWSNEST 46 ha	3	P	All Year				20		W		4P			
102	6 A3	CULTUS LAKE 656 ha	1	16P	Apr-Oct	Y	296		716	R C	F W	X	85F S 26P	X	X	11H W
103	28 B2	CUMMINS LAKES 6,109 ha	1	NO	June-Sept											
104	5 B2	CYPRESS 3,012 ha	1	10P	All Year				100				6P			60H W
105	38 B1	DAHL LAKE 750 ha	16	17G	All Year				X	C			1P	X	X	W
106	3 D3	D'ARCY ISLAND MARINE 81 ha	17	NO	May-Oct	Y			10				1P	X	X	1H W
107	7 B1	DARKE LAKE 1,470 ha	97	16G	May-Oct		5		X	C			1P	X	X	
108	5 D3	DAVIS LAKE 192 ha	7	20G	All Year									X	X	
109	1 D3	DAWLEY PASSAGE 154 ha	4	NO					C							
110	13 B4	DESOLATION SOUND MARINE 8,256 ha	101	NO	All Year				X	C			3P	X	X	H
111	33 C1	DIANA LAKE 233 ha	16	2G	May-Oct				180	C	F W		8P	X	X	2H
112	5 A3	DIONISIO POINT 142 ha	17	NO	All Year	Y		30	X				P	X	X	H
113	3 D4	DISCOVERY ISLAND MARINE 61 ha	17	NO	All Year	Y		X	X	C				X	X	H
114	11 D4	DIXIE COVE 156 ha	11	NO					C							
115	28 A4	DOWNIE CREEK 23 ha	23	P	May-Oct	Y	21		X	10R	F W		4P	X	X	
116	15 A1-2	DOWNING 100 ha	97	17P	May-Oct	Y	25		44		F W		4P	X	X	
117	9 A2	DREWRY POINT 21 ha	3A	NO	All Year		2		X				1P	X	X	
118	45 D2	DRIFTWOOD CANYON 23 ha	16	10G	Apr-Oct				15				2P			W
119	2 D3	DRUMBEG 20 ha	1	F 12P	All Year				10				2P	X	X	
120	18 C3	DRY GULCH 29 ha	93	1G	Apr-Oct	Y	26				F W		6F 8P			
121	14 D3	DUFFEY LAKE 2,379 ha							X	C			1P		X	
122	56 D2	DUNLEVY RA 110 ha	29	25P	May-Sept					R			2P		X	
123	27 A4	DUNN PEAK														
124	27 A4	EAKIN CREEK CANYON														
125	27 A4	EAKIN CREEK FLOODPLAIN														
126	57 B3	EAST PINE 14 ha	97	1G	May-Sept				7	R C	F		4P			
127	12 B2	ECHO BAY MARINE 2 ha	19	NO	All Year			X	X	R					X	
128	16 D4	ECHO LAKE 154 ha	6	20G	Apr-Oct				X	C			2P	X	X	
129	15 A1	EDGE HILLS 11,883 ha	97	R G												
130	15 B2	ELEPHANT HILL														
131	1 D1	ELK FALLS 1,087 ha	28	P	All Year	Y	122		30		F W	X	2F 26P	X	X	6H
132	19 A3	ELK LAKES 17,245 ha	3	125 G	June-Sept	Y		20					3P		X	23H

No.	Ref	Park	Nearest Highway	Road Access	Operating Dates	Fee (Y) Reserv. (R)	Vehicle/Tent Campsites Group Camping (*)	Wilderness/Walk-in Campsites	Picnicking/Day Use (Car Spaces)	Boat Ramp (R) Canoe/Kayak (C)	Firewood (F) Drinking Water (W)	Sani-Station	Flush (F)/Pit (P) Toilets Showers (S)	Swimming	Fishing	Hiking (Km H)/Walking (W) Trails
133	10 A2	ELK VALLEY 81 ha	3	10G	Apr-Oct											
134	16 C4	ELLISON 219 ha	97	16P	Mar-Nov	Y R	12	54	120	C	F W		18F 4P	X	X	2H
135	26 D4	EMAR LAKES														
136	6 B2	EMORY CREEK 15 ha	1	P	Apr-Nov	Y R	34				F W		4F 2P		X	1H
137	7 B1	ENEAS LAKES 1,036 ha	97	20R	All Year			X		C					X	
138	2 C3	ENGLISHMAN RIVER FALLS 97 ha	4	8P	All Year	Y	105		105		F W		7F 26P	X	X	3H W
139	1 C3	EPPER PASSAGE 306 ha	4	NO						C						
140	8 D3	ERIE CREEK 315 ha	3	P												
141	48 B4	ESKERS 1,600 ha	97	20G	All Year				50	C	F W		5P		X	9H W
142	46 D3	ETHEL F. WILSON MEMORIAL 29 ha	16	24G	May-Oct	Y	10		10	R C	W F		2P	X	X	
143	44 C3	EXCHAMSIKS RIVER 18 ha	16	P	May-Oct	Y	20		20	R C	W F		4P		X	
144	6 A3	F. H. BARBER 9 ha	1	P	All Year											
145	2 B2	FILLONGLEY 23 ha	19	F 4P	All Year	Y	10		X		F W		4P	X	X	2H W
146	27 C3	FINN CREEK														
147	16 C4	FINERTY 360 ha	97	8P	Apr-Oct	Y R				C	F			X	X	
148	22 B1	FIORDLAND RA 91,000 ha	37	NO												
149	26 B4	FLAT LAKE 4,344 ha	97	G						C						
150	1 B3	FLORES ISLAND 7,113 ha	4	NO												
151	48 B2	FORT McLEOD HISTORIC 3 ha	97	P												
152	2 A3	FOSSLI 53 ha	4	NO	All Year				X	C			1P	X	X	3H
153	3 C4	FRENCH BEACH 59 ha	14	P	All Year	Y R	69		140		F W	X	16P	X	X	1H W
155	2 D3	GABRIOLA SANDS 5 ha	1	F 2P	All Year				25		W		4P	X		
156	2 C2	GARDEN BAY MARINE 163 ha	101	2G	All Year				X				1P			
157	5 C1	GARIBALDI 194,650 ha	99	NO	June-Oct	Y		196	X	C			25P		X	62H
158	1 C3	GIBSON MARINE 142 ha	4	NO	All Year									X	X	
159	9 D3	GILNOCKIE 2,842 ha	3	NO	June-Sept											
160	44 C4	GITNADOIX RIVER RA 58,000 ha	16	NO	All Year			X							X	
161	8 A3	GLADSTONE Texas Creek 39,322 ha	3	P	Apr-Oct	Y	48	10	X	R	F W		2P	X	X	
162	17 D4	GOAT RANGE Gerard 78,947 ha	31	G	Apr-Oct		5	X	X				2P		X	
163	11 C2	GOD'S POCKET MARINE 2,025 ha	19	NO						C	W				X	
164	1 C1	GOLD MUCHALAT 653 ha	28	NO											X	
165	5 C-D2	GOLDEN EARS 55,594 ha	7	10P	All Year	Y R	343*	X	1088	R C	F W	X	46F S 64P	X	X	60H W
166	15 B3	GOLDPAN 5 ha	1	P	All Year	Y	14		24	C	F W		8P		X	
167	3 D3	GOLDSTREAM 388 ha	1	P	All Year	Y R	159*		82		F W	X	28F S 20P	X	X	16H W
168	2 C4	GORDON BAY 51 ha	18	14P	All Year	Y R	130		120	R C	F W	X	19F S 16P	X	X	1H
169	3 D3	GOWLLAND TOD 1,219 ha	1	P	All Year								P	X		
170	8 A1	GRANBY 40,845 ha	3	24G											X	
171	35 A4	GREEN INLET MARINE 37 ha	37	NO											X	
172	26 B4	GREEN LAKE 347 ha	97	16P	May-Oct	Y R	121*		160	R	F W	X	4F 36P	X	X	
173	2 D2	GROHMAN NARROWS	3A	P	All Year				15				2P		X	1H W
174	57 B4	GWILLIM LAKE 9,200 ha	29	P	Apr-Oct	Y	49		32	R C	F W		8P		X	W
175	13 A4	HA'THAYIM (VON DONOP) 1,277 ha	19	NO	All Year					C	F				X	H
176	22 B3	HAKAI RA 122,998 ha	20	NO				X		C					X	
177	5 A2	HALKETT BAY MARINE 309 ha	99	NO	All Year			X	X				1P	X		H
178	28 B1	HAMBER 24,520 ha	93	NO	All Year			10			F		1P	X		H
179	27 C4	HARBOUR DUDGEON LAKES														
180	2 D1	HARMONY ISLANDS MARINE	101	NO	All Year										X	
181	15 B2	HARRY LAKE ASPEN														
182	7 C3	HAYNES POINT 38 ha	97	1P	Mar-Nov	Y R	41		33	R C	F W		8F 1P	X	X	
183	19 A3	HEIGHT OF THE ROCKIES 54,208 ha	93	NO	June-Oct										X	
184	2 B2	HELLIWELL 2,872 ha	19	F 21P	All Year				30				4P	X	X	6H W
185	2 D3	HEMER 93 ha	1	7P	All Year				8	C					X	
186	16 C2	HERALD 79 ha	1	13P	Apr-Oct	Y R	51		68	R	F	X	4F S 18P	X	X	
187	1 B2	HESQUIAT LAKE 62 ha	28	NO												
188	1 B2	HESQUIAT PENINSULA 7,891 ha	28	NO						C						
189	26 D4	HIGH LAKES BASIN														
190	2 B4	HITCHIE CREEK 226 ha	28	NO												
191	16 B2	HIUIHIL CREEK														
192	24 B4	HOMATHKO RIVER - Tatlayoko														
193	2 B2	HORNE LAKE CAVES 123 ha	19	16G	All Year				X				1P			2H
194	26 B1	HORSEFLY LAKE 148 ha	97	65P	May-Oct	Y	23	10	60	R	F W		6P	X	X	W
195	84 A3	HYLAND RIVER														
196	5 B2	INDIAN ARM 6,821 ha	7A	NO	All Year										X	
197	5 B2	INDIAN ARM MARINE 5 ha	7A	NO	All Year			X	X	C			2P	X		1H
198	7 C3	INKANEEP 21 ha	97	P	All Year	Y	7				F W		2P	X	X	
199	6 A3	INTERNATIONAL RIDGE 1,905 ha	1	NO	All Year											

PARK / MAP NUMBER	MAP REFERENCE	Park	NEAREST HIGHWAY	ROAD ACCESS	OPERATING DATES	FEE (Y) RESERVATIONS (R)	VEHICLE / TENT CAMPSITES GROUP CAMPING (*)	WILDERNESS / WALK-IN CAMPSITES	PICNICKING / DAY USE (Car Spaces)	BOAT LAUNCHING RAMP (R) CANOEING / KAYAKING (C)	FIREWOOD (F) DRINKING WATER (W)	SANI-STATION	FLUSH TOILETS (F) PIT TOILETS (P) SHOWERS (S)	SWIMMING	FISHING	HIKING TRAILS (Km H) WALKING TRAILS (W)
200	5 A-B4	ISLE-DE-LIS MARINE 5 ha	17	NO	All Year			3		C			2P	X	X	1H
201	24 A1	ITCHA ILGACHUZ 111,977 ha	20	NO												18H
202	37 A4	JACKSON NARROWS MARINE 71 ha	20	NO	All Year											
203	18 C3	JAMES CHABOT 14 ha	93	3P	Apr-Oct				82	R C	W		10F	X		
204	2 C2	JEDEDIAH ISLAND MARINE 243 ha	19	NO						C						
205	8 A3	JEWEL LAKE 49 ha	3	8G	June-Sept		26		X	R			2P	X	X	
206	9 C2	JIMSMITH LAKE 12 ha	3	2P	May-Oct	Y	29		58	R	F W		12P	X	X	
207	14 C3-4	JOFFRE LAKES RA 1,460 ha	99	20P G	June-Oct		X	X					2p			11H
208	3 D3	JOHN DEAN 173 ha	17A	5P	All Year				20		W		2P			3H W
209	7 D3	JOHNSTONE CREEK 38 ha	3	P	Apr-Oct	Y	16				F W		4P			1H
210	3 B3-4	JUAN DE FUCA MARINE TRAIL 700 ha	14	3G	All Year			X								
211	25 C3	JUNCTION SHEEP RANGE 4,573 ha	20	RG												
212	15 C2	JUNIPER BEACH 260 ha	1	P	Apr-Oct	Y	30		X	C	F W	X	6P	X	X	
213	50 A4	KAKWA RA 127,690 ha	16	NO	All Year								2P			
214	16 C4	KALAMALKA LAKE 978 ha	6	8P	All Year				85	C			7P	X	X	5H
215	16 C4	KEKULI BAY 57 ha	97	P	All Year					R C						
216	1 D4	KENNEDY LAKE 379 ha	14	RG						C						
217	1 D3	KENNEDY RIVER BOG 11 ha	14	RG												
218	6 D1	KENTUCKY-ALLEYNE 144 ha	5A	6P	Apr-Oct	Y	63		X	C	F W		13P	X	X	5H
219	7 B3	KEREMEOS COLUMNS 20 ha	3A	NO	All Year											H
220	7 D3	KETTLE RIVER RA 179 ha	33	P	Apr-Oct	Y	53	6	20		F W	X	10P	X	X	2H
221	44 B3	KHUTZEYMATEEN 44,902 ha	16	NO												
222	9 B2	KIANUKO 11,638 ha	3	15G				X							X	
223	7 B2	KICKININEE 49 ha	97	P	All Year				102	R	W		10F 3P	X	X	
224	10 A3	KIKOMUN CREEK 682 ha	3	11P	Apr-Oct	Y R	104*		596	R C	F W	X	24F S 5P	X	X	6H
225	6 A3	KILBY 3 ha	7	1P	All Year	Y	38		50	R C	F W		8F 4P	X	X	
226	60 D2	KINASKAN LAKE 1,800 ha	37	G	May-Oct	Y	50		10	R	F W		8P		X	2H
227	8 B3	KING GEORGE VI														
228	57 D3	KISKATINAW 58 ha	97	5P	May-Oct	Y	28				F W		6P		X	
229	35 C3	KITLOPE HERITAGE CONSERVANCY														
230	44 A4	KITSON ISLAND MARINE 45 ha	16	NO	All Year					C						
231	44 D2	KITSUMKALUM 40 ha	16	24G	All Year					C					X	
232	45 A3	KLEANZA CREEK 269 ha	16	P	May-Oct	Y	21		10		F W		4P S		X	1H
233	75 D2	KLEDO CREEK														
234	34 B1	KLEWNUGGIT INLET MARINE 1,733 ha	37	NO	All Year											
235	37 D3	KLUSKOIL LAKE 15,548 ha	97	RG												
236	8 D2	KOKANEE CREEK 260 ha	3A	P	Apr-Oct	Y R	132*		380	R C	F W		32F S 18P	X	X	4H
237	8 D1	KOKANEE GLACIER 32,035 ha	3A	16R	June-Oct	Y		12	70				8P		X	113 H
238	3 C3	KOKSILAH RIVER 210 ha	1	10G	All Year	Y									X	
239	18 A4	KOOTENAY LAKE Davis Creek 345 ha	31	P	Apr-Oct	Y	12	X	X		F		2P	X		
240	18 A4	KOOTENAY LAKE Lost Ledge 38 ha	31	P	Apr-Oct	Y	14		X		F		4P	X		
241	9 A2	KOOTENAY LAKE Midge Creek 223 ha	3A	NO	All Year				X						X	
242	64 A1	KWADACHA WILDERNESS 158,475 ha	97	NO	All Year			X								
243	11 B4	KWAKIUTL LAWN POINT 560 ha		NO					C							
244	15 D2	LAC DU BOIS GRASSLANDS														
245	26 A3	LAC LA HACHE 24 ha	97	P	May-Oct	Y	83		70	R	F W	X	18F 6P	X	X	
246	15 D3	LAC LE JEUNE 47 ha	5	8P	Apr-Oct	Y	144		104	R C	F W	X	S 34P	X	X	1H
247	5 B1	LAKE LOVELY WATER RA 1,300 ha	99	NO	May-Oct			X								H
248	45 A3	LAKELSE LAKE 362 ha	37	P	May-Oct	Y	156*		360	R C	F W	X	16F S 38P	X	X	3H
249	85 C4	LIARD RIVER HOT SPRINGS 976 ha	97	G	All Year	Y R	53		90		F W		12P	X		1H
250	2 B3	LITTLE QUALICUM FALLS 440 ha	4	P	All Year	Y	91		122		F W		18F 21P	X	X	6H W
251	9 A2	LOCKHART BEACH 3 ha	3A	P	Apr-Oct	Y	13		4		F W		4P	X		
252	9 A2	LOCKHART CREEK 3,751 ha	3A	P	Apr-Oct	Y	13	X			F				X	
253	15 B1	LOON LAKE	97	26P	May-Oct	Y	14				F W		4P	X		
254	3 B3	LOSS CREEK 21 ha	14	G	All Year											
255	12 D4	LOVELAND BAY 30 ha	28	20G	All Year	Y	24		X	R C	F		5P	X	X	
256	34 B3	LOWE INLET MARINE 767 ha	37	NO	All Year											
257	11 D3	LOWER NIMPKISH 265 ha	19	RG											X	
258	16 D3	MABEL LAKE 187 ha	6	35G	Apr-Oct	Y	81		30	R C	F W	X	16P	X	X	1H
259	2 B2	MacMILLAN 136 ha	4	P	All Year				40				6P		X	4H W
260	13 A4	MAIN LAKES CHAIN 2,454 ha	19	F 25					C							
261	6 C3	MANNING 66,884 ha	3	P	Apr-Nov	Y R	353*	70	630	R C	F W	X	34F S 63P	X	X	
262	13 A4	MANSONS LANDING MARINE 100 ha	19	F 21P	All Year				X				4P	X	X	W
263	1 B2	MAQUINNA 2,668 ha	4	NO	All Year				X	C	W				X	2H
264	16 D2	MARA 4 ha	97A	P	Apr-Oct				110	R	W		4F 4P	X	X	
265	3 D3	MARBLE CANYON 335 ha	99	P	Apr-Nov	Y	26		12	C	F W		4P	X	X	

Park/Map No.	Map Ref.	Park	Nearest Highway	Road Access	Operating Dates	Fee(Y) Res(R)	Vehicle/Tent Campsites Group(*)	Wilderness/Walk-in	Picnicking/Day Use	Boat(R) Canoe(C)	Firewood(F) Water(W)	Sani-Station	Toilets(F/P) Showers(S)	Swimming	Fishing	Hiking(H)/Walking(W)
266	15 A1	MARBLE RANGE														
267	11 C3	MARBLE RIVER														
268	28 D4	MARL CREEK														
269	17 B1	MARTHA CREEK 71 ha	23	P	Apr-Oct	Y	25		50	R	F W		6F 6P	X	X	H
270	87 B3	MAXHAMISH LAKE 520 ha	77	NO	May-Sept			X						X	X	
271	15 D3	McCONNEL LAKE														
272	5 A4	McDONALD 12 ha	17	2P	Mar-Oct	Y	51	7			F W		8P			
273	17 B-C4	McDONALD CREEK 468 ha	6	P	Apr-Oct	Y	28		24	R	F W		9P	X	X	
274	3 C3	MEMORY ISLAND 1 ha	1	NO	May-Sept				X	C			2P	X	X	
275	52 C2	MEZIADIN LAKE 335 ha	37	P	May-Oct	Y	46			R C	F		6P	X	X	
276	2 A1	MIRACLE BEACH 137 ha	19	3P	All Year	Y R	193		230		F W	X	22F S 29P	X	X	2H W
277	2 A1	MITLENATCH ISLAND NATURE 155 ha	19	NO	All Year				X				1P	X	X	1H
278	57 A3	MOBERLY LAKE 97 ha	29	3P	May-Oct	Y R	109*		80	R C	F W	X	16P	X	X	2H W
279	27 C4	MOMICH LAKES 1,848 ha	5	G	May-Oct		30			R C			4P	X	X	
280	17 B3	MONASHEE 7,515 ha	6	NO	All Year	Y		X	25				5P		X	24H
281	15 D4	MONCK 87 ha	5A	11P	Mar-Nov	Y	71		130	R C	F W	X	16F 6P	X	X	5H
282	49 B2-3	MONKMAN 32,000 ha	29	45G	May-Oct	Y	42	X	20	C	F W		8P		X	30H
283	5 A4	MONTAGUE HARBOUR MARINE 97 ha	17	F 10P	All Year	Y R	25	15	X	R C	F W		10P	X	X	5H
284	16 B3	MONTE CREEK														
285	16 B3	MONTE LAKE 8 ha	97	P												
286	26 A4	MOOSE VALLEY 2,323 ha	97	RG				X		C					X	
287	3 C2	MORDEN COLLIERY 4 ha	1	1P	All Year											
288	10 A2	MORRISSEY 5 ha	3	P	Apr-Oct				26		W		1P		X	
289	12 D4	MORTON LAKE 67 ha	19	20G	All Year	Y	24		30	R C	F W		10P	X	X	
290	18 C2	MOUNT ASSINIBOINE 39,050 ha	93	NO	All Year	Y		75			W		24P		X	176 H
291	60 C1	MOUNT EDZIZA 232,702 ha	37	NO	All Year			X								119 H
292	10 A2	MOUNT FERNIE 259 ha	3	P	May-Sept	Y	38		44		F W		12F 10P			1H
293	5 D2	MOUNT JUDGE HOWAY 6,180 ha	7	NO	All Year											
294	5 A4	MOUNT MAXWELL 199 ha	17	F 15P	All Year				15				1P			1H
295	40 D3	MOUNT ROBSON 219,535 ha	16	P	Apr-Oct	Y	144*	80	461	R C	F W	X	10F S 47P	X	X	62H
296	15 C2	MOUNT SAVONA														
297	5 B2	MOUNT SEYMOUR 3,508 ha	1	6P	All Year				150		F W		5P	X	X	21H W
298	40 C4	MOUNT TERRY FOX 1,930 ha	16	NO	All Year			X								H
299	9 C2	MOYIE LAKE 90 ha	3	1P	Apr-Oct	Y R	104		90	R C	F W	X	6F 22P	X	X	3H
300	27 C2	MUD LAKE DELTA														
301	74 D1-2	MUNCHO LAKE 88,420 ha	97	P	May-Oct	Y	30		X	R C	F W		19P	X		H
302	5 B2	MURRIN 24 ha	99	P	All Year				40		W		4P	X	X	
303	2 C1	MUSKET ISLAND MARINE 4 ha	101	NO	All Year										X	
304	32 D2	NAIKOON Agate Beach														1
305	32 C2	NAIKOON Misty Meadows 73,325 ha	16	P	May-Oct	Y	30		5		F W		6P	X	X	5H
306	14 C4	NAIRN FALLS 170 ha	99	P	Apr-Oct	Y	88		24		F W	X	18P		X	2H
307	8 B3	NANCY GREENE 203 ha	3	P	May-Oct	Y	10		50	C	W		4P	X	X	5H
308	25 A1	NAZKO LAKES 7,919 ha	20	G				X		C					X	
309	2 D3	NEWCASTLE ISLAND MARINE 336 ha	1	NO	All Year			18	X	C	W		13F 6P	X	X	19H
310	7 A-B2	NICKEL PLATE 105 ha	97	30P	All Year					C			1P		X	H
311	6 B2	NICOLUM RIVER 24 ha	3	P	May-Sept	Y	9		10		F W		4P		X	
312	11 D3	NIMPKISH LAKE 3,950 ha	19	G						C						H W
313	44 D1	NISGA'A MEMORIAL LAVA BED 17,683 ha	16	45P 55G	All Year			X		R C			3P			H W
314	16 B2	NISKONLITH LAKE 238 ha	1	8G	Apr-Oct	Y	32			C	F		6P	X	X	
315	2 B4	NITINAT RIVER														
316	9 D2	NORBURY LAKE 97 ha	93	16P	All Year	Y	46		110	R C	F W		18P	X	X	2H
317	27 A4	NORTH THOMPSON ISLANDS														
318	27 C1	NORTH THOMPSON Oxbows East														
319	27 A2	NORTH THOMPSON Oxbows Jensen Island														
320	17 C1	NORTH THOMPSON Oxbows Manteau														
321	27 A4	NORTH THOMPSON RIVER 126 ha	5	P	Apr-Oct	Y	61		78		F W	X	15P	X	X	5H
322	1 B4	NUCHATLITZ 2,135 ha		NO						C					X	
323	24 D3	NUNSTI 20,898 ha	20	G						C					X	
324	13 A4	OCTOPUS ISLANDS MARINE 109 ha	19	NO	All Year			X		C				X	X	
325	7 B3	OKANAGAN FALLS 2 ha	97	P	Apr-Oct	Y	25				F W		2F 10P	X		
326	7 B1	OKANAGAN LAKE 98 ha	97	P	Mar-Nov	Y R	168		70	R C	F W	X	35F S 3P	X	X	2H
327	7 B1	OKANAGAN MOUNTAIN 10,562 ha	97	15P	All Year			48	20				5P	X	X	24H
328	13 B4	OKEOVER ARM 4 ha	101	5P	All Year		5	4	X	R C	F W		2P	X	X	
329	22	OLIVER COVE MARINE 74 ha	20	NO												
330	75 A-B2	115 CREEK 51 ha	97	P	May-Oct	Y	8		10		W F		2P		X	
331	58 A4	ONE ISLAND LAKE 61 ha	2	33G	May-Oct	Y	30		15	R C	F W		8P	X	X	

Park/Map Number	Map Reference	Park	Nearest Highway	Road Access	Operating Dates	Fee (Y) Reservations (R)	Vehicle/Tent Campsites Group Camping (*)	Wilderness/Walk-in Campsites	Picnicking/Day Use (Car Spaces)	Boat Launching Ramp (R) Canoeing/Kayaking (C)	Firewood (F) Drinking Water (W)	Sani-Station	Flush Toilets (F) Pit Toilets (P) Showers (S)	Swimming	Fishing	Hiking Trails (Km H) Walking Trails (W)
332	15 B3	OREGON JACK														
333	6 C2	OTTER LAKE 51 ha	5A	32P	May-Oct	Y R	45		25	R C	F W		12P	X	X	
334	47 C3	PAARENS BEACH 43 ha	27	11P	May-Oct	Y R	65		100	R C	F W		15P	X	X	H
335	15 C2	PAINTED BLUFFS														
336	3 B3	PARKINSON CREEK 140 ha	14	P	All Year											
337	16 A2	PAUL LAKE 402 ha	5	17P	Apr-Oct	Y	111		290	C	F W	X	30P	X	X	7H
338	5 C3	PEACE ARCH 9 ha	99	P	All Year				240		W F		10F			
340	7 A1	PENNASK LAKE 244 ha	97C	50R	Apr-Oct		28		25	R C			7P	X	X	
341	22 C4	PENROSE ISLAND 2,013 ha	20	NO						C					X	
342	2 D3	PETROGLYPH 2 ha	1	P	All Year				25							1H W
343	9 A2	PILOT BAY 347 ha	3A	NO	All Year			X					2P	X	X	3H
344	5 C2	PINECONE BURKE 38,000 ha	7	NO	All Year										X	
345	38 C4	PINNACLES 124 ha	97	8P	May-Oct				30				1P			H
346	2 D3	PIRATES COVE MARINE 31 ha	1	NO	All Year	Y		12	X	C	W		6P	X	X	4H
347	5 A2	PLUMPER COVE MARINE 57 ha	101	NO	All Year	Y		20	X	C	F W		6P	X	X	2H
348	15 D2	PORCUPINE MEADOWS														
349	2 D2	PORPOISE BAY 61 ha	101	4P	All Year	Y R	84*		280	C	F W	X	16F S 9P	X	X	3H
350	5 B2	PORTEAU COVE 50 ha	99	P	All Year	Y R	59	15	100	R	F W	X	21F S 1P	X	X	W
351	9 D1	PREMIER LAKE 662 ha	93	16G	All Year	Y	56	14	20	R C	F W		14P	X	X	7H
352	13 D4	PRINCESS LOUISA MARINE 65 ha	101	NO	All Year			9	X		W		5P	X	X	3H
353	5 A4	PRINCESS MARGARET MARINE 575 ha	17	NO	All Year	Y		20	X	C	W		5P	X	X	7H
354	5 B4	PRIOR CENTENNIAL 16 ha	17	F 6P	Mar-Oct	Y R	17				F W		4P			1H
355	65 C1	PROPHET RIVER RA 115 ha	97	G	May-Oct	Y	45				F W		4P	X		
356	33 C1	PRUDHOMME LAKE 7 ha	16	P	Apr-Nov	Y	24			C	F W		4P	X		
357	38 C4	PUNTCHESAKUT LAKE 38 ha	97	32P	May-Oct				180	R C	W		10P	X	X	
358	18 B4	PURCELL WILDERNESS 198,183 ha	31	NO	All Year			X						X		171 H
359	39 A1	PURDEN LAKE 321 ha	16	2P	Apr-Sept	Y	78		150	R C	F W	X	8F 6P	X	X	7H W
360	32 C2	PURE LAKE 130 ha	16	P	All Year				15			X	2P	X	X	
361	27 C1	PYRAMID CREEK FALLS														
362	11 B3	QUATSINO 654 ha	19	NO						C						
363	11 B3	RAFT COVE 670 ha	19	75G	All Year			X	X	C				X	X	3H
364	2 C2-3	RATHTREVOR BEACH 347 ha	19	P	All Year	Y R	174	X	1116		F W	X	48F S 38P	X	X	5H W
365	13 A4	READ ISLAND 639 ha		NO						C						
366	40 C4	REARGUARD FALLS 49 ha	16	P	All Year				10				2P		X	2H
367	13 A4	REBECCA SPIT MARINE 177 ha	19	F 9P	All Year				100	R	W		9P	X	X	1H
368	46 C2	RED BLUFF 148 ha	16	48P	May-Sept	Y	64		22	R C	F W	X	16P	X	X	1H
369	5 A2	ROBERTS CREEK 40 ha	101	P	May-Sept	Y	25		20		F W	X	6P	X		1H
370	2 D3	ROBERTS MEMORIAL 14 ha	1	19P	All Year				10				1P	X	X	1H
371	12 B3	ROBSON BIGHT 6,608 ha	19	NO												
372	16 A3	ROCHE LAKE 2,100 ha	5A	G	May-Oct		75			R C			10P	X	X	
373	12 D4	ROCK BAY MARINE 526 ha	19	25G						R C						
374	16 B2	RODERICK HAIG-BROWN 988 ha	1	8P	Apr-Oct					C			6P		X	24H
375	5 D3	ROLLEY LAKE 115 ha	7	8P	All Year	Y R	64		120	C	F W	X	8F S 16P	X	X	6H W
376	13 B4	ROSCOE BAY MARINE 247 ha	101	NO	All Year			X					1P	X		H
377	17 C4	ROSEBERY 32 ha	6	P	Apr-Oct	Y	36				F W		6P			
378	2 B2	ROSEWALL CREEK 54 ha	19	P	All Year				10				2P		X	2H
379	45 C1	ROSS LAKE 307 ha	16	P	All Year				60	R			8P	X	X	5H
380	5 A4	RUCKLE 486 ha	17	F 9P	All Year	Y		50	25	C	F W		20P	X	X	2H
381	1 A4	RUGGED POINT MARINE 308 ha	4	NO	All Year					C				X	X	1H
382	26 C3	RUTH LAKE 30 ha	97	30P	May-Sept				14	R C			4P	X	X	
383	9 C3	RYAN 58 ha	3	P	June-Sept				10		W		2F			
384	2 C1	SALTERY BAY 69 ha	101	P	All Year	Y R	42	X	120	R	F W	X	12P	X	X	1H
385	2 D3	SANDWELL 12 ha	1	F 8P	All Year				X				1P	X		H
386	2 B2	SANDY ISLAND MARINE 18 ha	19	NO	All Year			8	X	C			2P	X	X	
387	1 A2	SANTA GERTRUDIS -BOCA DEL INFIERNO 435 ha		NO						C						
388	2 D2	SARGEANT BAY 57 ha	101	2P	All Year				X						X	X
389	6 A2	SASQUATCH 1,217 ha	7	12P	All Year	Y R	177		365	R C	F W	X	12F 24P	X	X	5H
390	15 C2	SAVONA 2 ha	1	P	Apr-Sept				30	C	W		4P			
391	12 B4	SCHOEN LAKE 8,430 ha	19	12R	All Year	Y	10	X		R C			2P	X	X	5H
392	26 C3	SCHOOLHOUSE LAKE 4,536 ha	97	NO												
393	11 A4	SCOTT ISLANDS 6,215 ha	19	NO												
394	2 D2	SECHELT INLETS MARINE RA 155 ha	101	NO	All Year			20	X	C			7P	X	X	
395	45 C1	SEELEY LAKE 24 ha	16	P	Apr-Sept	Y	20		12	C	F W		6P	X	X	
396	14 C2	SETON PORTAGE HISTORIC 1 ha	99	P												
397	5 B1	SHANNON FALLS 87 ha	99	P	All Year				108		W		8F			1H
398	16 B-C2	SHUSWAP LAKE 149 ha	1	19P	Apr-Oct	Y R	271		409	R C	F W	X	64F S 12P	X	X	5H

PARK / MAP NUMBER	MAP REFERENCE	Park	NEAREST HIGHWAY	ROAD ACCESS	OPERATING DATES	FEE (Y) RESERVATIONS (R)	VEHICLE / TENT CAMPSITES GROUP CAMPING (*)	WILDERNESS / WALK-IN CAMPSITES	PICNICKING / DAY USE (Car Spaces)	BOAT LAUNCHING RAMP (R) CANOEING / KAYAKING (C)	FIREWOOD (F) DRINKING WATER (W)	SANI-STATION	FLUSH TOILETS (F) PIT TOILETS (P) SHOWERS (S)	SWIMMING	FISHING	HIKING TRAILS (Km H) WALKING TRAILS (W)
399	16 D1-2	SHUSWAP LAKE MARINE 1,006 ha	1	NO	Apr-Oct	Y		44	X	C			29P	X	X	5H
400	5 A-B4	SIDNEY SPIT MARINE 400 ha	17	NO	All Year	Y		20	X	C	F W		14P	X	X	3H
401	16 D1	SILVER BEACH 130 ha	1	65G	Apr-Oct	Y	35	10	40	C	W		10P	X	X	1H
402	6 B3	SILVER LAKE 77 ha	1	6G	May-Oct	Y	30						2P		X	
403	16 D3	SILVER STAR 6,092 ha	97	20P	All Year				120				8P			
404	2 D2	SIMSON 461 ha	101	NO	All Year			X		C				X	X	H W
405	22 C1	SIR ALEXANDER MACKENZIE 5 ha	20	NO	All Year				X							
406	6 C3	SKAGIT VALLEY 27,948 ha	1	35G	All Year	Y	132*	X	86	R C	F W		16P	X	X	49H
407	15 B4	SKIHIST 33 ha	1	P	Feb-Dec	Y	56		33		F W	X	20F 7P			W
408	2 D1	SKOOKUMCHUCK NARROWS 123 ha	101	P	All Year				20				5P			4H
409	13 A4	SMALL INLET 487 ha	19	F 30P						C						
410	2 A1	SMELT BAY 16 ha	19	F 25P	All Year	Y	23		35		F W		4P	X	X	
411	2 D2	SMUGGLER COVE MARINE 182 ha	101	3G	All Year		4	2	10				3P	X	X	2H
412	3 C4	SOOKE MOUNTAIN 450 ha	14	NO	All Year											
413	3 C4	SOOKE POTHOLES 7 ha	14	1P	All Year				62				5P	X	X	
414	47 B3	SOWCHEA BAY RA 13 ha	27	16P	May-Oct	Y	30			R C	F W		4P	X	X	
415	27 A3	SPAHATS CREEK 270 ha	5	15P	Apr-Oct	Y	20		40		F W		10P			3H
416	62 A2	SPATSIZI PLATEAU WILDERNESS 656,785 ha	37	25G	May-Oct	Y		X		C			4P		X	100 H
417	3 D3	SPECTACLE LAKE 65 ha	1	2P	All Year				60	R	W		2p	X	X	
418	2 B2	SPIDER LAKE 65 ha	19	8G	All Year				60	C	W		5P	X	X	1H
419	16 B1	SPILLMAN BEACHES	16													
420	2 A3	SPROAT LAKE 39 ha	4	P	All Year	Y	59		200	R C	F W	X	8F S 16P	X	X	2H
421	2 C2	SQUITTY BAY MARINE 13 ha	19	NO	All Year			X	X	C	W		2P		X	
422	9 B1	ST. MARY'S ALPINE 9,146 ha	95A	63G	June-Sept											H W
423	8 D3	STAGLEAP 1,133 ha	3	P	All Year				30		F W		4P		X	1H
424	15 D3	STAKE-McCONNEL LAKES RA 189 ha	5	8P	Apr-Oct	Y	10		X	C	F W		9P	X	X	6H
425	2 A3	STAMP FALLS 234 ha	4	15P	All Year	Y	22		30		F W		6P		X	2H
426	2 A2	STAMP RIVER MONEY'S POOL 316 ha	4													
428	15 C2	STEELHEAD 38 ha	1	P	Apr-Oct	Y	32		10	C	F W		6F S 1P	X	X	
429	14 D4	STEIN VALLEY 107,191 ha	1	NO	Apr-Oct	Y		8					9P		X	
430	7	STEMWINDER 4 ha	3	P	All Year	Y	27			C	F W		6P		X	
431	61 C1	STIKINE RIVER RA 217,000 ha	37	NO	All Year			X		R C					X	H W
432	75 B3	STONE MOUNTAIN 25,691 ha	97	P	May-Oct	Y	28	X	5	R	W		7P		X	5H

PARK / MAP NUMBER	MAP REFERENCE	Park	NEAREST HIGHWAY	ROAD ACCESS	OPERATING DATES	FEE (Y) RESERVATIONS (R)	VEHICLE / TENT CAMPSITES GROUP CAMPING (*)	WILDERNESS / WALK-IN CAMPSITES	PICNICKING / DAY USE (Car Spaces)	BOAT LAUNCHING RAMP (R) CANOEING / KAYAKING (C)	FIREWOOD (F) DRINKING WATER (W)	SANI-STATION	FLUSH TOILETS (F) PIT TOILETS (P) SHOWERS (S)	SWIMMING	FISHING	HIKING TRAILS (Km H) WALKING TRAILS (W)
433	1 D1	STRATHCONA 253,773 ha	28	P	All Year	Y	161	26	37	R C	F W		54P	X	X	107 H
434	47 B3	STUART LAKE 315 ha	27	35G	All Year					C					X	X
435	58 A4	SUDETEN 5 ha	2	P	May-Oct	Y	15		25		F W		6P			
436	49 A1	SUKUNKA FALLS 360 ha	29	25G	Apr-Oct										X	
437	1 C2	SULPHUR PASSAGE 2,299 ha	4	NO						C						
438	5 D3	SUMAS MOUNTAIN 185 ha	1	4G	All Year											4H
439	16 C2	SUNNYBRAE 25 ha	1	6P	Apr-Oct				56	C	W		4F	X	X	
440	7 B2	SUN-OKA BEACH 30 ha	97	P	All Year				190		F W		11F 2P	X		
441	13 A4	SURGE NARROWS 586 ha	13	NO						C						
442	58 B4	SWAN LAKE 67 ha	2	4G	May-Oct	Y R	41*		75	R C	F W		12P	X		H
443	52 D3	SWAN LAKE - Kispiox River	52													
444	1 B2	SYDNEY INLET 2,774 ha	4	NO						C						
445	8 B2	SYRINGA CREEK 4,417 ha	3	19P	Apr-Oct	Y	60		220	R C	F W	X	22F 12P	X	X	5H
446	11 D4	TAHSISH KWOIS 10,829 ha	19	35G						C						
447	46 D1	TAKLA LAKE MARINE														
448	62 C4	TATLATUI 105,826 ha	37	NO	May-Nov			X							X	H
449	79 A4	TATSHENSHINI-ALSEK 958,000 ha	7	NO	All Year					C					X	H
450	26	TAWEEL														
451	2 A3	TAYLOR ARM 71 ha	4	P	All Year	*	60	15			F W		8P	X	X	1H W
452	57 C2	TAYLOR LANDING 2 ha	97	P	All Year				20	R			1P		X	
453	1 B4	TEAKERNE ARM MARINE 128 ha	101	NO	All Year										X	H
454	38 D3	TEN MILE LAKE 260 ha	97	P	May-Oct	Y R	131*		350	R C	F W	X	10F S 24P	X	X	H
455	75 C3	TETSA RIVER 115 ha	97	1G	May-Oct	Y	25		6		F W		4P		X	
456	5 A2	TETRAHEDRON														
457	8 A-B3	TEXAS CREEK 112 ha	3	P	Apr-Oct	Y	33		X		F W				X	
458	18 C4	THUNDER HILL 44 ha	93	P	Apr-Oct	Y	23				F W		6P			
459	13 A3	THURSTON BAY MARINE 389 ha	19	NO	All Year				X	C					X	H
460	9 D1	TOP OF THE WORLD 8,790 ha	93	54G	All Year	Y		24	20				6P		X	40H
461	46 C2	TOPLEY LANDING 12 ha	16	40P					45	C	W		4P	X	X	
462	1 D3	TRANQUIL CREEK 299 ha	4	NO												
463	2 B4	TRIBUNE BAY 95 ha	19	F 10P	All Year				100		W		6P	X		H
464	17 D3	TROUT LAKE 316 ha	31	P	Apr-Oct		5						2P		X	X
465	16 C4	TRUMAN DAGNUS LOCHEED 7 ha	97	P	All Year											

PARK / MAP NUMBER	MAP REFERENCE	Park	NEAREST HIGHWAY	ROAD ACCESS	OPERATING DATES	FEE (Y) RESERVATIONS (R)	VEHICLE / TENT CAMPSITES GROUP CAMPING (*)	WILDERNESS / WALK-IN CAMPSITES	PICNICKING / DAY USE (Car Spaces)	BOAT LAUNCHING RAMP (R) CANOEING / KAYAKING (C)	FIREWOOD (F) DRINKING WATER (W)	SANI-STATION	FLUSH TOILETS (F) PIT TOILETS (P) SHOWERS (S)	SWIMMING	FISHING	HIKING TRAILS (Km H) WALKING TRAILS (W)
466	13 D1	TS'Y-LOS 233,240 ha	20	RG		Y	32			R			4P		X	50H
467	15 D1	TSINTSUNKO LAKES														
468	48 B1	TUDYAH LAKE 56 ha	97	2G	May-Oct	Y	36*		40	R C	F W		6P	X	X	
469	15 C3	TUNKWA														
470	36 B3	TWEEDSMUIR NORTH 487,788 ha	16	NO	Apr-Oct			X		C	F			X	X	20H
471	36 B3	TWEEDSMUIR SOUTH 506,458 ha	20	20G	Apr-Oct	Y	38	11	63	R C	F W	X	28P	X	X	469 H
472	45 D2	TYHEE LAKE 33 ha	16	1P	Apr-Oct	Y	59*		200	R C	F W	X	16F S 18P	X	X	1H
473	34 C2	UNION PASSAGE MARINE 1,373 ha	37	NO	All Year											
474	27 C3	UPPER ADAMS RIVER														
475	8 C1	VALHALLA 49,800 ha	6	42G	All Year			X	X	C			9P	X	X	88H
476	1 C3	VARGAS ISLAND 5,970 ha	4	NO						C						
477	7 C3	VASEUX LAKE 12 ha	97	P	All Year	Y	12		5	C	F W		4P	X	X	
478	17 A2	VICTOR LAKE 15 ha	1	P												
479	5 A4	WALLACE ISLAND MARINE 72 ha	17	NO	All Year			20	X	C	F		3P	X	X	H
480	15 D3	WALLOPER LAKE 55 ha	5	P	Apr-Oct			10	X	C			2P	X		
481	13 B4	WALSH COVE MARINE 85 ha	101	NO	All Year									X	X	
482	9 D2	WARDNER 4 ha	3	2P	Apr-Oct				20		W		2P			
483	9 D1	WASA 144 ha	93	1P	All Year	Y R	104		500	R C	F W	X	47F 20P	X	X	2H
484	27 A1	WELLS GRAY 529,748 ha	5	40P	May-Sept	Y	88	23	321	R C	F W	X	68P	X	X	240 H
485	26 D3	WELLS GRAY (Mahood L.)	97	86 PG	Apr-Oct	Y	34		40	R C	F W		8P	X	X	11H
486	8 D2	WEST ARM														
487	38 C2	WEST LAKE 256 ha	16	13P	All Year		X		300	R C	F W		8F 10P	X	X	14H
488	3 C3	WEST SHAWNIGAN LAKE 9 ha	1	16P	All Year				120	C	F W		6P	X	X	
489	1 B1	WEYMER CREEK Karst														
490	2 D3	WHALEBOAT ISLAND MARINE 10 ha	1	NO	All Year					C				X	X	
491	48 C2	WHISKERS POINT 50 ha	97	P	May-Sept	Y	69		50	R C	F W	X	6F 6P	X	X	H
492	25 B2	WHITE PELICAN														
493	1 C1	WHITE RIDGE														
494	12 C4	WHITE RIVER POCKET WILDERNESS														
495	18 D4	WHITESWAN LAKE 1,994 ha	93	21G	All Year	Y	88	24	15	R C	F W	X	21P	X	X	8H
496	5 B4	WINTER COVE MARINE 91 ha	17	F 6G	All Year				10	R C	W		2P	X	X	2H
497	36 B1	WISTARIA 40 ha	35	40G	May-Oct			5	30	R			2P		X	
498	75 B3	WOKKPASH RA 37,800 ha	97	NO	All Year			X						X		H

PARK / MAP NUMBER	MAP REFERENCE	Park	NEAREST HIGHWAY	ROAD ACCESS	OPERATING DATES	FEE (Y) RESERVATIONS (R)	VEHICLE / TENT CAMPSITES GROUP CAMPING (*)	WILDERNESS / WALK-IN CAMPSITES	PICNICKING / DAY USE (Car Spaces)	BOAT LAUNCHING RAMP (R) CANOEING / KAYAKING (C)	FIREWOOD (F) DRINKING WATER (W)	SANI-STATION	FLUSH TOILETS (F) PIT TOILETS (P) SHOWERS (S)	SWIMMING	FISHING	HIKING TRAILS (Km H) WALKING TRAILS (W)
499	12 B4	WOSS LAKE														
500	9 C3	YAHK 9 ha	3	P	Apr-Oct	Y	26	30			F W		4P	X		
501	16 D2	YARD CREEK 61 ha	1	P	May-Oct	Y	90	14			F W	X	2F 14P	X		2H

BC Parks General Information

Fee period is generally April 1 to October 31.

BC resident seniors, 65 years of age or older, may camp before June 15 and after Labour Day at a 50% discount from the regular camping fee.

Disabled BC residents may camp free in Provincial Parks if they have applied for and received a disabled access card from BC Parks headquarters in Victoria.

Maximum stay in each provincial Park is 14 days per calendar year.

To cancel a reservation, call the reservation line after 7:00 pm and follow the recorded instructions. Cancellation policies do apply.

This park information is subject to change without notice.

National Parks within or bordering on British Columbia

For complete listing of facilities, see "Guide to Camping and Activities in National Parks" – available from Canada Parks Service Offices.

Park		NEAREST HIGHWAY	ROAD ACCESS	OPERATING DATES	FEE (Y) RESERVATIONS (R)	VEHICLE / TENT CAMPSITES GROUP CAMPING (*)	WILDERNESS / WALK-IN CAMPSITES	PICNICKING / DAY USE (Car Spaces)	BOAT LAUNCHING RAMP (R) CANOEING / KAYAKING (C)	FIREWOOD (F) DRINKING WATER (W)	SANI-STATION	FLUSH TOILETS (F) PIT TOILETS (P) SHOWERS (S)	SWIMMING	FISHING	HIKING TRAILS (Km H) WALKING TRAILS (W)
Page 18	BANFF	1 93	P	May-Sept		2800	X	X	R C	F W	X		X	X	H W
Page 17	GLACIER	1	P	Apr-Sept		394*	X	X		F W	X			X	H W
Page 20	GWAII HAANAS	16	NO				X						X	X	
Page 41	JASPER	16 93	P	May-Nov		1900	X	X	R	F	X		X	X	H
Page 78	KLUANE	7	P	June-Oct		41	X			F W		F P		X	H W
Page 18	KOOTENAY	93	P	May-Oct		450*	X	X	C	F W	X		X	X	H W
Page 17	MT. REVELSTOKE	1	P	All Year			X							X	H W
Page 1	PACIFIC RIM	4	P	All Year		175	X	X	C	X		F P	X	X	H W
Page 10	WATERTON	3	P	All Year		300	X	X	C	F W	X		X	X	H W
Page 18	YOHO	1	P	May-Oct		200	X	X		F W	X			X	H W

Ministry of Environment Contacts

Region 1 — Vancouver Island
Fish and Wildlife Regional Office
Nanaimo: 2080A Labieux Rd., V9T 6J9, (250) 751-3100

Conservation Officer Service District Offices
Campbell River: 101-370 S. Dogwood St., V9W 6Y7, (250) 286-7630
Duncan: 5785 Duncan St., V9L 5G2, (250) 746-1236
Nanaimo: 2080A Labieux Rd., V9T 6J9, (250) 751-3100
Port Alberni: 4515 Elizabeth St., V9Y 6L5, (250) 724-9290
Port Hardy: 8755 Granville St.,Bag 11000, V0N 2P0, (250) 949-6272
Vancouver Island Hatchery
Duncan: (250) 746-1425

Region 2 — Lower Mainland
Fish and Wildlife Regional Office
Surrey: 10334-152 A St., V3R 7P8, (604) 582-5200

Conservation Officer Service District Offices
Chilliwack: 9365 Mill St., V2P 4N3, (604) 795-8422
Maple Ridge: 20450 Dewdney Trunk Rd., V2X 3E3, (604) 465-4011 (24 hrs)
Powell River: 125-6953 Alberni St., V8A 2B8, (604) 485-3612
Sechelt: 102 Toredo Square, V0N 3A0, (604) 885-2004
Squamish: 37823 2nd Ave.,Box 187 V0N 3G0, (604) 892-5971
Surrey: 10334-152 A St., V3R 7P8, (604) 582-5200
Fraser Valley Trout Hatchery
Abbotsford: (604) 852-5388

Region 3 — Thompson-Nicola
Fish and Wildlife Regional Office
Kamloops: 1259 Dalhousie Dr., V2C 5Z5, (250) 371-6200

Conservation Officer Service District Offices
Clearwater: Box 490, V0E 1N0, (250) 674-3722
Clinton: 1423 Cariboo Hwy., Box 220, V0K 1K0, (250) 459-2341
Kamloops: 1259 Dalhousie Dr., V2C 5Z5, (250) 371-6200
Lillooet: 615 Main St., Bag 700, V0K 1V0, (250) 256-4636
Merritt: Box 4400, Station Main, V1K 1B8, (250) 378-8489
Loon Creek Hatchery
Cache Creek: (250) 459-2454

Region 4 — Kootenay
Fish and Wildlife Regional Offices
Nelson: Suite 401-333 Victoria St., V1L 4K3, (250) 354-6333
Cranbrook: 205 Industrial Rd. G, V1C 6H3, (250) 489-8540

Conservation Officer Service District Offices
Castlegar: 2205-14th Ave., V1N 3M7, (250) 365-8522
Cranbrook: 205 Industrial Rd. G, V1C 6H3, (250) 489-8570
Creston: 1000 Northwest Blvd., Box 1550, V0B 1G0, (250) 428-3220
Fernie: 1621-A 10th Ave., Bag 1000, V0B 1M0, (250) 423-7551
Golden: 903-9th St. S., Box 1313, V0A 1H0, (250) 344-7585
Invermere: 504-7th Ave., Box 2949, V0A 1K0, (250) 342-4266
Nakusp: 204-6th Ave. NW, Box 183, V0G 1R0, (250) 265-3714
Nelson: Suite 101-333 Victoria St., V1L 4K3, (250) 354-6397
Kootenay Trout Hatchery
Fort Steele: (250) 429-3214

Region 5 — Cariboo
Fish and Wildlife Regional Office
Williams Lake: Ste 400, 640 Borland St., V2G 4T1, (250) 398-4530

Conservation Officer Service District Offices
Alexis Creek: General Delivery, V0L 1A0, (250) 394-4343
Bella Coola: Box 907, V0T 1C0, (250) 799-5255
100 Mile House: 160 Cedar Ave. S, Box 187, V0K 2E0, (250) 395-5511
Quesnel: 350 Barlow St., V2J 2C1, (250) 992-4212
Williams Lake: Ste 400, 640 Borland St., V2G 1R8, (250) 398-4569

Region 6 — Skeena
Fish and Wildlife Regional Office
Smithers: Box 5000, 3726 Alfred St., V0J 2N0, (250) 847-7303

Conservation Officer Service District Offices
Atlin: Box 80, Second St., V0W 1A0, (250) 651-7501
Burns Lake: 33-3rd Ave., Box 285,V0J 1E0, (250) 692-7777
Dease Lake: Hwy. 37, Box 29, V0C 1L0, (250) 771-3566
Houston: 3459 10th St., Bag 2000, V0J 1Z0 (250) 845-7836
New Hazelton: Hwy. 16, Box 309, V0J 2J0, (250) 842-5319
Q.C. City: 126-2nd Ave., Box 370, V0T 1S0, (250) 559-8431
Smithers: Bag 5000, 3726 Alfred St., V0J 2N0, (250) 847-7261
Terrace: 104-3220 Eby St., V8G 5K8, (250) 638-3279

Region 7 — Omineca-Peace
Fish and Wildlife Regional Offices
Prince George: 3rd Fl., Plaza 400, 1011-4th Ave.,V2L 3H9, (250) 565-6135
Fort St. John: Rm 200, 10003-110th Ave.,V1J 6M7, (250) 787-3295

Conservation Officer Service District Offices
Chetwynd: 4729-51st St., Bag 105, V0C 1J0, 788-3611
Dawson Creek: 1201-103rd Ave., V1G 4J2, 784-2304
Fort Nelson: Bag 1000, #4 Govt. Bldg, 4640 Sunset Dr., V0C 1R0 (250) 774-3547
Fort St. John: Rm. 200, 10003-110th Ave.,V1J 6M7, (250) 787-3295
MacKenzie: 5-220 MacKenzie Blvd., Bag 5000, V0J 2C0, (250) 997-6555
Prince George: 3rd Fl., Plaza 400, 1011-4th Ave, V2L 3H9, (250) 565-6140
Valemount: Regency Place, Box 39, V0E 2Z0, 566-4398
Vanderhoof: Box 980, V0J 3A0, (250) 567-6304

Region 8 — Okanagan
Fish and Wildlife Regional Office
Penticton: Suite 201, 3547 Skaha Lake Rd., V2A 7K2, (250) 490-8200

Conservation Officer Service District Offices
Grand Forks: 7272-2nd St, Box 638, V0H 1H0, (250) 442-4310
Kelowna: 1690 Powick Rd., V1X 7G5, (250) 861-7670
Penticton: 3547 Skaha Lake Rd., V2A 7K2, (250) 490-8200
Princeton: 195 Bridge St, Box 1000, V0X 1W0, (250) 295-6343
Vernon: 3201-30th St., V1T 9G3, (250) 549-5558
Summerland Trout Hatchery
Summerland: (250) 494-0491

BC Forest Service Contacts

Forest recreation in B.C. involves dozens of activities, ranging from the passive enjoyment of scenery to the physically demanding challenges of mountaineering and kayaking. Approximately two million people annually take advantage of the more than one thousand recreation sites and thousands of kilometres of trails provided.

The sites are rustic and usually small without sophisticated amenities but do include basic facilities. They are located near lakes and rivers, blending in with the natural surroundings. The overall goal of the B.C. Forest Service recreation program is to provide opportunities for outdoor recreation by protecting the provincial forest recreation resource and managing its use. For more information regarding specific sites, please contact the nearest forest district office listed below.

Numbers in front of each District Office below identify the Forest Districts in British Columbia. These Districts are shown on the Key Map on pages I - II

65 Ministry of Forests
Box 65, Stum Lake Rd.
ALEXIS CREEK, B.C.
V0L 1A0
(250) 394-4700

21 Ministry of Forests
185 Yellowhead Hwy.
Box 269
BURNS LAKE, B.C.
V0J 1E0
(250) 692-2200

18 Ministry of Forests
370 S. Dogwood St.
CAMPBELL RIVER, B.C.
V9W 6Y7
(250) 286-9300

55 Ministry of Forests
845 Columbia Ave.
CASTLEGAR, B.C.
V1N 1H3
(250) 365-8600

31 Ministry of Forests
Box 4501, RR #2
Yellowhead Hwy. #5
CLEARWATER, B.C.
V0E 1N0
(250) 587-6700

51 Ministry of Forests
1902 Theatre Road
CRANBROOK, B.C.
V1C 4H4
(250) 426-1700

47 Ministry of Forests
9000-17th St.
DAWSON CREEK, B.C.
V1G 4A4
(250) 784-1200

29 Ministry of Forests
Stikine & Commercial
Gen. Del., Hwy 37
DEASE LAKE, B.C.
V0C 1L0
(250) 771-4211

16 Ministry of Forests
7233 Trans-Canada Hwy.
DUNCAN, B.C.
V9L 5G2
(250) 746-2700

49 Ministry of Forests
RR #1, Mile 301,
Alaska Hwy
FORT NELSON, B.C.
V0C 1R0
(250) 774-3936

45 Ministry of Forests
Stones Bay Road
Box 100
FORT ST JAMES, B.C.
V0J 1P0
(250) 996-5200

48 Ministry of Forests
8808 - 72nd St.
FORT ST JOHN, B.C.
V1J 6M2
(250) 787-5600

53 Ministry of Forests
800 - 9th St. North
Box 1380
GOLDEN, B.C.
V0A 1H0
(250) 344-7500

56 Ministry of Forests
136 Sagamore Ave.
Box 2650
GRAND FORKS, B.C.
V0H 1H0
(250) 442-5411

1A Ministry of Forests
Sawmill Road
Box 190
HAGENSBORG, B.C.
V0T 1H0
(250) 982-2000

24 Ministry of Forests
2210 West Hwy 62
Box 215
HAZELTON, B.C.
V0J 1Y0
(250) 842-7600

63 Ministry of Forests
Box 69
HORSEFLY, B.C.
V0L 1L0
(250) 620-3200

22 Ministry of Forests
2430 Butler Ave.
Bag 2000
HOUSTON, B.C.
V0J 1Z0
(250) 845-6200

52 Ministry of Forests
625 - 4th St.
INVERMERE, B.C.
V0A 1K0
(250) 342-4200

32 Ministry of Forests
1265 Dalhousie Dr.
KAMLOOPS, B.C.
V2C 5Z5
(250) 371-6500

37 Ministry of Forests
Bag 700, 650 Industrial Pl.
LILLOOET, B.C.
V0K 1V0
(250) 256-1200

46 Ministry of Forests
1 Cicada Rd.
Bag 5000
MACKENZIE, B.C.
V0J 2C0
(250) 997-2200

43 Ministry of Forests
Box 40
McBRIDE, B.C.
V0J 2E0
(250) 569-3700

36 Ministry of Forests
Bag 4400
Hwy 5A & Airport Rd.
MERRITT, B.C.
V1K 1B8
(250) 378-8400

57 Ministry of Forests
1907 Ridgewood Road
NELSON, B.C.
V1L 5P4
825-1100

64 Ministry of Forests
300 S. Cariboo Hwy
100 MILE HOUSE, B.C.
V0K 2E0
(250) 395-7800

35 Ministry of Forests
102 Industrial Pl.
PENTICTON, B.C.
V2A 7C8
(250) 490-2200

17 Ministry of Forests
4227 - 6th Ave.
PORT ALBERNI, B.C.
V9Y 4N1
(250) 724-9205

19 Ministry of Forests
2291 Mine Pl.
Box 7000
PORT McNEILL, B.C.
V0N 2R0
956-5000

15 Ministry of Forests
7077 Duncan St.
POWELL RIVER, B.C.
V8A 1W1
(604) 485-0700

41 Ministry of Forests
200 S. Ospika Bvld.
PRINCE GEORGE, B.C.
V2N 4W5
(250) 565-7100

28 Ministry of Forests
125 Market Place
PRINCE RUPERT, B.C.
V8J 1B9
(250) 627-0460

1B Ministry of Forests
1229 Cemetery Rd.
Box 39
QUEEN CHARLOTTE, B.C.
V0T 1S0
(250) 559-8447

61 Ministry of Forests
322 Johnston Ave.
QUESNEL, B.C.
V2J 3M5
(250) 992-4400

54 Ministry of Forests
1761 Big Eddy Road
Box 9158, RPO #3
REVELSTOKE, B.C.
V0E 3K0
(250) 837-7611

11 Ministry of Forests
9880 S. McGrath Rd.
Box 159
ROSEDALE, B.C.
V0X 1X0
(250) 794-2100

33 Ministry of Forests
Bag 100
2780 - 10th Ave. NE
SALMON ARM, B.C.
V1E 4S4
(250) 832-1401

23 Ministry of Forests
3333 Tatlow Rd.
Bag 6000
SMITHERS, B.C.
V0J 2N0
(250) 847-6300

13 Ministry of Forests
42000 Loggers Lane
SQUAMISH, B.C.
V0N 3G0
(250) 898-2100

25 Ministry of Forests
Room 200
5220 Keith Ave.
TERRACE, B.C.
V8G 1L1
(250) 638-5100

44 Ministry of Forests
1552 Hwy. 16
Box 190
VANDERHOOF, B.C.
V0J 3A0
(250) 567-6363

62 Ministry of Forests
2501 - 14th Ave.
VERNON, B.C.
V1T 8Z1
(250) 558-1700

34 Ministry of Forests
925 North 2nd Ave.
WILLIAMS LAKE, B.C.
V2G 4P7
(250) 305-2001

113

The Ferry number shown to the left of the ferry information is shown on the map as: **F19**

MINISTRY OF TRANSPORTATION AND HIGHWAYS FERRIES
4D-940 Blanshard Street, Victoria, B.C. V8W 3E6   Phone: (250) 387-3417

Inland Ferries

F1 Albion - Fort Langley Ferry – 10 min., 26 cars, 100 passengers
F2 Lytton Ferry* – 5 min., 2 cars or 1 truck, 20 passengers
F3 Big Bar Ferry* – 5 min., 2 cars, 12 passengers
F4 Marguerite Ferry* – 5 min., 2 cars, 12 passengers
F5 François Lake Ferry – 7 min., 32 cars, 150 passengers
F6 McLure Ferry* – 5 min., 2 cars, 12 passengers
F7 Little Fort Ferry* – 5 min., 2 cars, 12 passengers
F8 Shuswap Lake Ferry – Sicamous to Seymour Arm. Port of call Anstey Arm.
         Route time varies, 9 cars, 18 passengers
F9 Needles Ferry – Needles to Fauquier, 40 cars, 150 passengers
F10 Arrow Park Ferry – 5 min., 28 cars, 75 passengers
F11 Upper Arrow Lake Ferry – Shelter Bay to Galena Bay, 20 min., 41 cars, 150 passengers
F12 Kootenay Lake Ferry – Balfour to Kootenay Bay, 40 min., 38 cars, 150 passengers, also 42 cars, 150 passengers
F13 Glade Ferry – 3 min., 8 cars, 50 passengers
F14 Harrop Ferry – 5 min., 10 cars, 50 passengers
F15 Usk Ferry* – 5 min., 2 cars, 12 passengers

*denotes reaction ferry only - operation times vary; check with Ministry office or obtain local information.

BRITISH COLUMBIA FERRY CORPORATION
1112 Fort Street, Victoria, B.C. V8V 4V2 Ph: Victoria (250) 386-3431, Vancouver (604) 669-1211

Vancouver Island

F16 Vancouver (Tsawwassen) to Victoria (Swartz Bay) – 1 hour 35 min., 338 cars, 1360 passengers
F17 Vancouver (Tsawwassen) to Nanaimo (Departure Bay) – 2 hours, 300 cars, 1360 passengers
F18 Vancouver (Horseshoe Bay) to Nanaimo (Departure Bay) – 1 hour 35 min., 362 cars, 1500 passengers
F19 Brentwood (Saanich) to Mill Bay – 20 min., 16 cars, 134 passengers
F20 Denman Island Ferry – Buckley Bay to Denman Island, 10 min., 30 cars, 195 passengers
F21 Hornby Island Ferry – Denman Island to Hornby Island, 15 min., 16 cars, 138 passengers
F22 Comox - Powell River Ferry – Little River to Westview, 1 hour 15 min., 135 cars, 700 passengers
F23 Campbell River to Quathiaski Cove – 15 min., 30 cars, 200 passengers
F24 Cortes Island Ferry – Heriot Bay to Whaletown – 45 min., 16 cars, 150 passengers
F25 Alert Bay Ferry – Alert Bay (Cormorant I) to Sointula (Malcolm I) to Port McNeill, 30 cars, 150 passengers

Gulf Islands

F26 Vancouver (Tsawwassen) to Saltspring Island (Long Harbour), Pender Island (Otter Bay), Mayne Island (Village Bay), Galiano Island (Sturdies Bay) 2 hours 45 min., vehicle reservations required, 138 cars, 1000 passengers
F27 Vancouver Island (Swartz Bay) to Saltspring Island (Fulford Harbour) 30 min., 70 cars, 400 passengers
F28 Vancouver Island (Crofton) to Saltspring Island (Vesuvius Bay) – 20 min., 36 cars, 182 passengers
F29 Thetis Island Ferry – Chemainus to Thetis and Kuper Islands, 25 min., 25 cars,150 passengers
F30 Gabriola Island Ferry – Nanaimo to Gabriola Island, 20 min., 70 cars, 394 passengers

Sunshine Coast

F31 Vancouver (Horseshoe Bay) to Sechelt Peninsula (Langdale) – 40 min., 300 cars, 1000 passengers
F32 Vancouver (Horseshoe Bay) to Bowen Island (Snug Cove) – 20 min., 70 cars, 330 passengers
F33 Earls Cove to Saltery Bay – 50 min., 70 cars, 400 passengers
F34 Texada Island Ferry – Westview to Blubber Bay, 35 min., 30 cars, 200 passengers

Northern Services

F35 Vancouver Island (Port Hardy) to Prince Rupert – 15 hours, year round service to Bella Bella, 157 cars, 800 passengers
F36 Prince Rupert to Skidegate – year round service, 8 hours, reservations required,80 cars, 504 passengers; also 157 cars, 800 passengers
F37 Queen Charlotte Islands, Skidegate (Graham I) to Alliford Bay (Moresby I) 20 min., 80 cars, 504 passengers; also 157 cars, 800 passengers

CITY OF PRINCE RUPERT
424-3rd Avenue West, Prince Rupert, B.C. V8J 1L7 Ph: (250) 627-0937 Fax: (250) 627-0999

F38 Digby Island Ferry – Prince Rupert to Digby Island, 25 min., 40 passengers

WESTERN PACIFIC MARINE
North foot of Denman Street, Vancouver V6G 2W9
Phone (604) 681-5199 or Lasqueti (604) 333-8787

F39 Darrell Bay - Woodfiber – 25 min., 7 cars, 332 passengers
F40 Lasqueti Island Ferry – 1 hour, 65 passengers
F41 Barnston Island Ferry – Port Kells to Barnston Island, 5 min., 5 cars, 38 passengers, (50 passengers without vehicles)
F42 Prince Rupert to Kincolith – 3 hours, 40 passengers

METLAKATLA FERRY SERVICES LTD.
Box 224, Prince Rupert, B.C. V8J 3P6 Phone: (250) 628-3201 Fax:(250) 628-9259

F43 Prince Rupert to Port Simpson, 1 hour 30 min., 40 passengers

CLIPPER NAVIGATION LTD.
1000-A Wharf Street, Victoria, B.C. V8W 1T4
Victoria Reservations Phone: (250) 382-8100   Seattle Reservations Phone: (206) 448-5500

F44 Victoria to Seattle – 2 hours 30 min., approximately 300 passengers, year round service

ALBERNI MARINE TRANSPORTATION COMPANY
Box 188, Port Alberni, B.C. V9Y 7M7 Phone: (250) 723-8313

F45 Port Alberni to Ucluelet (via Broken Group Islands) – 10 hours round trip, 100 passengers, Seasonal: Monday, Wednesday, Friday
Port Alberni to Bamfield (waypoint Kildonan) – 9 hours round trip, 100 passengers, Tuesday, Thursday, Saturday

NOOTKA SOUND SERVICE LTD.
P.O. Box 57, Gold River, B.C. Phone: (250) 283-2515   Ship: (250) 283-2325

F46 Gold River – Ports of call: Tahsis, Ceepeecee, McCurdy Creek, Kendrick Arm, Plumper Harbour, Hayes Logging, Kyuquot, Blithelskund, Hecate Bay, Mooyah Bay, Blowhole Bay, 100 passengers

WASHINGTON STATE AND STATE OF ALASKA TO B.C.

BLACK BALL TRANSPORT INC.
430 Belleville St., Victoria, B.C. V8V 1W9 Phone: (250) 386-2202
Port Angeles (206) 457-4491

F49 Victoria to Port Angeles – 1 hour 35 min., 100 cars, 800 passengers

STATE OF ALASKA, DIVISION OF MARINE HIGHWAY SYSTEMS
Pouch R, Juneau, Alaska 99811   Phone: (907) 465-3941 Prince Rupert: (250) 627-1744

F50 Prince Rupert to Skagway – Ports of call: Ketchikan, Wrangell, Petersburg, Sitka, Juneau, Haines; from 34 to 58 hours, 100 cars, 500 passengers. Additional routes originate from some of the ports of call

WASHINGTON STATE FERRIES
Flair Hospitality Ltd., 2499 Ocean Ave., Sidney, B.C. V8L 1T3
Phone: Sidney (604) 656-1531 or (604) 381-1551 Seattle (206) 464-6400

F51 Sidney to Anacortes – San Juan Islands ports of call, 3 hours, 160 cars, 2000 passengers, daily departures year round

PRINCESS MARGUERITE
185 Dallas Road, Victoria, B.C. V8V 1A1
Phone: Canada 1-800-668-1167 USA 1-800-888-2325

F52 Victoria to Seattle – 4 hours 30 min., 200 cars, 1000 passengers
Leaves Victoria 7:30 am, leaves Seattle 1:00 pm

BC Gazetteer

Location references in this gazetteer consist of a page number and a letter/number combination indicating position on the page, according to the diagram below. In this example, 8D2.

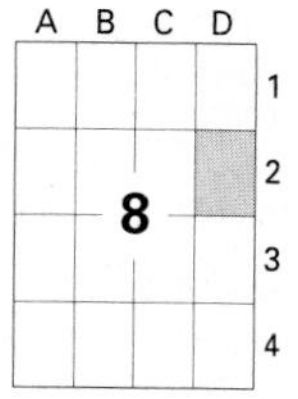

Place Names are shown in bold

● Hospital

❍ Diagognostic & Treatment Centre

A

Aaltanhash In ... 35A3
Aaltanhash R ... 35A3
Aaron Hill ... 8C3
● **Abbotsford ... 5D3**
Abbott Cr ... 26B1
Aberdeen L ... 16D4
Abies Cr ... 53C1
Abraham Cr ... 54C1
Abuntlet L ... 23D1
Aconitum Cr ... 82A4
Aconitum L ... 82A4
Actaeon Sd ... 11D2
Active Pass ... 3D2
Active Pass ... 5A-B4
Adam R ... 12B3
Adamant Mtn ... 28B3
Adams Cr ... 56C2
Adams L ... 16B1
Adams L ... 27C4
Adams Lake ... 16B2
Adams R ... 16B2
Adams R ... 27C4
Addenbroke I ... 22B4
Adolf Cr ... 27C1
Adoogacho Cr ... 62C2
Adsett Cr ... 76C4
Adsit L ... 71C-D2
Adsit L ... 72A2
Advance Mtn ... 56A2
Aeneas L ... 7B2
Aero ... 31A3
Aeroplane L ... 73B1
Aeroplane L ... 84B4
Agamemnon Chan ... 2C-D1
Agassiz ... 6A3
Ahbau Cr ... 38D3
Ahbau L ... 38D3
Ahclakerho Chan ... 11C1
Ahdatay Cr ... 47A-B1
Ahnuhati R ... 12D2
Ahousat ... 1C3
Ahwhichaolto In ... 11B3
Aid L ... 28C3
Aiken L ... 54D1
Aikman Cr ... 56D1
Ain R ... 30D1
Ain R ... 32B2
Ainslie Cr ... 6B1
Ainsworth Hot Springs ... 9A1
Airdrie ... 19D1
Airline L ... 47A1
Airplane L ... 81B3
Airport Cr ... 46C3
Airy Mtn ... 8B2
Aitken Cr ... 66A4
Aiyansh ... 44D1
Akamina Cr ... 10C3
Akamina Pass ... 10C3
Akehurst L ... 26D4
Akie Mtn ... 64A3
Akie R ... 64A2-3
Akluky Cr ... 65B2
Akokli Cr ... 9A2
Akokli Mtn ... 9A2
Akolkolex R ... 17B2
Aktaklin L ... 24A-B2
Akue Cr ... 75D3
Akue Cr ... 76B3
Alan Cr ... 82C3
Alan Cr ... 83A3
Alan Reach ... 35A2
Alans L ... 26C3
Alastair L ... 44C-D4
Albas ... 16D1
Alberni In ... 2B3
Albert Canyon ... 17B1
Albert Cr ... 17B1
Albert L ... 46D1
Albert L ... 54D4
Albert Pk ... 17B1
Albert R ... 18D3
Albert Snowfield ... 17C1
Alberta L ... 15A1
Alberta L ... 26A4
Alberts Hump ... 62C2
Albion ... 5C3
Albreda R ... 27C-D1
Alcantara Cr ... 18D2
Alces R ... 57D1
Alces R ... 58A1-2
Alcock L ... 57D4
Alcock L ... 58A4
Alder Cr ... 28C4
Alder Cr ... 44C4
Alder Pk ... 44C1
Aldergrove ... 5C3
Aldridge Cr ... 19B3
Alec Chief L ... 83B3
● **Alert Bay ... 12A3**
Alex Cr ... 16B1
Alex Graham L ... 25B2
Alexander Cr ... 10B1
Alexander Cr ... 57A1
Alexander Cr ... 66A4
Alexander In ... 22A1
Alexander In ... 35A4
Alexandra Pass ... 11B-C1
Alexandra Pk ... 1D1
Alexandria ... 38C-D4
Alexis Cr ... 25A2
Alexis Creek ... 25B2
Alexis Pk ... 48D1
Aley Cr ... 55D1
Aley Cr ... 56A1
Aleza Lake ... 48D4
Alford Cr ... 48C4
Alger Cr ... 61B4
Alice Arm ... 52B-C4
Alice Arm ... 52C4
Alice Cr ... 38D3
Alice Cr ... 44D3
Alice L ... 11C3
Alice Pk ... 44D3
Aline L ... 74D1
Aline L ... 85D4
Alison Sd ... 11D1
Alixon Cr ... 25D3
Alkali Cr ... 25D3
Alkali L ... 25D3
Alkali L ... 60B1
Alkali Lake ... 25D3
Allan Cr ... 27C1
Allan L ... 16A1
Allard L ... 22C-D4
Allen Cr ... 15A2
Allenby ... 6D2
Alleyne L ... 6D1
Alliford Bay ... 31A3
Alliford Bay ... 32C4
Allin Cr ... 46C4
Allison Cr ... 6D2
Allison L ... 6D1
Allison Pass ... 6C3
Allison Pk ... 10B1
Alma Cr ... 62B4
Alma Pk ... 62C4
Alma Russell Is ... 2A4
Almond Cr ... 8A3
Almond Gardens ... 7A3
Almond Mtn ... 8A3
Alna Pk ... 35B1
Alnus Cr ... 28B1
Alocin Cr ... 16B4
Alocin L ... 7B1
Alouette L ... 4B1
Alouette L ... 5D3
Alouette R ... 4B1
Alpha Cr ... 31D1
Alpha Cr ... 33C2
Alpha Cr ... 34A1
Alpha Mtn ... 60A3
Alsek R ... 78C3-4
Aluk Cr ... 53A3-4
Amai Creek ... 11D4
Ambition Mtn ... 60B2
America Cr ... 9C4
American Cr ... 52B2
Ames Cr ... 39A2
Amiskwi R ... 29A4
Amor de Cosmos Cr ... 12D4
Amor L ... 12D4
Amos Cr ... 26C1
Amos Cr ... 39B-C4
Amoth L ... 44B2
Anaconda ... 7D3
Anacortes ... 4B3
Anahim Cr ... 25B2
Anahim L ... 23D1
Anahim Lake ... 24A1
Anahim Pk ... 36D4
Anarchist Mtn ... 7C3
Anchor L ... 34D3
Anderson Cr ... 15A2
Anderson L ... 14D3
Anderson L ... 27B2
Anderson R ... 6B1
Andesite Pk ... 45B4
Andy Cr ... 55D2
Andy Cr ... 56A2
Andy Good Cr ... 10B2
Aneko Cr ... 24D1
Aneko Cr ... 25A1
Angel L ... 81C4
Angel Pk ... 75A3
Anger I ... 33D3
Anger I ... 34B2
Anglemont ... 16C2
Angly L ... 47B4
Angus Cr ... 2D2
Angus Cr ... 9C2
Angus Horne Cr ... 27B1
Angus Horne L ... 27B1
Angusmac Cr ... 48C3
Ankitree Cr ... 23B4
Ankwill Cr ... 54B4
Anstey Arm ... 16D1
Anstey R ... 16D1
Ant L ... 48B2
Anthony Cr ... 62A4
Anthony I ... 20B2
Anthracite Cr ... 62A4
Antle Is ... 31D2
Antle Is ... 33B-C3
Antler Cr ... 39B3
Antoine Cr ... 14D2
Antoine L ... 26B1
Anudol Cr ... 44C1
Anuk R ... 60A3
Anvil Mtn ... 14A1
Anvil Mtn ... 25A4
Anyox Cr ... 52B4
Anzac R ... 48D2
Anzus L ... 37A1
Apalmer Cr ... 16C2
Ape L ... 23B2
Apex Cr ... 8D2
Apex Mtn ... 7B2
Apex Mtn ... 28B2
Apple R ... 12D2
Appledale ... 8C2
Applegrove ... 8B1
Apsassin Cr ... 65D3
Aramis Ls ... 63D1
Arcat Cr ... 7A2
Archer Cr ... 26D2
Archer Cr ... 27A2
Archer Cr ... 39A3
Archie L ... 34D4
Arctic L ... 49A3
Argenta ... 18A4
Argentine Mtn ... 28B4
Argillite Cr ... 71D3
Argillite Cr ... 72A3
Argonaut Cr ... 28A3
Argonaut Mtn ... 28A3
Aristazabal I ... 21C-D1
Aristazabal I ... 34C4
Arlington ... 4C4
Arlington Ls ... 7C2
Arlington Pk ... 8D1
Armadillo Pk ... 60C-D2
Armadillo Pk ... 61A2
● **Armstrong ... 16C3**
Armstrong L ... 17C2
Arnell Cr ... 75C4
Arnell Cr ... 76A4
Arnhem Mtn ... 74D3
Arnoup Cr ... 34D3
Arras ... 57D3
Arras ... 58A3
Arrow Cr ... 9B3
Arrow Creek ... 9B3
Arrow Park Cr ... 17B4
Arrow Park L ... 17B4
Arrow Pass ... 12A2
Arrowhead ... 17B2
Arrowview Heights ... 2B3
Arthur I ... 33B2
Arthur I ... 43C4
Arthur L ... 16C3
Artlish R ... 11D4
Artlish R ... 12A4
Ash Mtn ... 71C-D1
Ash Mtn ... 72A1
Ash R ... 1D2
Ash R ... 2A2
Ashcroft ... 15B2
Asher Cr ... 17C3
Ashlu Cr ... 5A1
Ashlu Cr ... 14A4
Ashlulm Cr ... 23A3
Ashnola R ... 7A3
Ashton Cr ... 16D3
Ashton Creek ... 16D3
Asitka L ... 54B1
Asitka Pk ... 54B1
Asitka R ... 54B1
Askom Mtn ... 15A3
Asp Cr ... 6D2
Aspen Grove ... 6D1
Asseek R ... 23A3
Assiniboine Pass ... 18D2
Asulkan Br ... 17C1
Atan L ... 72C-D1
Athabasca Pass ... 28B1
Athalmer ... 18C3
Athlone I ... 22A2
Athlow B ... 30B2
Athlow B ... 32A3
Atick Cr ... 65C3
Atis Cr ... 39A4
Atlatzi R ... 12C1
Atli In ... 20B1
Atli In ... 31A4
Atlin ... 80D4
Atlin ... 81A4
Atlin L ... 69C1
Atlin L ... 70A1
Atlin L ... 80C3
Atlin L ... 81A3
Atlin Mtn ... 80C4
Atlin Mtn ... 81A4
Atlin R ... 80C4
Atlin R ... 81A4
Atluck ... 12A4
Atluck L ... 12A4
Atna L ... 35B1
Atna L ... 45B4
Atna R ... 35B1
Atna R ... 45B4
Atnarko ... 23C1
Atnarko R ... 23C1
Attachie ... 57B2
Attichika Cr ... 62D4
Attichika Cr ... 63B4
Attycelley Cr ... 63B3
Atwaykellesse R ... 12B1
Augier L ... 46D3
August L ... 88C3
Austerity Cr ... 28B3
Australian ... 38C-D4
Australian Cr ... 25D1
Australian Cr ... 38D4
Avalanche Pass ... 40B2
Averil Cr ... 48D4
Averil L ... 48D4
Avola ... 27C3
Avon Cr ... 25A2
Avun L ... 30C2
Avun L ... 32B3
Axelgold Pk ... 54C2
Axnegrelga Cr ... 52D3
Aylard Cr ... 56C2
Ayton Cr ... 33D1
Ayton Cr ... 44B4
Azouzetta L ... 56C4
Azuklotz Cr ... 54B2
Azuklotz L ... 54B2
Azure L ... 27A1
Azure Mtn ... 27A2
Azure R ... 27A1

B

B.X. Cr ... 16C4
Babcock Cr ... 49C2
Babcock L ... 39B3
Babiche Hill ... 53B2
Babine L ... 46C2
Babine R ... 53C4

Babine R 54A4
Baboon L 46B2
Bachelor Cr..............28B4
Back L 18D2
Bacon Cr.................69D3
Bacon Cr.................70A3
Badger Cr................16A1
Badger L 16A1
Badman Point 71B1
Baezaeko R..............37D4
Baezaeko R..............37B4
Bain Br 17C1
Baird Br 17D1
Baker Cr 7C3
Baker Cr 28A2
Baker Cr 38B-C4
Baker I 12B2
Baker In 33D2
Baker In 34B1
Balaklava I 11C2
Bald Mtn 25B4
Bald Range Cr 16B4
Balden Cr 55D1
Balden Cr 56A1
Balden Cr 64C4
Balden Cr 65A4
Baldface Mtn 37B4
Baldonnel **57C2**
Baldy Cr 7C3
Baldy Hughes.........**38C2**
Baldy Mtn 7C3
Baldy Mtn 8D2
Baldy Mtn 24A1
Baldy Mtn 27A4
Baldy Mtn 37A4
Baldy Mtn 55B4
Balfour................**9A2**
Ball Cr 60C3
Ball Cr 61A3
Ballenas Chan 2C2-3
Ballenas Chan 3B1
Ballenas Is 2C2
Balmoral **16C2**
Bamberton............**3D3**
Bambrick Cr 25B4
Bamfield...............**2A4**
Bamford Lagoon...........11D1
Bancroft Cr 1C2
Banff **18D1**
Banks I 31D2
Banks I 33C3
Banks I 34A-B2
Banks L 33C4
Banks L 34A2
Bannock Burn Cr...........8C1
Banon Cr 2D4
Banon Cr 3C2
Banshee L 16B2
Banting Cr 17A4
Baptiste Cr 47A2
Barbara L 49D4
Barbara L 50A4
Barbour Cr 18B3
Bardolph L 16D4
Bardswell Group........22A2
Barella Cr 26D1
Barella Cr 27A1
Barker Cr 62B4
Barker Cr 65C3
Barkers Cr 39B4
Barkerville **39A-B3**
Barkley Sd 1D4
Barkshack Cr 13C4
Barnes Cr 8B1
Barnes Cr 15C2
Barnes Cr 17B4
Barnes L 15B2
Barnes L 84C2
Barnes L 85A2
Baron I 33B1
Baron I 43C3
Barr Cr 1A1

Barr Cr 19A4
Barrett Lake **46A3**
Barrie Reach...........35A2
Barrier Pass 64A4
Barrier Pk 64A4
Barrière **16A1**
Barrière R 16A1
Barrière R 27B4
Barrington R...........60A1
Barton Hill 16B4
Barton L 38B2
Basalt L 36D4
Base Camp Cr 80C-D3
Base Camp Cr 81A3
Bassett Cr 26C2
Bastille Cr 40A1
Bastille Mtn 40B1
Bastion Bay **16C-D2**
Bat Cr 64D1
Bat Cr 65B1
Batchelor L 34B2
Bate Pass 11B2
Bates Cr 54C3
Batnuni L 37C2
Battle Br 17C1
Battle Gla 78B-C4
Battle L 12B2
Bay Tree **58B3**
Baynes Lake **10A3**
Baynes Sd 2B2
Bayton **2A2**
Beach Grove...........**5B3**
Beachcomber Bay......**16C4**
Beady Cr 71D2
Beady Cr 72B2
Beak Cr 16B4
Beale L 72D2
Beale Mtn 72C2
Bean Cr 10A3
Beano Cr 1A2
Beany Cr 56D2
Bear B 13A2
Bear Canyon **58B2**
Bear Cr 25B4
Bear Cr 71B4
Bear Creek Res 3C3
Bear Flat **57B2**
Bear Lake **48C3**
Bear L 17D4
Bear L 34D3
Bear L 53D2
Bear L 54A2
Bear Mtn 57D3
Bear Mtn 58A3
Bear R 13A2
Bear R 52B2-3
Bear R 53D2
Bear R 54A2
Bear River Gla 52B2
Bear River Pass 52B2
Bearcub Cr 47C4
Beard Cr 18B1
Bearpaw L 26B3
Beasley **8C2**
Beaton **17C2**
Beaton Cr 17C2
Beatrice Cr 8C1
Beatrice L 8C1
Beattie Cr 55D2
Beattie Cr 56A2
Beattie Pks 56C3
Beatton R 57C1
Beatton R 65D3
Beatton R 66B3
Beatton Ranch **65C4**
Beatton River **66B2**
Beatty Cr 71B3-4
Beauchamp Pk 75A2
Beauchemin Chan 21C1
Beauchemin Chan 34C4
Beaudette Cr 56D4
Beaumont Cr 25C3

Beauregard L 16A1
Beaver Cove 12A3
Beaver Cove **12A3**
Beaver Cr 8C3
Beaver Cr 26A1
Beaver Cr 65C1
Beaver Creek **2B2-3**
Beaver Har 11C2
Beaver In 12D3
Beaver L 25B2
Beaver Mines **10C2**
Beaver Pass 31D1
Beaver Pass 34A1
Beaver R 17C1
Beaver R 28C4
Beaver R 86B3
Beaverdell **7D2**
Beaverdell Cr 7D2
Beaverfoot R 18B1
Beaverley **38C1**
Beaverley Cr 38C1
Beaverlodge **50C1**
Beaverlodge L 50B1
Beaverlodge L 58B4
Beaverpond Cr 54C3
Beaverskin Cr 77D4
Becher B 3C-D4
Beckman Cr 75C-D4
Beckman Cr 76A4
Bedaux Pass 64A-B1
Bedingfield L 26B3
Bedji Cr 77C4
Bednesti L 38A1
Bedwell L 1D2
Bedwell R 1D2
Bedwell Sd 1C3
Beece Cr 14A1
Beece Cr 25A4
Beechey Head 3C4
Beedy Cr 25D1
Beef Trail Cr...........23C-D1
Beef Trail Cr 36C4
Beehive Mtn 19B4
Beggerlay Cr 61C1
Beggerlay Cr 72C4
Behrman Cr 18A3
Beirnes Cr 62A4
Belcarra **5B-C3**
Belcourt Cr 49D3
Belcourt Cr 50A3
Belcourt L 49D3
Belcourt L 50A3
Belgo Cr 7D1
Belize In 11D1
Bell Bay Cr 52B4
Bell Cr 25A2
Bell I 11C2
Bell L 70B-C1
Bell L 81C4
Bell-Irving R 52B1
Bell-Irving R 61B-C4
Bella Bella **22B2**
Bella Coola **23A1**
Bella Coola R 23A-B1
Belle Bay Cr 44B1
Belle Cr 63A2
Belleisle Sd 12B2
Bellevue **10C2**
Bellevue Cr 7C1
Bellingham **5C4**
Bellos L 38D3
Bells L 26B2
Ben Abel Cr 18C4
Ben L 25D1
Bend Mtn 63B2
Benhur Cr 8D1
Bennison Cr 17D1
Benno Mtn 51B1
Benny L 26B1
Benson Cr 57A3
Benson Lake **11D3**
Benson R 11D3

Bentinck Spire...........22D1
Bentzi L 37A-B1
Berendon Gla 52A2
Berendon Gla 51D2
Beresford **16A3**
Beresford B 30B1
Beresford Cr 32A2
Beresford Cr 42B4
Beresford I 11A4
Berg Cr 74B1
Berg Cr 85B4
Berg L 40C-D3
Bergeland Cr 35C1
Berman L 38B1
Bernadet Cr 57A1
Bernadet Cr 66A4
Bernard Cr 9A1
Bernhardt Cr 36B4
Berry Cr 71D2
Berry Cr 72A2
Bertha L 11C1
Besa R 64D2
Besa R 65A2-3
Besa R 65B2
Bessborough..........**57D3**
Bessborough..........**58A3**
Bessette Cr 16D4
Betty Cr 39C3
Bevan **2A1-2**
Bevel Cr 55C-D2
Bevel Mtn 55C2
Bews Cr 17A1
Bidwell Cr 24D3
Bidwell Ls 24C3
Big Arrow Cr 66C3
Big B 33C1
Big B 43D3
Big B 44A3
Big Bar Cr 14D1
Big Bar Creek **14D1**
Big Bar L 15A1
Big Bar L 26A4
Big Bay **13A3**
Big Beaver Cr 76C3
Big Bend Arm 37B2
Big Bend Cr 37B2
Big Cr 14B1
Big Cr 25B3
Big Cr 25B4
Big Creek **25B3**
Big Eddy Cr 17A1
Big Falls Cr 34B-C1
Big Falls Cr 44B-C4
Big Falls L 33D2
Big Falls L 34B1
Big Falls L 44B4
Big Goat Cr 7D2
Big Kettle Fumarole ...54B2
Big L 26A1
Big L 26B4
Big Lake Ranch **26A1**
Big Loon L 46C2
Big Mountain Cr 50D2
Big Sheep Cr 8B3
Big Silver Cr 6A1
Big Timothy Mtn 26C2
Big Valley Cr 39A3
Big White Mtn 7D1
Bighorn Cr 10B3
Bighorn Cr 80B4
Bighorn Mtn 74B4
Bigmouth Cr 28A3
Bigsby In 20A1
Bill Miner Cr 26D1
Billings Bay **2C1**
Billygoat Cr..............14C4
Bilou Cr 64B1
Bilou Pk 64B1
Bingay Cr.................19A4
Bingley Pk 41A4
Binta L 36D1

Birch Bay **5C4**
Birch Cr 28A3
Birch Island **27B4**
Birch L 26D4
Birch Mtn 80C4
Birch Mtn 81A4
Birches L 73B1
Bird Hill 53D1
Bird Hill 54A1
Bird L 37A2
Birdflat Cr 53D1
Birdflat Cr 54A1
Birk Cr 16B1
Birk Cr 27A4
Birken **14C3**
Birkenhead L 14C3
Birkenhead R 14C3
Birley Cr 66B2
Bish Cr 34D1
Bish Cr 44D4
Bishop B 34D2
Bishop Bluffs 37C3
Bishop L 26B4
Bishop R 13C2
Bissett Cr 57A3-4
Bissette Cr 57D3
Bissette Cr 58A4
Bisson L 17A4
Bitter Cr 8B3
Bitter Cr 52B2
Bivouac Cr 46D1
Black Angus Cr 84A3
Black Cr 2A1
Black Cr 66A-B2
Black Creek **2A1**
Black Diamond **19C2**
Black Fox Cr 61D1
Black L 2A4
Black Martin Cr 40B4
Black Mtn 80D3
Black Mtn 81A3
Black Night Mtn 7C1
Black Pines **16A2**
Blackbear Cr 26B1
Blackberry Cr 45B3
Blackcome Pk 14C4
Blackfish Sd 12A3
Blackfly Cr 71C1
Blackfly L 71C1
Blackfoot Cr 18D4
Blackfox Mtn 72C1
Blackhawk L 49D1
Blackhawk L 50A1
Blackhorn Mtn 24B4
Blackjack Mtn 55B4
Blackman Cr 28A1
Blackpine L 54D1
Blackpool **27A4**
Blackstock Cr 53B3
Blacktail Cr 9D4
Blackwater Cr 30D2
Blackwater Cr 32B3
Blackwater Cr 55D4
Blackwater Cr 56A4
Blackwater L 28D4
Blackwater Mtn 28C3
Blackwater Pk 53B1
Blackwater R 38B3
Blackwell L 16A3
Blaeberry **28D4**
Blaeberry R 29A4
Blaine **5C4**
Blair Cr 16B3
Blair Cr 65D4
Blair I 22B4
Blairmore **10C2**
Blais Cr 27D4
Blakeburn **6C2**
Blakeney Cr 3B3
Blanchard Cr 64A3
Blanchard R 79B3
Blanchet L 36B2

Blanchet R 36C2
Blanket Cr 17B2
Blanket Cr 17B2
Blazed Cr 9A3
Bleasdell Cr 19A3
Blewett **8C2**
Bligh I 1B2
Blind Bay **16C2**
Blind Channel **12D3**
Blind Cr 7B3
Blind Cr 12D2
Bliss Landing...........**13B4**
Blizzard Ls 75A3
Bloedel **12D4**
Blomley Cr 16B1
Bloom Cr 9D3
Bloomfield L 35A4
Blowhole Bay **1A1**
Blubber Bay **2B1**
Blue Canyon Cr 37A4
Blue Cr 14C1
Blue Earth L 15B3
Blue Grave Cr 56C1
Blue Joe Cr 9A4
Blue Joint Mtn 8A2
Blue L 7B3
Blue L 55B3
Blue Lead Cr 26D1
Blue Lead Cr 27A1
Blue Lead Cr 39D4
Blue Lead Cr 40A4
Blue R 27C2
Blue R 82D4
Blue R 83B4
Blue R 83C3
Blue River **27C2**
Blue Sheep Cr 73A-B2
Blue Sheep L 73A2
Blue Springs **16D4**
Blueberry Cr 8B3
Blueberry
    Mountain.............**52C-D3**
Blueberry R 57A-B1
Blueberry R 66A-B4
Bluejoint Cr 8A2
Bluewater Cr 28D3
Bluey L 6D1
Bluff Cr 74B3
Bluff Hill 64A4
Bluff L 24B3
Blunden B 11B-C1
Blunden I 1C3
Blunt Cr 45D1
Blunt Cr 46A1
Blunt Mtn 45D1
Blurton Cr 16D2
Blustry Mtn 15A3
Boat Basin **1B2**
Boat Cr 65D1
Bob Quinn L 60D4
Bob Quinn L 61A4
Bobb Cr 14C2
Bobbie Burns Cr 17D1
Bobbie Burns Cr 18A1-2
Bobbie Burns Mtn 16D3
Bobtail L 26A3
Bobtail Mtn 38B1
Bodega Hill 3D2
Bodega Hill 5A4
Bodel Cr 60B1
Boise Cr 5C2
Boitano L 25D3
Boivin Cr 10A1
Boivin Cr 19A4
Bold Point **13A4**
Bolean Cr 16B3
Bolean L 16B3
Bolton Cr 45A4
Bonanza.....................**58B3**
Bonanza Cr 17C4
Bonanza Cr 52B4
Bonanza L 12A3

Bonanza R 12A3
Bonaparte L 15D1
Bonaparte R 15B1
Bonaparte R 15C1
Bonaparte R 26C4
Bond Sd 12B-C2
Bone Cr 27C2
Bone Cr 35D3
Bone Cr 36A3
Bone Mtn 49C2
Bones B 12B3
Bones Bay **12B3**
Bongard Cr 16D3
Bonilla I 31C2
Bonilla I 32C2
Bonilla I 33B3
Bonnatie Cr 38B2
Bonneau Cr 16D4
Bonners Ferry **9B4**
Bonnington L 48B2
Bonwick I 12A2
Booker Lagoon 12A2
Boomerang L 11D1
Boomerang L 12A1
Bootleg Mtn 9C2
Borel L 37A1
Borgeson L 6D1
Boring Ranch **65C4**
Borrett Cr 76B4
Bosk L 26C2
Boss Cr 26C2
Boss Mtn 26D2
Boston Bar **6B1**
Boston Bar Cr 6B2
Boswell.......................**9A2**
Boswell In 11C1
Boswell In 22C4
Botanie Cr 15B4
Botanie L 15A3
Botanie Mtn 15A3
Botany In 31A4
Bottle Cr 26A1
Bottleneck Cr 36B4
Boucher Cr 54B4
Boucher L 57A3
Bouchie L 38C3
Bouchie Lake **38C3**
Boughey B 12C3
Bougie Cr 65C1
Boulder Cr 29B4
Boulder Cr 45C1
Boulder Pass 54C2
Bouldery Cr 26D1
Bouleau Cr 16B4
Bouleau L 16B4
Bouleau Mtn 16B4
Boundary B 4A2
Boundary B 5B3
Boundary Bay **5B3**
Boundary Cr 7D3
Boundary Cr 9A3
Boundary Cr 58A-B1
Boundary L 9A4
Boundary L 58B1
Bounding Cr 39C2
Bourgeaux Cr 60C-D2
Bourgeaux Cr 61A2
Bourne Cr 28A4
Bowen I 3D1
Bowen Island **5A2**
Bower Cr 63C2
Bowers L 26D3
Bowes Cr 38D1
Bowman L 11D2
Bowron L 39B3
Bowron R 38D1
Bowron R 39A2
Bowron R 39B3
Bowron R 48D4
Bowser **2B2**
Bowser L 52B1
Bowser R 52B1

Bowser R 52C1
Bowsprit Mtn 62B3
Boya Cr 73C1
Boya L 83D4
Boyd Cr 17C2
Boyd L 26B3
Boydell L 11C1
Boyds...........................**8B4**
Boyer Cr 7D2
Boyer Cr 70B1
Boyer Cr 81B4
Boyer L 15C1
Brackendale **5A2**
Braden Cr 3B3
Braden R 22C1
Bradley Cr 26C3
Bradley Lagoon 11D2
Brady Ranch **65C4**
Braeside **47C4**
Bragg Creek **19B2**
Braid Cr 74C4
Bralorne **14C2**
Bramham I 11C1
Brandon Pk 63C2
Brandt Cr 77A1
Brash Cr 16D3
Brassey Cr 57C4
Brazion Cr 56D4
Breadner Group 22A3
Breccia Pk 62C-D2
Breccia Pk 63A2
Brem R 13B3
Brem River **13B3**
Bremner Cr 5D2
Bremner Cr 17C4
Brenda L 7A1
Brenot Cr 56D2
Brentwood Bay...........**3D3**
Brew Bay **2C1**
Brew Cr 13A1
Brewer Cr 18C3
Brewery Cr 60A-B1
Brewster L 12D4
Brexton **14C2**
Briar Ridge **58B3**
Bridal Falls **6A3**
Bridesville **7C3**
Bridge Cr 26B3
Bridge L 26C4
Bridge Lake **26C4**
Bridge R 14A2
Bridge R 14D2
Briggs In 22B1
Brim R 35A2
Brimstone Cr 86A4
Brink L 11B2
Brink L 11B2
Brisco **18B2**
Britannia Beach **5B2**
Brittain R 13C4
Brittanny Cr 24D3
Brittanny L 24D3
Britton Cr 6C2
Broadview **16C2**
Broadview L 40A1
Brocket **10D2**
Broken Cr 7A2
Broken Group 1D4
Bromley Cr 6D2
Bronlund Pk 63B2
Bronson Cr 51C1
Bronson Cr 60B4
Brookmere **6C1**
Brooks B 11B4
Brooks Pen 11B-C4
Brothers L 62C3
Brothers Pks 62C3
Broughton I 12A2
Broughton Str 11D3
Broughton Str 12A3
Brousseau L 15C2
Brown Cr 15D1

Brown Cr 25A1
Brown Cr 26D4
Brown L 33D2
Brown L 34B1
Brown L 44B4
Brown Pass 33B1
Brown Pass 43C4
Brownie Mtn 73D3
Brownie Mtn 74B3
Browning Entrance 31C-D1
Browning Entrance 33B3
Browning In 11B3
Browning Pass 1C3
Brownlee L 80B4
Browns R 2A1
Browntop Mtn 39B4
Bruce Cr 18B3
Bruce Cr 62A2
Brucejack L 51D1
Brucejack L 52A1
Brûlé **41B3**
Brûlé Cr 10A1
Brundige In 43C3
Brunson L 25D2
Brunswick **5B2**
Brunt Cr 51B1
Bryan Arm 36D3
Bryant Cr 24A1
Bryce Cr 28D2
Bryden L 16B2
Brydon Cr 60A2
Bubbles Cr 66A3
Buchan In 33D4
Buchan In 34B2
Buchanan Cr 39D1
Buchanan Cr 40A1
Buck Chan 30C3
Buck Chan 32B4
Buck Cr 7D2
Buck Cr 11C3
Buck Cr 46B4
Buckhorn L 38C1
Buckhorn Ls 24C3
Buckinghorse Cr 62A2
Buckinghorse L 62A3
Buckinghorse R 65B-C2
Buckley Bay................**2B2**
Buckley L 60C1
Bucklin Cr 5C1
Buckskin L 25D2
Buckworth Cr 9A3
Buffalo Cr 26B3
Buffalo Creek **26B3**
Buffalo L 26B3
Buffalo Lake **50D1**
Buffalo Lake **58D4**
Bugaboo Cr 18B2
Bugle L 48B3
Buhl Cr 9C1
Buick Cr 66B4
Bulkley L 46C3
Bulkley R 45C1
Bulkley R 46A3
Bulkley R 46B-C3
Bull Cr 7B2
Bull Cr 66A2
Bull Cr 71D1-2
Bull Cr 72A1-2
Bull Cr 81B4
Bull Har 11B2
Bull Harbour **11B2**
Bull R 10A1
Bull R 19A4
Bull River **9D2**
Bulldog Cr 27D1
Bulldog Cr 40D4
Bullhead Mtn 56D2
Bullmoose Cr 49B1
Bullmoose Mtn 49A-B1
Bullock Chan 22B1

Bullock L 26B4
Bulman Cr 7C1
Bulman Cr 16C4
Bulson Cr 1D3
Bulwell Cr 86A4
Bunch Cr 65B1
Bunch Grass Hill 8A2
Buntzen L 4A1
Buntzen L 5C2
Burden L 55D4
Burden L 56A4
Burden Pk 48D2
Burdick Cr 45B1
Burgess Cr 25D1
Burke Chan 22C2
Burlington **4C3**
Burman L 1C2
Burman R 1D2
Burmis **10C2**
● **Burnaby** **5B3**
Burnaby I 20B1
Burned L 48C4
Burnie L 45C3
Burnie R 45B4
Burns L 46D4
Burnstead Cr 47D4
Burnstead Cr 48A4
Burnt Bridge Cr 23C1
Burnt R 57A4
Burrage Cr 60D3
Burrage Cr 61B3
Burrard In 4A1
Burrard In 5B3
Burrell Cr 8A2
Burton **8B1**
Burton **17B4**
Burton Cr 8B1
Burton Cr 44B2
Buse L 16A3
Bush Arm 28C3
Bush Cr 2D3-4
Bush Cr 3C2
Bush Cr 16B2
Bush Cr 28C2
Bush R 28C2
Buster L 26C2
Butchart L 3C3
Bute In 13A3
Butedale **34D3**
Butedale L 34D3
Buth Cr 48B1
Butsih Cr 82B4
Butte L 71C1
Butte L 72A1
Butterfield Cr 46D2
Butterfield L 46D3
Buttle L 1D1
Buxton Cr 26A1
Byman Cr 46B3
Byron Cr 46B2

C

Caamaño Pass 43C3
Caamaño Sd 34C4
Cab Cr 56D1
Cabin Cr 10B3
Cabin L 77B1
Cache Cr 15B2
Cache Cr 57B1
Cache Cr 71C2
Cache Cr 72A2
Cache Creek **15B2**
Cadboro Bay **3D3-4**
Cadomin **41C3**
Cadorna Cr 19A3
Cadorna L 19A3
Cadwallader Cr 14C2
Caen Mtn 75A4
Cahill Cr 7A2
Cahill L 8C1

Name	Ref
Cahilty Cr	16A2
Cahilty L	16B2
Cain Cr	16B3
Caine Cr	48C3
Cairie L	11C-D2
Cairn Needle	6A1
Cake Hill	72C4
Calamity B	33D4
Calamity B	34B3
Calder Cr	10B3
Cale Cr	38C1
Calendar Cr	88C3
Calf Cr	84A4
Calgary	**19C-D1**
Call In	12C3
Callaghan Cr	14B4
Callaghan L	14B4
Callahan L	25C2
Callazon Cr	56C4
Callbreath Cr	60B1
Calling L	15C3
Callison L	72B-C1
Calm Chan	13A4
Calnan Cr	64D4
Calnan Cr	65A4
Calvert I	22B4
Cambie	**16D2**
Camborne	**17C2**
Cambria Icefield	52B3
Camel Mtn	24A4
Cameo L	7B1
Cameo L	16B4
Cameron Cr	9B3
Cameron Cr	39C4
Cameron L	2B3
Cameron L	3A1
Cameron Lake	**2B3**
Cameron R	2B3
Cameron R	3A1
Cameron R	56D1
Cameron R	65D4
Camp Artaban	**5A2**
Camp Cr	27C1
Camp Cr	40C4
Camp Island L	71A3
Campania I	34C3
Campania Sd	34C3
Campbell Cr	9A1
Campbell Cr	16A3
Campbell I	22B2
Campbell Icefield	28D3
Campbell Icefield	29A3
● **Campbell Island**	**22B2**
Campbell L	1D1
Campbell L	12D4
Campbell L	16A3
Campbell Pk	74C1
Campbell River	**2A1**
Campbell River	**13A4**
Camper Cr	3A3
Campion Cr	40D3
Campobasso Mtn	75A-B4
Camsell L	47A3
Canal Flats	**18C4**
Candle L	27A3
Cane Cr	8A1
Canford	**15C4**
Canim L	26C-D3
Canim Lake	**26C3**
Canim R	26D3
Canimred Cr	26D3
Canoe	**16C2**
Canoe Cr	25D4
Canoe R	40C4
Canoe Reach	27D1
Canoona L	35A3
Cantin Cr	38D4
Canuck Cr	9C4
Canvas Cr	27C1
Canyon	**9B3**
Canyon City	**44C1**
Canyon Cr	17D1
Canyon Cr	18A1
Canyon Cr	45D2
Canyon Cr	46A2
Canyon Cr	51C1
Canyon Cr	53A2
Canyon Cr	71D2
Canyon Cr	72A2
Canyon Cr	85D4
Canyon Hotsprings	**17B1**
Canyon L	53B2
Cape Ball	31A1
Cape Ball	32D3
Cape Ball R	31A1
Cape Ball R	32C2
Cape Beale	2A4
Cape Calvert	22B4
Cape Caution	11B1
Cape Chroustcheff	31A3
Cape Chroustcheff	32D4
Cape Cook	11B4
Cape George	31C1
Cape George	33B2
Cape Horn Cr	17B3
Cape James	11B2
Cape Knox	32A1
Cape Knox	42B4
Cape Mudge	13A4
Cape Palmerston	11A3
Cape Parkins	11B3
Cape Russell	11A2
Cape Scott	11A2
Cape Scott	11B4
Cape St. James	20C3
Cape Sutil	11B2
Capilano L	4A1
Capilano L	5B2
Capilano R	4A1
Capilano R	5B2
Capoose L	37A3
Capot-Blanc Cr	87A4
Captain Cove	33C2
Captain Cove	34A1
Captain Cr	49C3
Captain Harry L	36C-D4
Captain L	83C3
Caput Mtn	26D1
Carabine Cr	15C2
Carbon Cr	56C3
Carbon L	56C3
Carbon Pk	56C2
Carcajou Cr	63D2
Carcross	**80B2**
Cardiff Mtn	24D4
Cardtable Mtn	14B1
Carey Cr	56D2
Cargill Cr	49B4
Cariboo Cr	72C3
Cariboo L	39B4
Cariboo Mtn	39A4
Cariboo R	26A1
Cariboo R	39A4
Cariboo R	39B4
Cariboo R	39C3
Caribou Cr	8C1
Caribou Cr	17C4
Caribou Mtn	23C2
Caribou Mtn	39B-C2
Carina L	55A1
Carlick Cr	82C3
Carlin	**16C2**
Carmanah Cr	2B4
Carmanah Cr	3A3
Carmanah Mtn	2B4
Carmi	**7C2**
Carmi Cr	7D2
Carnes Cr	17B1
Carney Cr	18A4
Carney L	52B4
Carnlick Cr	37A4
Caroline L	22D4
Caron Cr	57A4
Carp L	48B2
Carpenter B	20C2
Carpenter Cr	8D1
Carpenter Cr	17D4
Carpenter L	14C2
Carpot-Blane Cr	86C-D4
Carrier L	47D3
Carrier L	48A3
Carrigan Cr	53B4
Carrolls Landing	**17B4**
Carrs	**16C4**
Carruthers Cr	54B-C2
Carruthers Pass	54B2
Carry Cr	6C2
Carter L	35A4
Carter Pass	12A2
Cartmel L	61C1
Cartmel Mtn	61C1
Cartwright Sd	30C3
Cartwright Sd	32B4
Cascade	**8B3**
Cascade B	6A2
Cascade B	4D1
Cascade Cr	17D3
Cascade In	22C1
Casino	**8C3**
Cassiar	**72B1**
Cassiar R	73B3
● **Cassidy**	**2D3**
Castle Cr	6C3
Castle Cr	39D3
Castle Cr	40A3
Castle Junction	**18C1**
Castle Mtn	59D4
Castle Rock	**25C1**
● **Castlegar**	**8C3**
Castor Cr	18B2
Cat Thumb Cr	56B4
Catala I	1B4
Cataract Br	29B4
Cataract L	2A3
Cate Cr	10B3
Catfish Cr	39C2
Cathcart I	11C1
Cathcart I	22C4
Catkin Cr	86B4
Causqua Cr	45D1
Cautley Cr	66C1
Caven Cr	9D3
Caverhill L	26D4
Cawston	**7B3**
Caycuse	**2C4**
Caycuse R	2B4
Caycuse R	3A2
Cayenne Cr	27C4
Cayley	**19B3**
Cayoosh Cr	14D3
Cayuse Cr	8B2
Cayuse Cr	11C3
Cecelia L	40B1
Cecil Cr	45A4
Cecil L	57C1
Cecil Lake	**57D2**
Cecil Lake	**58A2**
Cecilia Cr	40B1
Cecilia Cr	50B4
Cedar	**2D3**
Cedar Cr	26B1
Cedar L	44B1-2
Cedarvale	**45A1**
Ceepeecee	**1A1**
Celista	**16C2**
Celista Cr	16D1
Central Saanich	**3D3**
Centre Cr	6B3
Centre Pk	54B3
Centurion Cr	57A-B3
Cerberus Mtn	23C3
Cerulean L	18D2
Cervus Cr	1C1
Cesford Cr	46C3
Chaatl	**30C3**
Chaatl	**32B4**
Chaatl I	30C3
Chaatl I	32B4
Chaba Pk	28C2
Chaimberlain Mtn	49A1
Chakluk Mtn	70B2
Chalco Mtn	40B2
Chalco R	40B2
Chalford Cr	85C-D4
Chambers Cr	44B2
Chamiss Bay	**11D4**
Champion Cr	6C2
Champion Cr	8C3
Champion Ls	8C3
Chancellor Chan	12D3
Chantslar L	24B2
Chapea Cr	62C2-3
Chapman L	46B2
Chapmans	**6B1**
Chappelle Cr	62C3
Chapperon Cr	16B4
Chapperon L	16A4
Chapple In	34D4
Charcoal Cr	16B3
Charles Cr	12B2
Charleson Cr	38C3
Charlie Chief Cr	83C4
Charlie Cole Cr	82A4
Charlie L	57C1
Charlie Lake	**57C2**
Charlotte L	23D2
Chartrand Cr	15C3
Chartrand L	15C1
Chase	**16B2**
Chase Cr	2D3
Chase Cr	16B2
Chase Mtn	55A1
Chase R	3C1
Chase River	**2D3**
Chasm	**15B1**
Chasm Cr	15B1
Chasm Cr	77D4
Chatfield I	22B2
Chatham Sd	33B1
Chatham Sd	43C-D3
Chatsquot Cr	35C3
Chatsquot Mtn	35C3
Chatter Cr	28C3
Chauncey C	19B4
Chaunigan L	24D4
Cheakamus L	5B1
Cheakamus L	14B4
Cheakamus Mtn	5C1
Cheakamus Mtn	14C4
Cheakamus R	5B1
Cheakamus R	14B4
Cheam Pk	4D1
Cheam Pk	6A3
Cheam View	**6A3**
Checleset B	11C4
Chedakuz Arm	37A2
Chedakuz Cr	37B3
Chee Mtn	73C1
Cheekye R	5B1
Cheeny Cr	60C-D1
Cheeny Cr	61A1
Cheewhat L	2B4
Cheewhat L	3A3
Chehalis Cr	81B-C3
Chehalis L	4C1
Chehalis L	5D2
Chehalis R	4C1
Chehischic Cr	38B2
Chelaslie Arm	36D2
Chelaslie R	36B2
Chelaslie R	36C2
● **Chemainus**	**2D4**
Chemainus R	2D4
Chemainus R	3C2
Cherry Cr	15D3
Cherry Cr	17A4
Cherry Creek	**2B3**
Cherry Creek	**15D2**
Cherry Point	**58B2**
Cherryville	**17A4**
Cheshi Cr	24C4
Cheslatta L	36D1
Cheslatta R	36D1
Chesterfield Cr	64A1
Chesterfield L	64A1
Chetarpe	**1C3**
Chettleburgh Cr	62B4
Chettleburgh Pk	62B4
● **Chetwynd**	**57A3**
Cheves Cr	75D3
Cheves Cr	76B3
Chezacut	**24C1**
Chezko R	36B3
Chiaz Cr	38D4
Chiaz Cr	39A4
Chic Chic L	22B4
Chichouyenily Cr	56B4
Chicken Cr	65B3
Chief L	48B4
Chief Louis Arm	36D1
Chief Louis L	36C2
Chief Mathews B	35B2
Chikoida Mtn	70B1
Chilako R	37D1
Chilako R	38A2
Chilako R	38B1
Chilanko Forks	**24C2**
Chilanko R	24B2
Chilcotin L	24C-D1
Chilcotin R	24B1
Chilcotin R	24D2
Chilcotin R	25B-C3
Chilcotin R	37B4
Chilko L	13C1
Chilko L	24C4
Chilko Mtn	13C1
Chilko R	24D3
Chilko R	25A2
Chilkoot Pass	80A3
● **Chilliwack**	**6A3**
Chilliwack L	6B3
Chilliwack R	4D2
Chilliwack R	6A3
Chimdemash Cr	45A3
Chimney Cr	25D2
Chimney Cr	86A4
Chimney L	26A3
China Butte	7D2
China Cr	2B3
China Cr	3A1
China Cr	7D2
China Creek	**2B3**
China Creek	**8C3**
China L	14D1
China L	25D4
China Nose Mtn	46B3
Chinaman L	56D2
Chinchaga Ls	66D3
Chinchaga R	66D3
Chinohchey Cr	48A4
Chinook Cove	16A1
Chinukundi Cr	32C4
Chinukundl Cr	30D3
Chipesia Cr	76B-C4
Chipmunk Pk	62C-D4
Chischa Pk	75B4
Chischa R	75B-C3
Chischa R	76A3
Chisel Cr	28B1
Chisholm L	45D4
Chisholm Pk	63D2
Chismaina L	71A1
Chismore Cr	61B3
Chist Cr	45A4
Chita Cr	14A1
Chlotapecta Cr	75C3
Chlotapecta Cr	76A3
Choate Cr	26A1
Choelquoit L	24C3
Choquette Gla	60A-B4

Chowade R 56B1
Chowade R 65B4
Chowika Cr 64B4
Chowika Mtn 64B4
Chris L 26C3
Christensen Cr 24A1
Christian Valley **7D2**
Christie 30C1
Christie R 32B2
Christina Cr 60A3
Christina Falls 56B1
Christina L 8A3
Christina Lake **8B3**
Christmas Cr 71A1
Christmas Cr 82A4
Chu Chua Cr 16A1
Chu Chua Cr 27A4
Chuatse Cr 76D2
Chub L 26B3
Chubb L 38C3
Chuchi L 47B1
Chuchinka Cr 48D3
Chuckwalla R 22D3
Chudelatsa L 55A2
Chuius Mtn 47B2
Chukachida L 63A2
Chukachida R 62C1
Chukachida R 63A1
Chukchida L 62D2
Chum L 16B2
Chunair L 37C2
Church House **13A3-4**
Church Pk 4D2
Church Pk 6A3
Churchill Cr 75A3-4
Churchill Pk 75A4
Churn Cr 14C2
Churn Cr 25C4
Chutani L 37B2
Chute Cr 1D1
Chute L 7C1
Chutine L 59D1
Chutine R 59D1
Chuunk Mtn 69D2
Chuunk Mtn 70B2
Chuwanten Cr 6D3
Chuwanten Mtn 6C3
Chuwhels Mtn 15D3
Chuyazea Cr 48C-D2
Cicero Cr 16B1
Cinema **38C-D3**
Circle L 38B1
Circle L 48B4
Circlet L 1D1
Circum L 47C4
Cirque Cr 28D4
Citroen Pk 74C4
Clabon Cr 17B1
Clachnacudainn
    Snowfield 17B1
Clairmont **50D1**
Clallam Bay **3B4**
Clanwilliam **17A2**
Clapp Cr 3C3
Clapperton Cr 15D4
Clark L 7D2
Clarke 76D2
Classy Cr 71C4
Clatse L 22B2
Claud Elliott L 12B4
Clauminchil L 48B4
Claw Mtn 62C2
Claw Mtn 63A2
Clayhurst **58B2**
Clayoquot **1C3**
Clayoquot Arm 1D3
Clayoquot L 1D3
Clayoquot Sd 1B-C3
Clayton Falls Cr 23A2
Clear Cr 44D2
Clear Cr 47C4
Clear L 13A4

Clear R 12B1
Clearbrook **5D3**
Cleardale **58C2**
● **Clearwater** **27A4**
Clearwater L 24A2
Clearwater L 27A2
Clearwater R 27A2
Clearwater R 27A3
Clearwater R 40A4
Clearwater R 56B3
Clemenceau Icefield 28B-C2
Clemina Cr 27D1
Clemretta **36B1**
Clemretta **46B4**
Clendenning Cr 13D3
Cleswunkut L 38B2
Clifford B 21C1
Clifford Cr 53A3
Clinchintampan Cr 24D1
Cline River **29B2**
Clint Cr 18A4
Clinton **15A1**
Clinton Cr 15A1
Clio Chan 12B3
Clipper **5D4**
Clisbako R 24C1
Clisbako R 25A1
Clisbako R 37C-D4
Clisbako R 38A4
Clo-oose **2B4**
Clore R 45B3-4
Cloudmaker Mtn 64A1
Cloutier Pk 80C3
Cloverdale **5C3**
Clowhom L 5A1
Clowhom R 5A1
Cluachon L 60D1
Cluculz Cr 37D1
Cluculz Cr 38A1
Cluculz L 37D1
Cluculz L 38A1
Clusko R 24D1
Clute Cr 9A1
Clute Cr 18A4
Cluxewe R 11D3
Clyak R 22D3
Clyde Cr 39D2
Clyde Cr 40A2
Coal Cr 10A2
Coal Cr 45B-C2
Coal Cr 57D3
Coal Cr 58A3
Coal Cr 65D2
Coal Harbour **11C3**
Coal I 3D3
Coal I 5A4
Coal River **84D3-4**
Coal River **85A3-4**
Coalgoat Cr 17A4
Coalmont **6D2**
Coates R 30C1
Coates R 32A3
Cobb L 37D1
Cobb L 38A1
Cobb L 47D4
Cobb L 48A4
Cochin L 24C3
Cochran Cr 18D3
Cochrane **19B1**
Cochrane Cr 8A2
Cocoa Crater 60C2
Coconino Cr 81D3
Coconino L 81D3
Coffee Crater 60C2
Coffee Crater 61A2
Coffeepot Mtn 48C3
Cogburn Cr 6A2
Coglistiko R 37C4
Cokato **10A2**
Colbourne Cr 48C1
Cold Fish L 61D2
Cold Fish Lake

Camp **61D1**
Coldscaur L 26D3
Coldstream **16C4**
Coldstream Cr 16C4
Coldstream Cr 57B-C3
Coldwater Cr 44D4
Coldwater R 6C1
Coldwater R 15C4
Colebank L 38C-D3
Coleman **10B2**
Coleman Cr 2B4
Coles L 35C2
Coles L 87C3
Colin Cr 19A4
Colin Cr 55D2-3
Colledge Cr 64D3
Colledge L 64C3
Colledge L 65A3
Colleen Cr 9C3
College Cr 65A3
Colleymount **36C1**
Colleymount **46C4**
Collie Cr 29A4
Collingwood Chan 3D1
Collingwood Chan 5A2
Collins Cr 55C1
Collins L 45D4
Colonel Cr 40D3
Colonial Cr 11C4
Colt Cr 56C1
Columbia Gardens **8C3**
Columbia Icefield 28D2
Columbia L 18C4
Columbia L 8C4
Columbia R 18B1-2
Columbia Reach 28B-C3
Colwell Cr 24A3
Colwood **3D4**
Comaplix Mtn 17C2
Comb Pk 54B2
Combatant Mtn 23D4
Comet Mtn 35D4
Commerce Cr 10C3
Commotion Cr 57A3-4
Community L 16A2
Como L 80D4
Como L 81A4
● **Comox** **2A-B2**
Comox L 2A2
Compass Cr 23B1
Compton Cr 12C4
Compton Gla 13C2
Compton Mtn 13C2
Compton Néve 13C2
Concrete **4D3**
Cone Hill 25A4
Cone Mtn 60A2
Confederation Gla 12D1
Conical Pk 63C4
Conkle L 7D3
Connel Cr 14C2
Connor Ls 19A4
Conroy Cr 66A1-2
Consolation Cr 80D3
Consolation Cr 81B3
Constable Pk 75A-B3
Conuna R 1B1
Convey **4B4**
Conway Cr 9A2
Cony Cr 8B1
Cook L 72B1
Cooke Cr 16D2
Cool Cr 7A3
Coolridge Mtn 60D1
Coolridge Mtn 61A1
Coombs **2C3**
Cooper Cr 17D4
Cooper Cr 25A1
Cooper Cr 25B4
Cooper Creek **18A4**
Cooper L 9C3
Cooper Reach 12D2

Copeland **9B4**
Copeland Cr 17A1
Copley L 37B1
Coplin Cr 57A1
Copper B 31A3
Copper B 32D4
Copper Cr 6C3
Copper Cr 31A3
Copper Cr 32D4
Copper Creek **15C2**
Copper I 69C1
Copper I 80C4
Copper I 81A4
Copper Mtn 7D3
Copper Mtn 8C2
Copper River **45A3**
Coppercrown Mtn 18B4
Copperstain Cr 17D1
Coquihalla Mtn 6C2
Coquihalla R 6B2
Coquitlam **5C3**
Coquitlam L 4B1
Coquitlam L 5C2
Coquitlam Mtn 4B1
Coquitlam Mtn 5C2
Coquitlam R 4B1
Coquitlam R 5C2-3
Coral Mtn 18B1
Corbin **10B2**
Corbin Cr 10B2
Corbin Pk 17C1
Corbold Cr 5C2
Cordero Chan 12D3
Cordova Bay **3D3**
Corkscrew Cr 24A1
Corkscrew Cr 37C1
Cormier Cr 83C3
Cormorant Chan 12A3
Corn Cr 9A3
Corning Cr 16B2
Cornwall Cr 15B2
Cornwall In 34D3
Corona Pk 45B4
Corral Cr 6D2
Corrigan Cr 2B3
Corrigan Cr 3A2
Corsica L 26D3
Cortes Bay **13A4**
Cortez I 13A4
Cortiana Cr 8A1
Corya Cr 45C1
Cosens Cr 16C4
Cossack L 26B2
Costello Pk 12D1
Cotsworth L 37D3
Cotsworth L 38A3
Cotter Cr 1C2
Cottonwood **38D3**
Cottonwood R 38C3
Cottonwood R 71D1
Cottonwood R 72A1
Cottonwood R 82D4
Cottonwood R 83A4
Cougar Cr 8C1
Cougar L 34D3
Couldrey Cr 10B3
Coulee Cr 57C3
Coulter Cr 51D1
Coulter Cr 52A1
Coupeville **4B4**
Courcelette Pk 19B4
Coursier L 17B2
Courtenay **2A1**
Courtney L 6D1
Courvoisier Cr 77A1
Cous Cr 2A3
Cousins Cr 52C1
Cousins In 22C1-2
Coutlee **15C4**
Cow Cr 56D1
Cow Ls 72B2
Cowart Cr 55D2

Cowart Cr 56A2
Cowichan B **3C-D3**
Cowichan Bay **5A4**
Cowichan L 2C4
Cowichan L 3B2
Cowichan R 2D4
Cowichan R 3C3
Cowie Cr 57B4
Cowley **10C2**
Cox I 11A2
Cox I 11B4
Coyote Cr 9D1
Coyote Cr 18D4
Coyote Cr 61B1
Crab L **35A2**
Cracroft **12B3**
Cracroft I 12B3
Crag Cr 23B1
Crag Cr 36B4
Cragg Cr 3C3
Craig Cr 17C3
Craig R 51B-C1
Craig R 60B4
Craigellachie **16D2**
Cranberry Cr 17B2
Cranberry Junction **53A4**
Cranberry Mtn 17B2
Cranberry R 53A4
Cranberry Rapids 84C3
Cranberry Rapids 85A3
● **Cranbrook** **9C-D2**
Cransvick L 64D3
Cranswick L 65A3
Craster L 16D4
Crater L 80A3
Crater Mtn 7A3
Crawfish L 1A1
Crawford Bay **9A1**
Crawford Cr 9A1
Crawford Cr 17B2
Crazy Cr 17A1
Crazy Cr 24A4
Crease I 12A3
Crehan Cr 64C-D1
Crehan Cr 65A1
Creighton Cr 16D4
Creighton Valley **16D4**
Crescent Bay **8D2**
Crescent Beach **5B3**
Crescent In 31A4
Crescent L 39A3
Crescent Mtn 62A2
Crescent Spur **39C2**
Crescent Valley **8C2**
● **Creston** **9B3**
Creston Mtn 9A3
Criccieth Mtn 64A1
Cridge Pass 34C3
Cridland Cr 76C2
Cripple L 47C2
Criss Cr 15C2
Crocker Cr 48B4
Crocker Cr 48D2
Crofton **5A4**
Cronin Cr 46A2
Crooked L 16C4
Crooked L 26D2
Crooked L 85B3
Crooked R 26D2
Cross Cr 16C1
Cross R 18D2
Crow Cr 46C3
Crow R 86A3
Crown Mtn 1C1
Crowned Cr 1C1
Crowsnest **10B2**
Crowsnest Pass 10B2
Croydon **40B3**
Croydon Cr 54C1
Cruickshank R 2A2
Cruiser L 26C2
Crusty Cr 75A1

Cry L 72D2
Crystal Butte 7D2
Crystal L.....26C4
Cuisson Cr.....25D1
Cuisson L.....25D1
Cullite Cr.....3A3
Culliton Cr.....5B1
Cullivan Cr.....61D1
Cullon Cr.....53B3
Cultus Cr.....9A3
Cultus L.....4C2
Cultus L.....6A3
Cultus Lake.....**6A3**
○ **Cumberland**.....**2A2**
Cumming Cr.....45C3
Cummings Cr.....10A1
Cummins Cr.....28B2
Cumsack Cr.....13A2
Cumsack Mtn.....13A2
Cumshewa.....**31A3**
Cumshewa In.....31A3
Cunningham Cr.....39B4
Cunningham I.....22B2
Cunningham L.....15B1
Cunningham L.....26B3
Cunningham L.....47A3
Cup Cr.....81B3
Cup L.....7D2
Cupola Cr.....28C4
Cupola Mtn.....28C4
Curlew.....**8A3**
Currie Cr.....17A4
Currier Cr.....62A4
Curve L.....55C3
Curwen Cr.....17A3
Curzon.....**9C3**
Cushing Cr.....39D2
Cushing Cr.....40A2
Cushing Cr.....62D2
Cushing Cr.....63A2
Cusson Cr.....17B4
Cutbank Cr.....54C-D1
Cutbank Cr.....63D4
Cutbank L.....50A-B1
Cutbank L.....58A-B4
Cutfoot Cr.....53B1
Cutfoot Cr.....62B4
Cutoff Cr.....37B2
Cutoff Cr.....63C2
Cyclops Pk.....64C2
Cypre R.....1C3
Cypress B.....1C3
Cypress Cr.....65B4

D

D'Arcy.....**14C3**
D'Arcy I.....3D3
d'Easum Cr.....87B3
Daer Cr.....18C2
Dagaichess Cr.....60B-C1
Dagger L.....15D1
Dago Cr.....8B1
Dahl Cr.....38B1
Dahl Cr.....44D2
Dahl Cr.....66C2
Dahl L.....38B1
Dahlaks Cr.....35A1
Dainard Cr.....18B1
Dainard Cr.....28A2
Dairy Cr.....15D2
Dairy Ls.....15C3
Dais Gla.....13A1
Dais Gla.....24A4
Daisy L.....5B1
Daisy L.....14B4
Dak Cr.....52C4
Dala R.....35A1
Dale Cr.....7C2
Dale L.....38D4
Dall L.....73B-C3

Dall R.....73B2
Dallery Cr.....22D4
Dalton Cr.....72C1
Damdochax Cr.....53A-B1
Damdochax L.....53B1
Damfino Cr.....7D1
Damshilgwit Cr.....53B1
Damshilgwit L.....53B1
Dana In.....31A4
Daniels Cr.....65C2
Daniels R.....13C4
Danville.....8A4
Darb Cr.....54C1
Darb L.....54C1
Darber Cr.....65D4
Darby Chan.....22C4
Darby L.....48B4
Dardanelles L.....16A3
Darfield.....**27A4**
Dark Mtn.....72C3
Darke Cr.....7B1
Darke L.....7B1
Darlington Cr.....16A1
Darlington Cr.....27A4
Darrell Bay.....**5B1**
Darrington.....**4D4**
Darsmith Cr.....60A4
Darwin Sd.....20A1
Darwin Sd.....31A4
Dash Cr.....3B2
Dash Cr.....14C1
Dashwood.....**2B2**
Dasque Cr.....44D3
Dastaiga Cr.....56A-B4
Datcin Cr.....77C2
Date Cr.....45B1
Date Cr.....53B4
Datlamen Cr.....30C2
Datlamen Cr.....32B3
Dave Henry Cr.....40D4
David L.....35A4
Davidson Cr.....30C1
Davidson Cr.....32B2
Davidson Cr.....37A-B3
Davie Cr.....73B1
Davie L.....48C3
Davie R.....12B4
Davies Cr.....45B4
Davies L.....56D1
Davis Cr.....37D4
Davis Cr.....38A4
Davis L.....6C1
Davis R.....55B1
Davis R.....64B4
Dawson Cr.....28A2
Dawson Cr.....57D3
Dawson Cr.....58A3
● **Dawson Creek**.....**57D3**
Dawson Creek.....**58A3**
Dawson In.....30C3
Dawson In.....32B4
Dawson R.....62A2
Day L.....46B3
Dayeezcha Mtn.....36D1
Dazo Cr.....77B4
De Winton.....**19C-D2**
Deacon Cr.....38D4
Dead Dog Cr.....75C4
Deadhorse Cr.....57A1
Deadhorse Cr.....66A4
Deadman L.....15C1
Deadman R.....15C1
Deadwood Cr.....73A1
Deadwood R.....73A1
Dean Chan.....22C2
Dean Chan.....35D4
Dean Chan.....36A4
Dean R.....23D2
Dean R.....36B4
Dean R.....36D4
Deana Cr.....32C4
Dear Mtn.....6C2

Dease Cr.....71D3
Dease Cr.....72A3
Dease L.....71D2-3
Dease L.....72B3
Dease Lake.....**71D3**
Dease Lake.....**72B3**
Dease R.....71D2
Dease R.....72B1-2
Dease R.....83D3-4
Dease R.....83D4
DeBeck Cr.....5C2
Deception Cone.....64B4
Deception Cr.....26D2
Deception Cr.....26D3
Deception L.....46B2
Deception Mtn.....26D2
Dechamps Cr.....13C1
Decker Cr.....46D4
Decker L.....46C4
Dede Cr.....66C4
Dee L.....16C4
Deeker Cr.....60A2
Deena Cr.....30D3
Deep Bay.....**2B2**
Deep Canoe Cr.....53B3
Deep Cove.....**5A4**
Deep Cr.....16C3
Deep Cr.....46A3
Deep Creek.....**16C3**
Deep Har.....12A-B2
Deer I.....11C2
Deer L.....16C4
Deer L.....34D3
Deer Park.....**8B2**
Deer Pass.....13A4
Deer R.....85C4
Deerhorn Cr.....26B2
Deerhorn Hill.....36D2
Deescius Mtn.....46C-D2
Dehacho Cr.....77A4
DeHorsey I.....33C1
DeHorsey I.....44A4
Deka Cr.....26C4
Deka L.....26C3
Dekontha L.....65C1
Del Cr.....64A2-3
Delano Cr.....75A3
Delkluz Cr.....55A1
Delkluz L.....64A4
Delkpay Cr.....87B4
Della Falls.....1D2
Della L.....1D2
Delphine Cr.....18B3
● **Delta**.....**5B3**
Delta Cr.....63B3
Delta Pk.....52C1
Delta Pk.....61C4
Deltaic Cr.....52C1
Delure Cr.....71D2
Delure Cr.....72A2
Delusion Pk.....24A4
Demers Cr.....27A4
Demers Ls.....8C1
Deming.....**5D4**
Dempsey L.....26B3
Denain Cr.....14B1
Denetiah Cr.....73C3
Denetiah Cr.....74A3
Denetiah L.....73C3
Denetiah L.....74A3
Denison Cr.....53D4
Denkman Cr.....64C4
Denkman Cr.....65A4
Denman I.....2B2
Denman Island.....**2B2**
Dennis Pk.....62D3
Dennis Pk.....63A3
Denny I.....22B2
Denys Cr.....45C-D3
Departure Bay.....**2D3**
Depot Cr.....6B3
Deroche.....**5D3**

Derrick Cr.....53A3
Des Cr.....48B2
Desan Ls.....77C1
Desan Ls.....88C4
Deserters Cr.....38C4
Deserters Group.....11C2
Deserters Pk.....64A4
Desolation Sd.....13B4
Destilida L.....48C2
Destlay L.....47C2
Deszen Cr.....87B3
Detiaten Cr.....60C1
Detiaten Cr.....71C4
Detiaten Cr.....72A4
Detna Cr.....36C3
Detna L.....36C3
Detni Cr.....54C2
Deuce Cr.....45B1
Devar Pk.....62D4
Devastation Chan.....34D2
Devereux Cr.....12D1
Devereux Pk.....75B3-4
Devil Cr.....60D3
Devil Cr.....61A-B3
Devil L.....60D3
Devil L.....61A3
Devils Paw.....69D2
Devils Paw.....70A2
Devils Thumb.....59D3
Devine.....**14C3**
Devoe Cr.....26C1
Devoe Cr.....39B-C4
Devon L.....33D3
Devon L.....34B2
Dewar Cr.....9B1
Dewar L.....26A2
Dewar Pk.....63A-B4
Dewdney.....**5D3**
Dewdney Cr.....6B2
Dewdney I.....34B4
Dewdney Pk.....4C1
Dewdney Pk.....5D3
Dezadeash.....**79A1**
Diagonal Mtn.....62C4
Diana I.....2A4
Dick Booth Cr.....11C2
Dick Cr.....51B1
Dick Cr.....79B3
Dickebusch Cr.....57A-B4
Dickson L.....4C1
Dickson L.....5D3
Didene Cr.....61D3
Dieppe Mtn.....74D3
Digby I.....33C1
Digby I.....43D4
Digby I.....44A4
Dillabough L.....26B1
Dilly Cr.....87D3
Dimsdale.....**50D1**
Dimsdale L.....49D4
Dimsdale L.....50A4
Dina L.....56B4
Dinan B.....30C1
Dinan B.....32B3
Diorite Cr.....9D1
Dipper L.....9C2
Dirst Cr.....59D2
Dirty Cr.....56D1
Discovery Cr.....55A3
Discovery I.....3D4
Discovery Pass.....12D4
Disella L.....70D1
Diskangieq Cr.....44C1
Diver L.....54C3
Diver Pk.....54C3-4
Divergence Pk.....28B1
Divers L.....1D1
Diversion Res.....3C3
Divide L.....52B2
Dixie L.....69D1
Dixie L.....70B1
Dixie L.....80D4

Dixie L.....81B4
Dixon Cr.....16A1
Dixon Entrance.....32B1
Dixon Entrance.....42D3
Dixon L.....16B1
Doan Cr.....75C3
Doan Cr.....76A3
Dobbin B.....12A2
Dobbin L.....16B4
Docken Cr.....49C2
Docs Cr.....48B4
Doctor Cr.....18C4
Dodd Cr.....38B1
Dodd L.....2C1
Dodd L.....13C4
Dodjatin Cr.....60B1
Doe Cr.....57D3
Doe Cr.....58A3
Doe River.....**58A-B2**
Doebay Village.....**5C4**
Dog Cr.....8B2
Dog Cr.....25D4
Dog Cr.....47C4
Dog Creek.....**25D4**
Doig R.....57C-D1
Doig R.....58A1
Doig R.....66C-D4
Dokdaon Cr.....60A2
Dokie Cr.....57A3
Dolly Varden Cr.....18C2
Dolphin I.....31D1
Dome Cr.....39B2
Dome Creek.....**39C1**
Dome Mtn.....46B2
Dome Mtn.....72C3
Dominion Cr.....27D1
Dominion Cr.....39B2
Dominion L.....48C3
Dominion Mtn.....8D2
Dominion Mtn.....59D3
Don Pen.....22A-B1
Donahue Cr.....52B4
Donald Cr.....28D4
Donald Landing.....**46D3**
Donald Station.....**28D4**
Donelly Cr.....14B3
Donner L.....1C1
Donnie Cr.....65D2
Dooley Cr.....10A2
Doos Cr.....23A4
Dooza L.....84A4
Doran Cr.....13B1
Doreen L.....16C4
Doreen L.....26C2
Doré R.....39D3
Doré R.....40A3
Doris L.....22C4
Doris L.....46B2
Doriston.....**2D1**
Dorothy Cr.....23D4
Dorothy Gla.....23D4
Dortatelle Cr.....54B-C1
Dortatelle Pk.....54C1
Dottay Cr.....65C1
Douglas.....**5C3**
Douglas.....**70B4**
Douglas Chan.....34C3
Douglas Cr.....5D1
Douglas Cr.....44D2
Douglas In.....30D4
Douglas L.....16A4
Douglas Lake.....**16A4**
Douse L.....53A4
Dousé Cr.....53A4
Dove Cr.....2A1
Dowager I.....22A1
Dowling Cr.....56D3
Downie Cr.....28B4
Downie L.....17B1
Downie L.....28A4
Downie Pk.....28A4
Downton Cr.....14D3

Downton Cr ...24B1
Downton Cr ...37B4
Downton L ...14B2
Doyle I ...11C2
Dragon L ...38D4
Dragon L ...44D1
Dragon L ...52D4
Dragon Mtn ...38D4
Drake I ...11C3
Draney In ...22C4
Dream Cr ...54D4
Dresser Cr ...56D2
Drewry L ...26C3
Drift L ...53D2
Drift L ...54A2
Driftpile Cr ...63C1
Driftpile Cr ...74C4
Driftwood Cr ...18B2
Driftwood Cr ...45D2
Driftwood Cr ...46A2
Driftwood L ...11D1
Driftwood R ...53D2
Driftwood R ...54A2
Driftwood R ...54B3
Drimmie Cr ...17B2
Drinkwater Cr ...1D2
Driscoll Cr ...39B1
Drury In ...11D2
Dry Gulch ...**18C3**
Dry L ...6D2
Dryas Pk ...64A1
Drybrough Pk ...62D3
Drybrough Pk ...63A3
Drymeat L ...65C1
Ducette Cr ...56B3
Ducette Pk ...56B3
Duck Cr ...9B3
Duck L ...9A3
Duckfoot L ...24C3
Duckling Cr ...54D3
Duckling L ...26C3
Duckworth L ...25D1
Dudgeon Cr ...27C4
Dudido R ...71A3
Dudidontu R ...71A2
Dudley Cone ...13B4
Duff L ...79C3
Dufferin I ...22A2
Duffey L ...14D3
Duffield Cr ...65A2
Dugan L ...26A2
Dum L ...26D4
Dum L ...27A4
Dumbell L ...24A4
Dunbar Cr ...18B2
● Duncan ...2D4
Duncan Bay ...**13A4**
Duncan I ...11C2
Duncan L ...17D3
Duncan L ...18A3
Duncan L ...62D3
Duncan L ...63B3
Duncan R ...17D2
Dundas I ...43C3
Dunedin R ...75B2
Dunedin R ...75C1
Dunedin R ...86C4
Dungate Cr ...46B3-4
Dungeness ...**4A4**
Dunira I ...33B1
Dunira I ...43C3
Dunlevy Cr ...56D2
Dunlevy L ...56D2
Dunn Cr ...18A3
Dunn Cr ...27A4
Dunn L ...27A4
Dunsapie L ...16A1
Dunsmuir ...**2B2**
Dunster ...**40B3**
Durand Cr ...15C2
Durham Cr ...60D3
Durham Cr ...61A-B3

Durieu ...**5D3**
Durkin Cr ...75C-D4
Durkin Cr ...76A4
Dust Cr ...54C4
Dutch Cr ...18B4
Dutch Cr ...18C4
Duteau Cr ...16D4
Duti R ...62B4

E

Eagan L ...26C4
Eagle Bay ...**16C2**
Eagle Cr ...8A1
Eagle Cr ...26B2
Eagle Cr ...26C3
Eagle Cr ...46C4
Eagle Creek ...**26C3**
Eagle L ...24C3
Eagle L ...26B2
Eagle R ...16D2
Eagle R ...72B-C2
Eagle R ...72C3
Eaglehead L ...72C-D3
Eaglenest Cr ...61C2
Eaglet L ...48D4
Eakin L ...26D4
Ealue L ...61B1
Ear L ...35C3
Earl Grey Pass ...18B4
Earle Cr ...2D1
Earle L ...26C4
Earls Cove ...**2D1**
East Anderson R ...6B1
East Arrow Park ...**17B4**
East Barrière L ...16B1
East Barrière R ...16B1
East Barrière R ...27B4
East Cache Cr ...57B1
East Cr ...18A2
East In ...33D3
East In ...34B1
East Kelowna ...**7C1**
East Kispiox R ...53A3
East Pine ...**57B3**
East Port ...**9B4**
East Redonda I ...13B4
East Seebach Cr ...48D3
East Sooke ...**3C4**
East Sound ...**5B4**
East Thurlow I ...12D3
East Tutshi R ...80A3-4
East Twin Cr ...17B1
East Twin Cr ...39D2
East Twin Cr ...40A2
East Wellington ...**2D3**
East White R ...19A4
Easter L ...1C2
Eastman Cr ...60D2
Eastman Cr ...61A-B2
Echo Bay ...**12B2**
Echo Cr ...18A3
Echo I ...4D1
Echo I ...6A2
Echo L ...16C4
Echo L ...16D4
Echo Pk ...54C2
Echoes L ...9C1
Eclipse Nrs ...12A1
Ecoole ...**2A4**
Ecstall L ...34C1
Ecstall R ...34B-C1
Ecstall R ...44B4
Ed Asp Cr ...71D1
Ed Asp Cr ...72A1
Ed Asp L ...71D1
Ed Asp L ...72A1
Ed Bird Cr ...63D4
Ed Bird L ...64A4
Eddontenajon ...**61B1**
Eddontenajon L ...61B1

Eddy ...**40A-B3**
Eddy Cr ...40A3
Eden I ...12A2
Eden L ...30C1
Eden L ...32B2
Edgar L ...80C4
Edgegrain Cr ...50A4
Edgewater ...**18C2**
Edgewood ...**8B1**
Edinburgh Mtn ...2C4
Edinburgh Mtn ...3B3
Edison ...**4B3**
Edith L ...15D3
Edmond Cr ...13D1
Edmund L ...26B4
Edney Cr ...26A1
Edney L ...26A1
Edozadelly Mtn ...62C2
Edwards Cr ...16A2
Edwards L ...26C3
Edwards Ls ...10A3
Edye Pass ...33B2
Edye Pass ...43D4
Effingham I ...2A4
Effingham In ...2A3
Effingham R ...2A3
Egeria Mtn ...31D1
Egeria Mtn ...33C2
Egeria Mtn ...34A1
Egeria Reach ...35B3
Egmont ...**2D1**
Egnell Cr ...71A4
Egnell Ls ...84B-C3
Ehaheezetle Mtn ...61B1
Ehatisaht ...**1A1**
Eholt Cr ...8A3
Eight Mile Cr ...57D2
Eight Mile Cr ...58A2
Eight Mile Cr ...75A1
Eightythree Cr ...26B3
Eightythree L ...26B4
Ejas L ...26D3
Ejas L ...27A3
Eklund Cr ...55C3
Ekwan Cr ...77C3
Ekwan L ...77C3
Elaho R ...14A3
Elbow Cr ...65C3
Elbow L ...26C2
Elbow Mtn ...51A1
Elcho Har ...22C1
Elder Cr ...10C3-4
Elder Cr ...10C4
Eldred R ...13C4
Eleven Mile Cr ...56C3
Elfin Cove ...**68C4**
Eliguk L ...36D4
Eliza Dome ...1B4
Elizabeth L ...22C3
Elk Bay ...**12D4**
Elk Cr ...18D4
Elk Pass ...19A3
Elk R ...1C1
Elk R ...10B1
Elk R ...19A3
Elkford ...**19A4**
Elkhorn Mtn ...1C1
Elkin Cr ...24D4
Elkin L ...24D4
Elko ...**10A3**
Ella Cr ...62B3
Ella Frye Cr ...27B1
Ella Frye Cr ...40B4
Elleh Cr ...77A3
Elleh R ...77B3
Ellen L ...1B2
Ellen L ...7A1
Ellen L ...16A4
Ellerslie L ...22B1
Elliot Cr ...13B2
Elliot L ...47A1
Elliot Res ...3C3

Elliott Cr ...45C3
Ellis B ...11C1
Ellis Cr ...7C2
Ellis L ...13B4
Ellison ...**7C1**
Ellison L ...16C4
Elmworth ...**50B-C1**
Elsie L ...2A2
Elwin L ...46B3
Elwyn Cr ...60C1
Embree Cr ...64D3
Embree Cr ...65A3
Emerslund Cr ...56B1-2
Emerslund Ls ...56B1
Emile Cr ...87C3
Emily L ...22B1
Emory Cr ...6B2
Empress Mtn ...3C4
Encampment Cr ...28A2
End L ...55B2
Endako ...**47A4**
Endako R ...46C3
Endako R ...46D4
● **Enderby** ...**16C3**
Endless Cr ...53C2
Eneas Cr ...7B1
Enerald L ...29B4
Engen ...**37C1**
Engen ...**47C4**
Engineer Mtn ...80C4
Englefield B ...30D4
English B ...4A1
English B ...5B3
English L ...26D4
Englishman Cr ...9C3
Englishman R ...2C3
Englishman R ...3B1
Enright Cr ...76B4
Ensign Cr ...29A4
Enterprise ...**26A3**
Enterprise Cr ...8D1
Entiako L ...36D3
Entiako R ...36D3
Entrance ...**41C2**
Eon Mtn ...18D2
Equesis Cr ...16C3
Eric Cr ...1D2
Erickson ...**9B3**
Erickson Cr ...10B1
Erickson L ...38B2
Erie ...**8D3**
Erie Cr ...8C3
Erie L ...8D3
Erie Mtn ...8C3
Erlandsen Cr ...44D3
Errington ...**2C3**
Escalante R ...1B2
Eskai Cr ...77A4
Esker L ...38B1
Esker L ...84C3
Eskona Mtn ...73C2
Esling Cr ...8B3
Esperanza ...**1A1**
Esperanza In ...1B4
Esperon Cr ...16B4
Espinosa In ...1A1
Espinosa In ...1B4
Esquimalt ...**3D4**
Estall R ...33D2
Estella Cr ...64A4
Estella Ls ...64A4
Estero Basin ...13A3
Estevan Group ...34B3
Estevan Pt ...1B2
Estevan Sd ...34C3
Estsine L ...88A3
Etane Cr ...75D1
Etane Cr ...76A1
Etcho Cr ...76D1
Etschitka Cr ...54D2
Etset L ...88A-B4
Etsho Cr ...87D4

Etthithun L ...66D1
Etthithun R ...66C-D1
Etthithun R ...77C4
Euchiniko Ls ...37C3
Euchiniko R ...37C2
Euchu Reach ...36D2
Eugene L ...26D4
Eulatazella L ...37D1
Eulatazella L ...38A1
Eureka ...**10A4**
Eureka River ...**58D1**
Europa Reach ...35A2
Eutsuk ...**36A2**
Eutsuk L ...35D2
Eutsuk L ...36A2
Eutsuk Pk ...36C3
Eva L ...11C1
Evans Cr ...8C1
Evans In ...22B-C2
Evans L ...8C1
Eve R ...12B3
Eveline L ...38D4
Everett Cr ...39B1
Everson ...**5D4**
Evie L ...76B2
Evindsen Cr ...52C3-4
Ewart Cr ...7A3
Ewart L ...1A1
Ewe Mtn ...74D1
Ewin Cr ...10B1
Ewin Cr ...19B4
Exchamsiks R ...44C3
Excursion Inlet ...**68C3**
Exeter ...**26B4**
Exshaw ...**19A1**
Exstew R ...44C4
Extension ...**2D3**

F

Face L ...15D3
Factor Ross Cr ...55B1
Fadear Cr ...16A1
Fair Harbour ...**11D4**
Fairfax In ...30D4
Fairless Cr ...25C4
**Fairmont
Hot Springs** ...**18C3-4**
Fairview ...**7B3**
Fairweather Mtn ...67C2
Fairy Cr ...3B3
Fairy L ...64C2-3
Fairy L ...65A3
Faith Cr ...8B2
Falaise ...75A3
Falcon Gla ...13C2
Falcon Mtn ...13C2
Falk Cr ...75D3
Falk Cr ...76A3
Falkland ...**16B3**
Fall Cr ...16D3
Fall R ...54C3
Falling Cr ...56D4
Falls Cr ...27A2
Falls R ...14A1
Falls R ...35A1
False Ears ...11D4
False L ...80B4
Fang Cr ...17B1
Fang Pk ...23C4
Fanny Bay ...**2B2**
Fantali L ...80B4
Far Cr ...36D4
Farmington ...**57D3**
Farmington ...**58A3**
Farnham Cr ...18B3
Farrant I ...34C3
Farrell Cr ...56D2
Farrell Creek ...**57A2**
Farwell Cr ...25C3
Faulkner Cr ...72D3

121

Fauquier	8B1	
Favels Cr	57B3	
Fawn Cr	26C4	
Fawn L	26C4	
Fawnie Cr	36D3	
Fawnie Cr	37A3	
Feak Cr	44C4	
Fearless Cr	49C2	
Feather L	30D2	
Feather L	32C3	
February Cr	53D1	
February Cr	54A1	
February L	88C-D3	
Federal Ranch	56D1	
Felker L	26A3	
Fellers Heights	57D4	
Fennell Cr	8D1	
Fennell R	27B4	
Fenton L	36B2	
Fenwick Cr	18D3	
Ferguson	17C2	
Ferguson Cr	17C2	
Fern L	64B1	
Fern Pk	64A1	
Ferndale	5C4	
● **Fernie**	10A2	
Ferrer Pt	1B4	
Ferris Gla	67C1	
Ferris Gla	68A1	
Ferriston Cr	54C2	
Ferry Cr	72D3	
Fiddes Cr	65B4	
Fiddler Cr	45A2	
Field	29B4	
Fife Cr	17B4	
Fife Sd	12A-B2	
Fiftynine Cr	15A1	
Fiftyone Cr	15A1	
Fiftyseven Cr	15A1	
File Cr	27B2	
Filer Cr	13C2	
Filer Gla	13C2	
Fin I	34C3	
Findlay Cr	9B1	
Findlay Cr	18B-C4	
Findlay L	46B3	
Finger L	37C2	
Finger Mtn	12B1	
Finlay R	62D3	
Finlay R	63B3	
Finlayson Arm	3D3	
Finlayson Chan	22A1	
Finlayson I	43D3	
Finley R	63C-D2	
Finn Cr	27C3	
Fintry	16C4	
Fir Cr	10B2	
Fire Cr	5D1	
Fire Cr	25B4	
Fire Cr	77D3	
Fire L	5D1	
Fireside	84C-D3	
Fireside	85A3	
Firesteel R	62D3	
Firesteel R	63A3	
First Nrs	23A3	
Firth Cr	48C2	
Firth L	48C2	
Firvale	23B1	
Fiset L	26C4	
Fish Cr	52C2	
Fish Hawk Ls	7D1	
Fish Hawk Ls	16D4	
Fish L	17D4	
Fish L	72B3	
Fish L	81B3	
Fishem L	13D1	
Fisher Chan	22B2	
Fisher Cr	56D4	
Fisher L	48C3	
Fisherman B	11A2	

Fisherman R	11A2	
Fishing Cr	84D4	
Fishing Cr	85A-B4	
Fishing L	84D4	
Fishing L	85B4	
Fishing Ls	63B2	
Fishpot L	37D4	
Fishtrap Cr	16A1	
Fissure Cr	28A4	
Fitch Cr	17D2	
Fitz Hugh Sd	22B3-4	
Fitzsimmons Cr	14B4	
Fitzstubbs Cr	17C4	
Fizzle Mtn	51B1	
Fizzle Mtn	60B4	
Flack Cr	75C3	
Flack Cr	76A3	
Flameau Cr	63C4	
Flamingo In	20B2	
Flat Cr	17C1	
Flat Cr	72D3	
Flat L	48B4	
Flat R	52C3	
Flat Top Mtn	63B1	
Flatbed Cr	49C1	
Flathead	10B-C3	
Flathead	10B2	
Flathead R	10B3	
Flatrock Cr	57D2	
Flatrock Cr	58A2	
Fleet Cr	39D2	
Fleet Cr	40A2	
Fleet Pk	63C4	
Fleet R	3C3	
Flemer R	79C3	
Fleming Cr	46D2	
Fleming I	2A4	
Fleming L	46D2	
Fletcher L	25B3	
Fleurbaix Cr	27B2	
Flint Cr	45A2	
Float Cr	18B1	
Float Cr	29B4	
Floe Cr	18C1	
Floe L	18C1	
Flood Cr	55A1	
Flood Cr	64A4	
Flood Gla	60A3	
Flood L	60A3	
Floods	6A2	
Florence Cr	30D2	
Florence Cr	32C3	
Florence L	13A3	
Florence Pen	22B1	
Florencia B	1D4	
Flores I	1C2-3	
Flourmill Cr	27A2	
Flume Cr	50A-B3	
Fly Cr	39A1	
Flyfish L	16C4	
Foch L	34C1	
Focus Mtn	70B1	
Foerster L	54B2	
Fog Lag	34D1	
Foghorn Cr	27B4	
Foghorn Mtn	27A4	
Foisey Cr	10B2	
Foley Cr	6A3	
Fontaine Cr	39A4	
Fontas	77A4	
Fontas R	66D1	
Fontas R	77B4	
Fontas R	77D4	
Fontoniko Cr	49B3	
Foot L	63D3	
Forbes Cr	13B4	
Forbes Cr	13B4	
Forbes L	26A3	
Forcier L	74C1	
Forcier L	85C4	
Ford Pass	61C1	
Fording	19A-B4	

Fording Mtn	10B1	
Fording R	19B4	
Fording River Pass	19A4	
Forest Grove	26C3	
Forgetmenot Cr	39D1	
Forgetmenot Cr	40A1	
Forres Mtn	63D4	
Forrest Ker	60C4	
Forsight Mtn	35C3	
Forster Cr	18B3	
Forsyth Cr	19A3	
Fort Babine	46B1	
Fort Babine	54B4	
Fort Casey	4B4	
Fort Cr	53C1	
Fort Fraser	47B4	
Fort Langley	5C3	
Fort Liard	86D2	
Fort Liard	87B2	
Fort Mtn	53C1	
● **Fort Nelson**	76C2	
Fort Nelson R	75C-D1	
Fort Nelson R	76A-B1	
Fort Nelson R	76C-D3	
Fort Nelson R	86C4	
Fort Nelson R	87A4	
Fort Rupert	11C2	
● **Fort St. James**	47C3	
● **Fort St. John**	57C2	
Fort Steele	9D2	
Fortine	10A4	
Fortress L	28C1	
Fortress Mtn	28C1	
Fortune Chan	1C-D3	
Fortune Cr	87D3	
Fortynine Cr	8C2	
Forward In	11B3	
Forward Pk	36B4	
Foster Cr	27D2	
Foster Cr	53B1	
Foster L	50B1	
Foster Pk	18C1	
Fosthall	17B3	
Fosthall Cr	17B3	
Foul B	33C4	
Foul B	34A2	
Four Ls	22C2	
Four Mile Cr	75A2	
Four Mile L	81D3	
Four Mile R	72C2	
Four Mile Rapids	84A3	
Fourth of July Cr	80D3-4	
Fourth of July Cr	81A3-4	
Fowler Cr	60A4	
Fox Cr	57C1	
Fox Cr	57C3	
Fox Cr	66B4	
Fox L	63C1	
Fox Pk	63C1	
Fox R	63C1	
Foxy Cr	46C4	
Framstead Cr	49C3-4	
Frances Cr	18B2	
Frances Cr	18B2	
Francis L	38D1	
François L	36C1	
François L	46C4	
François Lake	46D4	
Frank Cr	39B4	
Frank Cr	55B1	
Frank Mackie Gla	51D2	
Frank Mackie Gla	52A2	
Frank Ward Cr	16B4	
Franklin Arm	13C1	
Franklin Camp	2B4	
Franklin Cr	8A2	
Franklin Gla	12D1	
Franklin Gla	23D4	
Franklin R	2B3	
Franklin R	3A2	
Franklin R	12D1	

Fraser	80A3	
Fraser Cr	18B1	
Fraser L	12B2	
Fraser L	47B4	
○ **Fraser Lake**	47B4	
Fraser R	6B1	
Fraser R	14D1	
Fraser R	15A3	
Fraser R	25C-D1	
Fraser R	25D4	
Fraser R	28A1	
Fraser R	38C2	
Fraser R	39B1	
Fraser R	40A2-3	
Fraser R	40D4	
Fraser R	48C4	
Fraser Reach	34C3	
Fred Wright L	52D3	
Freda Cr	2C1	
Freda L	13C4	
Freda L	33D3	
Freda L	34B1	
Freddie L	75B4	
Frederick Arm	13A3	
Frederick I	30B1	
Frederick I	32A2	
Frederick Sd.	12A1	
Fredrikson Cr	63B3-4	
Fredrikson L	63B4	
Freil L	2D1	
Frembd L	6C2	
French Bar Cr	14D1	
French Cr	2B3	
French Cr	2C2	
French Cr	3A1	
French Cr	28A3	
French L	26C4	
French Pk	53D4	
French Pk	54A4	
French Pks	27D2	
French R	83C4	
Frenchman Cr	22C1	
Frenchy Cr	6C2	
Freshwater Bay	12A3	
Friday Harbor	4A3	
Friday L	46B1	
Friday L	54B4	
Friendly L	26D4	
Fries Cr	55C3	
Frisby Cr	17A1	
Frog R	62C-D1	
Frog R	63A1	
Frog R	73D3	
Frog R	73D4	
Frog R	74A4	
Frontier Cr	23D4	
Frontier Mtn	24A4	
Frosty Mtn	6C3	
Froth Cr	27C2	
Fruitvale	8C3	
Fry Cr	18A4	
Frye Cr	38D3	
Frypan Cr	54C4	
Frypan Pk	54B4	
Fulford Harbour	5A4	
Fulmore L	12C3	
Fulton L	46B2	
Fulton R	46B2	
Fumar Cr	54B2	
Funter	70A4	
Furry Cr	5B2	
Fusilier Pk	75A3	

G

Gable Cr	8A2	
Gable Mtn	7D2	
Gable Mtn	35D3	
Gable Mtn	36A3	
Gable Mtn	49A3	
Gabriola	2D3	

Gabriola I	2D3	
Gabriola I	3C1	
Gaffney Cr	55C4	
Gagnon Cr	48B1	
Gagnon Cr	56B-C4	
Gain Cr	3B3	
Gainer Cr	17D2	
Galbraith Cr	9D1	
Gale L	36B1	
Galena	17B3	
Galena B	17B3	
Galena Bay	17B3	
Galene Cr	6B3	
Galiano	5A4	
Galiano I	3D2	
Galiano I	5A4	
Gallic L	83C4	
Galloping Mtn	8A1	
Galloway	10A2	
Gambier Harbour	5A2	
Gambier I	3D1	
Gambier I	5A2	
Gamble L	34C3	
Gammer Cr	75D3	
Gammer Cr	76A3	
Gamsby R	35C3	
Gang Ranch	25D4	
Ganges	5A4	
Gannett L	27C4	
Ganokwa Cr	45D2	
Garbutt Cr	86A4	
Garden Bay	2D2	
Gardener Canal	35A-B2	
Gardom L	16C3	
Garibaldi	14B4	
Garibaldi Heights	5B1	
Garibaldi L	5B1	
Garnett Cr	4D1	
Garvin Cr	38C1	
Gaspard Cr	25C4	
Gaspard L	25C4	
Gataga Mtn	73D3	
Gataga Mtn	74A3	
Gataga Mtn	73D3	
Gataga R	74B3	
Gataga R	74D4	
Gatcho L	36D4	
Gate Cr	88A4	
Gates Cr	17A3	
Gates R	14C3	
Gathto Cr	64B1	
Gathto Cr	75C4	
Gathto Cr	76A4	
Gautier Pk	64B1	
Gauvreau Cr	55D2	
Gauvreau Cr	56A2	
Gauvreau Pk	55D1	
Gauvreau Pk	56A1	
Gavin L	26A1	
Gay L	25A3	
Gaylard Cr	56C2	
Geddes Cr	84D4	
Geddes Cr	85B4	
Geen Ls	7C1	
Geesdale Cr	65B4	
Geese Cr	62C1	
Geese Cr	63A1	
Geikie Cr	28A1	
Gellatly	7B1	
Gem Hill	8B3	
Gem Pass	54C4	
Gemini Ls	73C1	
Gemini Ls	84C4	
Genelle	8C3	
Genevieve L	38D3	
Genier Ls	16A1	
George Cr	38D2	
George Pass	12A2	
Georgetown Mills	43D3	
Georgetown Mills	44A3	
Georgie L	11C2	
Georgie R	52A-B3	

Geremi Cr	38D4
Germaine L	48B4
German L	58B1
Germansen L	55A-B3
Germansen Landing	**55B3**
Germansen R	55B3
Gerow Cr	46C4
Gething Cr	56D3
Getzuni L	36D1
Ghita Cr	40D4
Ghitezli L	36B2
Ghost Cr	30D2
Ghost Cr	32B-C4
Ghost L	39C4
Gibbons Cr	26B1
Gibsons	**5A2**
Gidegingla L	47C1
Giegerich Cr	17D2
Giegerich Pk	63B3
Gifford Pen	13B4
Gil I	34C3
Gil Pk	62B3
Gilbert Gla	13C2
Gilbert L	52B1
Gilford I	12B2
Gillies B	2B1
Gillies B	2B2
Gillies Bay	**2B-C1**
Gilliland Cr	85B3
Gilliland Ls	84D3
Gilliland Ls	85B3-4
Gillis Cr	9A1
Gillis Cr	18A4
Gillis Cr	55B4
Gilnockie Cr	9D3
Gilpin	**8A3**
Gilttoyees Cr	34C1
Gilttoyees In	34D1
Ginmiltkun Cr	53A4
Gisborne L	15C2
Giscome	**48D4**
Gitnadoix R	44C4
Glacial Mtn	72C4
Glacier	**6A4**
Glacier Cr	18A4
Glacier Cr	81A3
Glacier L	5D1
Glacier L	80D3
Glade	**8C2**
Gladsheim Pk	8C1
Gladstone Cr	8B2
Gladys L	81C3
Gladys R	81C3
Gladys R	81C4
Glatheli L	36B2
Gleason Cr	49B4
Glen Eden	**5B2**
Glen Vowell	**45C1**
Glenannan	**37A1**
Glenannan	**47A4**
Glendale Cr	12D3
Glendale L	12D3
Gleneden	**16C2**
Glenlyd Cr	54C2
Glenogle Cr	29A4
Glenora	**60B1**
Glenrosa	**7B1**
Glimpse L	16A4
Glossy Mtn	15B3
Gloucester Cr	8A2
Gloyazikut Cr	46D2
Glundebery Cr	71A1
Gnat Cr	72B4
Gnawed Mtn	15C3
Goat Cr	23C2
Goat Cr	26D1
Goat Cr	27A1
Goat Cr	44D2
Goat Har	34D2
Goat I	13C4
Goat L	13C4
Goat Pk	7D2

Goat Pk	28C3
Goat R	9B2
Goat R	9B3
Goat R	39C2
Goatcanyon Cr	8C1
Goatcanyon Cr	17C4
Goathead Cr	53C3
Goathorn Cr	45D3
Goathorn Cr	46A3
Goatskin Cr	8A1
Goering Cr	25A1
Goguka Cr	76C3
Gold Bridge	**14C2**
Gold Cr	9D3
Gold L	1C1
Gold L	12C4
Gold Mtn	9D3
Gold R	1C1
Gold R	4B1
Gold R	5C2
Gold R	28B4
○ **Gold River**	**1C1**
● **Golden**	**18A1**
Golden Gate	80C4
Golden Hinde	1C-D1
Golden Mtn	80C4
Goldeneye L	63D4
Goldstream	**3D3**
Goldstream L	3C3
Goldstream R	28A4
Goldway Pk	54B-C1
Goleta Chan	11B-C2
Good Hope L	72C1
Good Hope L	83C4
Good Hope Mtn	13C1
Goodfare	**50B1**
Goodfellow Cr	28D3
Goodlow	**57D1-2**
Goodlow	**58A1-2**
Goodrich Cr	57A4
Goodrich L	36B2
Goodrich Pk	48D1
Goodrich Pk	56D4
Goodwin Cr	81D4
Goose B	22C4
Goose Bay	**22C4**
Goose Group	22A3
Goose L	16C4
Goosly L	46B4
Gopher Cr	18B3
Gopherhole Cr	55B2
Gordon Chan	11C2
Gordon Cr	15C4
Gordon Cr	16C2
Gordon Cr	57B4
Gordon Head	**3D3**
Gordon Horne Pk	27D3
Gordon L	47D4
Gordon L	48A4
Gordon R	2C4
Gordon R	3B3
Gordondale	**58C3**
Gore I	1B2
Gorge Cr	15C1
Gorman Cr	17D1
Gorrie Cr	64D3
Gorrie Cr	65A3
Goschen I	31C-D1
Goschen I	33B2
Gosling I	22A3
Gosnell Cr	45C4
Gotchen L	26C2
Gott Cr	14D3
Gott Pk	14D4
Government Cr	38C2
Gowan Cr	5D1
Gowgaia B	20B1
Gracey Cr	51D2
Gracey Cr	52A2
Graham Cr	80C3-4
Graham Cr	81A3-4
Graham I	30C-D1

Graham I	30C1
Graham I	32B2
Graham I	42C4
Graham I	43C-D4
Graham In	81A4
Graham Inlet	80C4
Graham R	56B1
Graham R	56C1
Graham Reach	35A3
Grain Cr	26B1
Grain Cr	39B4
Gramophone Cr	45D2
Granby R	8A2
● **Grand Forks**	**8A3**
Grand Mtn	17C1
Grand Pacific Gla	67C1
Grand Pacific Gla	68A1
Grand Rapids	**47B2**
Grande Cache	**40C1**
Grande Prairie	**50D1**
Grandview Bench	**16C3**
Granger R	65B2
Granisle	**46C2**
Granite	**8D2**
Granite Bay	**13A4**
Granite Cr	6C2
Granite Cr	55C3
Granite Knob	8D1
Granite L	71B2
Granite Mtn	6C2
Granite Mtn	25D1
Granite Pk	13A2
Grant B	11B3
Grant Brook	40D3
Grant Cr	7A2
Grant Cr	14B1
Grant Cr	84D4
Grant Cr	85B4
Grant L	84D4
Grant L	85B4
Grant Pk	48D1
Granthams Landing	**5A2**
Grasmere	**10A3**
Grass Cr	9A4
Grass Cr	60D1
Grass Cr	61A1
Grassham L	47B3
Grassy Cr	65C2
Grassy Mtn	9C2
Grassy Mtn	65C1
Grassy Plains	**36C1**
Grassy Plains	**46C4**
Grave Cr	10B1
Grave L	10B1
Grave Mtn	63D3
Gravel Cr	26B1
Gravell Cr	14C4
Graveyard Cr	57B3
Graveyard L	73C1
Graveyard L	74A1
Gray B	31A3
Gray B	32D4
Gray Cr	2D2
Gray Cr	12D3
Gray Creek	**9A2**
Graybank Cr	86A4
Grayling L	48B1
Grayling R	85C3
Grayling R	85D4
Great Beaver L	47D3
Great Beaver L	48A3
Great Central	**2A2-3**
Great Central L	2A2
Great Glacier	60A4
Great Snow Mtn	64C2
Greata Cr	7B1
Greaves I	11C1
Greely	**17B1**
Greely Cr	17B1
Green Cove	**2A4**
Green Cr	2C3
Green Cr	3B2

Green Cr	65C2
Green In	35A4
Green L	14B4
Green L	26B3
Green Lagoon	35A4
Greenbank	**4B4**
Greenbush L	17A2
Greendrop L	6B3
Greenstone Cr	1D1
Greenstone Cr	12D4
Greenstone Mtn	15D3
Greenville	**44B-C1**
Greenville Chan	33C-D2
Greenville Chan	34B1
Greenwood	**7D3**
Greer Cr	37B1
Gregg Cr	38B1-2
Grewatch Cr	65D3
Grey Eagle L	8D1
Grey Pk	64A1
Grey Wolf Mtn	8C1
Greyback Mtn	7C2
Greyling Cr	56D1
Gribbell I	34D2
Grice B	1D3
Griffin Pass	22A1
Griffith Cr	62A2
Grilse Cr	1C1
Grilse Cr	12C4
Grinder Cr	25D4
Grindrod	**16C3**
Griz Cr	18A3
Grizzly Bear Cr	39A1
Grizzly Cr	8B2
Grizzly Cr	17D1
Grizzly Cr	28D4
Grizzly Ls	27A3
Grizzly Mtn	27A3
Grohman Cr	8D2
Grossman Pk	62B4
Ground Birch Cr	56D1
Ground Birch Cr	57A1
Groundbirch	**57C3**
Groundhog Cr	25B4
Groundhog Mtn	62B4
Groundhog Pass	62A4
Grouse Cr	7D2
Grouse Cr	27D1
Grouse Cr	39B3
Grovedale	**50D1**
Guess Cr	46B2
Guess L	46B2
Guichon Cr	15C3
Guilbault Cr	55D1
Guilbault Cr	56A1
Guise B	11A2
Guise B	11B4
Guish Cr	53B2
Gulatch L	26A3
Gullwing Cr	46D3
Gun Cr	14B1
Gun L	14B1
Gun L	71A2
Gunanoot L	53D3
Gunanoot L	54A3
Gundahoo R	73D1
Gundahoo R	74B1
Gundy	**58B4**
Gundy Cr	65D4
Gunn L	50B2
Gunnell Cr	77A2
Gunniza L	48C4
Gurd I	31C-D1
Gurd I	31C1
Gurd I	33B2
Gurney Cr	5C2
Gustafsen L	26A4
Gustavus	**68C3**
Gutah Cr	66B1
Gutah Cr	66C1-2
Gutah Cr	77B4
Gwillem Ls	8C1

Gwillim Cr	8C1
Gwillim L	49B1
Gwillim L	57B4
Gwillim R	57B4
Gwunya Cr	52B-C4
Gyllenspetz Cr	23B-C2

H

Haan Cr	52C4
Hackett R	71A4
Hackney Hills	56C1
Haddo L	16D4
Hadow Cr	17B2
Haffner Cr	18C1
Hagan Arm	46C1-2
Hagensborg	**23B1**
Haggard Cr	16B1
Haggen Cr	39B2
Haggen L	16B2
Haha Cr	9D2
Haha Cr	54D3
Hahas L	9C1
Haida	**30D1**
Haida	**32C2**
Haida	**42D4**
Haig	**6B2**
Haig Br	10A3
Haina	**30D3**
Haina	**32C4**
Haines	**68D1**
Haines Cr	25A3
Haines L	25B3
Hakai Pass	22B3
Halcourt	**50C1**
Halden Cr	76B3
Hale Mtn	80B4
Halfmoon Bay	**2D2**
Halfmoon L	39B1
Halfmoon L	72B2
Halfway R	17C3
Halfway R	56C-D1
Halfway R	57A1
Halfway R	64D4
Halfway R	65A-B4
Halfway R	65C4
Halfway Ranch	**56D1**
Hall	**8D2**
Hall Cr	7D2
Hall Cr	8D2
Hall Cr	9B3
Hall L	9B2
Hall L	81D3
Haller Cr	9D3
Hallett L	37B1
Hambrook Cr	49C2
Hamill Cr	18A4
Hamill Gla	18A-B4
Hamilton Bay	**59A4**
Hamling Cr	17C4
Hamling Ls	17C4
Hammer L	15D1
Hammett Cr	48B2
Hanawald Cr	53D3-4
Hanawald Cr	54A3-4
Hanceville	**25B3**
Hancock R	30D1
Hancock R	32C2
Handy Cr	2A3
Haney	**5C3**
Haney L	47A3
Hanington Cr	49D4
Hanington Cr	50A4
Hankin Cr	72B2
Hankin L	45C2
Hankin L	72A-B2
Hankin Pk	60C3
Hanklin Cr	40A3
Hanklin Cr	71D2
Hanklin L	71D2
Hanna Cr	52C2

123

Hannah L 6A1
Hannah L 15A4
Hansard L 48D4
Hansen B 11A2
Hansen B 11B4
Hanson I 12A3
Hanson L 47A4
Happy Cr 62B3
Happy L 62A-B3
Harbledown I 12B3
Harbour Cr 27C4
Hard Cr 72D3
Hard L 72D3
Hardscrabble Cr 45A2
Hardwicke I 12C3
Hardwicke Island 12C3
Hardy B 11C2
Hardy I 2C1
Hardy In 22C3
Hare L 84C4
Harmac 2D3
Harmer Cr 10B1
Harmon L 6D1
Harmon L 15D4
Haro Strait 3D3
Harold Cr 39B3
Harold Price Cr 45D1
Harold Price Cr 46A1
Harper Cr 16B2
Harper Cr 27B4
Harper L 16B2
Harper Reed Cr 71A4
Harris Cr 2C4
Harris Cr 3B3
Harrison Hot Springs 6A3
Harrison L 4D1
Harrison L 6A2
Harrison Mills 6A3
Harrison R 4D1
Harrison R 6A3
Harrogate 18B2
Harrop 8D2
Harrymel Cr 51D1
Harrymel Cr 52A1
Hart L 26A1
Hartell 19C3
Hartley Bay 34C3
Hartley Cr 10A2
Hartwig L 26C4
Hartz Cr 71C4
Harvey Cr 10B3
Harvey L 83D4
Harveys Cr 39B4
Harvie Heights 18D1
Harwood I 2B1
Haslam Cr 2D3
Haslam Cr 3C2
Haslam L 2C1
Hasler Cr 56D4
Hastings Arm 52B4
Hat Cr 15A2
Hat Mtn 13B3
Hatchau L 71A4
Hatchery Cr 45A3
Hatdudatehl Cr 47B-C2
Hatdudatehl L 47B2
Hathaway Cr 11B3
Hathaway L 26C4
Hatlin L 71A3
Hatzic L 4C1
Hatzic 5D3
Haul L 46B1
Haul L 54B4
Hautête Cr 46C1
Haven L 35D3
Haven L 36A3
Hawk Cr 18C1
Hawkesbury I 34C4
Hawkins Cr 9C3
Hawkins L 26C3
Hawkley Cr 26D1
Hawks Cr 25D2

Haworth L 64A1
Hay R 77D3
Hayes Cr 6D2
Hayes Cr 7A2
Hayes Pk 81D4
Haynes L 7C1
Hayward Cr 33D2
Hayward Cr 44B4
Hayward L 33D2
Hayward L 44B4
Hazel Cr 9C3
Hazelmere 50B1
● **Hazelton 45C1**
Hazelton Cr 45B1
Hazelton Pk 45B1
Hazelton Pk 53B4
Head B 1A2
Headquarters 2A1
Headstone Cr 65B3
Headwall Cr 13C2
Heakamie Gla 13B1
Health B 12B2
Health Bay 12B2
Healy Cr 17D3
Heard I 11C2
Heart Cr 8B1
Heart Pks 71A3
Heather L 31A3
Heather L 32D4
Heather L 56B4
Heber R 1C1
Hecate I 22B3
Hecate Str 20C-D1
Hecate Str 21A-B1
Hecate Str 33A3
Hecate Str 31B2
Hecate Str 34A3
Heck Cr 66C2
Heckman Cr 17A4
Heckman Pass 23C1
Hedges Pk 63C1
Hedley 7A2
Hedley Cr 7A2
Hedrick Cr 49C4
Hedrick L 49B-C4
Heffley Cr 16A2
Heffley Creek 16A2
Heffley L 16A2
Hela Pk 8C1
Helen L 82A3
Helena L 26A3
Helene L 47A4
Helicopter Cr 66C1
Hellroar Cr 27C2
Hellroarer Cr 7D2
Hellroaring Cr 9B2
Hellroaring Cr 39D2
Hells Gate 6B1
Helmcken Falls 27A3
Helmcken In 34D4
Helmcken L 34D4
Helmer L 15D4
Helmut 88C4
Help L 28C4
Helveker Cr 60A-B2
Hemlock 6A2
Hemp Cr 27A3
Hen Ingram L 26C1
Henderson Cr 7D3
Henderson L 2A3
Hendrix Cr 26C2
Hendrix L 26C2
Hendrix Lake 26C2
Henkel Cr 46C4
Henning L 47C3
Henretta Cr 19B4
Henri L 25B2
Henrietta Cr 47A4
Henry Cr 75B3
Henry House 41B4
Henry I 31C1
Henry I 33B2

Henry I 43C4
Henshaw Cr 1D2
Herchmer Pass 55C1
Herd Dome 45C4
Hereron L 7C1
Hereron L 16C4
Herkyelthtie L 38C3
Hernando I 2A1
Hernando I 13A4
Herrick Cr 49B3
Herring Cr 48D4
Hesquiat 1B2
Hesquiat Har 1B2
Hesquiat L 1B2
Hesquiat Pen 1B2
Hetty Pk 80A4
Hevenor In 33C-D3
Hevenor In 34B2
Hevenor Lagoon 33D3
Hevenor Lagoon 34B2
Hewer Cr 64C2
Hewer Cr 65A2
Heydon L 12D3
Hiamadam Cr 63A2
Hibbard L 11D1
Hibben I 30D4
Hickethier Ranch 56D1
Hicks L 4D1
Hicks L 6A2
Hidden Cr 8D3
Hidden L 16D3
Hidden Valley Cr 73B1
Hiding Cr 50A-B2
Hiellen R 31A1
Hiellen R 32D2
Hiellen R 43A4
Higgins L 26C4
Higgins Pass 21D1
High Cr 2D1
High River 19D3
High Tuya L 71C1
High Tuya L 72A1
Highhat R 57A4
Highland Valley 15C3
Highrise Cr 56D3
Hihium Cr 15B1
Hihium L 15C1
Hilary L 53D3
Hilary L 54A3
Hilda L 39C4
Hilda Pk 8B1
Hill Cr 17C2
Hill L 38D4
Hillcrest Mines 10C2
Hillgren Ls 84C3
Hillgren Ls 85A3
Hilliers 2B3
Hillis Cr 13B3
Hills 17C4
Hinton 41C2
Hinton Trail 50C1
Hippa 30B2
Hippa 32A3
Hippa I 30B2
Hippa I 32A3
Hird Ls 8C1
Hiren Cr 17A1
Hirsch Cr 45A4
Hirschfeld Cr 81C4
Hisnit In 1A2
Hitchcock Cr 80D3
Hitchcock Cr 81A3
Hiuhihill Cr 16B2
Hiusta Meadow 71C4
Hixon 38C2
Hixon Cr 38C2
Hizaza Cr 73C2-3
Hizaza Cr 74A2-3
Hizaza Hill 84B3
Hkusam Mtn 12C3
Hluey Ls 71D4
Hluey Ls 72A-B4

Hobiton L 2B4
Hoboe Cr 69C1
Hobson Arm 26B1
Hobson Cr 27A1
Hobson Cr 40A4
Hobson L 26D1
Hobson L 27A1
Hobson L 40A4
Hockey Cr 66A2
Hodder Cr 61B4
Hoder Cr 8C1
Hoeya Sd 12C2
Hoffard Cr 76D2
Hogem Pass 54C-D4
Hogg Cr 9C2
Hogsback L 37D1
Hohoae I 11D4
Holberg 11B3
Holberg In 11C3
Hold Cr 12B2
Hold Cr 28D4
Holder Cr 48B1
Holdich Cr 17A1
Holdich Cr 28A4
Hole in the Wall Mtn 60A4
Holman Cr 66A3
Holman L 37D1
Holman L 38A2
Holmes Cr 46B-C3
Holmes L 17A4
Holmes R 40B2
Holobia L 55A4
Holt Cr 17D1
Holte Cr 24A1
Holtry Cr 24A1
Holy Cross L 37A1
Holy Cross Mtn 37A1
Holy Cross Mtn 39C1
Homan L 80A3
Homan R 80A3
Homathko Pk 24B4
Homathko R 13A1
Homathko R 24B4
Homathko Snowfield 13B1
Homer Cr 5C2
Homfray Chan 13B4
Homfray Cr 13B4
Hominka R 49A2
Honakta Cr 69D2
Honakta Cr 70B2
Honeymoon Bay 2C4
Honna R 30D3
Honna R 32C4
Hooch L 24A2
Hoodoo Cr 12D1
Hoodoo Cr 23D4
Hoodoo Gla 60B4
Hoodoo L 7D2
Hoodoo Ls 48B4
Hoodoo Mtn 60B4
Hook Cr 49B2
Hook Cr 82B3
Hook L 49B2
Hooker Icefield 28B1
Hoole Cr 74C1
Hoole Cr 85C4
Hoonaln 68D4
Hoop B 11C1
Hoopatatkwa L 15D1
Hoover L 15D1
Hope Cr 17D3
Hope I 11B2
● **Hope 6B2**
Hope Mtn 6B2
Horetzky Cr 35B2
Horn Cr 49A4
Horn Cr 50C4
Horn Cr 55D1
Horn Cr 56A1
Horn Cr 64D4
Horn Cr 65A4
Horn L 24B3

Horn Pk 54C2
Hornby I 2B2
Hornby Island 2B2
Horne Cr 27D3
Horne L 2B3
Horne L 3A1
Horneline Cr 73C-D1
Horneline Cr 74A1-2
Hornet Cr 6A2
Hornway Cr 54C2
Horse Cr 18A1
Horse L 26C4
Horse Range Cr 65C-D1
Horsefeed Cr 70C1
Horsefly 26B2
Horsefly L 26C1
Horsefly R 26B-C2
Horseranch L 83D4
Horseshoe Bay 5B2
Horseshoe Cr 56C1
Horseshoe L 2C1
Horseshoe L 9D2
Horsethief Cr 18B3
Horsfall I 22A2
Hoskins Cr 27D3
Hoskyn Chan 13A4
Hosmer 10A2
Hospital Cr 29A4
Hospital Cr 48D4
Hossitl Cr 88A3
Hostli Cr 88D4
Hostli L 88D4
Hot L 72C1
Hot L 83C4
Hotel Cr 72B3
Hotfish L 26D3
Hotham Sd 2C-D1
Hotlesklwa L 62B3
Hotnarko L 23D1
Hotnarko R 23C-D1
Hotsprings Cove 1B2
Hottah L 73B4
Hoult Cr 45B4
Hound Cr 17A3
House Mtn 13A2
○ **Houston 46B3**
Houston Cr 17D2
Houston Pass 3D2
Houston Pass 5A4
Houston R 1B2
Houston Stewart In 20C2
Houston Tommy Cr 45D3-4
Houston Tommy Cr 46A4
Hovel B 13B2
Howard Cr 27D1
Howarth Cr 6C1
Howe B 20C2-3
Howe Cr 8A2
Howe Sd 3D1
Howe Sd 5A2
Howell Cr 10B3
Howser 18A4
Howser Cr 18A3
Howson Cr 45C3
Howson Cr 62C4
Hoy L 62C4
Huaskin L 11D2
Huaskin L 12A2
Huble Cr 49A4
Huckey Cr 39B3
Hudson Bay Mtn 45C2
Hudson Bay Pass 43C3
○ **Hudson's Hope 57A2**
Hugh Allan Cr 28A1
Hugh Cr 34D1
Huguenot Cr 50A3
Hulcross Cr 56D3
Humamilt L 16D1
Humbug Cr 39C1
Hume Cr 17D2
Humphrey L 54D4
Hunaechin Cr 13D4
Hunakwa L 16D1

Hungary Cr 39A-B1
Hunger L 10B3
Hungry Cr 9B1
Hungry Valley Cr 25B4
Hunter Chan 22B2-3
Hunter Cr 7B3
Hunter Cr 45B4
Hunter I 22B3
Hunter Mtn 75A-B3
Hunters Ls 66B2
Huntingdon **5D3**
Hunts Inlet **33C2**
Hunts Inlet **43D4**
Hunts Inlet **44A4**
Hurley R 14B2
Hurricane Cr 70C1
Hurricane Cr 81C4
Hurst I 11C2
Hustan L 12A4
Hutchinson Cr 8A2
Hutchinson Cr 84D3
Hutchison Cr 85B3
Hutsigola L 81D4
Hutton In 20B1
Huxley I 20B1
Hyas L 16A2
Hydaburg **42C1**
Hyde Cr 39A3
Hyde Creek **11D3**
Hyder **52A-B3**
Hydraulic Cr 7C1
Hydraulic L 7C1
Hyland Cr 60B1
Hyland L 71A1
Hyland L 82A4
Hyman Cr 47C3
Hythe **50C1**
Hythe **58C4**

I

Ian L 30C1
Ian L 32B2
Ice Cr 8C1
Ice Mtn 49B3
Ice R 18B1
Icefall Brook 28D3
Icewall Cr 13C2
Ickna Cr 23A2
Iconoclast Mtn 28C4
Idabel L 7C1
Idaho Pk 80D4
Idaho Pk 81B4
Ideal L 7D1
Ideal L 16D4
Idol L 39D1
Idol Cr 40A1
Ignatieff Cr 55D2
Ignatieff Cr 56A2
Ikesumka L 22C1
Iknouk R 44B1
Ilgachuz Range 36D4
Illal Cr 6C2
Illecillewaet R 17B1
Illiance R 52C4
Iltasyuko L 36B4
Iltasyuko R 36C4
Iltcoola Cr 7A2
Impa L 65B2
Imperial Cr 49B2
Imperial Eagle Chan 2A4
Incomappleux R 17C1
Indata L 47A1
Indata L 55A4
Index L 16A4
Indian Arm 4A1
Indian Arm 5B2
Indian Cr 57C1
Indian Cr 80D3
Indian Cr 81A3
Indian I 11C1

Indian L 39B2
Indian L 80D3
Indian L 81B3
Indian Pk 18D2
Indian R 5B2
Indianpoint 39B2
Indianpoint L 39B3
Ingenika Arm 64A4
Ingenika Cone 64A4
Ingenika Crag 64A4
Ingenika R 63B4
Ingenika R 63C-D4
Ingraham B 30B1
Ingraham B 32A2
Ingram Cr 7D3
Ingram Cr 16B3
Inhini R 51B1
Inhini R 60A-B4
Ink L 1D2
Inkaneep **7C3**
Inkaneep Cr 7C3
Inkikuh Cr 15B3
Inklin R 70C2
Inland L 2C1
Inlet Cr 18D4
Inner Basin 1A1
Inonoaklin Cr 8A1
Inonoaklin Cr 17A4
Inonoaklin Mtn 8A1
Inonoaklin Mtn 17A4
Insect Cr 45A1
Inskip Ch 30D3
Inspector Pk 73B-C2
Intata Reach 36D2
Intersection Mtn 40B1
Intlpam Cr 15A3
● **Invermere** **18C3**
Inzana Cr 47A-B2
Inzana Cr 47B-C2
Inzana L 47B2
Inziana R 23A3
Ioco **5B3**
Ione **8C4**
Ipec L 64B2
Ireland Cr 16D3
Irene L 75B1
Irene L 86B4
Irish Cr 16C3
Irishman Cr 9C3
Iron Cr 10A2
Iron Mtn 15C4
Iron R 1D1
Ironside Cr 53B4
Ironside Mtn 30C1
Ironside Mtn 32A3
Iroquois Cr 28A1
Iroquois L 48B2
Irvines Landing **2C2**
Irving Cr 52D2
Isaac R 39B3
Isaak L 39C3
Isadore Cr 48C2
Isaiah Cr 26C1
Isaiah Cr 39C4
Ishkheenickh R 44C2
Ishkloo Cr 39B4
Isintok Cr 7B2
Iskut **61B1**
Iskut Mtn 51A1
Iskut Mtn 60A4
Iskut R 51B-C1
Iskut R 60B4
Iskut R 60D2
Iskut R 60D3-4
Iskut R 61A2
Iskut R 61A4
Islaht L 16B4
Islam Cr 53D1
Islam Cr 54A1
Island L 16C4
Island L 26A3
Island L 60D1

Island L 61B1
Island L 72A-B4
Island Morchuea L 71D4
Island Mtn 39A3
Isle Pierre **38B1**
Isle Pierre **48B4**
Isola Cr 64A4
Isolation Mtn 60A1
Italia L 26D3
Italy Cr 8B3
Itautso L 26B3
Itcha L 37B4
Itcha Mtn 37B4
Ithaca Gla 64C2
Ittsi Cr 86D3
Ittsi Cr 87B3
Iverson Cr 82D4
Iverson Cr 83A4
Ivor Cr 27A2
Ivor Cr 64A4
Ivor Cr 64A4

J

Jack Cr 7B1
Jack Frost L 26C4
Jack Lee Cr 62D2
Jack Lee Cr 63A2
Jack of Clubs Cr 39A3
Jack of Clubs L 39A3
Jack Stone Cr 73C4
Jack Stone Cr 74A4
Jack Wilson Cr 60A1
Jackfish C 55B3
Jackfish Cr 76C3
Jackfish L 57A-B3
Jackknife Cr 76C4
Jacklah R 1C2
Jackpine Cr 49C1
Jackpine L 7B1
Jackpine L 26A1
Jackson B 12C3
Jackson Pass 22A1
Jacobie Cr 26A1
Jacobsen Gla 23C2
Jacques L 26C1
Jade L 28A1
Jade L 41A4
Jade L 52C3
Jaffray **10A2**
Jakes Corner **80C1**
Jakes Corner **81A1**
Jalun R 42C4
James Cr 49A-B3
James I 3D3
James I 5A4
James L 7C1
Jamieson Cr 15D1
Jamieson Cr 16A1
Jane Smith Cr 85B-C3
Janet Cr 23C1
Jarvis Cr 49C4
Jarvis Cr 50A4
Jarvis Ls 49D4
Jarvis Ls 50A4
Jasper **41B4**
Jayam **2C3**
Jean Marie Cr 47B1
Jedney Cr 65D3
Jeffrey Cr 28B2
Jekill R 51B1
Jellicoe Cr 62C3
Jenkins Cr 62A3
Jennings Lakes 82C3-4
Jennings Ls 83A3
Jennings R 82A4
Jenny In 22C2
Jensen Cr 63B4
Jensen Pk 63B4
Jerky Cr 25D1
Jerky Cr 38D4

Jerry Cr 38D2
Jervis In 2C-D1
Jervis In 13D4
Jesmond **15A1**
Jesmond Cr 15A1
Jesse Cr 34D1
Jesson Cr 64D3
Jesson Cr 65B3
Jeune Landing **11C3**
Jewakwa Gla 13B1
Jewakwa R 13A1
Jewel L 8A3
Jezebel Cr 57B4
Jim Brown Cr 13C4
Jim Cr 26C3
Jim Kelly Cr 6C2
Jim L 26C4
Jim L 84A3
Jim May Cr 55A2
Jim Smith L 9C2
Joan L 7D2
Joanne Cr 48B3
Joanne L 48B3
Jobin Cr 23D3
Jock Cr 62D3
Jock Cr 63B3
Joe Irwin L 72B2
Joe Poole Cr 63D1
Joe Rich Cr 7C1
Joe Ross L 15C1
Joes L 25D3
Joffre Cr 14C4
Joffre Cr 19A3
Johanson Cr 54B1
Johanson L 54C1
Johiah L 73D4
Johiah L 74B4
John Bennett Cr 56C4
John Boyd Cr 38D3
John Brown Cr 45C1-2
John Cr 16B1
John Cr 17D4
John Hart L 12D4
John L 26A3
Johnny L 36D3
Johns Cr 7A3
Johns Cr 22D3
Johnsen Cr 56D4
Johnson Chan 22B2
Johnson Cr 16B1
Johnson Cr 56D3
Johnson Gla 60A4
Johnson L 16B1
Johnson R 60A4
Johnsons Crossing ...**80D1**
Johnsons Crossing ...**81A1**
Johnsons Landing **18A4**
Johnston Canyon **18C1**
Johnston Cr 8A1
Johnston Cr 22C4
Johnston L 34C1
Johnstone Str 12B3
Jones L 26A2
Jones L 80C3
Jones L 81A3
Jones Pk 56C2
Joplin Cr 75B4
Jordan R 3C3
Jordan R 17A1
Jorgensen Cr 24B-C2
Joseph Cr 9D2
Joseph Cr 27A4
Josephine Cr 71C1
Josephine Cr 72A1
Joss Mtn 17A2
Juan de Fuca Strait ..3B-C4
Juan Perez Sd 20B1
Jubilee Mtn 7D1
Jubilee Mtn 12D1
Julian Cr 72D1
Julienne Cr 65D3
Juliet Cr 6C1

July Cr 8A3
July L 88C3
July Mtn 6C1
Jumble Mtn 36B4
Jumbo Cr 18B2
Jumbo Mtn 18B3
Jump Across Cr 23A1
Jump L 2C3
Jump L 3B2
Jumping Cr 17C1
Junction Cr 14D2
June Cr 7B2
June L 88C-D3
Juneau **70B-C4**
Juniper Cr 7A3
Juniper Cr 45C1
Juniper Heights **16A3**
Junker L 23C2
Junkers Cr 62D2
Junkers Cr 63A2
Juskatla **30D2**
Juskatla **32C3**
Juskatla In 30D2
Juskatla In 32B3
Justice Cr 56B1
Justine L 47A4

K

Kachook Cr 82A4
Kadah L 62C-D2
Kadah L 63A2
Kadeen Cr 44C4
Kagan B 30D3
Kagan B 32C4
Kah Cr 88C4
Kah L 77C1
Kaha Cr 71A2
Kahan Cr 71B1
Kahan Cr 82B4
Kahntah **77C3**
Kahntah R 66C1
Kahntah R 77C4
Kahta Cr 65C2
Kaien I 33C1
Kaien I 43D4
Kaien I 44A4
Kain Cr 18A2
Kains L 11C2
Kaiput Cr 12A4
Kaiput L 12A4
Kaisun **30C3**
Kakawis **1C3**
Kaketsa Mtn 71A4
Kakiddi Cr 60D1
Kakiddi Cr 61A1
Kakiddi L 60D2
Kakiddi L 61A2
Kakuchuya Cr 71A3
Kakwa L 40A1
Kakwa L 50A4
Kakwa Pass 40A1
Kakweiken R 12C2
Kalahin Mtn 51C1
Kalamalka **16C4**
Kalamalka L 16C4
Kalder Cr 47C2
Kaleden **7B2**
Kalone Cr 36A-B4
Kalone Pk 23B1
Kalone Pk 36B4
Kamano R 35B1-2
● **Kamloops** **15D2**
Kamloops **16A3**
Kamloops L 15C-D2
Kamma Cr 9B2
Kanaka Bar 15B4
Kananaskis **19A1**
Kane Cr 17D4
Kane L 6C1
Kane L 15D4

Kanish B 12D4
Kano In 30C3
Kano In 32B4
Kaouk In 11D4
Kaouk R 12A4
Kapella R 35C3
Kapoose Cr 1A4
Kappan Cr 23D1
Kappan Cr 23D1
Karlukwees 12B3
Kashutl In 11D4
Kasiks R 44C3
Kaska Cr 84A3
● **Kaslo 9A1**
Kaslo Cr 9D3
Kaslo R 8D1
Kaslo R 17D4
Kastberg Cr 54B2
Katah Cr 66B1
Katakose Cr 65B2
Kataleen Cr 77C3
Kate Cr 17A3
Kate 59A4
Kate L 17A3
Kateen R 44B3
Kates Needle 59D3
Katete R 51A1
Katharine Cr 63B2
Katina Cr 70B1
Kaufmann L 18B1
Kaustua Cr 70C-D2
Kauwinch R 11C4
Kawdy Cr 71B2
Kaykay L 48A-B4
Kaza L 54B2
Kaza Pk 54C2
Kazchek Cr 47A2
Kazchek L 47A2
Keap Cr 45A-B3
Keary L 14C2
Keats Island 5A2
Kechika R 63C1
Kechika R 73C1
Kechika R 73D3
Kechika R 74A2
Kechika R 74B4
Kechika R 84B4
Kechika R 85A4
Kedahda L 71A-B1
Kedahda R 71A1
Kedleston 16C4
Keecha L 33D4
Keecha L 34B3
Keefer L 17A4
Keen Cr 8D1
Keene Cr 17D4
Kehlechoa R 72D4
Keily Cr 64C2
Keily Cr 65A2
Keith L 26B4
Keith R 11B3
Keithley Cr 39A-B4
Keithley Creek 39B4
Kelechoa R 61D1
Kellie Cr 17C2
Kellington L 26D3
Kellogg Cr 38B1
Kelly Cr 15A2
Kelly L 15A1
Kelly L 50A-B1
Kelly Lake 15A1
Kelly Lake 50B1
Kelly R 7C3
● **Kelowna 7C1**
Kelowna Cr 7C1
Kelowna Cr 16C4
Kelsall L 79B3
Kelsall R 79B3
Kelsey Bay 12C3
Kelskiist Cr 44B1
Kelskiist Cr 52B4
Kemano 35B2

Kemano B 35B2
Kemess Cr 62D3-4
Kemess Cr 63B3-4
Ken L 83D3
Kenai Cr 66B1
Kenai Cr 77B4
Kendell 5D4
Kennedy I 33C2
Kennedy I 34A1
Kennedy I 44A4
Kennedy L 1D3
Kennedy R 1D3
Kenneth Cr 39A1
Kennicott L 71A4
Kenny Cr 54D4
Keno L 26B1
Kent 6A3
Kentucky L 6D1
Keogh R 11D3
○ **Keremeos 7B3**
Keremeos Cr 7B3
Kerouard Is 20C3
Kerry L 48C2
Kersley 38D4
Kersley R 38D4
Ketchikan 43A1
Ketchikan 51A4
Ketchum L 71A3
Kettle In 21C1
Kettle In 34C4
Kettle R 7D1
Kettle R 7D3
Kettle R 8A4
Kettle R 17A4
Kettle Valley 7D3
Kewquodie Cr 11C3
Keystone Mtn 8D3
Khartoum L 2C1
Khtada L 44C4
Khtada R 44C4
Khutze In 35A3
Khutzeymateen In 44A-B2
Khutzeymateen R 44B3
Khyer R 33D1
Khyex R 44B3
Kiakho L 9C2
Kianuko Cr 9B2
Kibbee L 39B3
Kicking Horse Pass 29A4
Kicking Horse R 18A1
Kicking Horse R 29B4
Kid Cr 9B3
Kidney L 23C2
Kidprice L 35C1
Kilbella B 22C3
Kilbella R 22D3
Kildala Arm 35A1
Kildala R 35A1
Kildidt Lagoon 22B3
Kildidt Sd 22B3
Kildonan 2A3
Kilkerran 57D3
Kilkerran 58A3
Killam Cr 39C2
Killarney L 71D2
Killarney L 72A2
Killdog Cr 26D1
Kilmarnock Cr 19B4
Kilpala R 11D3
Kilpoola L 7B3
Kiltik Cove 22B3
Kiltuish In 35A2
Kiltuish R 35A3
Kimball Cr 39B4
● **Kimberley 9C1**
Kimea Cr 88C4
Kimea L 88C4
Kimpton Cr 18C3
Kimsquit L 35C3
Kimsquit R 35D3
Kinaskan L 60D2
Kinaskan L 61A-B2

Kinbasket L 28A-B2
Kinbasket L 40D4
Kinbasket L 28B2
Kincolith 44B1-2
Kincolith R 44B1
King Cr 51C1
King I 22C2
King Pk 75A4
King Salmon Cr 70B2
King Salmon L 70C2
Kingcome 12C2
Kingcome In 12B2
Kingcome Inlet 12B2
Kingcome In 12C1
Kingfisher 16D3
Kingfisher Cr 16D2
Kingkown In 31D2
Kingkown In 33C3
Kingkown In 34A2
Kingsgate 9B3
Kingsvale 6C1
Kinnear L 5D2
Kinney L 40C3
Kinskuch L 52C3
Kinskuch Pk 52D3
Kinskuch R 52D3-4
Kinuseo Cr 49B2
Kinuseo Falls 49B2
Kirby Cr 3C4
Kirbyville Cr 27D4
Kirk Cr 60A2
Kirkpatrick Cr 65C1-2
Kirkup Cr 17A1
Kisgegas Pk 53C3
Kishinena Cr 10C3
Kiskatinaw R 49D1
Kiskatinaw R 50A1
Kiskatinaw R 57C-D3
Kiskatinaw R 58A3-4
Kiskosh In 34C3
Kispiox 45C1
Kispiox 53B-C4
Kispiox Mtn 53B4
Kispiox R 53A3
Kistakok L 62B3
Kitamaat Village 35A1
Kitamaat Village 45A4
Kitasu B 21D1
Kitchener 9B3
Kitchener Crag 62C3
Kitchener L 62C3
Kitchi Cr 39D1
Kitchi Cr 49D4
Kiteen R 44D1
Kiteen R 52D4
● **Kitimat 45A4**
Kitimat R 45A4
Kitkatla 31D1
Kitkatla 33C2
Kitkatla 34A1
Kitkatla Chan 31D1
Kitkatla Chan 33B2
Kitkiata In 34C3
Kitkiata R 34C1
Kitlangas Cr 53B2
Kitlope L 35B3
Kitlope R 35C3-4
Kitnayakwa R 45B3
Kitsault L 52C3
Kitsault R 52C3-4
Kitseguecla 45B1
Kitseguecla Mtn 45B1
Kitseguecla R 45A-B1
Kitsumkalum L 44D2
Kitsumkalum R 44D2
Kitsuns Cr 45B2
Kitwancool 45B1
Kitwancool Cr 45A1
Kitwanga 45B1
Kitwanga L 45B1
Kitwanga L 53A-B4
Kitwanga R 45B1

Kitza Cr 84B4
Kitza L 84B4
Kiwa Cr 40B4
Kiwetinok R 29B4
Kiwigana R 87B-C4
Kiwigana R 87D4
Klahowya L 62A3
Klaklakama Ls 12B4
Klakring Cr 54C2
Klanawa R 2B4
Klanawa R 3A2
Klappan R 61B1
Klappan R 61C3
Klaskino In 11C4
Klaskish In 11B-C4
Klaskish R 11C4
Klastline R 60C1
Klastline R 61A1
Klattasine Cr 13A-B1
Klattasine Cr 13A1
Klawdetelle Cr 47B1
Klawli L 47B1
Klawli L 55B4
Klawli R 47B1
Klawli R 55B4
Klaytahnkut L 46D2
Kleana Cr 45A3
Kledane In 35A3
Kledo Cr 75C2
Kledo Cr 76A2
Kleena Kleene 24B3
Kleeptes Cr 1B1
Klehini R 79B4
Kleindale 2D2
Klekane R 34D3
Klemtu 22A1
Klenteh Cr 87C4
Klesilkwa R 6B3
Kli Cr 88B3
Klicho Cr 77B2
Klinaklini Gla 12C1
Klinaklini Gla 23C4
Klinaklini L 23D3
Klinaklini L 12D1
Klinaklini R 23D3-4
Klinaklini R 24A3
Klingzut Mtn 65B2
Klinit Cr 82B4
Klinkit L 82B4
Klite Cr 13C3
Klitsa Mtn 2A3
Kliweguh Cr 62A1
Kliyul Cr 54C1
Kliyul L 25B3
Klo Cr 7C1
Klo Cr 46B4
Kloakut L 25A4
Klock L 47A1
Klonas L 22D4
Klootchlimmis Cr 11C3
Klowee L 76B-C3
Klowkut Pk 54D4
Kloye Cr 84A3
Klua Cr 65D1
Klua Cr 76D3
Klua Ls 76C4
Kluachesi Cr 64D1
Kluachesi Cr 65A1
Kluachesi Cr 75D4
Kluachesi Cr 76A4
Kluachesi L 65A1
Kluachesi L 75C4
Kluachesi L 76A4
Kluachon L 61B1
Kluakaz Cr 61D3
Kluantantan R 62A3
Kluantantan R 62A-B4
Kluayaz Cr 62B3
Kluayaz L 62A-B3
Kluayetz Cr 62A3
Kluea L 61B1
Kluk Cr 47B4

Klukshu 79A2
Klukwan 79C-D4
Kluskoil L 37C3
Kluskus Ls 37B3
Knapp Cr 37A1
Knapp L 37A1
Knappen Cr 8A2
Knife L 26A2
Knight Cr 47D4
Knight In 12C2-3
Knob Hill 11B2
Knoll Cr 24B2
Knot Ls 23D3
Knouff Cr 16A2
Knouff L 16A1
Knox L 25D2
Knutsford 16A3
Knutson Cr 27B1
Kobes Cr 56D1
Koch Cr 8B1
Kodak Cataract 63B2
Koeye Cr 22C3
Koeye R 22C3
Kohasganko Cr 36C4
Kokanee Cr 8D1
Kokanee L 8D1
Kokish 12A3
Kokish R 12A3
Koksilah 2D4
Koksilah R 2D4
Koksilah R 3C3
Koller Cr 65B3
Komie Cr 76D1
Komie L 77A1
Konigus Cr 61C-D4
Konni L 24D4
Konthil Cr 61A1
Konthill Cr 60D1
Kookipi Cr 6A1
Kooryet L 33D4
Kooryet L 34B2
Kootenay Bay 9A-B1
Kootenay Crossing 18C2
Kootenay In 30D4
Kootenay L 9A1
Kootenay L 18A4
Kootenay R 8C2
Kootenay R 9D1
Kootenay R 18B-C2
Kootenay R 18D3
Koprino Har 11B3
Koshin R 71A2
Kostal L 27B2
Koster Cr 25D4
Kostering Cr 15A1
Kostick Cr 85D4
Kotcho L 77B1
Kotcho R 77B1
Kotcho R 77C2
Kotsine R 54B3
Kotsinta Cr 53A1
Kowatua Cr 70D3
Kowesas R 35B3
Kravac Cr 64D1
Kravac Cr 65A1
Krestova 8C2
Kruger Cr 39B2-3
Kruger I 39B3
Ksedin Cr 44B-C1
Ksemamaith Cr 44C1
Kshadin Cr 52D4
Kshwan R 52B3
Kuachesi L 64C1
Kubicek Pass 62B3
Kuldo Cr 53A3
Kuldo Mtn 53B3
Kulee Cr 23A4
Kumdis Cr 30D2
Kumdis Cr 32C3
Kumdis Slough 30D1
Kumealon L 33D2
Kumealon L 34B1

Kunghit I 20C2
Kunishma Cr 60B1
Kunlin L 1C1
Kunnum Cr 12B4
Kuper I 3C2
Kushya R 37B4
Kuskanax Cr 17C4
Kuskonook 9A-B3
Kutcho Cr 73A3
Kutcho Cr 73A4
Kuthai L 69D1
Kuthai L 70B1
Kuttat Cr 9B2
Kuyakuz Mtn 37B3
Kuzkwa R 47B2
Kwadacha Gla 64A1
Kwadacha Mtn 63D2
Kwakshua Chan 22B4
Kwanika Cr 55A4
Kwashona Cr 69D2-3
Kwashona Cr 70B2-3
Kwatna In 22C2
Kwatna R 22D2
Kwatsi B 12B2
Kwikoit Cr 16C1
Kwinageese L 52D2
Kwinageese R 52D2
Kwinamass Mtn 44B2
Kwinamass R 44B2
Kwinamuck L 44C-D1
Kwinamuck L 52C-D4
Kwinatahl R 52C4
Kwoiek Cr 15A4
Kwoiek Needle 15A3
Kwoiek Pk 15A3
Kwokullie L 77C1
Kwotlenemo L 15A3
Kwun Cr 45D1
Kxngeal L 33D2
Kxngeal L 34B1
Kye B 2B1
Kyklo Cr 77B3
Kynoch In 35B4
Kyuquot 11C4
Kyuquot Chan 1A4
Kyuquot Chan 11D4
Kyuquot Sd 11C-D4

L

L. Magog 18D2
L. McArthur 18B1
L. O'Hara 18B1
L. O'Hara 29B4
I. McArthur 29B4
La Conner 4B4
La Forme Cr 17B1
La France Cr 9A2
La Glace 58C-D4
La Guarde Cr 57D1
La Guarde Cr 58A1
La Pierre Cr 38D1
La Prise Cr 66A2
La Salle Cr 39D2
Labouchere Chan 11D2
Labouchere Chan 22D1
Labour Day L 2C3
Labour Day L 3B2
Lac des Roches 26D4
Lac La Hache 26B3
Lac la Hache 26B3
Lac Le Jeune 15D3
Lac Le Jeune 15D3
Lachine Cr 18C2
Lacoma Cr 7B1
Ladner 5B3
Lady Douglas I 22A1-2
Lady King L 16B3
Lady Laurier L 55D1
Lady Laurier L 64D4
Lady Laurier L 65A4

Ladybird Cr 8B2
Ladybird Mtn 8B2
● **Ladysmith 2D4**
Lafferty Cr 55C1
Lagoon In 31A4
Lagoon In 31A4
Laib Cr 9A2
Laidlaw 6A3
Laidlaw L 81B3
Laidman L 37A3
Laird L 6D2
Lake Cowichan 2C4
Lake Cr 17D3
Lake Eileen 18C3
Lake Enid 18C3
Lake Errock 5D3
Lake Louise 29C4
Lake Lovely Water 5B1
Lake Mtn 22A1
Lake of the Hanging
    Glacier 18B3
Lake of the Mountains ...11B2
Lake of the Trees 26B3
Lake Revelstoke 17A1
Lake Revelstoke 28A3-4
Lakelse L 45A3
Lakelse Lake 45A3
Lakelse R 44D3
Lakeview Cr 7A3
Lakeview Mtn 7A3
Lama Pass 22B2
Lamarque Pass 73C4
Lamb Cr 9C3
Lambert Chan 2B2
Lambert Cr 16D3
Lambly Cr 7B1
Lambly Cr 16B4
Lamming Mills 39D2
Lamming Mills 40A2
Lamprey Cr 45D4
Lamprey Cr 46A4
Lanberi's Gla 64A1
Landslide Cr 38C4
Lanes Cr 15D2
Lanes Cr 16A2
Lanezi L 39C3
Lang Bay 2C1
Lang Cr 2C1
Lang Cr 28D4
Lang L 26C3
Langara I 42B4
Langara Island 32A1
Langdale 5A2
Langford 3D4
● **Langley 5C3**
Lantzville 2C3
Lanz I 11A-B4
Lapan L 12C3
Lapie Cr 85B-C4
Lapie L 74C1
Lapie L 85C4
Lapierre Cr 55D1
Lapierre Cr 56A1
Lapp Cr 66C2
Larchwood L 9C1
Lard Cr 35B4
Lardeau 18A4
Lardeau Cr 17C2
Lardeau R 17D3
Laredo Chan 34D4
Laredo In 34D4
Laredo Sd 21D1
Larman Cr 75C4
Larson Cr 13B3
Lasca Cr 8D2
Laskeek B 31A4
Laslui Cr 62B2
Lasqueti 2C2
Lasquiti I 2C2
Lasquiti I 3B1
Lassie L 7D2

Lassiter B 11C1
Lastman L 13D1
Lastman L 24D4
Latelle Cr 12D3
Latewhos Cr 17A3
Laundry Cr 18C3
Laurel 5C2
Laurier 8B4
Laurier Pass 64D4
Laurier Pass 65B4
Lava L 44D1
Lavender Pk 52C4
Lavigure L 16B4
Lavington 16D4
Law Cr 18B3
Lawless Cr 6C2
Lawnhill 31A2
Lawnhill 32C-D4
Lawrence 5D4
Lawson L 80B3
Lawyers Cr 62C2-3
Lawyers Pass 62C3
Lay Cr 54C1
Lazo 2A1
Lazy L 9D1
Le Bourdais L 39A4
Le Moray Cr 56D4
Leach Cr 10B2
Leach L 9A3
Leader L 1D2
Lean-to Cr 45A4
Lean-to Mtn 45A4
Lebahdo 8C2
Leckie B 22B3
Leckie Cr 14B2
Ledge Cr 17B3
Leduc Gla 51D2
Leduc Gla 52A2
Lee Creek 16C2
Lee L 11D2
Leech R 3C3
Legate Cr 45B2
Leguil Cr 84C3
Leguil Cr 85B2
Lehman Cr 24A1
Leigh Cr 38B2
Leighton L 15C3
Leiner R 1B1
Lejac 47B4
LeMare L 11B3
Lemieux Cr 27A4
Lemieux Cr 80A3
Lemon Cr 8C1
Lempriere Cr 27C1
Lens Cr 3B3
Leo Cr 46D1
Leo L 83D3
Leon Cr 14D2
Leonora L 11C1
Lepine Cr 86A4
Leslie Cr 10B3
Lessard Cr 23D1
Lessard Cr 23D1
Lessard L 36D4
Lesser Fish L 26C4
Letain Cr 72D4
Letain Cr 72D4
Leventie Cr 35C2
Leverson L 33D1
Leverson L 44B3
Lew Cr 17C3
Lewis Chan 13A-B4
Lewis Pass 34C3
Lexau Ranch 56D1
Liard Hot Springs 85C4
Liard R 74D1
Liard R 84B3
Liard R 85B4
Liard R 86B3-4
Liard R 87A3-4
Liard River 85C4

Liberty Cr 28A4
Lichen Cr 77B2
Lichen Mtn 16C1
Lick Pk 28B1
Lickskillet Cr 26D1
Lickskillet Cr 27A1
Lightning Cr 6C3
Lightning Cr 38D3
Lightning Pk 8A1
Lignite Cr 30C1
Lignite Cr 32B2
Likely 26A1
Lilie L 24A1
Lillian L 1B2
Lillian L 18C3
● **Lillooet 15A2**
Lillooet Gla 13D2
Lillooet L 14C4
Lillooet R 5D1
Lillooet R 14A3
Lillooet R 14C4
Lily L 36D4
Lily L 37B1
Lily L 65C3
Lily Pad L 26B3
Limestone Pk 72B1
Limonite Cr 45B3
Limpoke Cr 60A1
Lina I 30D3
Lina I 32C4
Lindell Beach 5D3
Lindeman L 80A3
Linden 5C4
Lindmark Cr 17A2
Lindquist Cr 16A1
Lindquist L 35C2
Line Cr 10B1
Line L 81C4
Lingfield Cr 24C4
Link L 7A1
Link L 22C1
Linklater Cr 10A3
Lion Cr 54B3
Lions Bay 5B2
Liri Mtn 75A4
Lister 9B3
Little Beaver Cr 76C4
Little Beaverdam Cr ...66C-D4
Little Big Bar L 15A1
Little Big Bar L 26A4
Little Blue R 83B-C4
Little Bobtail L 38A1
Little Boulder Cr 56C4
Little Bridge Cr 26B4
Little Buffalo R 77D4
Little Cedar R 44D2
Little Charlotte L 23D2
Little Cloudmaker Mtn 64A1
Little Dease Cr 71D3
Little Dease Cr 72A3
Little Dease L 71D3
Little Dease L 72A3
Little Eagle R 72B3
Little Fort 27A4
Little Hay R 77D3
Little Hixon Cr 38C2
Little Horse L 26B3
Little Iskut R 60D2
Little Iskut R 61A2
Little Klappan R 61C-D2
Little L 26A1
Little Momich L 16C1
Little Moyie R 9B3
Little Paw Cr 52D3
Little Prairie Cr 49D3
Little R 39B4
Little Rancheria R 82C-D3
Little Rancheria R 83A3-4
Little River 2A-B1
Little Sand Cr 10A2
Little Sheep Cr 8D3

Little Shuswap L 16B2
Little Slocan Ls 8C2
Little Slocan R 8C2
Little Swift R 39A4
Little Tahltan R 71A-B4
Little Toba R 13C3
Little Wedeene R 44D4
Little White L 15A1
Little White Mtn 7C1
Little Whitesail L 35C2
Littlefield Cr 39B2
Litttle Tuya R 71C3-4
Livingstone Cr 57C3
Liz Cr 61B4
Lizard Cr 10A2
Lizette L 35B4
Lizzie Cr 14C4
Lizzie L 14D4
Lladnar Cr 10A1
Llangorse L 81C4
Llangorse Mtn 81C4
Llewellyn Gla 69C1
Llewellyn Gla 70A1
Llewellyn In 69C1
Llewellyn In 70A1
Llgitiyuz Mtn 36D1
Lloyd George Gla 64A1
Lloyd George Icefield 64A1
Loakin Cr 16B2
Loch Drinkie 16B4
Loch Katrine 7D1
Loch Lomond 15B1
Loch Lomond 26B3
Lockhard Gordon Cr 22D4
Lockhart Cr 9A2
Lodestone Mtn 6C2
Lodge Mtn 9C3
Lodgepole Cr 10A3
Lodi L 38D2
Log Cr 15A4
Logan Cr 3A3
○ **Logan Lake 15C3**
Logjam Cr 82A3
Lois L 2C1
Lois R 2C1
Loki Cr 9A1
Lombard Pk 64B1
Lone Butte 26B4
Lone Cabin Cr 14D1
Lone Cabin Cr 25D4
Lone Goat Cr 14B2
Lone Mtn 6C3
Lone Pk 9D2
Lone Prairie 57B4
Lone Valley Cr 14C1
Lonesome L 23D2
Lonesome Mtn 62A-B4
Long Beach 1D3
Long Cr 39C4
Long Harbour 5A4
Long I 4D1
Long I 6A2
Long In 30D3
Long In 32C4
Long John Cr 38B4
Long L 11D1
Long L 24A2
Long L 52B2
Long Mountain Cr 73D1
Long Mountain Cr 74B1
Long Mountain L 73D1
Long Mountain L 74B1
Long Mountain L 84D4
Long Mountain L 85B4
Long Mtn 74B1
Longbeach 8D2
Longbow L 26C4
Longview 19C3
Longworth 39B1
Lookout Mtn 7A2
Lookout Pk 4D1
Lookout Pk 6A2

127

Loomis 7B4
Loomis L 24D1
Loomis L 25A1
Loon Cr 15B1
Loon L 10A3
Loon L 15B1
Loon Lake **15B1**
Looncry L 73A1
Loop Br 17C1
Loos **39C2**
Loose L 12B2
Lopez **4A3**
Loranger Cr 65B3
Lord Mayor Pk 75B4
Lord R 14A2
Lorna L 14B1
Lorne Cr 45A2
Lorne L 6D2
Loss Cr 3B3
Lossy Cr 16D3
Lost Cabin Cr 55D2
Lost Cabin Cr 56A2
Lost Cr 8D3
Lost Cr 18C2
Lost Dog Cr 9C1
Lost Mtn 8D3
Lost Shoe Cr 1D3
Lost Valley Cr 14D3
Lostway Cr 39B4
Lottie L 39A3
Loudon Chan 1D4
Loughborough In..........12D3
Louis Cr 16A1
Louis Creek **16A1**
Louis L 16A2
Louis Lee Cr 28A3
Louise I 31A4
Louise Nars 31A4
Loup Cr 2C4
Loup Cr 3B3
Louscoone In 20B-C2
Lovola Cr 9B2
Low Fog Cr 78D3
Lowe Cr 19A4
Lowe L 34C3
Lower Arrow L 8B2
Lower Belle L 62D2
Lower Belle L 63A2
Lower Blue L 49C3
Lower Elk L 19A3
Lower L 26B2
Lower Nicola **15C4**
Lower Post **84A3**
Lowrie B 11A2
Lowry L 2A2
Lowry L 80B4
Lucas L 37A2
Luck Mtn 24C1
Ludwig Cr 63B1
Ludwig Cr 74B4
Lue Cr 74C2
Luke Cr 9C1
Lull Cr 12C2
Lulu I 4A1
Lulu I 5B3
Lumby **16D4**
Lumby Junction..........**16C4**
Lumme L 32D2
Lumme L 43A4
Lummi **5C4**
Lunar Cr 62C1
Lunch L 24C3
Lund **13B4**
Lundbreck **10C2**
Luno Cr 45C1
Lupin Ls 15D1
Lupin Ls 26D4
Lupin Ridge 64A1
Lussier Cr 9D1
Lussier R 18D4
Lutz Cr 83D3
Luxana B 20C2

Luxor Cr 18C2
Lyell Cr 28D3
Lyell I 20B1
Lyell I 31A4
Lyell Icefield 28D3
Lymburn **50B1**
Lymburn **52B4**
Lynch Cr 8A3
Lyne Cr 25D2
Lynx Cr 26D1
Lynx Cr 57A2
Lynx Mtn 40D3
Lyon Cr 45D2
Lyon Cr 46A2
Lys Cr 27B1
● **Lytton** **15A4**

M

Mab L 15D4
Mabel L 16D3
Mabel Lake **16D4**
Macaulay Cr 18C2
MacDonald Cr 75A2
MacDonald L 47A1
Machete Cr 26D4
Machete L 26D4
Machmell R 23B4
Macjack R 11B3
Mackay R 26D1
● **Mackenzie** **48B1**
Mackenzie **56B4**
Mackenzie Cr 17C3
Mackenzie Cr 39C1
Mackenzie L 12B2
Mackenzie Sd 12A2
Mackie Cr 56D2
Mackin Cr 25C2
Macktush Cr 2B3
Macleod Cr 39C2
Mad R 27B2
Madden Cr 17D3
Madden L 25C2
Madeira Park **2D2**
Madeline L 33D2
Madeline L 34B1
Madely Cr 52D2
Maeford L 39C4
Magar Cr 44D4
Maggie L 1D4
Magna Bay **16C2**
Mahatta Cr 11B3
Mahatta River............**11B-C3**
Mahood Falls **26D3**
Mahood L 26D3
Mahood L 27B3
Mahood R 27A3
Maiden Cr 15A2
Main L 13A4
Mainguy L 24D4
Maitland I 34D1
Majerus Falls 27A2
Major Hart R 73A-B2
Majuba L 36D3
Maka Cr 6C1
Makinson **17B4**
Malachite Cr 18A1
Malakwa **16D2**
Malaput L 36D4
Malaspina Pen 2B1
Malaspina Pen 13B4
Malaspina Pk 1B1
Malaspina Str 2C1-2
Malcolm I 11D3
Malkope In 11C4
Mallandaine Cr 9B2
Malloch Cr 62B4
Malloch Pk 62B4
Malloy Cr 18A2
Mamalilaculla............**12B3**
Mamin R 30D2

Mamin R 32B-C3
Mamit L 15C3
Mamit L 15C3
Mamquam L 5B1
Mamquam Mtn 5C1
Mamquam R 5B1
Manatee Cr 13D3
Mann Cr 26D3
Mann Cr 27A4
Manning Park **6D3**
Mansfield Cr 71C4
Manson Creek............**55B3-4**
Manson Ls 55C4
Manson Pass 2B1
Manson R 55B-C4
Mansons Landing **13A4**
Manteau Cr 27C1
Mantle Gla 13B1
Many Bear Cr 45B3
Mapes **37C-D1**
Maple Bay **5A4**
Maple Falls **5D4**
● **Maple Ridge** **5C3**
Maquilla Cr 12B4
Mara **16D2**
Mara Cr 16D2
Mara L 16D2
Marble Dome 81C3
Marble I 30C3
Marble I 32B4
Marble R 11C3
Marcus Pass 33C1
Marcus Pass 43D4
Marcus Pass 44A4
Margaret L 1D2
Margaret L 47D4
Margaret L 48A4
Margie L 17B3
Margison Cr 75C3
Marguerite **25D1**
Maria Cr 71D1
Maria Cr 72A-B1
Maria L 71D1
Maria L 72B1
Marian L 30C1
Marian L 32B2
Marion L 11D2
Marion L 12A2
Marion L 65B3
Mark Cr 9C1
Marietta **5C4**
Marina I 13A4
Marion L 11D2
Marl Cr 28D4
Marl L 10B3
Marmot Cr 38A4
Marmot Mtn 6B3
Marmot R 52B3
Maroon Cr 44D2
Maroon Mtn 45A2
Marron Valley **7B2**
Mars Cr 17A1
Mars Cr 28A4
Mars I 12A2
Marsh Adams Cr 17D2
Marsh Cr 8C3
Marsh Lake **80B1**
Marshall Cr 14C2
Marten Cr 10B2
Marten Cr 39C4
Martin Cr 29A4
Martin Cr 57A4
Martin Cr 66A2
Martin L 24B3
Marvin Cr 38C3
Mary Cr 38D3
Marysville **9C2**
Mason Cr 65C3
Mason L 65C2
Masset **30D1**

Masset **32C2**
Masset **42D4**
Masset In 30D1
Masset In 32C3
Masset Sd 30D1
Masset Sd 32C2
Massive **18C1**
Mat Cr 17D4
Matchlee B 1C2
Matchlee Mtn 1C2
Matetlo Cr 54D2
Mather Cr 9C1
Mathers Cr 31A3
Mathers Cr 31A4
Mathers L 31A4
Mathieson Chan 22A-B1
Mathieson Chan 35B4
Matilpi **12C3**
Matsatu Cr 71A3
Matsiu Cr 12C2
Matsqui **5D3**
Matterhorn Pk 23B2
Matthew Cr 9C1
Matthew R 39C4
Matulka Cr 73D2
Matulka Cr 74A2
Matzentzel Mtn 46C2-3
Maud Cr 39A4
Maud L 39A4
Maude I 30D3
Maude I 32C4
Maunsell B 12A1
Maurelle I 13A4
Maurice Cr 57A2-3
Maurier Cr 8D1
Maury L 26D3
Maury L 27A3
Maxan Cr 46C3-4
Maxan L 46C4
Maxhamish L 86D3
Maxhamish L 87B3
Maxwell Cr 24D1
May L 13A4
Mayer L 30D1
Mayer L 32C3
Mayer R 31A2
Mayer R 32C3
Mayfield L 84A3
Mayne **5B4**
Mayne I 3D2
Mayne I 5B4
Mayo Cr 44D2
Mayson L 15D1
Maze L 26A3
McAllister Cr 56C3
McArthur Cr 18B1
● **McBride** **40A3**
McBride L 1D2
McBride L 45C4
McBride R 61C1
McBride R 72C4
McCannel L 13D4
McCauley I 31D1
McCauley I 33C3
McCauley I 34A1-2
McClair Cr 62C2
McClair Cr 63A2
McClinchy Cr 24A2
McClinchy L 23D2
McClinton B 30C1
McClinton B 32B3
McColloch **7C1**
McConachie Cr 76C2
McConachie Pk 62B3-4
McConnell Cr 63B4
McConnell Gla 64A1
McConnell L 15D3
McConnell Ls 63B4
McConnell Pass 63B-C2
McCook R 63C1
McCool Cr 10A2
McCreight L 12D4

McCrum 49A1
McCullagh Cr 49C4
McCully Cr 53B4
McCurdy Cr 1B1
McCusker Cr..................64C3-4
McDame **72C1**
McDame Cr 72C1
McDermid Cr 10A2
McDermott Cr 25A3
McDonald L 80D3
McDonald L 81A3
McDonell L 45C2
McDougal Cr 17C1
McDougall Falls 27A2
McDougall L 27B2
McDougall R 48A-B2
McEvoy Cr 10B2
McEwan L 48C3
McEwen Cr 25C3
McFarland Cr 38A4
McFarlane Cr 8A1
McGavin Cr 70B2
McGillivray **10B2**
McGillivray Cr 14C3
McGillivray Cr 16B2
McGillivray L 16B2
McGraw Pk 63D3
McGregor **49A4**
McGregor R 39C-D1
McGregor R 49A-B4
McGregor R 49C4
McIntire Cr 48B1
McIntosh Cr 39D3
McIntosh Ls 26B2
McIntyre B 32C2
McIntyre B 43A4
McKale R 39D2
Mckale R 40A2
McKay Cr 2C4
McKay Cr 3B2
McKay Cr 15A2
McKay Cr 45A4
McKay Reach 34D3
McKean Ls 8B1
McKearney Ranch **56C-D1**
McKee Cr 80D4
McKee Cr 81A-B4
McKelvey L 47A2
McKelvie Cr 1B1
McKendrick Cr 46A-B2
McKian Cr 17D4
McKinley Cr 81B4
McKinley L 26C2
McKinney Cr 7C3
McKinnon Lagoon 11D1
McKnab L 47B3
McKusky Cr 26C2
McLean Ranch **56D1**
McLeary L 39C3
McLeese Lake **25D1**
McLennan R 40C4
McLeod L 15D3
McLeod L 48B2
McLeod Lake **48B2**
McLeod R 48B2
McLure **16A1**
McMicking I 33C2
McMicking I 43D4
McMicking I 44A4
McMillan Cr 38C1
McMurdo **18A1**
McMurdo I 17D1
McMurray **4C4**
McNab Cr 5A2
McNab Creek **5A2**
McNab L 84A3
McNair Cr 5A2
McNaughton Cr 82B3
McNaughton Group 22A3
McNeil Cr 9C2
McNeil L 26D2
McNeil R 33D1

128

McNeil R 44B4
McNomee Cr 16D1
McNomee Cr 27D4
McNulty Cr 7A2
McParlon Cr 14B2
McPhail Cr 6C1
McPherson L 22B1
McPherson L 35B4
McQuarrie L 46B3
McTavish L 84A3
McWater L 57D4
McWater L 58A4
Meachen 9B2
Meachen Cr 9B2
Meade Cr 2C4
Meade Cr 3B2
Meadow Cr 15C3
Meadow Cr 17D4
Meadow Cr 27C4
Meadow Creek 18A4
Meadow L 15A1
Meadow L 26A4
Meadows 8C3
Meager Cr 14A3
Meares I 1C3
Meason Cr 25D3
Medana Cr 65D2
Medicine Cr 15B2
Meehaz Mtn 71B1
Meek L 72C2
Meers Cr 12C1
Megatushon Cr 71B3
Megin R 1C2
Mehatl Cr 14D4
Meikle Cr 49B1
Melanistic Pk 62C4
Melbern Gla 67C1
Melbern Gla 68A1
Melbern Gla 78D4
Meldrum Cr 25C2
Meldrum Creek 25D2
Meldrum L 25C2
Mellersh Cr 13A2
Mellin Cr 16A4
Mellin L 16A4
Melville I 33B1
Melville L 43C3
Memekay R 12C4
Memory L 1D2
Menard Cr 63B4
Menhinick Cr 17C2
Mercer L 32A3
Mercers Pk 75B4
Merchant Taylors Pks ..75B4
Mereworth Sd 11C-D1
● **Merritt 15C4**
Merston Cr 38B4
Merton Cr 48B3
Merton L 48B3
Merville 2A1
Merzer L 30C2
Mesachie Lake 2C4
Mesilinka R 54C1
Mesilinka R 55A1
Mess Cr 60B1
Mess Cr 60C2
Mess L 60C2
Meszah Pk 71B3
Metah Mtn 71B1
Metchosin 3D4
Metlahdoa Cr 77B2
Metlakatla 33C1
Metlakatla 43A-B1
Metlakatla 44D3
Metlatulin Mtn 70C3
Metsantan L 62C2
Metsantan Pass 62C2
Meyers Pass 22A1
Meziadin Junction 52C2
Meziadin L 52C2
Mica Cr 28A2
Mica Pk 55B1

Michel 10B1
Michel Cr 10B2
Michel Cr 36C2
Michel L 36B2
Michel Pk 36B2
Michelle Cr 37D4
Michelle Cr 38A4
Midas Cr 62D2
Midas Cr 63A2
Midas L 62D2
Middle Cr 71B4
Middle Fork Cr 65C2
Middle Kootenay Pass ..10C3
Middle L 24A-B3
Middle Memekay R 12C4
Middle R 47A2
Middle River 47A2
Midge Cr 9A2
Midsummer I 12A-B3
Miduski Cr 76B2
Midway 7D3
Midwinter Cr 88C3
Midwinter L 88C3
Miette Hotsprings 41B3
Milbanke Sd 21D1
Milburn L 38C3
Milburn Pk 48D1
Miledge Cr 27C1
Miles Cr 25A1
Milk Cr 45C3
Milk R 39C2-3
Mill Bay 5A4
Mill Bay 44B1-2
Mill Cr 5B1
Mill Cr 45B1
Millar Chan 1C2
Millarville 19C2
Miller Cr 14B3
Miller L 16B3
Millet Cr 65B3
Milligan Cr 66C4
Milliken Cr 64D1
Milliken Cr 65B1
Milnes Landing 3C4
Milo Cr 76B3
Milo L 76B3
Milton R 22C3
Mimenuh Mtn 15B4
Minaker R 65B-C2
Minaret Cr 53C1
Minaty Bay 5B2
Mincho L 71C4
Miner L 24A3
Mineral Cr 18B3
Miners Cr 45B3-4
Minerva L 33C1
Minerva L 44B4
Minette B 35A1
Minette B 45A4
Ministik Cr 49D1
Ministik Cr 50A1
Mink Cr 12D2
Mink Cr 62A2
Mink I 13B4
Mink L 36B3
Minnie L 6D1
Minnie L 15D4
Minstrel Island 12B3
Minton Cr 25B3
Miocene 26A2
Mirror Lake 9A1
Mischinsinlika Cr 48C1
Misinchinka R 48C1
Misko Cr 18B1
Missezula L 6D1
Missezula Mtn 6D1
Missinka R 49A3
● **Mission 5D3**
Mission Cr 7C1
Mission Cr 9B4
Mission Cr 16D4
Mission L 7D1

Mission L 16D4
Missioner Cr 25D2
Missusjay Cr 60A2
Mistahae Cr 65C2-3
Mistanusk Cr 50A-B3
Mit L 38C3
Mitchell B 12A3
Mitchell Bay 12A3
Mitchell L 39C4
Mitchell R 18D2
Mitchell R 39C4
Mitla Cr 1C2
Mitlenatch I 2A1
Mitre Cr 17C1
Mitre Mtn 52B2
Mizzen Mtn 37A4
Moakwa Cr 12C4
Moat L 1D1
Mobbs Cr 17D3
Moberly L 57A3
Moberly Lake 57A3
Moberly R 56D3
Moberly R 57B2
Moccasin Cr 54C2
Moesmoos Cr 55B4
Moffat Cr 16C3
Moffat Cr 26B2
Moffatt L 84B3
Moh Cr 13B3
Moha 14D2
Mohawk Cr 17C2
Mohun L 12D4
Moira L 27A3
Moketas I 11D4
Molen Cr 27A2
Mollice L 36D1
Mollimarn L 15D1
Molson Cr 28A2
Molybdenite Cr 26C2
Momich L 16C1
Momich L 27C4
Momich R 16C1
Momich R 27C4
Monarch Mtn 23C3
Monashee Cr 17A4
Monashee Pass 17A4
Monckton In 34B3
Monias L 57B2
Monitor Cr 17D4
Monkman Cr 49B2-3
Monkman L 49B3
Monkman Pass 49B3
Monkton Cr 39B3
Monmouth Mtn 13D1
Monroe L 9C2
Mons Cr 28D3
Mons L 25B3
Montague Chan 5B2
Montague Cr 12B-C4
Montana L 26D4
Monte Cr 16B3
Monte Creek 16A-B3
Monte L 16B3
Monte Lake 16B3
Monticola L 26D4
Montney 57C1
Montrose 8C3
Montrose Cr 13C3
Moodie Cr 73C2
Moody Cr 8A3
Moon L 80B3
Moonbeam Cr 27D1
Moonlight Cr 58B2
Moonlit Cr 53B4
Moore B 12B2
Moore Chan 30D4
Moore Cr 15D4
Moore Is 21C1
Moore Is 34C4
Moore L 34C3
Moore Pk 15A2

Moose Cr 18B1
Moose Cr 61C1
Moose Cr 72C4
Moose Cr 81B3
Moose Heights 38C3
Moose L 26D3
Moose L 40D4
Moose L 49B1
Moose L 74D2-3
Moose Ls 72B3
Moose Lick Cr 65C3
Moose R 40D3
Moosecall L 56D3
Moosehorn Cr 62C2
Moosehorn Cr 63A2
Moosehorn L 62C2
Moosehorn L 63A2
Moosevale Cr 63B4
Mooto L 22B1
Mooto L 35B4
Mooyah B 1B2
Mooyah R 1B2
Morchuea Cr 60D1
Morchuea Cr 61A-B1
Morchuea L 61B1
Morchuea L 72A-B4
More Cr 60C3
More Cr 61A3
Moresby Camp 30D3
Moresby I 3D3
Moresby I 5B4
Moresby I 20B1-2
Moresby I 30D4
Morfee Ls 48B1
Morfee Ls 56B4
Morice L 35C1
Morice L 45C4
Morice R 45D4
Morice R 46A4
Moricetown 45C1
Morkill R 39D1
Morkill R 40A1
Morley 19B1
Morrell Cr 8A3
Morrisey L 16B2
Morrison L 46B1
Morrissey Cr 10A2
Morte L 13A4
Morte L 13A4
Moses In 22C3
Moses L 38A3
Moskow Cr 18D4
Mosley Cr 13B1
Mosley Cr 24A4
Mosque Mtn 53C1
Mosque R 53C1
Mosquito L 30D3
Moss Cr 77A-B2
Moss Mtn 62A-B4
Mossvale L 48B3
Motase L 53D2
Motase L 54A2
Motase Pk 53D2
Motase Pk 54A2
Mouat B 2B-C2
Moul Cr 27B3
Mould Cr 85C4
Moule Cr 85D4
Mount Cr 38C4
Mount Currie 14C4
Mount Robson 40C3
Mountain Cr 28C4
Mountain Cr 56C-D4
Mountain Point 43A-B1
Mountain Portage
  Rapids 84C-D4
Mountain Portage
  Rapids 85A4
Mouse Cr 44B3
Mouse Mtn 38D3
Mow Cr 15D1
Mowchilla L 60D2

Mowchilla L 61A2
Mowdade L 60D2
Mowdade L 61A2
Mowhokam Cr 15B4
Mowich L 15C1
Moxley Cr 39A1
Moyeha R 1C2
Moyez Cr 62C2
Moyie 9C3
Moyie L 9C3
Moyie R 9C2
Moyie R 9C3
Moyie Springs 9B4
Mt Hazel 82A3
Mt McCallum 69D1
Mt. Abbi 49A2
Mt. Abbot 17D3
Mt. Abel 18B4
Mt. Abruzzi 19A3
Mt. Adrian 1D1
Mt. Aida 75B4
Mt. Aitken 48D1
Mt. Albert Dease 62C1
Mt. Alcock 63D2
Mt. Alex Graham 25B2
Mt. Alexander 47B1
Mt. Alger 61B4
Mt. Anderson 52B1
Mt. Armour 78B3
Mt. Armstrong 19B3
Mt. Armstrong 80B3
Mt. Arrowsmith 2B3
Mt. Arrowsmith 3A1
Mt. Arthur Meighen 40C4
Mt. Arthurs 8A1
Mt. Ashmun 79C3-4
Mt. Assiniboine 18D2
Mt. Averil 48D3
Mt. Aylesworth 78A-B3
Mt. Bagot 69A1
Mt. Bagot 80A4
Mt. Baker 6A4
Mt. Baker 9D2
Mt. Baldy Hughes 38B2
Mt. Balourdet 63C2
Mt. Barham 80D3
Mt. Barham 81B3
Mt. Barker 39B4
Mt. Barnard 67D1
Mt. Barnard 68A1
Mt. Barr 56C2
Mt. Barrington 60A1
Mt. Barton 49B3
Mt. Basnet 63C2
Mt. Bates 54C3
Mt. Bayard 51D2
Mt. Bayard 52A2
Mt. Beals 47B3
Mt. Beauregard 48D3
Mt. Becker 49C3
Mt. Bedaux 64A-B1
Mt. Beelzebub 23C3
Mt. Begbie 17A2
Mt. Begbie 30C2
Mt. Beirnes 62A4
Mt. Bell 23D4
Mt. Bell-Irving 52C2
Mt. Benedict 12B1
Mt. Bennett 49C1
Mt. Bennett 63D2
Mt. Benson 2C3
Mt. Benson 3B1
Mt. Berendon 51D2
Mt. Berendon 52A2
Mt. Berkeley 12D3
Mt. Bertha 64D3
Mt. Bertha 65A3
Mt. Bess 40B-C2
Mt. Bigfoot 76C4
Mt. Bigger 79B4
Mt. Bisson 55D4
Mt. Blaine 51D2

Mt. Blair 73B4	Mt. Crocker.................48D2	Mt. Garbitt 56C4	Mt. Hooker....................2C3	Mt. Leonard.................81B3
Mt. Blake 12D2	Mt. Crompton.............75B4	Mt. Gardiner 13A3	Mt. Hooker....................3B2	Mt. Leslie 16B2
Mt. Blanchard 64A3	Mt. Cronin.................45D2	Mt. Garibaldi 5B1	Mt. Hooker....................9A2	Mt. Lester Jones 70B2
Mt. Blanchet 46C-D1	Mt. Cronin.................46A2	Mt. Garland 45A2	Mt. Hooper...................2B3	Mt. Lewis Cass 51C1
Mt. Blane 35C3	Mt. Crosby.................64A1	Mt. Geddes 23D4	Mt. Hooper...................3A2	Mt. Light 44D4
Mt. Blanshard 4B1	Mt. Crysdale 56A3	Mt. Geodfrey 62B4	Mt. Horetzky............53D3-4	Mt. Lodge 67C1
Mt. Blanshard 5C2	Mt. Cummings 28A2	Mt. George 38D2	Mt. Horetzky............54A3-4	Mt. Loki 9A1
Mt. Bleasdell 19A3	Mt. Cushing 63A-B2	Mt. Germansen 55A-B4	Mt. Hosmer 10A2	Mt. Lolo 16A2
Mt. Blenheim 2A4	Mt. D'Arcy 22B2	Mt. Geryon 23C3	Mt. Hoy 62C4	Mt. Longstaff...........40C3
Mt. Bodine 54C4	Mt. Daer 18C2	Mt. Gething 56D2	Mt. Hulcross 56D3	Mt. Lorenz 47A4
Mt. Bolom 35C2	Mt. Dalgleish 13D2	Mt. Gil 34C3	Mt. Huntingdon.........44B1	Mt. Loring 45C4
Mt. Bonney 17C1	Mt. Dalton 72C2	Mt. Gilbert 13C2	Mt. Irish 63C2	Mt. Lowe 12D1
Mt. Boofus 81B3	Mt. Davidson 37A3	Mt. Gilliland 48D1	Mt. Irma 35C2	Mt. Ludington 56B1
Mt. Bower 63C2	Mt. Davies 45B4	Mt. Gilliland 56D4	Mt. Irvine 9A1	Mt. Lyall 19B4
Mt. Bowman 15A1	Mt. Dawson 17C1	Mt. Gladstone 8B3	Mt. Irving 34D4	Mt. Lyell 28D3
Mt. Bracey 48D2	Mt. DeCosmos 2C3	Mt. Gladstone 52B2	Mt. Isola 64A4	Mt. Mabel 17A2
Mt. Brandes.............11B3	Mt. DeCosmos 3B1	Mt. Glenora 60B1	Mt. Jackson 62A-B4	Mt. Machray 40D3
Mt. Breakenridge 6A1	Mt. Del 64A3	Mt. Goddard 13D1	Mt. Jacobsen 23B-C2	Mt. Mackenzie 23C1
Mt. Brent 7B2	Mt. Dent 37C4	Mt. Gomm 75B4	Mt. James Turner 14C4	Mt. Mackenzie King ..40B4
Mt. Brenton 2D4	Mt. Denver 8A1	Mt. Goodsir 18B1	Mt. Jancowski 52B1	Mt. Mackie 8B3
Mt. Brenton 3C2	Mt. Derby 12C3	Mt. Gordon 29A4	Mt. Jane 22A1	Mt. Mackinnon 47D2
Mt. Brew 15A3	Mt. Dewdney 6C3	Mt. Gordon 60B1	Mt. Jardine 17D4	Mt. Mackinnon 48A2
Mt. Brewer...............18B3	Mt. Dick 51B1	Mt. Gordon 62B4	Mt. Jefferson Coolidge .51D2	Mt. Madely 52D2
Mt. Brewster............56B2	Mt. Dickie 52B3	Mt. Gordonia 62D2	Mt. Jefferson Coolidge .52A2	Mt. Madge 52A1
Mt. Brock 61C1	Mt. Dimsdale 39D1	Mt. Gordonia 63A2	Mt. Jette 78A3	Mt. Mansfield 79B3
Mt. Brown 28A1	Mt. Dimsdale 49D4	Mt. Gorman 50B4	Mt. Jobe 40B2	Mt. Manville 69D2
Mt. Brundage 70B4	Mt. Disraeli 52B2	Mt. Gottfriedsen 7B1	Mt. Joffre 19A3	Mt. Manville 70A-B2
Mt. Buchanan 40A1	Mt. Dobose 35B2	Mt. Grahame 55B1	Mt. John Jay 51D2	Mt. Mara 16D2
Mt. Bud 47B4	Mt. Donnaker 60A2	Mt. Graves 62D2	Mt. John Jay 52A2	Mt. Marconi 19A3
Mt. Bulman 16A3	Mt. Dopp 64D2	Mt. Graves 63A2	Mt. Johnny 51C1	Mt. Marion 17D4
Mt. Burden 56A2	Mt. Downton 24B1	Mt. Greene 56B2	Mt. Johnson 52B2	Mt. Mark 74C4
Mt. Burkett 59D3	Mt. Downton 37B4	Mt. Greer 37B1	Mt. Johnston 21D1	Mt. Marvin 23C2
Mt. Burnett 9A3	Mt. Drew 2D1	Mt. Grenville 13B2	Mt. Jones 13A3	Mt. Mary Henry 75B3
Mt. Buxton 22B4	Mt. Drewry 9A1	Mt. Griffin 17A2	Mt. Jorgensen 62D4	Mt. Mathison 12B2
Mt. Byng 11C3	Mt. Dudzic 49A2	Mt. Grohman 8D2	Mt. Jorgensen 63A4	Mt. McAllister 56C3
Mt. Cain 12B4	Mt. Duff 78B3	Mt. Guanton 52B3	Mt. Josefina 63C1	Mt. McArthur 29A4
Mt. Callaghan 14A4	Mt. Dunn 51C1	Mt. Guichon 15D3	Mt. Joseph 9D2	Mt. McCallum 70A1
Mt. Cambridge 13D4	Mt. Dyer 12D2	Mt. Gunanoot 61D3	Mt. Josephine 71C1	Mt. McClennan 27B4
Mt. Cameron 80C4	Mt. Earle 84B3	Mt. Gunnel 76A2	Mt. Josephine 72A1	Mt. McClure 14A1
Mt. Cameron 81A4	Mt. Edziza 60C1	Mt. Gunnell 75C2	Mt. Judge Howay 4C1	Mt. McCook 63C1
Mt. Canning 69B1	Mt. Elise 8D2	Mt. Guyet 39B3	Mt. Judge Howay 5D2	Mt. McCrae 63D2
Mt. Cardin 34D3	Mt. Elphinstone 3B1	Mt. Halkett 85C4	Mt. Kappan 23D1-2	Mt. McCullagh 49C4
Mt. Carl 31A4	Mt. Elphinstone 5A2	Mt. Halvorson 39D3	Mt. Kaslo 9A1	Mt. McCusker 64C3
Mt. Carlyle 8D1	Mt. Elsie 54C-D1	Mt. Hamill 18A4	Mt. Katharine 62D2	Mt. McCusker 65A3
Mt. Carnarvon 29A4	Mt. Elwin 33C2	Mt. Hamilton 15D4	Mt. Katharine 63B2	Mt. McDame 72B1
Mt. Caro Marion 22C1	Mt. Elwin 34B1	Mt. Hammell 39C2	Mt. Kathleen 7A1	Mt. McDame 83B4
Mt. Carruthers 54B2	Mt. Espinosa 1A1	Mt. Haney 69D2	Mt. Kelly 8C3	Mt. McDonnell 79B4
Mt. Carter 80D3	Mt. Evans 9B2	Mt. Haney 70A2	Mt. Kennedy 12D2	Mt. McEvoy 62A4
Mt. Carter 81A3	Mt. Everard 12D1	Mt. Hanington 50A4	Mt. Kenney 44D3	Mt. McGavin 71D1
Mt. Cartier 17B2	Mt. Evindsen 52B4	Mt. Hannah 2A3	Mt. Kenny 64D4	Mt. McGavin 72A1
Mt. Casey 9D3	Mt. Fagervik 6B2	Mt. Hansen 11B3	Mt. Kenny 65A4	Mt. McGregor 9A2
Mt. Chapleau 33C2	Mt. Faith 8A2	Mt. Harkin 18C2	Mt. Keyes 22B1	Mt. McGuire 4D2
Mt. Chapleau 34B1	Mt. Farnham 18B3	Mt. Harris 68B1	Mt. Kimmel 27C1	Mt. McGuire 6A3
Mt. Chapleau 44B4	Mt. Farrow 13C1	Mt. Haskin 72C1	Mt. Kimmel 40C4	Mt. McInnes 15C4
Mt. Chapman 28A3	Mt. Fawsett 51B1	Mt. Haskin 83C4	Mt. King Albert 18D2	Mt. McKay 9B2
Mt. Chapperon 16B4	Mt. Femont Morse.......69D3	Mt. Hawkins 12C3	Mt. King Edward 28C2	Mt. McLearn 74D1
Mt. Charlie Cole 82A4	Mt. Ferguson 55A1	Mt. Haworth 63D2	Mt. King George 18D3	Mt. McLeod 14A1
Mt. Cheadle 27D1	Mt. Fergusson 14C2	Mt. Hay 67C1	Mt. Kinney 48D1	Mt. McLeod 71D3
Mt. Chief Davie 63D2	Mt. Fernie 10A2	Mt. Headman 70B2	Mt. Kitchener 59D1	Mt. McLeod 72A-B3
Mt. Churchill 2D1	Mt. Ferris 54C2	Mt. Hedrick 49B-C4	Mt. Klappan 61D3	Mt. McMaster 70B1
Mt. Churchill 13D4	Mt. Ferroux 7C2	Mt. Heger 26D3	Mt. Knudsen 49C3-4	Mt. McMaster 81B4
Mt. Circe 64C2	Mt. Filberg 1D1	Mt. Heimdal 8C1	Mt. Kobau 7B3	Mt. McNamara 62C1-2
Mt. Clive 80B3	Mt. Filer 13C2	Mt. Heinze 8C3	Mt. Kruger 39B2-3	Mt. McNamara 63A1-2
Mt. Cochrane 8A2	Mt. Findlay 18B4	Mt. Helen 64C3	Mt. Lady Laurier 56A1	Mt. McNeil 43D3
Mt. Colley 46C4	Mt. Finlay 63C2	Mt. Helen 65A3	Mt. Lady Laurier 64D4	Mt. McNeil 44A3
Mt. Colonel Foster 1C1	Mt. Fisher 9D2	Mt. Helveker 60B2	Mt. Lady Laurier 65A4	Mt. McQuillan 2B3
Mt. Columbia 28C2	Mt. Forde 67C1	Mt. Henderson 45B4	Mt. Laidlaw 62B4	Mt. McQuillan 3A2
Mt. Connaught 16C3	Mt. Forde 68A1	Mt. Hendrix 26D2	Mt. Lang 12D2	Mt. Meehaus 71C4
Mt. Connell 9D3	Mt. Forrest 62D4	Mt. Henning 6C2	Mt. Lanning 80B3	Mt. Meehaus 72A4
Mt. Conover 60A2	Mt. Forrest 63B4	Mt. Henri 55B1	Mt. Lasca 8D2	Mt. Melvin 63C4
Mt. Cooper 17D4	Mt. Forsyth 19A4	Mt. Henry 12D2	Mt. Laurier 64D4	Mt. Merrick 49A1
Mt. Cornelia 24A4	Mt. Foster 79D3	Mt. Hentig 75B4	Mt. Laurier 65B4	Mt. Middleton 51D2
Mt. Cote 51A1	Mt. Fosthall 17A3	Mt. Herbert 78B3	Mt. Laussedat 28D4	Mt. Midgeley 9A3
Mt. Coulahan 71C-D2	Mt. Fougner 23A2	Mt. Hewett 62C3	Mt. Laussedat 29A4	Mt. Milburn 38C3
Mt. Coulahan 72A2	Mt. Frank Roy 56D3	Mt. Hickman 60B3	Mt. Lavoie 63D2	Mt. Milligan 47C1
Mt. Coutlee 33C2	Mt. Fraser 28A1	Mt. Hickson 24A4	Mt. Lawson 80B4	Mt. Milton 27C1
Mt. Coutlee 34B1	Mt. Fraser 41A4	Mt. Hills 12D2	Mt. Lay 54D1	Mt. Minto 80C3
Mt. Coutlee 44B4	Mt. Frederic 12C2	Mt. Hoadley 44D1	Mt. Le Hudette 56D4	Mt. Minto 81A3
Mt. Crawford 9A1	Mt. Fremont Morse......70B3	Mt. Hobson 37B1	Mt. Learmonth 21D1	Mt. Mitchell 39C4
Mt. Creswell 23B1	Mt. Freshfield 28D3	Mt. Hogue 27B1	Mt. Learmonth 34D4	Mt. Mobley 16C1
Mt. Cridge 12D2	Mt. Freshfield 29A3	Mt. Holben 64A1	Mt. Lempriere 27D1	Mt. Moloch 17B1
Mt. Crocker..............48D2	Mt. Gallatin 60A4	Mt. Holmes 40B-C2	Mt. Leonard 80D3	Mt. Moloch 28B4

Mt. Monckton....................84A3
Mt. Monkley 44B2
Mt. Moodie 55C2
Mt. Moore 7D1
Mt. Moriarty 2C3
Mt. Moriarty 3A1
Mt. Morice 46A4
Mt. Morris 47C3
Mt. Morrison 33C-D1
Mt. Morrison 44B4
Mt. Morse 33C1
Mt. Morse 43D3
Mt. Morse 44A3
Mt. Mortella 35B1
Mt. Mowat 40D4
Mt. Muir 3C3
Mt. Mummery 29A4
Mt. Munday 13A1
Mt. Munday 24A4
Mt. Murray 17C3
Mt. Murray 39B3
Mt. Musclow 35D3
Mt. Myhon 49B2
Mt. Nagle 28A2
Mt. Nation 47A1
Mt. Neal 14C4
Mt. Needham 30D3
Mt. Needham 32C4
Mt. Nelson 18B3
Mt. Nemaia 24C4
Mt. Neptune 8B3
Mt. Nesselrode 69C2
Mt. New 74B4
Mt. Nicola 15D4
Mt. Niord 8C1
Mt. Niord 17C4
Mt. Nivelle 19A3
Mt. O'Keefe 70B1
Mt. O'Leary 8A1
Mt. Oakes 62B3
Mt. Oates 28B1
Mt. Odin 17B3
Mt. Ogden 54D3
Mt. Ogden 69D3
Mt. Ogden 70B3
Mt. Ogilvie 69C2
Mt. Olson 9C3
Mt. Osmington 12D3
Mt. Outram 6B3
Mt. Ovington 49D4
Mt. Ozzard 1D4
Mt. Palmer 24C-D2
Mt. Palsson 49A1
Mt. Pambrun 18B4
Mt. Parry 34D4
Mt. Parton 79B3
Mt. Patcha 53D2
Mt. Patcha 54A2
Mt. Patterson 29A3
Mt. Patterson 80B3
Mt. Pattullo 52B2
Mt. Paul 63D2
Mt. Pauline 40B2
Mt. Pearce 28C4
Mt. Peck 19A4
Mt. Pender 34C3
Mt. Pendleton 72C1
Mt. Penelope 64C3
Mt. Pereleshin 60A3
Mt. Perseus 26D1
Mt. Phillips 40C3
Mt. Pierce 4D2
Mt. Pierce 6A3
Mt. Pike 6C1
Mt. Pitt 5C1
Mt. Poelzer 60D1
Mt. Poelzer 61B1
Mt. Poletica 69B1
Mt. Pondosy 36A3
Mt. Pool 17C2
Mt. Pootlass 23A1
Mt. Pope 47C3

Mt. Pope 53B3
Mt. Pounder 51-B-C1
Mt. Pratt 59D4
Mt. Preston 36A-B3
Mt. Prideaux 12C2
Mt. Priestley 44D1
Mt. Prince 47C3
Mt. Prinsep 79B4
Mt. Procter 10A2
Mt. Prudence 74C-D1
Mt. Prudence 85D4
Mt. Ptolemy 10B2
Mt. Puggins 57C4
Mt. Quanstrom 40A4
Mt. Queen Bess 13B1
Mt. Queen Bess 24B4
Mt. Queen Mary 18D3
Mt. Quincy Adams 67C2
Mt. Raleigh 13C2
Mt. Ratcliff 23C2
Mt. Rath 71D2
Mt. Rath 72A2
Mt. Ratz 59D2
Mt. Read 12B2
Mt. Reesor 49B1
Mt. Reid 85B4
Mt. Remo 44D3
Mt. Renshaw 40B2
Mt. Reynolds 48D1
Mt. Richard Bennett......40B4
Mt. Rider 39D2
Mt. Ritchie 52C1
Mt. Robb 64D4
Mt. Robb 65A4
Mt. Robert 57B4
Mt. Robinson..................11C1
Mt. Robson 40C3
Mt. Rodell 12D1
Mt. Roderick Dhu 8A3
Mt. Rodney 13B2
Mt. Rogeen 60A1
Mt. Rogers 28C4
Mt. Rognaas 62C3
Mt. Rognaas 63A3
Mt. Ronayne 14C3
Mt. Roosevelt 74D3
Mt. Root 67C2
Mt. Ross 55B1
Mt. Ross 64A-B4
Mt. Rothenberg 74D1
Mt. Russel 63D3
Mt. Ruth 40A1
Mt. Ruth 50A4
Mt. Rykert 9A3
Mt. Sandin 84C3
Mt. Sanford 81C4
Mt. Sarah 22A1
Mt. Saugstad 23B2
Mt. Scaia 8A1
Mt. Scriven 12C3
Mt. Seaton 45D1
Mt. Sedgwick 5A1
Mt. Selwyn 55D3
Mt. Selwyn 56A3
Mt. Sepulchre 75B3
Mt. Severeid 49A4
Mt. Seymour 4A1
Mt. Seymour 5B2
Mt. Shawcross 75B4
Mt. Sheba 14B1
Mt. Sheffield 64B1
Mt. Shields 8B3
Mt. Sidney Williams 46D2
Mt. Sinclair 18C3
Mt. Sir Alexander 39D1
Mt. Sir Alexander 40A1
Mt. Sir Alexander 50A4
Mt. Sir Douglas 19A2
Mt. Sir Francis Drake 13B2
Mt. Sir Richard 5C1
Mt. Sir Richard 14C4
Mt. Sir Sandford 28B3

Mt. Sir Wilfrid Laurier....40B4
Mt. Skinner 24C3
Mt. Skowill 61C4
Mt. Skuyhil 53A2
Mt. Slocomb 63C1
Mt. Smallpiece 81C4
Mt. Smith 13A2
Mt. Smythe 64A1
Mt. Snowdon 81D3
Mt. Sparling 69D2
Mt. Sparling 70A-B2
Mt. Spieker 49B1
Mt. Spranger 39C4
Mt. Sproat 17B2
Mt. St. George 75B3
Mt. St. Magnus 75B3
Mt. St. Mary 9B1
Mt. St. Mary 61C1
Mt. St. Mary 72C-D4
Mt. St. Paul 75B2
Mt. St. Thomas 8B3
Mt. Stalin 75B4
Mt. Stearns 65B3
Mt. Stephen 29A4
Mt. Stephens 12A2
Mt. Stephens 52D2
Mt. Stevenson 14B-C1
Mt. Stevenson 39B4
Mt. Stockdale 18B3
Mt. Stoeckl 51C1
Mt. Strong 69D3
Mt. Strong 70A3
Mt. Suprenant 49A1
Mt. Suprenant 57A4
Mt. Swannell 37A2
Mt. Sweeney 35C1
Mt. Sylvester 47C1
Mt. Sylvester 55C4
Mt. Sylvia 75B4
Mt. Talbot 60A4
Mt. Tanner 8A2
Mt. Tantalus 5A1
Mt. Tatlow 24D4
Mt. Taylor 10B2
Mt. Tegart 18C3
Mt. Tellot 24A4
Mt. Temple 18B1
Mt. Temple 29A4
Mt. Templeman 17D3
Mt. Terraze 62B3
Mt. Terry Fox 40C4
Mt. Thoen 53D4
Mt. Thoen 54A4
Mt. Thomlinson 53C4
Mt. Thor 17B3
Mt. Thule 62A3
Mt. Thurston 4D2
Mt. Thurston 6A3
Mt. Thynne 6C1
Mt. Tiedemann 24A4
Mt. Tinniswood..............13D4
Mt. Tinsdale 39B3
Mt. Toby 18B4
Mt. Tod 16B2
Mt. Todd 2D4
Mt. Todd 3C3
Mt. Tom 14B1
Mt. Tom 25B4
Mt. Tom 54D4
Mt. Tommy Jack 53B2
Mt. Trimble 64D3
Mt. Trimble 65A3
Mt. Truax 14C2
Mt. Trygve 62C4
Mt. Tsaydizkun..............64A4
Mt. Tuam 3D3
Mt. Turner 67C1
Mt. Turner 68A1-2
Mt. Tuxford 19B4
Mt. Tyrrell 18A4
Mt. Ulysses....................64C2
Mt. Umbach 62A3

Mt. Upshur 51D2
Mt. Upshur 52A2
Mt. Urquhard 6A2
Mt. Valpy 44D4
Mt. Van Wagenen 80A3
Mt. Vaux 18B1
Mt. Vedder 4C2
Mt. Vedder 5D3
Mt. Vingolf 17C4
Mt. Vreeland 49B3
Mt. Waddington 24A4
Mt. Wade 78B3
Mt. Wadman 75B3
Mt. Wakefield 12D2
Mt. Walbran 2B4
Mt. Walbran 3B3
Mt. Walker 23C1
Mt. Ward 63C3
Mt. Wardle 18C2
Mt. Warne 44C2
Mt. Warner 14B1
Mt. Warren 26B1
Mt. Watson 12D2
Mt. Watson 67C1
Mt. Weart 14C4
Mt. Weber 53A4
Mt. Wendt 49A1
Mt. West 56C4
Mt. Whipple 51A1
Mt. White-Fraser............51D2
Mt. White-Fraser............52A2
Mt. Whymper 2C4
Mt. Whymper 3B2
Mt. Wiley 39A3
Mt. Will 61D2
Mt. William Brown 44C-D3
Mt. Willibert 51D2
Mt. Willibert 52A2
Mt. Winston 73C3
Mt. Winston 74A3
Mt. Withrow 65B3
Mt. Wooliever 65B3
Mt. Yakatchie 65C1
Mt. Young 12D2
Mt. Yuen 64A2
Mt.Edziza 61A1
Mt.Vernon **4B4**
Muchalat In 1B-C2
Muchalat R 1B1
Muckaboo Cr 52D1
Muckaboo Cr 61D4
Mud B 4A2
Mud B 5B3
Mud Bay **2B2**
Mud Cr 14C1
Mud Cr 27D2
Mud Gla 60A3-4
Mud L 27C2
Mud River **38B1**
Muddy Cr 33D2
Muddy Cr 34B1
Mugaha Cr......................56B4
Muinok Mtn 49D3
Muinok Mtn 50A3
Muir Cr 3C4
Muller Cr 49C3-4
Mulvaney Cr..................62D2
Mulvehill Cr 17B2
Mulvey Ls 8C1
Mumm Pk 40C3
Muncho Cr 74D2
Muncho L....................74C-D2
Muncho Lake **74D2**
Munro Cr 55C4
Munro L 47C1
Munro L 55C4
Murch L 48B4
Murchison I 20B1
Murder Cr 53B4
Murphy Cr 8B3
Murray Cr 15B3
Murray Cr 39B3

Murray Cr 47C4
Murray L 6C1
Murray L 37A2
Murray R 49B2
Murray R 57B4
Murtle L 27B2
Murtle R 27A2
Musgrave Cr..................16C3
Muskeg L 49C1
Muskeg L 57C4
Muskeg R 48B3
Muskeg River **41A1**
Muskovite Ls 55C3
Muskwa **76C2**
Muskwa R 64C1
Muskwa R 65A1
Muskwa R 75D3-4
Muskwa R 76A2-3
Muskwa R 76A4
Mussel In 35B4
Mussel R 35B3
Mustela Cr 84B4
Myers Cr 7D3
Mylor Pen 44A2
Myoff Cr 16D1
Myra Cr 1D2
Myrtle Point................**2B-C1**

N

Nabesche R 56B1-2
Nadahini Cr 79B3
Naden Har 30C1
Naden Har 32B2
Naden Har 42C4
Naden R 30C1
Naden R 32B2
Nadila Cr 14B1
Nadila Cr 25B4
Nadina L 35D1
Nadina L 36A1
Nadina Mtn 45D4
Nadina Mtn 46A4
Nadina R 35D1
Nadina R 36A1
Nadina R 46A4
Nadsilnich L 38C1
Nagle Cr 27D2
Nahatlatch L 6A1
Nahatlatch L 15A4
Nahatlatch Needle 6A1
Nahatlatch Needle 15A3
Nahatlatch R 5D1
Nahatlatch R 15A4
Nahlin Mtn 70D2
Nahlin R 71A2
Nahlin R 71B2
Nahlouza Cr..................36C3
Nahlouza L 36C3
Nahlouza L 36C3
Nahmint **2B3**
Nahmint L 2A3
Nahmint R 2A3
Nahounli L 47C3
Nahun **16C4**
Nahwitti L 11B2
Nahwitti R 11B2
Naka Cr 12B3
Nakina L 70D1
Nakina R 70B2
Nakina R 70D1
Nakinilerak L 46C1
Nakonake R 69D2
Nakonake R 70B2
● **Nakusp** **17B-C4**
Nakusp Cr 17C4
Nalachaga Mtn..............71B3
Nalau I 22B3
Nalbeelah Cr 45A4
Nalmet L 8D1
Naltesby L 38A2

Name	Ref		Name	Ref		Name	Ref		Name	Ref		Name	Ref
Namu	22B3		Nazko L	25A1		Niagara Cr	26D1		Noke Cr	9C2		Notch Hill	16C2
Namu L	22B3		Nazko R	25A1		Niagara Cr	39B4		Nolaka Cr	39B4		Notch Pk	54C2
● Nanaimo	2D3		Nazko R	37D4		Niagara Mtn	70B2-3		Nomans L	26D4		Notchtop Pk	53C1
Nanaimo Ls	2C3		Neah Bay	3A4		Nicholl L	48B4		Nomash R	1A1		Notsah Cr	65C1
Nanaimo Ls	3B2		Nechako R	37B1		Nicholls Cr	28A3		Nomash R	12A4		Nowish In	22A1
Nanaimo R	2C3		Nechako R	37C-D1		Nichols Cr	14A2		Nome Cr	82C3		Nowitka Mtn	9B1
Nanaimo R	3B2		Nechako R	38A-B1		Nicholson	18A1		Nome L	82C4		Noyse Cr	3B3
Nancy Cr	66D3-4		Nechako R	47C4		Nichyeskwa Cr	53D4		Nonda Cr	74D2		Nuaitch Cr	15B4
Nancy L	84B3		Nechako R	48A4		Nichyeskwa Cr	54A4		Nooksack	5D4		Nuchatlitz	1A1
Nangeese R	53A3		Neck L	38D3		Nicklen Cr	16D4		Noomst Cr	23B1		Nuchatlitz In	1B4
Nanika L	35C1		Necleetsconnay R	23A1		Nicklen L	16D4		Nooseseck R	22D1		Nude Cr	24B4
Nanika Mtn	45C4		Necoslie R	47C4		Nickoll Pass	12B2		Nooseseck R	23A1		Nugent Sd	11C-D1
Nanika R	35C1		Neds Cr	16B3		Nicoamen R	15B4		Noosgulch R	23B1		Nukko L	48B4
Nanika R	45C4		Neechanz R	23A4		Nicola	15D4		Nooskulla Cr	36A4		Nukko Lake	48B4
Nanitsch L	54B2		Needa L	26D4		Nicola L	15D4		Nooskulla Pk	36A4		Nulki L	37C1
Nankai Pk	54C3		Needham Cr	56A-B1		Nicola R	15B3		Nootka	1A-B2		Numas I	11D2
Nancut	47A3		Needles	8B1		Nicola R	16A4		Nootka I	1A1		Nuntzum L	38A3
Nanna L	47B-C3		Neekas In	22B1		Nicolum R	6B2		Nootka I	1A1		Nusash Cr	22D1
Nanoose Bay	2C3		Negro Cr	9C2		Nielsp Cr	47B3		Nootka Sd	1A-B2		Nusash Cr	23A1
Nanoose Cr	2C3		Nehatl Cr	5D1		Nig Cr	66A3		Nootum R	22C3		Nusatsum R	23B1
Nanoose Cr	3B1		Nekite R	22D4		Nigei I	11C2		Noralee	36B1		Nustlo Cr	84B3
Nanoose Har	2C3		Nelles Pk	69C2		Nighthawk	7B4		Noralee	46B4		Nutli L	36B-C2
Nanton	19D3		Nelles Pk	70A2		Nikwikwaia Cr	16B2		Nordegg	29C1		Nuttlude Cr	61A1
Naramata	7B2		Nels Bight	11A2		Nile Cr	2B2		Nordquist L	85D4		Nuttlude L	60D1
Naramata Cr	7C2		● Nelson	8D2		Nile Cr	3A1		Nordschow Cr	23C2		Nyland L	38D4
Narboe Cr	10A1		Nelson Cr	52C2		Nilkitkwa L	46B1		Norgate Cr	1B1			
Narcosli Cr	25C1		Nelson Forks	86C4		Nilkitkwa L	54A-B4		Norge Cr	9C3		**O**	
Narcosli Creek	38C4		Nelson Forks	87A4		Nilkitkwa R	53D3		Norman Cr	38A1			
Narraway R	49D4		Nelson I	2C2		Nilkitkwa R	54A3		Norman L	38A1		O'Connor L	11D3
Narraway R	50A4		Nelson Kenny Cr	38C3		Niloil Cr	85A4		Norman Wood Cr	28B3		O'Connor R	79A4
Narrow L	39A2		Nelson Kenny L	38C3		Niloil L	84D4		Norns Cr	8C2		O'Donnel R	69D1
Narrowgut Cr	1B4		Nelson L	69C1		Niloil L	85A4		Norrie L	57C3		O'Donnel R	70B1
Narrowgut Cr	11D4		Nelson L	80C4		Nimbus Mtn	45B4		Norrish Cr	4C1		O'Donnel R	80D4
Narrows Cr	9A2		Nelson R	44D2		Nimbus Mtn	70C-D1		Norrish Cr	5D3		O'Donnel R	81B4
Narrows In	2D1		Nelway	8D3		Nimmo B	12A2		North Aitken Cr	66B3-4		O'Dwyer R	53B2
Nascall L	22C1		Nemaia Cr	24C-D4		Nimpkish	12A3		North Anzac R	48D1-2		O'Ne-el Cr	46D2
Nascall R	22C1		Nemaiah Valley	24D4		Nimpkish Heights	11D3		North Arm	26C1		Oak Bay	3D4
Nash Cr	35C4		Nemo Cr	8C1		Nimpkish L	11D3		North Arm	39C4		Oak Beck Cr	22D2
Nash Cr	16B4		Nenahlmai Lagoon	11D2		Nimpkish L	12A3		North Barrière L	16B1		Oak Harbor	4B4
Nasko R	38A4		Nep Pk	54B2		Nimpkish R	12A4		North Barrière L	27B4		Oasis	8C3
Nasoga Gulf	44A2		Nepah Lagoon	12A2		Nimpo L	24A1		North Bend	6B1		Obed	41D2
Nasparti In	11C4		Nepean Sd	34B3		Nimpo Lake	24A1		North Bentinck Arm	23A-B1		Oblique Cr	82C4
Nass B	44B2		Nepopekum Cr	6C3		Nina Cr	55A-B3		North Blue R	27C2		Obo L	62D1
Nass Camp	44D1		Neroutsos In	11C3		Nina L	55B3		North Bonaparte	26C4		Obo L	63B1
Nass R	44C1		Nesabut Pks	46D1		Nine Mile Cr	45C1		North Broughton I	12A2		Obo L	73D4
Nass R	52C2		Nesakwatch Cr	6A3		Nine Mile Cr	60B1		North Burnt R	48D1		Obo L	74B4
Nass R	53A1		Nesook B	1A2		Nine Mile Narrows	8D2		North Cache Cr	57B1		Obo R	63B1
Nass R	61D4		Nesook B	1B1		93 Mile House	26B4		North Cr	14B3		Obole Cr	75C-D1
Nasswald Pk	18D1		Ness L	38B1		Ningunsaw R	60D4		North Cr	71D1		Obole Cr	76A1
Naswhito Cr	16B3		Ness L	48B4		Ningunsaw R	61A4		North Cr	72A1		Observatory In	44B1
Nata Cr	46A2		Netalzul Mtn	46A1		Ningunsaw R	61B4		North Fork Pass	10B1		Ocean Falls	22C1
Natadesleen L	61A2		Netson Cr	73D2		Nipple Mtn	7C2		North Galbraith Cr	10A1		Ocean Grove	2A1
Natadesleen I	60D2		Netson Cr	74A-B2		Nisconlith Cr	16B2		North Galiano	5A4		Ocean Park	5B3
Natal	10B1		Netson L	73D2		Nisconlith L	16B2		North Hill	37C4		Ochre Cr	18B1
Natalkuz L	37A2		Netson L	74B2-3		Nisconlith L	16B2		North Horseshoe Gla	23C3		Ocock L	47D3
Nataniko Cr	37D1		Nettie Cr	10C3		Niska Ls	52C-D3		North Klinaklini R	23C-D3		Ocock R	47C3
Nathinan Mtn	71B2		Nettle I	2A4		Nissen Bight	11A2		North Kootenay Pass	10B2		Octopus Cr	8B1
Nation Ls	47A1		Nevada Mtn	8D3		Nitaga Cr	38D3		North Kwadacha R	64A1-2		Odayin Cr	75C1
Nation Pk	61D2		Nevertouch L	7D1		Niteal Cr	77B4		North Moyie R	9C2		Odayin Cr	76A1
Nation R	47C1		Neveu L	16A4		Nithi Mtn	37A-B1		North Pass	11B1		Odin Cr	17B2
Nation R	48A1		Nevis Cr	64D2		Nithi Mtn	47A-B4		North Pass	22B4		Oerns Cr	51A1
Nation R	54D4		Nevis Cr	65B2		Nithi R	37A1		North Pender I	3D4		Oetata Cr	57C-D4
Nation R	55D4		New Aiyansh	44D1		Nitinat	2B4		North Pender I	5B4		Oetata Cr	58A4
Nation R	56A4		New Clew	31A3		Nitinat L	2B4		North Pine	57C1		Og L	18D2
Natlan Cr	53C-D4		● New Denver	17C-D4		Nitinat L	3A3		North Seakinnish Cr	52D4		Ogden	14C2
Natlan Pk	53C-D4		New Hazelton	45C1		Nitinat R	2B4		North Seakinnish Cr	44D1		Ogden Chan	31D1
Natlan R	45D1		New L	9C2		Nitinat R	3A2		North Star Cr	39C2		Ogden Chan	33C2
Natowite L	46C1		New Moon L	62D2		Niven Pk	62D4		North Star Hill	9C1		Ogden Chan	34A1
Natsy L	25C2		New Moon L	63A2		Niven Pk	63A4		North Star Mtn	9A3		Ogden Cr	54D3
Natulzul Mtn	45D1		● New Westminster	5B3		Niven Pk	62D4		North Tetsa R	75B3		Ogilvie Cr	60D4
Natuza L	36C3		Newcastle Cr	12C3		Niven R	63A4		North Thompson R	16A2		Ogilvie Cr	61A-B4
Natuza L	36C3		Newcombe Har	33C3		Nixon Cr	2C4		North Thompson R	27B-C1		Ogston L	47A-B3
Naumulten Mtn	8B1		Newcombe Har	34B1		Nixon Cr	3B2		North Thompson R	27B4		Oie L	26B2
Naver L	38D2		Newcombe In	30D4		Nizi Cr	72D1		North Thompson R	27C2		Okanagan Centre	16C4
Navy Chan	3D2		Newcombe L	35D1		Noaxe Cr	14C1		● North Vancouver	5B2		Okanagan Falls	7B2
Navy Chan	5A-B4		Newcombe Pk	30D3		Noble Mtn	33C3		North White R	19A3-4		Okanagan L	7B1
Navy Cr	28D3		Newgate	10A3		Noble Mtn	34A1		Northeast Arm	17B2		Okanagan L	16C4
Naysash In	11D1		Newstubb L	37A2		Nodales Chan	12D3		Northport	8C4		Okanagan Landing	16C4
Naysash In	22D4		Newton	5C3		Noeick R	23B2		Northwest Arm	46C1		Okanagan Mission	7C1
Nazcha Cr	71B1		Newton Cr	6C2		Noel Cr	14C2					Okanagan Mtn	7B1
Nazko	38A3		Next Cr	9A3		Noel Pk	59D2					Okanagan R	7B3
Nazko Falls	25A1		Neyasri L	37A4		Nogah Cr	77A3						
						Noisy Cr	17A2						

Oke Cr 9D3
Okeover In 2B1
Okeover In 13B4
Okisollo Chan 13A4
Okotoks **19D2**
Oksa 60A2
Oktwansh R 1C1
Olalla **7B3**
Olalla Cr 7B3
Olatine Cr 51C1
Old Baldy 30D2
Old Baldy 32B-C4
Old Baldy Mtn 9C2
Old Fort **46B1**
Old Fort Mtn 46B1
Old Fort Nelson **76C2**
Old Friend Mtn 48C1
Old Glory Mtn 8B3
Old Wifes Mtn 50A2
Olh Cr 52B4
● **Oliver** **7B3**
Oliver Cr 27D3
Oliver Cr 45A2
Olivia Cr 10A2
Olivine Cr 6C2
Olivine Mtn 6C2
Olsson Cr 48D3-4
Omega Hill 50B3
Omega Mtn 30B1
Omineca Arm 55C2
Omineca R 54B-C2
Omineca R 54D3
Omineca R 55B3
Ominicetla Cr 54C2
One Ace Mtn 83C3
One Eye L 24B3
One Island L 49D1
One Island L 50A1
One Island L 57D4
One Island L 58A4
One L 25A2
● **100 Mile House** **26B4**
103 Mile L 26B3
108 Mile L 26B3
111 Mile Cr 26B3
130 Mile L 26A3
150 Mile House **26A2**
Onerka L 53D3
Onerka L 54A3
Onion Cr 49C2
Onion Cr 76C1
Onion L 49C3
Onyx Cr 16C1
Oona L 47B4
Oona River **31D1**
Oono River **33C2**
Oona River **34A1**
Oona River **43D4**
Ootischenia **8C3**
Ootla Cr 88A3
Ootsa L 36B1
Ootsa Lake **36C1**
Ootsanee L 36D1
Open Bight 22C4
Operator Mtn 62B4
Opitsat **1C3**
Oppy Cr 36B3
Oppy L 36B3
Orcas **4A3**
Oregon Jack Cr 15B3
Oregon L 84C3
Oregon L 85A3
Orford B 13B3
Orford R 13B3
Orient **8B4**
Orion Cr 54D1
Ormond Cr 47A-B4
Ormond Cr 47B4
Ormond L 47B4
Oroville **7C4**
Ortona Mtn 75A-B4
Osborn R 57D1

Osborn R 58A1
Osborn R 66D4
Oscar L 38C2
Oscar Pass 22A1
Oscar Pk 44D2
Osgood Cr 13D4
Oshinow L 1D2
Osilinka R 54D2
Osilinka R 55A-B2
Oso **4C4**
Osoyoos **7C3**
Osoyoos L 7C3
Ospika Arm 55C2
Ospika R 55C1
Ospika R 64C4
Osprey L 7A2
Oswald B 34B3
Otard Cr 30C1
Otard Cr 32A2
Otelsas Cr 74C2
Otsi Cr 62A3-4
Ottarasko Cr 24B4
Ottarasko Mtn 24B4
Ottawa Cr 17D3
Otter Chan 34C3
Otter Cr 6C1
Otter Cr 6D1
Otter Cr 27C3
Otter Cr 49A3
Otter Cr 80D4
Otter Cr 81B4
Otter L 6C2
Otter L 16C3
Otter L 49A3-4
Otter Pass 33D4
Otter Pass 34B3
Otter Point **3C4**
Ottertail R 18B1
Ottertail R 29B4
Otto Cr 29A4
Otun R 32C2
Otun R 42D4
Ouffield Cr 64D2
Ououkinsh In 11C4
Ououkinsh R 11C4
Outaanetday L 77B1
Outlet Cr 17A3
Oval B 31C1
Oval B 33B2
Oval B 43C4
Ovington Cr 49C3-4
Ovis Cr 27A1
Oweegee Cr 52B1
Oweegee L 52B1
Owen Bay **13A4**
Owen L 46A4
Owens Pk 59C1
Owikeno L 22D3
Owikeno L 23A3-4
Owl Cr 14C3
Owl Cr 61B4
Owlet Cr 61B4
Owossitsa L 1A1
Owossitsa L 1B4
Owyacumish Cr 35A2
Oyama **16C4**
Oyama Cr 16C4
Oyama L 16C4
Oyster B 2A1
Oyster R 1D1
Oyster River **2A1**

P

Pablo Cr 25D2
Pachena B 2A4
Pachena Pt 2A4
Pacific Cr 28B1
Pacific L 49A3
Pacific Ocean 30A2
Pacific Ocean 42A2-3

Pack L 11C1
Pack R 48B1
Packhorse Pk 10B3
Packsaddle Cr 40D4
Paddy Cr 73D3-4
Paddy Cr 74A3-4
Paddy L 70C1
Paddy L 8D1
Paddy Pk 17D4
Pagoda Pk 24B4
Paint Cr 56B3
Paint Pot Cr 56D1
Paldi **2D4**
Palliser Pass 18D2
Palliser R 18D3
Palliser R 19A3
Palmer Cr 24B-C1
Palmer Cr 28B3
Palmer L 25B1
Palmer L 80D4
Palmer L 81A-B4
Pan Cr 37A4
Panorama **18B3**
Panorama Cr 62A4
Panorama Mtn 62A4
Pantage Cr 38B3
Pantage L 38B3
Papoose L 39B1
Paradise Cr 14B1
Paradise L 7A1
Paradise Pk 69D1
Paradise Pk 70A-B1
Paradise Point **16C2**
Parallel Cr 82C4
Parallel Cr 83A4
Pardonet Cr 56B2-3
Pardonet Hill 56B2
Park Cr 17A1
Park Cr 28A4
Park Mtn 17A3
Park Rill 7B3
Park Siding **8C3**
Parkdale **5A2**
Parker Cr 76C4
Parker L 26A1
Parkers Cr 9B2
Parkland **57C-D3**
Parksville **2C3**
Parminter Cr 26A1
Parrott Cr 46B4
Parrott Ls 46B4
Parry Pass 32A1
Parry Pass 42B4
Parsnip R 48C2
Parsnip R 48D2-3
Parsnip R 49A3
Parsnip Reach 48B1
Parsnip Reach 56A-B4
Parson **18A-B1**
Parsons Cr 2B3
Parsons Cr 3A2
Parting Ls 26B4
Parton R 79A-B3
Partridge L 80A3
Partridge R 79D3
Pasayten R 6D3
Pashleth Cr 23B4
Pashleth Gla 23B-C4
Paska L 15D3
Pass Cr 8A3
Passby Cr 45C2
Passmore **8C2**
Pasulko L 15B3
Pat Cr 27D3
Patcha C 53D2
Patcha Cr 54A2
Paterson **8B3**
Paterson L 12D4
Patmore Cr 59D2
Patricia B 3D3
Patricia B 5A4
Patricia L 26D3

Patry Cr 86D4
Patry Cr 87A4
Patry L 75D1
Patry L 76B1
Patry L 86D4
Patry L 87B4
Patterson L 24B3
Pattinson L 7A1
Pattinson L 16A4
Pattinson Pk 55D2
Pattinson Pk 56A2
Paul Cr 7A3
Paul Cr 16A2
Paul L 16A2
Paul R 64A2
Paula Cr 46D2
Pavilion **15A2**
Pavilion Cr 15A2
Pavilion L 15A2
Paw Cr 52D3
Payne Cr 17B3
Payne Cr 17B4
Peace R 57A-B2
Peace Reach 55D2
Peace Reach 56A2
Peace River 58A2
Peachland **7B1**
Peachland Cr 7B1
Peacock Cr 46A3-4
Pearl L 1D1
Pearse Can 43D2
Pearse Can 44A2
Pearse I 43D2
Pearse I 44A2
Pearson Cr 7D1
Pearson Pk 49C-D4
Peavine Cr 9C2
Peavine Cr 58A4
Pebble Cr 14A2
Peck Cr 56C3
Peculier L 48B-C3
Peel I 11C2
Peel In 30D4
Peeve Cr 6D3
Peffer Cr 66B1-2
Pefferle L 7A1
Pefferle L 16A4
Peggy Pk 54B2
Pekisko **19C3**
Pelican **68C4**
Pelican L 37D3
Pelican L 38A3
Pelly Cr 63C3
Pelly Cr 63D3-4
Pelly L 63D4
Pelly Pk 63D4
○ **Pemberton** **14C4**
Pemberton B 34C4
Pemberton L 16A2
Pement L 16B2
Pend Oreille R 8D3
Pendant Gla 59D2
Pender Har 2C2
Pender Island **5B4**
Pendleton B 46D3
Pendrell Sd 13B4
Penfold Cr 39C4
Pennask Cr 7A1
Pennask L 7A1
Pennask L 16A4
Pennask Mtn. 7A1
Pennie L 15C2
Penny **39B1**
Penrose I 22C4
Penteuch Pass 35B2
● **Penticton** **7B2**
Penticton Cr 7D2
Pentreath Cr 75D4
Pentreath Cr 76B4
Peridotite Cr 14C2
Perkins Pk 24A3
Perpendicular Mtn 12B1

Perry B 3D4
Perry Cr 9C2
Perry Cr 17A4
Perry Cr 49B1
Perry R 1B1
Perry R 16D1
Perrys **8C2**
Perseverance Mtn 40B2
Pesh Cr 77D1
Pesika Cr 64A3
Pesika Mt 64A4
Peter Aleck Cr 46A4
Peter Cr 8B3
Peter Hope L 16A4
Peters L 39A3
Peters L 17A3
Petersburg **59C4**
Peterson Cr 16A1
Peteyaz Pk 53D2
Peteyaz Pk 54A2
Petitot R 88A3
Petitot R 88C-D4
Petrel Chan 33C3
Petrel Chan 34A1-2
Petrie Cr 64C2
Petrie Cr 65A2
Phacops Cr 60A2
Phair Cr 14D3
Phelix Cr 14C3
Pheno Mtn 60B4
Phililloo L 26A3
Philip Cr 47D3
Philip Cr 48A1
Philip L 47D4
Philip Ls 48A1
Phillips Arm 12D3
Phillips Cr 1D2
Phillips Cr 10A3
Phillips L 12D3
Phillips L 16B2
Phillips R 13A3
Phoenix **8A3**
Pickell Cr 66B3
Pickle L 84A3
Pierre Cr 46C3
Piers I 3D3
Piers I 5A4
Pike L 69D1
Pike L 70B1
Pike R 69D1
Pike R 70A-B1
Pike R 80D4
Pike R 81B4
Pillar L 16B3
Pillar Pk 45B4
Pillman Cr 69D1
Pillman Cr 70A1
Pilot Cr 62D4
Pilot L 63A-B4
Piltz Pk 25B4
Pimainus Cr 15B3
Pimainus Ls 15C3
Pimpernel Cr 45D4
Pimpernel Cr 46A4
Pimpernel Mtn 45D4
Pimpernel Mtn 46A4
Pinantan L 16A2
Pinantan Lake **16B2**
Pinaus L 16B3
Pincher **10D2**
Pincher Creek **10D2**
Pinchi **47B3**
Pinchi L 47B-C3
Pinchi Mtn 47B2-3
Pinder Pk 12A4
Pine Cr 45C-D2
Pine Cr 80D4
Pine Cr 81A-B4
Pine Cr 81B4
Pine R 57B3
Pine River 56C-D4
Pine Valley **56D4**

Pinecone Cr ... 5C2
Pinecone L ... 5C1
Pinenut Cr ... 53C4
Pinetree L ... 72B1-2
Pingel Cr ... 57C2
Pingston Cr ... 17B3
Pingston L ... 17B2
Pink Mountain ... **65C3**
Pink Mtn ... 65C3
Pinkerton Pk ... 39B2
Pinkut Cr ... 46C3
Pinkut Cr ... 46D3
Pinkut L ... 46D3
Pinnacle Cr ... 18B2
Piper R ... 22D4
Piper R ... 23A4
Pipestem In ... 2A3
Pisima L ... 16C1
Pisima Mtn ... 16C1
Pitka Cr ... 47B4
Pitka Mtn ... 47B4
Pitman R ... 62B1
Pitman R ... 73A4
Pitoney Cr ... 38D1
Pitoney L ... 38D2
Pitt I ... 33D3
Pitt I ... 34B2
Pitt L ... 4B1
Pitt L ... 5C2
Pitt Meadows ... **5C3**
Pitt R ... 4B1
Pitt R ... 5C1
Pitt R ... 5C2
Pitts Cr ... 18C2
Pivot Mtn ... 30B1
Pivot Mtn ... 32A2
Pivot Mtn ... 42B4
Pivot Mtn ... 63D3
Place L ... 26A3
Placer Cr ... 6D3
Plaghat Mtn ... 55B3
Plaid L ... 9A1
Plant Cr ... 17B3
Plate Cr ... 82C3
Plate L ... 82C3
Plate L ... 83A3
Plateau Cr ... 80C4
Plateau Cr ... 81A4
Plateau L ... 16A4
Pleasant Camp ... **79B4**
Plumper Sd ... 3D3
Plumper Sd ... 5B4
Pocahontas ... **41B3**
Pocketknife Cr ... 65B2
Point No Pt ... 3C4
Point Roberts ... **5B4**
Poison Cove Cr ... 35B4
Poison Cr ... 12D3
Poison Cr ... 53B2
Poison Mtn ... 53B2
Polaris Cr ... 54D1
Polebridge ... **10C4**
Police Cr ... 64B4
Police Cr ... 76C2
Polley L ... 26A1
Pomeroy Cr ... 39B3
Pondosy L ... 36A3
Pool Cr ... 17C2
Pooley Cr ... 72C1
Pooley I ... 22A1
Pooley I ... 35A4
Poorman L ... 72C1
Poorman L ... 83C4
Poplar Cr ... 17D3
Poplar Cr ... 46B4
Poplar Creek ... **17D3**
Poplar L ... 48B3
Poquette L ... 39B4
Porcher I ... 31D1
Porcher I ... 33B-C2
Porcher I ... 34A1
Porcher I ... 43D4

Porcher I ... 44A4
Porcher In ... 31D1
Porcher In ... 33B-C2
Porcher In ... 34A1
Porcher Pen ... 31C1
Porcher Pen ... 31C1
Porcher Pen ... 33B2
Porcupine Cr ... 8D3
Porcupine Cr ... 18A1
Porcupine Cr ... 25D4
Porcupine Cr ... 29A4
Porcupine Gla ... 60B4
Porcupine L ... 71D2
Porcupine L ... 72A2
Porcupine R ... 60A3
Pork Cr ... 18B4
Porky Cr ... 62A3
Porphyry Cr ... 45C1
● **Port Alberni** ... **2B3**
Port Albion ... **1D4**
● **Port Alice** ... **11C3**
Port Alworth ... **68B4**
Port Angeles ... **3D4**
Port Chilkoot ... **68D1**
Port Clements ... **30D1**
Port Clements ... **32C3**
Port Coquitlam ... **5C3**
Port Douglas ... **5D1**
Port Edward ... **33C1**
Port Edward ... **43D4**
Port Edward ... **44A4**
Port Eliza ... 1B4
Port Elizabeth ... 12B2
Port Essington ... **33D1**
Port Essington ... **44B4**
● **Port Hardy** ... **11C2**
Port Harvey ... 12B3
● **Port McNeill** ... **11D3**
Port Mellon ... **5A2**
● **Port Moody** ... **5C3**
Port Neville ... 12C3
Port of Roosville ... **10A4**
Port Renfrew ... **3B3**
Port San Juan ... 3B3
Port Simpson ... **43D3**
Port Simpson ... 43D3
Port Simpson ... **44A3**
Port Simpson ... 44A3
Port Stanley ... **4A3**
Port Stephens ... 33D4
Port Stephens ... 34B2
Port Townsend ... **4A-B4**
Portage Brûlé Rapids ... 84D4
Portage Brûlé Rapids ... 85A4
Portage Cr ... 56D2
Portage L ... 49A3
Portage Mtn ... 56D3
Porteau ... **5B2**
Porter Cr ... 39A4
Porthill ... **9B4**
Portland Canal ... 43D1
Portland Canal ... 44A-B1
Portland Canal ... 52B4
Portland I ... 3D3
Portland I ... 5A4
Portland In ... 44A2
Porto Rico ... **8B2**
Postern Mtn ... 28A1
Postern Mtn ... 41A4
Postill L ... 7C1
Postill L ... 16C4
Pothole Cr ... 6D1
Potlatch Cr ... 28A2
Pouce Coupe ... **57D3**
Pouce Coupe ... **58A3**
Pouce Coupe R ... 58A3
Pounder Cr ... 51B-C1
Poutang Cr ... 55D1
Poutang Cr ... 56A1
Powder Cr ... 9A1
Powder L ... 16A1
Powell Cr ... 14A1

Powell L ... 2B1
Powell L ... 13B-C4
Powell Pk ... 35B2
Powell R ... 13C3-4
● **Powell River** ... **2B1**
Powers Cr ... 7B1
Powles Cr ... 34D4
Prairie ... **4C3**
Prairie L ... 71A2
Prairie Mtn ... 63D2
Prattle Cr ... 28C3
Premier L ... 9D1
Prescott I ... 33B2
Prescott I ... 43C4
Prespatou Cr ... 66B3-4
Pressy L ... 26C4
Pretty Girl L ... 1B2
Prevost I ... 3D2
Prevost I ... 5A4
Price Cr ... 1D2
Price I ... 21D1
● **Prince George** ... **38C1**
Prince of Wales Reach ... 2D1
● **Prince Rupert** ... **33C1**
Prince Rupert ... **43D4**
Prince Rupert ... **44A4**
Prince Rupert Har ... 33C1
Prince Rupert Har ... 43D4
Prince Rupert Har ... 44A4
Princess Gla ... 23C3
Princess Louisa In ... 13D4
Princess Royal Chan ... 34D3
Princess Royal I ... 21D1
Princess Royal I ... 34D4
Princess Royal Reach ... 13D4
● **Princeton** ... **6D2**
Principe Chan ... 33C3
Principe Chan ... 34A-B2
Pritchard ... **16B2**
Prochniak Cr ... 74C1
● **Procter** ... **9A2**
Procter L ... 10C3
Progress ... **57C3**
Projectile Mtn ... 24A4
Prophet R ... 64C2
Prophet R ... 65B1
Prophet R ... 76C4
Prophet River ... **76C4**
Prospect Cr ... 15B4
Prospect Lake ... **3D3**
Prospector Cr ... 55A2
Prouix L ... 81B3
Prudential Mtn ... 62B3
Prudhomme L ... 33C1
Prudhomme L ... 44A4
Pryce Chan ... 13B4
Pt. Grey ... 3D1
Pt. Grey ... 5B3
Ptarmigan Cr ... 27D1
Ptarmigan Cr ... 39C2
Ptomaine Cr ... 40A-B1
Pub Cr ... 8B2
Puder Cr ... 64D1
Puder Cr ... 65B1
Pugh Cr ... 11B2
Pukaist Cr ... 15B3
Pukeashun Mtn ... 16C1
Pulpit L ... 62D2
Pulpit L ... 63B2
Pulpit Pk ... 62D2
Pulpit Pk ... 63B2
Punch Bowl ... 6C3
Punchaw ... **38B2**
Punchaw L ... 38B2
Pundata Cr ... 39A3
Pundata Cr ... 39A3
Punkutlaenkut Cr ... 24B1
Punkutlaenkut L ... 24B1
Puntataenkut Cr ... 38B3

Puntateankut L ... 38B4
Puntchesakut L ... 38C4
Punti L ... 24D2
Puntledge ... **2A2**
Puntledge R ... 2A2
Puntzi Cr ... 24B2
Puntzi Cr ... 24C2
Puntzi L ... 24C2
Purden L ... 39A1
Purvis L ... 46D1
Putnam Cr ... 16D3
Pye L ... 12D4
Pyne L ... 34D4
Pyper L ... 24C2
Pyramid Bluff ... 62B4
Pyramid Cr ... 27C1
Pyramid Cr ... 72B2
Pyramid Mtn ... 9B1
Pyramid Mtn ... 72B2
Pyrrhotite Cr ... 71A4
Pys Cr ... 57A3

Q

Quaal R ... 34C1
Quadra I ... 13A4
Qualcho L ... 36C3
Qualicum B ... 2B2
Qualicum Beach ... **2C2**
Qualicum R ... 2A2
Qualicum R ... 3A1
Quarrie Cr ... 19A4
Quarry B ... 2C2
Quartcha Cr ... 22B1
Quartz Cr ... 28C4
Quartz Cr ... 39C2
Quartz Cr ... 71C-D2
Quartz Cr ... 72A2
Quartzite Cr ... 54D3
Quartzrock Cr ... 72B-C1
Quash Cr ... 60D1
Quash R ... 61A1
Quatam R ... 13B3
Quathiaski Cove ... **13A4**
Quatlena R ... 22C2
Quatse L ... 11C3
Quatse R ... 11C3
Quatsino ... **11C3**
Quatsino Sd ... 11B3
Quattoon In ... 44A3
Queen Bess Gla ... 13B1
● **Queen Charlotte** ... **30D3**
Queen Charlotte ... **32C4**
Queen Charlotte Chan ... 3D1
Queen Charlotte Chan ... 5A-B2
Queen Charlotte Is ... 30B2-3
Queen Charlotte Sd ... 11A-B1
Queen Charlotte Sd ... 21C3-4
Queen Charlotte Str ... 11D2
Queen Mary Cr ... 18D3
Queens Bay ... **9A-B1**
Queens Reach ... 13D4
Queens Sd ... 22A3
Queest Cr ... 16D1
Quenada Cr ... 54B1
Quentin L ... 64A1
Quenville Cr ... 15C3
● **Quesnel** ... **38C4**
Quesnel Forks ... **39A4**
Quesnel L ... 26B-C1
Quesnel L ... 27A1
Quesnel L ... 39C4
Quesnel R ... 26A1
Quesnel R ... 38D4
Quilchena ... **15D4**
Quilchena Cr ... 6D1
Quilchena Cr ... 7A3
Quilchena Cr ... 15D4
Quilchena Cr ... 16A4
Quill Cr ... 45A2
Quiltanton L ... 15C3

Quinn Cr ... 10A1
Quinn L ... 26B4
Quinsam L ... 1D1
Quinsam R ... 1D1
Quintette Mtn ... 49C2

R

Rabbit Cr ... 10B3
Rabbit R ... 73D1
Rabbit R ... 74A1
Rabbit R ... 74B2
Rabbit R ... 84C4
Rabbit R ... 85A4
Race Rocks ... 3D4
Racine Cr ... 80B3
Racine L ... 80B3
Racing R ... 75A3
Racoon Cr ... 13C3
Radium Hot Springs ... **18C3**
Radnor ... **19B1**
Radnor Cr ... 81C4
Raffuse Cr ... 5B1
Raft Cove ... 11A3
Raft Mtn ... 27B3
Raft R ... 27B4
Raging R ... 11D3
Rail Cr ... 26B3
Rail L ... 26B3
Railroad Cr ... 17A4
Rainbow Cr ... 12A1
Rainbow Cr ... 47C1
Rainbow L ... 33C1
Rainbow L ... 36D4
Rainbow L ... 44A4
Rainbow Ls ... 73A3
Rainbow R ... 74B4
Rainy Hollow ... **79B4**
Raleigh Cr ... 13C2
Raleigh Gla ... 13C2
Raley Cr ... 44D4
Ralph R ... 1D2
Ram Cr ... 75A2
Ramage ... **16A2**
Ramillies Chan ... 5A2
Ramose Cr ... 13D2
Rampalo Cr ... 8A1
Rampart Cr ... 6D2
Ramsay Arm ... 13A3
Ramsay I ... 20B1
Ramsey Cr ... 25B1
Ramsey Cr ... 36B4
Ramsey Pk ... 36B3
Ranch Cr ... 17C4
Ranger Cr ... 62A3
Ranhorn Cr ... 73A2
Rankine Is ... 20C2
Rapid Cr ... 17D3
Rapid R ... 72D2
Rapid Roy Cr ... 81C4
Rapids Cr ... 71C1
Rapids of the Drowned ... 74D1
Raspberry Cr ... 60C2
Raspberry Cr ... 75D2
Raspberry Cr ... 76B2
Rat L ... 7A1
Rat L ... 16A4
Rat L ... 49D2
Ratchford Cr ... 16D1
Ratchford Cr ... 27D4
Raush Gla ... 27B1
Raush Gla ... 40B4
Raush R ... 40B3
Raven L ... 25C2
Raven Mtn ... 51B1
Raven Mtn ... 60B4
Ravenal Cr ... 55A1
Ravenal Cr ... 64A4
Ravenal Pk ... 63D4
Rawlings L ... 16D4
Rayfield R ... 15C1

Rayfield R 26C4
Raymond Pass 22A2
Raymond Pk 79C3
Raza I 13A4
Raza Pass 13A4
Razor Cr 24B3
Razorback Mtn 24B4
Read I 13A4
Read Island **13A4**
Reco Mtn 8D1
Reco Mtn 17D4
Red Bluff L 34C3
Red Canyon Cr 45B2
Red Cr 7A2
Red Cr 53D1
Red Cr 54A1
Red Cr 57B1
Red Crag 62C3
Red Deer Cr 49C-D3
Red Deer Cr 50A3
Red L 15C2
Red Pass **40D4**
Red R 73A1
Red R 84A4
Red Ridge Pk 75B3
Red Rock **38C1**
Red Rock Cr 38C1
Red Rock L 38C1
Redburn Cr 29A4
Redding Cr 9B2
Redfern L 64C2
Redfern L 65A2
Redfern Mtn 64C2
Redfern Mtn 65A2
Redfern Rapids 36C3
Redfish Cr 82B3
Redfish L 36B3
Redonda Bay **13A4**
Redpot Cr 85D3
Redrocky Cr 48C2-3
Redrocky L 48C3
Redslide Mtn 35C1
Redstone **25A2**
Redtop Cr 46B3
Redwater Cr 37D3
Redwater Cr 38A3
Redwater L 37D3
Redwillow R 49D2
Redwillow R 50A2
Reef I 31A4
Reef Icefield 40D3
Rees Cr 2A2
Reflector L 27A3
Refuge Cove **13B4**
Refuge L 60D2
Refuge L 61A-B2
Reg Christie Cr 27B-C4
Reid B 12A2
Reid L 48B4
Reid Lake **38B1**
Reid Lake **48B4**
Reienecker Cr 16C2
Reimer Cr 64D1
Reimer Cr 65A1
Reiseter Cr 45D2
Reiseter Cr 46A2
Reiswig **16D4**
Reiter Cr 17A3
Relay Cr 14B1
Relay Mtn 14B1
Reliance Mtn 24B4
Reliance Mtn. 13B1
Remac **8C3**
Remote Cr 23D4
Remote Mtn 23D4
Renata **8B2**
Rendell Cr 7D1
Renfrew Cr 3B3
Rennell Sd 30C2
Rennell Sd 32B4
Renner L 25C2
Rennison I 34C4

Reno Mtn 8D3
Renolds Cr 48C1
Rentoul Cr 46C3
Republic **7D4**
Resplendent Cr 40D3
Resplendent Mtn 40D3
Retreat Pass 12A-B2
Return Chan 22B2
● **Revelstoke** **17B1**
Rexford **10A4**
Rey Cr 15C3
Réné L 57A3
Rhone **7D3**
Rice Brook 28D2
Rich Cr 37A4
Richards Chan 11C2
Richards Cr 64D2
Richards Cr 65A2
Richardson **4A4**
Richardson I 31A4
Richfield Cr 46B-C3
Richie Cr 27B3
● **Richmond** **5B3**
Richmond Centre **5B3**
Richmond I 9B2
Riddle Cr 7B2
Ridgeway Cr 9C3
Ridgeway L 63B1
Ring Cr 5B1
Ring Reid Cr 66D1
Riondel **9A1**
Rioulx Cr 17B4
Rioux L 26D3
Ripley L 22B1
Ripon I 22C4
Ripple Mtn 8D3
Ripple Pass 11C2
Riske Cr 25C2
Riske Creek **25C3**
Ritchie Cr 52C1
Ritchie L 78C3
Rithet Cr 3C3
River Bight 34D3
River Jordan **3B-C4**
River L 66B2
River Ls 15A1
Rivers In 22C4
Rivers Inlet **22D3**
Rivers Ls 26A4
Rivers Pk 36B3
Riverside Mtn 19A3
RN Mtn 60D3
RN Mtn 61B3
Roan Horse Cr 65D1
Roaring Cr 39B4
Roaring R 26C1
Roaring R 39C4
Robb **41D3**
Robbins Cr 16B3
Robert Arm 22C4
Roberts Creek **5A2**
Roberts L 12D4
Roberts Pk 39D4
Robertson Cr 15A2
Robertson Cr 65C4
Robinson Cr 7B2
Robinson Cr 48A1
Robson **8C2**
Robson Bight 12B3
Robson Cr 35D3
Robson Pass 40C-D3
Robson R 40C3
Roche Cr 10C3
Roche Harbor **4A3**
Roche L 16A3
Rochester Cr 61C4
Rock Bay **12D3-4**
Rock Cr 7C3
Rock Creek **7D3**
Rock L 18C2
Rockbluff L 9D1
Rocky Pk 63C1

Roderick I 22A1
Roderick I 35A4
Roderick L 22A1
Rododendron Cr 75A2-3
Roe Lake **26C4**
Roger L 26C3
Rogers Cr 14C4
Rogers Ls 85B3
Rogers Pass **28C4**
Rolla **57D3**
Rolla **58A3**
Rolla Cr 57D3
Rolla Cr 58A3
Rollie Cr 39A-B4
Ronning Cr **11B3**
Roosville 10A3
Rory Cr 18A3
Rosario **5B4**
Roscoe In 22B-C1
Roscoe L 15C3
Rose In 20C2
Rose L 26A2
Rose Pass 9A1
Rose Prairie **57C1**
Rose Spit 32D1
Rose Spit 43A4
Rosebery **17C-D4**
Rosedale **6A3**
Roseland Cr 57C1
Rosella R 83C4
Rosen L 10A2
Rosewall Cr 2B2
Rosita L 25B1
Ross Cr 16C1
Ross Cr 24D1
Ross Cr 25A1
Ross Cr 71C3
Ross Cr 72A3
Ross L 25C2
Ross Moore L 15D3
Ross R 62B2
Ross Spur **8C3**
Rossé L 24C3
● **Rossland** **8C3**
Rosswood **44D2**
Rostrum Pk 28D3
Rothwell Pk 79D3
Rottacker Cr 47A1
Rottacker Cr 55A4
Rough B 11D3
Rough Cr 3C3
Round L 16C3
Round L 26B3
Round Mtn 60D2
Round Mtn 61B2
Round Prairie **19A4**
Rowland Cr 12A4
Roy L 30C1
Roy L 32B2
Royal Chan 35A3
Royal Oak **3D3**
Royal Roads 3D4
Royston **2A2**
Rubi Cr 6A2
Ruby Cr 4D1
Ruby Cr 80D3
Ruby Cr 81B3
Ruby Creek **6A2**
Ruby L 2D1
Rubyred Cr 64A4
Rubyrock Cr 46D3
Rubyrock L 47A3
Ruddock Cr 27D3
Ruddy Cr 56D2
Rudolf B 21D1
Rugged Mtn 1A1
Rugged Mtn 12A4
Rugged Mtn 60A1
Rumble Beach **11C3**
Rupert Cr 80C4
Rupert In 11C3
Ruric Cr 38C4

Rush Cr 2C3
Rush Cr 3B2
Rush L 16A4
Ruskin **5C3**
Russel Cr 63D3
Russell Cr 9B3
Russian Cr 39B3
Ruth L 26C3
Ruth L 70C1
Ruth Redfern Cr 26D2
Rutherford Cr 14B4
Ryan R 14B3
Rycroft **58D3**
Rykerts **9B3**

S

● **Saanich** **3D3**
Saanich In 3D3
Saanich In 5A4
Saar Cr 5D3
Sabine Chan 2C2
Sabine L 36C2
Sable Cr 17C2
Sachs Cr 31A3
Sachs Cr 32C4
Saddle Mtn 60A3
Sadie Cr 2B3
Sadie Cr 3B2
Safety Cove 22B4
Sagar L 22B-C2
Sage Cr 10C3
Sahara Heights **2B3**
Sahcho Cr 77C2
Sahdoanah Cr 77C1
Sahdoanah Cr 88B4
Sahtaneh R 76D1
Saiya L 54B2
Sakeniche R 46C1
Sakinaw L 2D1
Sakumtha 36A3
Sakumtha Pass 36A-B4
Saladamis Cr 52D2
Salahagen Cr 35D3
Salal Cr 14A2
Salient Cr 35D3
Salient Cr 36A3
Salix Cr 53D2
Salix Cr 54A2
Salloomt R 23B1
Sally Cr 8A1
Sallysout Cr 53A2
Salmo **8D3**
Salmo R 8D3
Salmon Arm 12A1
● **Salmon Arm** **16C2**
Salmon Arm 16C2
Salmon Chan 12A2
Salmon Gla 52A2
Salmon In 2D2
Salmon In 5A1
Salmon L 16A4
Salmon L 47D2
Salmon L 48A2
Salmon R 1C1
Salmon R 12C4
Salmon R 16C3
Salmon R 47D2
Salmon R 48A2
Salmon R 48B3-4
Salmon Valley **48C4**
Saloon L 71B4
Salt Cr 57C4
Salt Lagoon 31D1
Salt Lagoon 33C2
Salt Lagoon 34A1
Salt Lagoon 43D4
Salt Lagoon 44A4
Salter L 33D3
Salter L 34B2
Saltery Bay **2C1**

Saltspring I 3D2
Saltspring I 5A4
Sam Green Cr 53B-C3
Samatosum Mtn 16B1
Samboo Cr 84A3
Samotua R 70D4
San Jose R 26A2-3
San Josef **11B2**
San Josef R 11B2
San Joseph B 11A3
San Juan R 2D4
San Juan R 3B3
San Juan R 3C3
Sanabar Cr 62B2
Sanca **9A2**
Sanca Cr 9A2
Sand Cr 8A3
Sand Cr 10A2
Sand L 10A2
Sand L 44D2
Sandell L 22C4
Sandell R 22C-D4
Sandford I 2A4
Sandifer Pk 35C2
Sandilands I 30D3
Sandilands I 32C4
Sandner Cr 8A3
Sandon **8B1**
Sandpile Cr 73B1
Sandpile Ls 73B1
Sandspit **31A3**
Sandspit **32D4**
Sandwick **2A1**
Sandy Cr 86D3
Sandy Cr 87A-B3
Sandy L 39B3
Sandy Point **16C2**
Sangan R 31A1
Sangan R 32C2
Sangrida Pk 8B1
Sangster I 2C2
Sansixmor Cr 53B1
Sanskisoot Cr 52D2
Sansum Nrs 3D2
Sansum Nrs 5A4
Sanyam Cr 52D2
Sapeye L 24B3
Sarah I 22A1
Sarah I 35A4
Saratoga Beach **2A1**
Sardine Cr 38D4
Sardis **6A3**
Sarita **2A4**
Sarita L 2B4
Sarita R 2B4
Sartine I 11A4
Saskatoon Cr 57D3
Saskum L 27B4
Saskum Mtn 16B1
Saskum Mtn 27B4
Sass Cr 65C1
Satah Mtn 24B1
Satellite Chan 3D3
Satellite Chan 5A4
Satsalla R 12C1
Saturna **5B4**
Saturna I 5B4
Saunders Cr 63A2
Saunier Cr 7D2
Savary I 2B1
Savary Island **2B1**
Savio Mtn 75B4
Savona **15C2**
Saw Cr 39A1
Sawmill Cr 6B2
Sawyer Cr 9B1
Saxon Cr 50B3-4
Saxton Cr 48A4
Saxton L 38B1
Saxton L 48A-B4
Sayward **12C3**
Scaffold Cr 75A1

Scallon Cr 25B4
Scallon Cr 45C3
Scallop Mtn 54B2
Scar Cr 13A1
Scarcity Mtn 63C1
Scarp Mtn 28A1
Scatter R 86A3
Schaft Cr 60C2
Schoen Cr 12B4
Schoen L 12B4
Schoolbuckhand Cr 45A3-4
Schooler Cr 56C2
Schwarzenberg Lagoon 11D1
Scimitar Cr 24A4
Scimitar Gla 24A4
Scoop L 73C1
Scot Cr 15C1
Scotch Cr 16C2
Scotch Creek **16C2**
Scotia R 44B-C4
Scott Chan 11A2
Scott Chan 11B4
Scott Cr 52B1
Scott Cr 55D3
Scott Cr 56A3
Scott Is 11A4
Scott L 57C3
Scottie Cr 15B2
Scovil Cr 48B1
Screw Cr 82B3
Scrip Cr 27D3
Scud Gla 60B2-3
Scudamore Cr 14D4
Scum L 25A3
Scuzzy Cr 6A1
Scuzzy Mtn 6A1
Sea I 4A1
Sea I 5B3
Sea Lion Pk 36B4
Sea Otter Cove 11A3
Seabird L 12C3
Seaford **13B4**
Seaforth Chan 22A-B2
Seal I 32B3
Seal In 30C2
Seal In 32B3
Seaside Park **5A2**
Seaskinnish Cr 44D1
Sebalhall Cr 1B1
● **Sechelt** **2D1**
Sechelt Cr 5A1
Sechelt In 2D1-2
Sechelt Pen 2D2
Second Nrs 23A3
Secret Cove **2D1**
Section Mtn 80C4
Section Mtn 81A4
Security In 30D3
Secus Mtn 49D3
Secus Mtn 50A3
Sedan Cr 45A1
Sedgwick B 20B1
Sediesh Cr 53C4
Sedro Woolley **4C3**
Seebach Cr 48D3-4
Seebe **19A1**
Seeds Cr 65B1
Seeds Cr 76B4
Seel L 35C2
Seguthooth Cr 71A-B2
Sekiu **3B4**
Selish Mtn 6C1
Selish Mtn 15C4
Seller Cr 26B1
Seller Cr 39B4
Seltat Cr 79B4
Seltat Pk 79B4
Selwyn Cr 55D3
Selwyn Cr 56A3
Selwyn In 31A4
Senio Mtn 75A4
Sentinel Mtn 80D4

Sentinel Mtn 81B4
Sentinel Pk 49A2
Sentry Mtn 28C3
Septimus Cr 57C2
Serac Cr 18C1
Serb Cr 45C2
Serpentine Cr 27C1
Serrated Pk 63B3
Seshal Cr 13D4
Seton L 14D2
Seton Portage **14D2**
Settea Cr 72D4
Seven Mile Corner **57D3**
Seven Mile Corner **58A3**
Seven Mile Corner 56C3
Seven Sisters 45B2
70 Mile House **26B4**
Severide Cr 17A4
Sewall **30D1**
Sewall **32C2**
Sewell In 31A4
Sewell Inlet **31A4**
Sexsmith **50D1**
Sexsmith **58D4**
Seymour Arm **16D1**
Seymour Cr 28A4
Seymour In 11C1
Seymour In 12A1
Seymour L 4A1
Seymour L 5B2
Seymour L 45D2
Seymour Nrs 12D4
Seymour R 4A1
Seymour R 5B2
Seymour R 12B1
Seymour R 16D1
Seymour R 23B4
Seymour R 27D4
Shadwell Pass 11B2
Shag Cr 37A4
Shakan Cr 15B4
Shakatah Cr 71B1
Shaker Cr 80C3
Shaker Cr 81A3
Shaker L 80C3
Shaker L 81A3
Shakes Cr 60A1
Shalalth **14B2**
Shames Cr 44D3
Shana Cr 70B2
Shandalope Cr 53A2
Shangweshi Cr 56D3
Shanley L 47D4
Shannon Bay **30C2**
Shannon Bay **32B3**
Shannon Cr 17C4
Shannon L 12C3
Shanoss Cr 52D1
Sharktooth Mtn 73B3
Sharpe L 15C1
Sharpe L 26C4
Shaslomal Cr 53B1
Shass Mtn 47B3
Shatford Cr 7B2
Shaw Cr 2C4
Shaw Cr 3B2
Shaw Cr 9A3
Shaw Cr 84D3
Shaw Cr 85B3
Shawatum Mtn 6D3
Shawl B 12B2
Shawnigan L 3C3
Shawnigan Lake **5A4**
Shazah Cr 69D2
Shazah Cr 70A2
Shea L 6C1
Shearer Dale **58A-B2**
Shedi Cr 53C3
Sheemahant R 23B3
Sheep Cr 8D3
Sheep Cr 72D1
Sheep L 8B3

Sheep Pass 35A4
Sheephorn Cr 71A-B1
Shegisic Cr 53C4
Shegunia R 45C1
Shegunia R 53C4
Sheilds I 32B4
Shekilie R 77D1-2
Shekilie R 88D4
Sheladamus Cr 53B2
Shelagyote Pk 53D3
Shelagyote R 53C-D3
Shelagyote R 54A3-4
Shell Cr 25C2
Shelley **38C1**
Shelley **48C4**
Shelley L 15D1
Shelter B 11C2
Shelter Bay **17B3**
Shelter In 1C2
Shelter Point **2A1**
Shelton L 2C3
Shelton L 3B1
Shenismike Cr 53C3
Shepherd Cr 1D2
Shepp Cr 10B3
Sheppard Pk 59C1
Sheraton Cr 46D4
Sherbrooke L 29B4
Sheridan Cr 25D1
Sheridan L 26C4
Sheslay R 70D3
Sheslay R 70D4
Shields I 30D2
Shiko L 26B1
Shilahou Cr 53B1
Shingle Cr 7B2
Shingle Creek **7B2**
Shinish Cr 7A2
Shirley **3C4**
Shoal L 55C3
Shonektaw Cr 71A1
Shonektaw Cr 82B4
Shoreacres **8C2**
Shoreholme **17B4**
Shorts Cr 16B4
Shotgun Cr 37A1
Shotnana L 10A3
Shovel Cr 47A4
Shovel Cr 55B1
Shovelnose Mtn 6C1
Shrimpton Cr 6D1
Shroud Mtn 44C3
Shulaps Cr 14D2
Shumal Cr 44C1
Shumway L 16A3
Shush Cr 76D1
Shushartie Mtn 11B2
Shushartie R 11B2
Shuswap **18C3**
Shuswap Cr 18C3
Shuswap Falls **16D4**
Shuswap L 16C2
Shuswap R 16D3
Shuswap R 17A3
Shuttleworth Bight 11B2
Shutty Bench **18A4**
Sialun Cr 32A1
Sialun Cr 42B4
Sibley Cr 27D4
Sicamous **16D2**
Sicamous Cr 16D2
Sicily L 26D3
Sicily Mtn 75A4
Sicintine R 53B2
Sidenius Cr 64C-D3
Sidenius Cr 65A3
Sidina Mtn 53C4
Sidney **5A4**
Sidney Cr 46D2
Sidney I 3D3
Sidney I 5B4
Sierra **77B2**

Sifton Pass 63C1
Sigutlat Cr 36C4
Sigutlat L 36B-C4
Sihun Cr 1D1
Sikanni Chief **65C3**
Sikanni Chief R 64C-D3
Sikanni Chief R 65D1
Sikanni Chief R 77A4
Sikanny Chief R 65B3
Silence L 27B3
Silent L 25C2
Silica 8B3
Silt Cr 18C3
Silt L 79D3
Silver Cr 16C3
Silver Cr 54D3
Silver Creek **6B2**
Silver Creek **16C3**
Silver L 6B3
Silver Ls 66B2
Silver Mtn 17C4
Silver Salmon R 70B1
Silver Star Mtn 16D3
Silver Valley **58C2**
Silverado Cr 1B2
Silverhope Cr 6B3
Silverthrone Mtn 23C4
Silvertip Cr 17C2
Silvertip Mtn 6B3
Silverton **8D1**
Silverton Cr 8D1
Simem Cr 7A1
Similk Beach **4B4**
Similkameen R 6D3
Similkameen R 7B3
Simma Cr 51B-C1
Simma Mtn 51B1
Simmons L 12D3
Simmons L 72B1
Simonds Group 22A3
Simoom Sound **12B2**
Simpson Cr 69D1
Simpson Cr 70A1
Simpson L 34C3
Simpson L 69D1
Simpson L 70A-B1
Simpson Pass 18C1
Simpson Pk 82A-B3
Simpson R 18C2
Simpson Ranch **56D1**
Sims Cr 13D4
Sinawa Eddy Mtn 70C1
Sinclair Mills **39A1**
Sinclair Mills **49A4**
Sinkut L 37C1
Sinkut Mtn 37C1
Sinkut R 37C1
Sinmax Cr 16B1
Sinta Cr 46C1
Sinta Cr 54C4
Sinwa Cr 70B2
Sinwa Mtn 69D2
Sinwa Mtn 70B2
Siphon Cr 57D1
Siphon Cr 58A1
Sirdar **9B3**
Siska Cr 15B4
Sitchiada Mtn 54A-B2
Sitkum Cr 8D2
Sitkum Cr 17A3
Sitkum L 17A3
Sitlika Cr 54C3
Sittakanay Gla 70B3
Sittakanay Mtn 69D3
Sittakanay Mtn 70B3
Sittakanay R 69D3
Sittakanay R 70A-B3
Siwash B 12C2
Siwash Cr 6B2
Siwash Cr 6D1
Siwash L 7A1
Siwash Mtn 8C2

Siwash Rock Mtn 16B3
Siwhe Cr 15A3
Siwhe Mtn 15A3
Six Mile Cr 56A3-4
Six Mile Point **16D2**
Sixtyone Cr 15B1
Skaat Har 20B1
Skadi Mtn 62A2
Skagit R 6C3
Skagway **80A4**
Skaha L 7B2
Skaist Mtn 6C3
Skaist R 6C3
Skedans **31A4**
Skeena R 44C-D3
Skeena R 45A-B1
Skeena R 45B1
Skeena R 53B3
Skeena R 53C1
Skeena R 62A3-4
Skelhorne Cr 62A3
Skelly L 80B3
Skelton Cr 25D1
Skelu B 30C2
Skelu B 32A3
Skidegate **31A3**
Skidegate **32C4**
Skidegate Chan 30C2
Skidegate Chan 30D3
Skidegate Chan 32C4
Skidegate In 30D3
Skidegate In 32C4
Skidegate L 31A3
Skidegate L 32C4
Skidegate Mission **31A3**
Skidegate Mission **32C4**
Skidigate Chan 32B4
Skihist Mtn 15A3
Skim L 2C1
Skimikin L 16C2
Skinkuttle In 20B2
Skins L 36C1
Skmana L 16B2
Skonun Cr 5B1
Skonun R 30D1
Skonun R 32C2
Skookum Cr 5B1
Skookum L 15C1
Skookumchuck **9D1**
Skookumchuck Cr 9C1
Skookumchuck Cr 18C4
Skookumchuck Mtn 9B1
Skowill Cr 52B1
Skowill Cr 61C4
Skowootum Cr 16A1
Skowquiltz R 22D1
Skowquiltz R 35C4
Skud R 60A3
Skuhun Cr 15C4
Skull Cr 15D1
Skull Cr 16A1
Skundale L 30C1
Skundale L 32B3
Skunk L 55C4
Skwawka R 13C2
Skwim L 13C4
Slamgeesh L 53B1
Slamgeesh R 53B1
Slate Cr 71D2
Slate Cr 72A2
Slave Cr 77A3
Sleigh Cr 85C3
Slender L 48B3
Slesse Cr 6A3
Slesse Mtn 4D2
Slesse Mtn 6A3
Slewiskin Cr 17C4
Sliammon **2B1**
Sliammon L 2B1
Slick Cr 17C1
Slim Cr 14B2
Slim Cr 39B1
Slim L 39B1

Slim R 12D1
Slingsby Chan 11C1
Slocan **8C1**
Slocan L 8C1
Slocan L 17C4
Slocan Park **8C2**
Slocan R 8C2
Slok Cr 15A2
Sloko L 69D1
Sloko L 70A1
Sloko R 69D1
Sloko R 70B1
Slollicum Pk 4D1
Slollicum Pk 6A2
Sloquet Cr 5D1
Slousiska Cr 22D2
Slowmaldo Cr 53A1
Slowmaldo Mtn 53A-B1
Slowmaldo Mtn 62A-B4
Smaby Cr 35D3
Small Cr 40C3
Smanit Cr 13D4
Smart R 82A3
Smelter Ls 6D2
Smith Cr 7A2
Smith Cr 37B1
Smith I 33C1
Smith I 43D4
Smith I 44A4
Smith In 11C-D1
Smith In 22C-D4
Smith R 85B3
Smith River **85B3**
Smith Sd 11B-C1
● **Smithers** **45D2**
Smithers **46A2**
Smithers Landing **46B1**
Smitley R 23A2
Smoke Cr 27C2
Smoke Mtn 35D1
Smokehouse Cr 11D1
Smokehouse Cr 12A1
Smokehouse Cr 23A4
Smyth Cone 12C2
Smyth Cr 17A3
Snake Cr 75B2
Snake L 36B1
Snake River **76D1**
Snake R 76D2
Snaking R 38A3-4
Snass Cr 6C3
Snass Mtn 6C3
Snehumption Cr 7B3
Snippaker Cr 51C1
Snippaker Mtn 51C1
Snippaker Mtn 60C4
Snohoosh L 15C1
Snook Cr 82A4
Snow Cr 8C1
Snow Dome 28D2
Snow Pk 71D3
Snow Pk 72A3
Snowball Cr 8A3
Snowbank Cr 61B4
Snowcap Cr 5C1
Snowcap L 5C1
Snowdon Cr 81D3
Snowdrift Cr 72C4
Snowfall Cr 77D4
Snowside Mtn 23B2
Snowtop Mtn 69A1
Snowtop Pk 64A-B4
Snowy Mtn 7B3
Snyder Cr 66B4
Soards Cr 27D2
Sob L 37D1
Sob L 38A1
Sock L 27A3
Soda Cr 25D2
Soda Creek **25D1**
Soda L 26B3
Sointula **11D3**

Soles Cr 18B2
Solillock Pk 6B3
Solitary L 73B1
Solo Cr 54C1
Solsqua **16D2**
Sombrio Pt 3B3
Sombrio R 3B3
Somerville I 43D2
Somerville I 44A2
Songhees Cr 11C2
Sonora I 13A3
Soo R 14B4
Sooke **3C4**
Sooke Basin 3C4
Sooke In 3C4
Sooke L 3C3
Sooke R 3C4
Sorcerer Cr 28B4
Sorcerer Mtn 28B4
Sorrento **16C2**
South Anahim Cr 25B2
South Barrière L 16B1
South Bentinck Arm 23A2
South Canoe **16C2**
South Cr 14B3
South Cr 36B3
South Cranberry Cr 17B2
South Fosthall Cr 17B3
South French Bar Cr 14B1
South Gataga R 63D1
South Gataga R 74D4
South Germansen R 55B4
South Hawks Cr 25D2
South Hazelton **45C1**
South Kootenay Pass 10C3
South Nanaimo R 2C3-4
South Nanaimo R 3B2
South Pass 11B1
South Pass Pk 53D1
South Pass Pk 62C-D4
South Pass Pk 63A4
South Pender **5B4**
South Pender I 5B4
South Redwillow R 49D2
South Redwillow R 50A2
South Riske Cr 25C3
South Salmo R 8D3
South Shekilie R 77D1
South Slocan **8C2**
South Thompson R 16A2
South Unuk R 51D1
South Unuk R 52A1
Southbank **36D1**
Southbank **46D4**
Southgate R 13B2
Sovereign Cr 39A4
Sovereign Mtn 39A3-4
Sowaqua Cr 6B2
Sowchea Cr 47B3
Sowsap Cr 16D3
Spa Cr 16C3
Spa L 16C3
Spahats Cr 27B3
Spahomin Cr 16A4
Spahomin L 16A4
Spaist Mtn 15C3
Spakwaniko Cr 49B-C3
Spallumcheen L 16C3
Spanish Cr 26B1
Spanish Cr 26D3
Spanish Cr 27D2
Spanish L 16C3
Spanish L 26B1
Spanish Mtn 26B1
Spapilem Cr 16B1
Sparkling Cr 33D2
● **Sparwood** **10A-B1**
Spatsizi R 61D2-3
Spatsizi R 62A2
Spatsum **15B3**
Spawning L 54B-C1
Specs Ls 16D4

Spectacle Ls 39B3
Spectre Pk 63D1
Spectrum Cr 17A3
Specularite L 46D3
Spence L 31A1
Spence L 32D2
Spences Bridge **15B3**
Spey Cr 38D1
Sphaler Cr 60B3
Sphinx Cr 72B2
Sphinx Mtn 9A2
Sphinx Mtn 72B2
Spicer I 31D1
Spider I 33C3
Spider I 22A3
Spike Mtn 72B2
Spiked Pk 62D2
Spiked Pk 63B2
Spiller Chan 22B1-2
Spiller In 22B1
Spillimacheen **18B2**
Spillimacheen R 17D1
Spillimacheen R 18A1
Spillman Cr 16B1
Spinel Cr 63B1
Spinel L 63B1
Spirit River **58D3**
Spittal Cr 40C3
Spius Cr 6C1
Spius Cr 15C4
Splinter Hill 24C3
Split Cr 7D1
Split Cr 29A4
Split Pk 18C1
Split Top Mtn 74B3
Spokin L 26A2
Spout L 26B3
Sprague Cr 16A1
Spring Cr 83C4
Spring House **25D3**
Spring L 26B3
Spring Mtn 38D1
Springer Cr 8C1
Sproat L 2A3
Sproat Lake **2A-B3**
Sproule Cr 8C2
Spruce Cr 14D3
Spruce Cr 39A1
Spruce Cr 80D4
Spruce Cr 81A-B4
Spruce Hill 62B2
Spruce L 14B1
Spuzzum **6B1**
Spuzzum Cr 6A1
Squalicum L 2B4
Squally Chan 34C3
Square L 36C1
Squaw Cr 10B2
Squaw Fish L 36D2
Squaw Mtn 49D2
Squaw Mtn 50A2
Squawk L 26A2
Squiness L 36C4
Squingula R 53C-D2
Squingula R 54A2
Squirrel Cove **13A-B4**
St. Annes Cr 8A2
St. Eugene Mission **9D2**
St. George Cr 38B1
St. Ives **16C2**
St. John Cr 57C1
St. Julien Cr 27B1
St. Leon Cr 17C3
St. Mary L 9C2
St. Mary R 9B1
St. Mary R 9C2
St. Thomas B 35D2
St. Thomas B 36A2
St. Thomas R 36B2

Stafford L 12D2
Stafford R 12D2
Stagleap Cr 8D3
Stagnant Gla 64A1
Stagoo Cr 44B1
Stakawus Cr 13D4
Staki B 20B2
Stalk Ls 62C3
Stalk Pk 62B3
Stamp R 2A2
Standard Cr 28A4
Stanislas Cr 87D3
Stanley **39A3**
Stanley Cr 79B3
Stanley Pk 18C1
Stanner Cr 85D4
Stanolind Cr 76B1
Stanwood **4B-C4**
Star Cr 17A3
Star Cr 44D2
Star L 27A4
Starbird Gla 18A3
Stark Cr 18B4
Starlike L 26B2
Starr Cr 45C3
Starvation Cr 10C4
State Cr 7D2
Statlu Cr 4C1
Statlu Cr 5D2
Staubert L 17C2
Stave Falls **5D3**
Stave L 4C1
Stave L 5D2
Stave R 5C2
Stawamus R 5B1
Steamboat Cr 75D2
Steamboat Cr 76A2
Steamboat Mtn 75C2
Steamboat Mtn 76A2
Steamer Pass 43D2
Steamer Pass 44A2
Steele Cr 12A4
Steele L 48B4
Steep Canyon Cr 53A4
Steeple Mtn 9A3
Steffens Cr 15C4
Stein Mtn 15A3
Stein R 15D4
Stelkuz Cr 63D3
Stelkuz L 63D3
Stella L 12D4
Stenstrom Cr 45A1
Stephen L 39A2
Stephen Pk 53B1
Stephens I 33B1
Stephens I 43C4
Stephens Pass 2C2
Stephney Cr 17C2
Stepp L 35C1
Stepp L 45C4
Sterling Cr 44D1-2
Stern L 47A-B4
Steven Cr 7A2
Stevens Cr 17D2
Stevens Ls 16B3
Stevens Ls 27B3
Steveston **5B3**
Steward Cr 45B3
Stewardson In 1B2
Stewardson Inlet **1B2**
● **Stewart** **52B3**
Stewart Cr 57B3
Stikelan Cr 24C4
Stikine R 51A1
Stikine R 60A4
Stikine R 60B1
Stikine R 61C1
Stikine R 62B1
Stikine R 62A3
Stikine R 71C4
Stikine R 72A4
Stillwater **2C1**

Stirling Cr 7C2
Stirling I 22B3
Stitt Cr 28B3
Stobart Cr 25C4
Stockdale Cr 18A3
Stocke Cr 5D1
Stoddart Cr 18C3
Stoddart Cr 57B1
Stone Cr 38C2
Stone Cr 57A3-4
Stone Mtn 75B2
Stonehouse R 79B3-4
Stoner **38C2**
Stony Cr 37C1
Stony L 39A2
Stony L 49D2
Stopper Is 1D4
Storie Cr 57D4
Stork Cr 19A4
Storm Cr 10B3
Storm Hill 7D3
Storm Mtn 18C1
Stormking Cr 27B1
Stovel Pk 80C3
Stoyoma Cr 6B1
Stoyoma Mtn 6B1
Stoyoma Mtn 15B4
Strachan B 11C1
Straight Pass Cr 63A2
Strait Cr 27B2
Strait L 26B3
Strait L 27B2
Strait of Georgia 2B1
Strait of Georgia 3C1
Strait of Georgia 5B4
Stranby R 11B2
Strange I 1A-B1
Stranger L 26D1
Stranger L 27A1
Strata Cr 60A2
Strata Mtn 60A2
Strathnaver **38C3**
Stratton Cr 27B3
Streak L 16C4
Strohn Cr 52B-C2
Strutell Cr 8A1
Strutell Cr 17A4
Stryen Cr 15A4
Stryker **10B4**
Stuart Chan 2D3-4
Stuart Chan 3C2
Stuart Island **13A3**
Stuart L 47B3
Stuart R 47C4
Stuart R 48A4
Stuhini Cr 69D3
Stuhini Cr 70B3
Stuie **23C1**
Stukemapten L 16C1
Stukemapten L 27C4
Stum L 25B2
Stump L 15D3
Stupendous Mtn 23B-C1
Sturdee R 62C3
Sturdee R 63A3
Styx Gla 13C2
Success Cr 23C-D3
Succour Cr 28C3
Succour L 63D2
Sucha Cr 37C3
Sucha L 37B3
Suck Cr 18A3
Sucker Cr 24B2
Sucker Cr 26B2
Sucker L 16B4
Sucker L 24B2
Sucker L 26B3
Sucwoa R 1B1
Sue Cha 34D1
Suey L 26C1
Sugar Cr 17A3
Sugar L 17A3

Sugarbowl Mtn 39A1
Sugarcane **26A2**
Sugarloaf Mtn 15D4
Suhm Cr 88C3
Suka Cr 6B2
Sukunka R 49A1
Sukunka R 49A2
Sukunka R 57A4
Sullivan Hill 9C1
Sullivan L 16A2
Sullivan R 28B3
Sulphur Cr 10A2
Sulphur Cr 74D1
Sulphurets Cr 51D1
Sulphurets Cr 52A1
Sulphurous L 26C4
Sumallo R 6B3
Sumas Mtn 4C2
Sumas Mtn 5D3
Sumas R 4C2
Sumas R 5D4
Summer L 9D1
● **Summerland** **7B2**
Summers Cr 6D2
Summit Cr 9A3
Summit Cr 39B3
Summit L 17C4
Summit L 25A2
Summit L 48C4
Summit L 52B2
Summit L 75B3
Summit L 80A3
Summit Lake **48C4**
Summit Lake **75B2-3**
Summit Pass 75B3
Summit Pk 17C4
Sumquolt Cr 23B3
Sunday Cr 6D3
Sunday In 20A1
Sunday Pk 80C3
Sundberg L 39A4
Sunderland Chan 12C3
Sundown Cr 9C3
Sundown Cr 57C4
Sunnybrae **16C2**
Sunrise Cr 9C3
Sunrise Valley **57C3**
Sunset Cr 27C4
Sunset Cr 57C3
Sunset L 46B3
Sunset Mtn 8D1
Sunset Prairie **57C3**
Sunsets Cr 45C-D3
Sunshine L 84B4
Superb Mtn 13B2
Surel L 35D3
Surge Narrows **13A4**
Surgeon Mtn 79B4
Surprise **80D4**
Surprise **81A-B4**
Surprise Cr 18D2
Surprise Cr 52C2
Surprise L 80D4
Surprise L 81B3-4
● **Surrey** **5C3**
Surrey L 15D3
Survey B 31D2
Survey B 33C4
Survey B 34A2
Survey Cr 30D2
Survey Cr 32C4
Survey Mtn 3C3
Surveyors Cr 52B-C1
Susan I 22A1
Susap Cr 7B3
Suschona Cr 47C1
Susie Cr 60B1
Suskwa Pass 45D1
Suskwa Pass 46A1
Suskwa Pass 53D4
Suskwa Pass 54A4
Suskwa R 45C1

Suskwa R 46A1
Suskwa R 54A4
Sussex L 15D3
Sustut L 54B1
Sustut Pk 54B1
Sustut R 53D2
Sustut R 54A2
Sustut R 54B1
Sustut R 63B4
Sutherland Cr 8B3
Sutherland R 47A3
Sutil Chan 13A4
Sutlahine R 70C3
Sutlej Chan 12A2
Sutslem Cr 35D4
Sutton Cr 2C4
Sutton Cr 3B2
Sutton R 52B3
Suzanne L 10A3
Suzannie L 25C1
Swakum Mtn 15D4
Swallop Cr 23A1
Swallop Cr 36A4
Swalwell L 16C4
Swamp L 48B-C4
Swan Cr 28B3
Swan L 16C3
Swan L 52D3
Swan L 58B4
Swan L 82B3
Swannell R 54D1
Swanson Cr 37B1
Swanson I 12A3
Swanson R 69B1
Swanson R 80B4
Swartz Bay **5A4**
Swede Cr 38C1
Sweden Cr 38B1
Sweeney L 35D1
Sweetin R 53A3
Sweetwater **57D3**
Sweetwater **58A3**
Swehaw Cr 8B3
Swift Cr 8D3
Swift Cr 40C4
Swift L 82A3
Swift R 38D4
Swift R 39A4
Swift R 81D3
Swift R 82B3
Swift River **82B2**
Swindle I 22A1
Sydney In 1B2
Sydney R 1B2
Sylvester Cr 47C1
Sylvester Pk 72C-D1
Sylvestre Cr 50B2
Symond Cr 18C1
Syncline Mtn 10B2
Syringa Cr 8B2

T

T Mtn 59D3
Table Cr 56D2
Table Hill 31D2
Table Hill 33C3
Table Hill 34A2
Table Mtn 62A-B4
Table Mtn 80C4
Table Mtn 81A3-4
Table R 48D2
Tabletop Cr 62D4
Tabletop Cr 63A4
Tabor Cr 38C1
Tabor L 38C1
Tacheeda Ls 48C2
Tacheeda Mtn 48C-D2
Tachek Cr 46C2
Tachick L 37C1
Tachie **47B3**

Tachie R 47B2
Tachilta Ls 71C3
Tachintelachick Cr 38B1
Taft Cr 52C1
Tagai L 37D1
Tagai L 38A2
Tagetochlain L 35D1
Tagetochlain L 36A1
Tagetochlain L 45D4
Tagetochlain L 46A4
Taghum **8C2**
Taginchil L 48B4
Tagish **80B-C2**
Tagish L 80C3
Tahaetkun Mtn 16B4
Taharti L 25B1
Taharti L 25B1
Tahini R 79C3
Tahla L 6C1
Tahlo Cr 54B4
Tahltan **71B-C4**
Tahltan L 60A1
Tahltan L 71A4
Tahltan R 60A1
Tahltan R 71B4
Tahoots Cr 71B1
Tahoots Cr 82B4
Tahsis In 1A1
Tahsis Mtn 1B1
Tahsis R 1A1
Tahsish In 11D4
Tahsish R 11D4
Tahtsa L 35C1
Tahtsa Reach 35D1
Tahtsa Reach 36A1
Tahtsedle Cr 61D3
Tahultzu L 37B1
Tahumming Gla 13B-C2
Tahumming Mtn 13C2
Tahumming R 13B3
Tahuntesko L 36B-C3
Tahyesco R 23B1
Tahyesco R 36C4
Taiataeszi Cr 36C4
Taite Cr 8B1
Takatoot L 47A1
Takia R 36C4
Takla L 46D1
Takla L 54C4
Takla Landing **54C4**
Tako Cr 38B2
Taku Arm 80C4
Taku R 69D3
Taku R 70A3
Takush Har 11C1
Takush R 11C1
Takysie Cr 36C-D1
Takysie Lake **36C1**
Talaha B 81A3
Talaha Bay 80C3
Talbot Cr 1C2
Talchako Gla 23C3
Talchako Mtn 23C2
Talchako R 23C2
Taleomey Gla 23B3
Taleomey R 23B2-3
Tally Cr 53B2
Taltan **60B-C1**
Taltapin L 47A4
Taltapin Mtn 47A3
Talunkwan I 31A4
Tam O'Shanter Cr 9A1
Tamarack L 9C1
Tamihi Cr 6A3
Tan Mtn 30C2
Tan Mtn 32B3
Tanah Cr 71A1
Tandzie Cr 74C-D2
Tangier R 17B1
Tangier R 28B4
Tangle Cr 18D2

Tangle Pk 18D3
Tanglefoot Cr 9D2
Tanilkul L 25A1
Tanswanket Cr 36D4
Tanu I 31A4
Tanya Ls 36C4
Tanzilla Butte 72B3
Tanzilla R 71C-D4
Tanzilla R 72A4
Tanzilla R 72B4
Taper Mtn 64A3
Tappen **16C2**
Tarnezell Cr 47A2
Tarnezell L 47A2
Tarrys **8C2**
Tartu In 30C2
Tartu In 32B3
Taseco R 14A1
Taseko Ls 14A1
Taseko Ls 25A4
Taseko R 24D3-4
Taseko R 25A3
Taslincheko Cr 47C2
Tasse L 26C1
Tasu **30D4**
Tasu Sd 30D4
Ta Ta Creek **9C1**
Tatalaska L 36C1
Tatalrose **36C1**
Tatalrose **46C4**
Tatalrose L 36C1
Tatalrose L 46C4
Tatchu Cr 1B4
Tate Cr 57D4
Tate Cr 58A4
Tatelkuz L 37B3
Tatelkuz Mtn 37B3
Tatin L 47A4
Tatisno Cr 84B3
Tatisno Mtn 84B3
Tatla Hill 24B3
Tatla L 24B-C2
Tatla Lake **24B3**
Tatla Lake Cr 24C2
Tatlatui L 62C4
Tatlatui L 63A4
Tatlatui Pk 62C4
Tatlayoko **24C3**
Tatlayoko L 24C4
Tatley Cr 18C3
Tatogga L 60D1
Tatogga L 61B1
Tatsadah L 47D4
Tatsamenie L 70D3
Tatsatua Cr 70D3
Tatshenshini R 78D3
Tatshenshini R 78D4
Tatshenshini R 79A-B3
Tatshenshini R 79A4
Tatsho Cr 71D3
Tatsho Cr 72A3
Tatsho Mtn 71D3
Tatsho Mtn 72B3
Tatsutnai Cr 47B4
Tatton **26B3**
Tatuk L 37C2
Tatzille Cr 84B-C3
Taurus L 7D3
Tautri Cr 25A1
Tautri L 25B1
Tavistock Gla 13C2
Tavistock Mtn 13C2
Taweel L 26D4
Taweel L 27A4
Taweh Cr 60C1-2
Tawina L 69D1
Tay Cr 48C4
Taylor **57C2**
Taylor Cr 14C2
Taylor L 26B4
Taylor Pk 62A3
Taylor R 1D3

Taylor R 52D1
Taylor R 61D4
Taynton Cr 18C3
Taysen Cr 70C1
Tchaikazan R 13D1
Tchentlo L 47A1
Tchentsut Mtn 47A-B2
Tchesinkut Cr 46C-D4
Tchesinkut L 46D4
Tchesinkut Lake **46D4**
Tchitin R 52D4
Tea Cr 18A3
Teakerne Arm 13A-B4
Teapot L 38D2
Teapot Mtn 48C3
Teaquahan Mtn 13B1
Teaquahan R 13B2
Tedideech Cr 71A2
Tedideech L 71A2
Teditua Cr 70D2
Teepee Cr 9D3
Teepee Cr 80B3
Teeta Cr 11C3
Teeter Cr 85C4
Teetzel Cr 9A3
Teh Cr 82A4
Tehran Pk 75A4
Teigen Cr 61B4
Teigen L 60D4
Teigen L 61A4
Teklo Cr 77C3
Telegraph Cove **12A3**
Telegraph Cr 23D1
Telegraph Cr 80D3
Telegraph Cr 81A3
Telegraph Creek **60B1**
Telegraph Pass 33C2
Telegraph Pass 34A1
Telegraph Pass 44A4
Telford Cr 10A1
Telkwa **45D2**
Telkwa **46A2**
Telkwa Pass 45C3
Telkwa R 45C3
Telkwa R 46A2
Tellot Cr 24A4
Tellot Gla 13A1
Tellot Gla 24A4
Telsequah Gla 70A2
Temapho L 24D1
Temple Cr 65D1
Templeton R 18B2
Ten Mile Cr 56C3
Ten Mile L 38C-D3
Ten Mile L 83D3
Tenaka Cr 75D4
Tenaka Cr 76B4
Tenakihi Cr 54D2
Tenas Cr 14C3
Tenas Cr 45D3
Tenas L 23D2
Tenderfoot Cr 17D3
Tennent L 1D2
Tenquille Cr 14C3
Tentsi Cr 75A3
Tepee Cr 49C1
Tepee Cr 65D2
Tepee Mtn 75C-D2
Tepee Mtn 76A2
Teresa I 80C-D4
Teresa L 81A4
Terminus Mtn 73D2
Terminus Mtn 74A2
● **Terrace** **45A3**
Terrace Cr 16B4
Terrace Mtn 16B4
Terraced Pk 7D2
Terrahina Cr 81C4
Terry Cr 38C2
Tescla Cr 65C2
Teseko Mtn 14A1
Tesla L 36B3

Teslin 81C2
Teslin R 71A-B2
Teslin R 71A1
Teslin R 81D4
Tetachuck L 36C3
Tetachuck R 36D2
Tete Hill 25A4
Tetsa Pk 75B3
Tetsa R 75B3
Tetsa R 76A3
Texaco Ls 77A1
Texada I 2C2
Texas Cr 8B3
Texas Cr 15A3
Tezwa R 35B3-4
Tezzeron Cr 47C2
Tezzeron L 47B2
Tezzeron Mtn 47C2
Tête Angela Cr 25A3-4
Tête Cr 40B4
Tête Jaune Cache 40C4
Thaba Mtn 48C1
Thabah Mtn 56C4
Thalia L 6C1
Thane 70C4
Thane Cr 54D2
Thatue Mtn 61B1
Thautil R 45C4
The Bookworm 5B1
The Elbow 65C4
The Jaws 35B2
The Knob 60A4
The Lions 4A1
The Monarch 18C1
The Nipple 6A1
The Old Settler 6A2
The Pillar 62D3
The Pillar 63A3
The Pinnacles 17B4
The Red Pillar 1D2
The Steeples 9D2
The Thumb 54A-B2
The Wart 6D1
Thelwood Cr 1D2
Thenatlodi Mtn 72B4
Theodosia R 13B4
Thetis I 2D3
Thetis I 3C2
Thetlaandoa Cr 77B1
Thetlaandoa Cr 88B4
Thibert Cr 71C-D2
Thibert Cr 72A2
Thinahtea Cr 88D3-4
Thinahtea L 88D3
Third Nrs 23A3
Thirty Mile Cr 81D4
Thirty Mile L 71C4
Thirty Mile L 72A4
Thomas Cr 45B3
Thomas Cr 60D3
Thomas Cr 61A3
Thomas Pk 62D3
Thomas Pk 63A3
Thomlinson Cr 53C4
Thompson Cr 46A3
Thompson Pass 28D2
Thompson R 15B3-4
Thompson Sd 12C2
Thompson Sound 12C2
Thone Cr 7D2
Thor Cr 17B3
Thorald Cr 18C3
Thormanby Is 2C2
Thormanby Is 3C1
Thornbrough Chan 3D1
Thornbrough Chan 5A2
Thorne L 63B4
Thornhill 45A3
Thorpe Cr 85C-D3
Thorsen Cr 23A2
Thorwald Cr 22D2
Three Brothers Mtn 6C3

Three Forks Cr 72D2
3 Mile Cr 26A1
Three Mile L 15A1
Three Valley 17A2
Through Cr 74B4
Thrums 8C2
Thudaka Cr 62D1
Thudaka Cr 63B1
Thule Cr 62A3
Thulme R 44B3
Thunder Cr 49D2
Thunder Cr 50A2
Thunder Mtn 23B1
Thunder Mtn 24C1
Thunder R 27C2
Thurlow 12D3
Thurston Bay 13A3
Thutade Cr 62C4
Thutade L 62D4
Thutade L 63A4
Thuya Cr 26D4
Thuya Cr 27A4
Thynne L 6C1
Tibble Cr 38B4
Tie L 9D2
Tiedemann Gla 13A1
Tiedemann Gla 24A4
Tiger 8C4
Tighe Cr 27A1
Tightfit L 87C4
Tildesley Cr 46D2
Tiletown L 37D3
Till L 25D2
Tiltzarone L 38B4
Timberwolf Cr 77D3
Timothy Cr 26B3
Timothy L 26B3
Tin Cup L 26B3
Tingle Cr 4B1
Tingle Cr 5D2
Tingley Cr 25C1
Tingley Cr 25C1
Tinmusket Cr 25D4
Tinsdale Cr 39B3-4
Tintina Cr 52C2
Tintlhohtan L 26D4
Tipella Cr 5D1
Tipperary L 18D3
Tisdall L 26C2
Tisimtack L 34C3
Tlakwa Mtn 11D4
Tlatlos Cr 12B3
Tlell 31A2
Tlell 32C3
Tlell R 30D2
Tlell R 32C3
Tlools Cr 1C1
Tlupana In 1A2
Tlupana R 1B1
Toad Hot Springs 75A2
Toad Mtn 8D2
Toad R 74D3
Toad R 75A1-2
Toad R 86A-B4
Toad River 75A2
Toba Gla 13C-D2
Toba In 13B3
Toba Pk 13C2
Toba R 13C3
Tobacco Cr 15C1
Tobe L 26D4
Tobin L 55C2
Toboggan Cr 45C-D2
Toby Cr 18B3
Toby Creek 18B3
Toby Gla 18B4
Tochcha L 46C2
Todagin Cr 61B2
Todagin L 61B2
Todd Cr 52B1-2
Todd Cr 81B4
● **Tofino 1C3**

Tofino Cr 1D3
Tofino In 1D3
Tokumm Cr 18B1
Tolmie Chan 35A4
Tom Browne L 12C3
Tom Cr 54D4
Tom Mackay L 51D1
Tom Mackay L 52A1
Tomias L 55A1
Tomias Mtn 62B2
Tommy Cr 14C2
Tommy Jack Cr 53C2
Tommy L 6D1
Tommy L 15D4
Tommy Ls 66A1
Tomslake 58A4
Tonasket 7C4
Toneko L 39B1
Tonquin Cr 41A4
Tony Cr 56B4
Toodoggone L 62D2
Toodoggone L 63A2
Toodoggone Pk 62D2
Toodoggone Pk 63A2
Toodoggone R 63A2
Tooga Cr 77D1
Tooga L 77C1
Toon L 44B3
Toon R 44B3
Tootsee L 82C3
Tootsee L 83A3
Tootsee R 82D3
Tootsee R 83A3
Toozaza Cr 82D4
Toozaza Cr 83A4
Topaze Har 12C3
Topknot L 11B3
Topley 46B3
Topley Landing 46C2
Toquart B 1D3
Toquart R 1D3
Tornado Mtn 10B1
Tornado Mtn 19B4
Tornado Pass 10B1
Tornado Pass 19B4
Torpid Cr 75B1
Torpy R 39B1
Torpy R 39B1
Torres Chan 81A4
Torres Channel 80C4
Tortoise L 26D4
Tosh Cr 14B1
Tower Cr 9B2
Tower L 57D2
Tower Mtn 75A-B3
Towkuh Cr 39A3
Towler Cr 38D4
Town Cr 17C2
Townsend Cr 38C4
Townsend Cr 65D4
Townsley Cr 64D2
Townsley Cr 65B2
Townsoitoi Cr 77C3
Towydkin L 25A3
● **Trail 8C3**
Trail Cr 36D4
Trail Cr 62A4
Trail Creek 10C4
Trail L 87D4
Tranquil Cr 1D3
Tranquille 15D2
Tranquille L 15D2
Tranquille R 15D2
Trap Mtn 3C3
Trapline Cr 45B3
Trapp L 16A3
Trapper Cr 57B4
Trapper L 70C3
Trapping Cr 38C2
Trapping L 38C2
Treat Cr 2D1
Treaty Cr 52B1

Treble Mtn 52B3
Tregillus Cr 39A3
Trego 10B4
Tremblay Cr 57C3
Trembleur L 47A2
Tremor Mtn 14C4
Trent R 2A2
Trepanier 7B1
Trepanier Cr 84A3
Tretheway Cr 5D2
Trevor Chan 2A4
Trevor L 11D1
Trépanier Cr 7B1
Trial Is 3D4
Triangle I 11A4
Triangle L 84D3
Triangle L 85B3
Tribune Chan 12B2
Trident Mtn 28B3
Trident Pk 64C4
Trimble Cr 64D3
Trimble Cr 65A3
Trimble L 64D3
Trimble L 65A3
Trincomali Chan 3D2
Trincomali Chan 5A4
Trinity B 12A2-3
Trinity Cr 16D3
Trinity Valley 16D3
Trio L 26A1
Triple L 53D2
Triple L 54A2
Triplex Mtn 23C4
Triumph Cr 59D2
Triumph Gla 59D2
Troitsa Cr 35D2
Troitsa L 35C2
Troitsa Pk 35D2
Troitsa Pk 36A2
Troitsa Pk 36A2
Trophy Mtn 27B3
Trout Cr 7B2
Trout Cr 45C2
Trout L 17C3
Trout L 81C3
Trout Lake 17C3
Trout Mtn 17C3
Trout R 74C1
Trout R 74C2
Trout R 85C4
Troutline Cr 72B1
Troy Cr 8A3
Truax Cr 14C2
Truncate Mtn 64A3
Trutch 65C1
Trutch Cr 65C1
Trutch I 33D4
Trutch I 34B3
Trygve L 62C4
Tsable L 2A2
Tsable R 2A2
Tsacha L 37A-B3
Tsachehdza Cr 76B3
Tsah Cr 47C4
Tsai Cr 45C3
Tsalit Mtn 45D4
Tsalit Mtn 46A4
Tsar Cr 28B3
Tsartus I 2A4
Tsatia Cr 61B2
Tsatia Mtn 61B2
Tsawwassen 5B3
Tsayakwacha L 36D3
Tsaybahe Cr 60D1
Tsaybahe Cr 61B1
Tsaybahe Pass 61B1
Tsaydaychuz Pk 36B3
Tsaydiz Cr 63D3
Tsayta L 54D4
Tsaytis R 35B3
Tsaytut B 53D2
Tsaytut B 54A-B2

Tsazia Mtn 60D1
Tsazia Mtn 61A-B1
Tschick L 36D3
Tsea Ls 87D4
Tsea R 88A4
Tseax R 44D1
Tsedeka Cr 48B1
Tsedeka Cr 56B4
Tsenaglode L 71D4
Tsenaglode L 72B4
Tsenglode Mtn 61C1
Tseta Cr 70D1
Tsetia Cr 61C-D2
Tsetogamus Cr 61B1
Tsetzi L 37A4
Tsezakwa Cr 46A-B1
Tsezakwa Cr 46B1
Tsezakwa Cr 54A4
Tsia Cr 84C3
Tsia L 84B3
Tsibass Lagoon 11D1-2
Tsichgass L 46B4
Tsikhini Cr 60B1
Tsikwustum Cr 27C4
Tsikwustum L 27C4
Tsilbekuz L 37A4
Tsilcoh Cr 47C3
Tsimeh Cr 76C1
Tsimeh Ls 76C2
Tsimpsean Pen 43D3
Tsimpsean Pen 44A3
Tsimpson Pen 33C1
Tsinhia Cr 87B4
Tsinhia L 87B4
Tsinitla Cr 84B-C3
Tsintsunko Cr 15D1
Tsintsunko L 15D1
Tsirku Gla 68B1
Tsirku Gla 79B4
Tsitika R 12B3
Tsitsutl Mtn 46D2
Tsitsutl Pk 36D4
Tsoloss Cr 24D4
Tsolum R 2A1
Tsoo Cr 75D1
Tsoo Cr 76A-B1
Tsuh Cr 7B1
Tsuh L 25B3
Tsuius Cr 17A3
Tsuius Mtn 17A2
Tsulquate R 11C2
Tsuniah L 24C4
Tsus Cr 39A1
Tsusiat L 2A4
Tuaton L 62B3
Tuaton Pk 62A-B3
Tubbs L 26B3
Tucha Cr 63C4
Tucha Cr 63C-D4
Tucho L 73B2
Tucho R 73A4
Tuchodi Ls 75B4
Tuchodi R 64B1
Tuchodi R 75B4
Tuchodi R 76A4
Tuck In 33C1
Tuck In 43D3
Tuck In 44A3
Tuck L 2B4
Tuck L 3A2
Tudyah L 48B1
Tuff Pk 62C2
Tugulnuit L 7C3
Tugwell Cr 3C4
Tuktakamin Mtn 16B3
Tuktsayda Mtn 60D1
Tulameen 6C2
Tulameen Mtn 6C2
Tulameen R 6C2
Tulameen R 6C3
Tulip Cr 8B2
Tullin Mtn 24C4

Tulsequah Gla	69C-D2
Tulsequah L	69C-D2
Tulsequah L	70A2
Tulsequah R	69D2
Tulsequah R	70A2
Tumbler Ridge	**49C1**
Tumeka Cr	61C3
Tumeka L	61C3
Tumtum L	27D3
Tumuch L	39B1
Tumult Gla	12C1
Tunjony L	70C3
Tunkwa L	15C3
Tupper	**58A-B4**
Tupper Cr	57D4
Tupper Cr	58A4
Tupper R	58B4
Turn Cr	81C4
Turnagain L	72C-D4
Turnagain R	72D3
Turnagain R	73A-B2
Turner Cr	39C3
Turner L	23C2
Turner Pk	30D3
Turner Pk	32C4
Turner Valley	**19C2**
Turning Mtn	49B2
Turning Mtn	49B2
Turnoff Cr	65B3
Turnour L	12B3
Turret I	1D4
Turtle L	80C3
Tusulko R	23D1
Tuta L	56B4
Tutachi L	63D4
Tutchi R	80A3
Tutesheta Cr	71B4
Tutiai Mtn	37A3
Tutizzi L	54D2
Tutizzi L	54D2
Tutshi L	80B3
Tutshi R	80B-C3
Tutsingale Mtn	71C2
Tuwartz L	34C3
Tuwasus Cr	5C1
Tuya L	71C1
Tuya L	72A1
Tuya R	71C-D1
Tuya R	71C2
Tuya R	71C4
Tuya R	72A1
Tuya R	72A3
Tuzcha L	13D1
Tuzcha L	14A1
Tuzcha L	25A4
Tuzo Cr	7D2
Twaal Cr	15B3
Twain Cr	46C2
Twan Cr	25C1
Tweedsmuir Gla	78B-C3
Tweedsmuir Pk	36B2
Twelve Mile Cr	18A1
Twenty Mile Cr	55A3
Twidwell Cr	49A1-2
Twig Cr	16B3
Twin Bays	**9A2**
Twin Butte	**10D3**
Twin Cr	55A4
Twin Gla	60B4
Twin Is	2A-B1
Twin Is	13A4
Twin Island L	73B1
Twin L	9D3
Twin Ls	7B3
Twin Ls	50A1
Twin One Cr	14C4
Twin Two Cr	14D4
Twina L	70B1
Twist Cr	24A4
Twist L	24A4
Two Bid Cr	65B3
Two Cr	49B1

Two Fish Cr	72D3
Two Island L	87D4
Two L	25A2
Two Lake Cr	53D1
Two Lake Cr	54A1
Two Mile Rapids	84A3
Two Rivers	**57D2**
Two Rivers	**58A2**
Two Sisters Mtn	39A3
Twobit Cr	8B2
Tyaughton Cr	14B-C1
Tyaughton L	14C2
Tyee L	25D1
Tyhee L	45D2
Tyhee L	46A2
Tzahny L	62B4
Tzahny Mtn	62B3-4
Tzazati L	25A1
Tzeetsaytsul Pk	23B1
Tzenzaicut L	25C1
Tzenzaicut L	38C4
Tzeo R	23A3
Tzoonie R	2D1

U

Ucluelet	**1D4**
Ucona R	1C1
Uduk L	36C2
Udy Cr	38A-B4
Ulkatcho	**36D4**
Umbach Cr	66B3-4
Umiti Cr	38D3
Uncha Cr	36D1
Uncha L	36D1
Uncha Mtn	36D1
Uncha Mtn	46D4
Union Bay	**2A-B1**
Union Cr	81B4
Union I	1A4
Union I	11D4
Union I	44A3
Union In	43D3
Union L	43D3
Union L	44A3
Union Mtn	80D4
Union Mtn	81A-B4
Unna L	39B3
Unuk Finger Mtn	51D1
Unuk Finger Mtn	52A1
Unuk R	51D1
Unuk R	52A1
Unuk R	60D4
Unuk R	61A4
Upana L	1B1
Upana R	1C1
Upper Arrow L	17B3
Upper Bell L	62D2
Upper Belle L	63A2
Upper Blue L	49C3
Upper Campbell L	1D1
Upper Elk L	19A3
Upper Fraser	**49A4**
Upper Habour L	27C4
Upper L	26B3
Upper Liard	**83D2**
Upper Loon L	15C1
Upper Quinsam L	1D1
Upright Cr	40D3
Upright Mtn	40D3
Upset Cr	66B4
Ure Cr	14C4
Urquhart Cr	6A2
Ursula Chan	34D2
Ursula Cr	56B2
Ursus Cr	1D2
Useless Cr	31D1
Useless Cr	33B2
Uselss Cr	43D4
Usk	**45A3**
Uslika L	55A2

Ussa L	26B1
Utahn Cr	76D2
Uztlius Cr	6B1

V

Vachon Cr	27B2
Valanciennes R	28D3
Valdes I	3C-D2
Valdes I	5A3
Valemont Mtn	74B4
○ **Valemount**	**40C4**
Valentine Mtn	3C3
Valhalla Centre	**58C4**
Valhalla Mtn	60A2
Valleau Cr	47A-B1
Valleau Cr	55A4
Vallee Cr	46A3
Valley Cr	8A1
Vallican	**8C2**
Vama Vama Cr	38D1
Van Horne Br	17C1
Van In	30C3
Van In	32B4
Van Zandt	**5D4**
Vananda	**2B1**
Vance Cr	16D4
● **Vancouver**	**5B3**
Vancouver I	1D2
Vancouver I	3A-B2
Vancouver I	11C-D3
Vancouver R	2D1
● **Vanderhoof**	**37C1**
Vanderhoof	**47C4**
Vansittart I	11C2
Vanstone Cr	17B3
Vanwyk Cr	17A2
Vargas I	1C3
Varrick Cr	64D1
Varrick Cr	65A1
Varrick Cr	75D4
Varrick Cr	76A4
Vaseux Cr	7C3
Vaseux L	7C3
Vavenby	**27B4**
Vedan Cr	25C3
Vedan L	24D4
Vedder Crossing	**6A3**
Vega Cr	55A2
Venables L	15B3
Ventego Cr	28C4
Ventego L	28C4
Vents	73D1
Vents R	74B1
Vents R	84D4
Vents R	85B4
Verdant Cr	18C1
Vermilion Crossing	**18C1**
Vermilion R	18C1
Vermillion Pass	18C1
Vermont Cr	18A2
Vern Ritchie Gla	78B-C3
Verney Pass	34D2
● **Vernon**	**12B4**
Vernon	**16C4**
Vernon Cr	7C1
Vernon Cr	16C4
Vernon Hill	16C4
Vernon L	1B1
Vernon L	12B4
Verrett R	60B-C4
Vert L	25D4
Vertical Mtn	9D1
Vesuvius	**3D2**
Vevey Cr	8D1
Vic L	14B1
Vickers Cr	5C2
● **Victoria**	**3D4**
Victoria Cr	38D4
Victoria L	11C3
Victoria L	70D2

Victoria Pk	12C4
Vidette	**15C1**
View L	1D2
View Royal	**3D4**
Vignal Pk	64B1
Vigue Cr	17A3
Vile Cr	53A1
Village I	12B3
Vincent L	83D4
Viner Sd	12B2
Vines L	72B1
Viola L	11D2
Violin L	8C3
Virago Sd	32B2
Virago Sd	42C4
Vizer Cr	85D3
Vlem Cr	16D3
Voght Cr	6C1
Volcano L	1C1
Vowell Cr	18A2
Vuich Cr	6C2

W

Waddington Chan	13B4
Waddington Gla	13A1
Waddington Har	13B2
Wadin Cr	84B4
Waglisla	**22B2**
Wagner Ranch	**56D1**
Wahkash Cr	12D1
Wahla L	36B3
Wahleach Cr	4D1
Wahleach Cr	6A3
Wahleach L	6A3
Wahpeeto Cr	12B1
Wahshihlas B	12D1
Wahthinli Mtn	64B-C1
Waiparous	**19B1**
Waitabit Cr	28D4
Waitabit Cr	29A4
Waitabit L	29A3
Wakeman R	12B1
Wakeman R	23B4
Wakeman Sd	12B1-2
Walbran Cr	2B4
Walbran Cr	3A3
Walbran I	22C4
Wales Cr	25B4
Wales I	43D2
Wales I	44A2
Walhachin	**15C2**
Walker Cr	39C1
Walker Cr	73A1
Walker Group	11C2
Walker L	22B2
Walkum B	11D1
Walkum B	22D4
Walkus L	23B4
Wall Cr	7A3
Wall Cr	16C3
Wall L	10C3
Wallensteen L	16C3
Waller B	33C4
Waller B	34A2
Waller L	33C4
Waller L	34A2
Wallop Mtn	39D1
Walt L	2C1
Waneta	**8C3**
Wann L	69C1
Wann R	80B-C4
Wannock R	22D3
Wanokana Cr	11C3
Wansa Cr	38D1
Wap Cr	17A2
Wap L	17A2
Wapistan Cr	65C3
Wapiti	**50C-D2**
Wapiti L	49C3
Wapiti Pass	49C3

Wapiti R	49D2-3
Wapiti R	50A2
Wapoose L	36D1
Wapta L	29B4
Wapumun L	40A1
Wapumun L	50A4
War L	48B2
Ward Cr	9D3
Ward Cr	14D1
Wardner	**9D2**
Ware	**63D2**
Warfield	**8C3**
Wargen Ls	66B2
Warm Beach	**4B4**
Warm Cr	80B4
Warn B	1D3
Warneford R	63D2
Warner Pk	63C1-2
Warren Cr	18A2
Warren L	16A2
Warsaw Mtn	28A2
Wasa	**9D1**
Wasa L	9D1
Wash Cr	62A3
Washwash R	23D3
Wasi Cr	55A2
Wasi L	55A2
Wasko Ls	26C1
Waskulay Cr	65B2
Wasley L	16A4
Wasp Cr	14B3
Watch L	26C4
Watching Cr	15D2
Watchman Mtn	26D1
Waterlily L	47D4
Waterloo Mtn	2D4
Waterloo Mtn	3C3
Waterton Park	**10D3**
Watson B	22A1
Watson Bar Cr	14D1
Watson I	12A2
Watson L	26B3
Watson Lake	**83D2**
Watson Lake Airport	**83D2**
Watson Pk	48D1
Watt Cr	39C4
Watt L	39C4
Watta Cr	1C2
Wauconda	**7D4**
Waump Cr	12A1
Wavey L	26D4
Wawa L	24A1
Weare L	34C3
Weasel Cr	56B2
Weaver Cr	9C2
Weaver L	6A2
Weaver Pk	49C3
Webber L	47D4
Webber L	48A4
Webberly L	47C1
Weber C	53A4
Webster Cr	25C1
Webster L	22B2
Wedeene Mtn	44D4
Wedeenne R	44D4
Wedge Cr	14C4
Wedge Mtn	14C4
Wedge Pk	55D2
Wedge Pk	56A2
Wee Sandy Cr	8C1
Wee Sandy Cr	17C4
Wee Sandy L	8C1
Wee Sandy L	17C4
Weedon Cr	48B2
Weedon L	48B2-3
Weeks L	3C3
Weewanie Cr	34D1
Weigert Cr	10A1
Weir Mtn	81C3-4
Weissener Cr	63D1
Weissener L	63D1
Welch Pk	4D1

Welch Pk.....................6A3
Wellington.....................**2C3**
Wells.....................**39A3**
Wells Cove.....................20B2
Wells Cr.....................36C1
Wells Gray Pk.....................36B2
Wells Pass.....................12A2
Wembley.....................**50C-D1**
Wendle Cr.....................39A2
Wendle Cr.....................39C3
Wendy Cr.....................66B2
Wendy L.....................66B2
Weneez.....................**47C-D4**
Wenger Cr.....................64D1
Wenger Cr.....................65B1
Wentworth Cr.....................38A-B4
Wentworth L.....................15D2
Werner B.....................20B1
Wesach Cr.....................44D2
West Arm.....................8D2
West Cache Cr.....................57A1
West Churn Cr.....................14C1
West Churn Cr.....................25C4
West Conroy Cr.....................66A2
West Grenville Gla.....................13B2
West Gutah Cr.....................66B2
West Kettle R.....................7D1
West Kiskatinaw R.....................49C-D1
West Kiskatinaw R.....................58A4
West Kiskatinow R.....................57D4
West Klua Cr.....................76C4
West Kwanika Cr.....................54D4
West L.....................2C1
West L.....................85B3
West Landing.....................**54C4**
West Milligan Cr.....................66C3
West Nabesche R.....................56B2
West Nadila Cr.....................25B4
West Redonda I.....................13B4
West Road
  (Blackwater)R.....................37A4
West Road
  (Blackwater)R.....................37C3
West Road
  (Blackwater)R.....................38A3
West Sound.....................**5B4**
West Taylor R.....................52D1
West Thurlow I.....................12D3
West Toad R.....................74C3
West Torpy R.....................49A-B4
West Twin Cr.....................17B1
West Twin Cr.....................39D2
West Vancouver.....................**5B2**
West Yahk R.....................9C4
Westbank.....................**7B1**
Westbridge.....................**7D3**
Westfall Cr.....................17D2
Westham I.....................3D2
Westham I.....................5B3
Westman Cr.....................26B3
Westmere L.....................7A1
Weston Cr.....................55D3
Weston Cr.....................56A3
Westside.....................**7C1**
Westwick L.....................25D2
Westwold.....................**16B3**
Weyman Cr.....................16A3
Whalen L.....................34D3
Whaletown.....................**13A4**
Whatshan L.....................8B1
Whatshan L.....................17B4
Whatshan Pk.....................17B4
Whatshan R.....................17B4
Wheaton Cr.....................72D3-4
Wheeler Cr.....................10B2
Whelakis Lagoon.....................11D2
Whidbey Reach.....................35B2
Whiffle L.....................26B1
Whip Cr.....................17A3
Whipsaw Cr.....................6D3
Whirlpool Pass.....................28B1

Whiskey Cr.....................25D2
Whistle Cr.....................7A3
Whistler.....................**14B4**
Whistler Basin.....................54B-C1
Whistler Mtn.....................14B4
Whitburn.....................**58C3**
White Boar L.....................9B2
White Cr.....................9B1
White Cr.....................44D3
White Eye L.....................36D2
White Grouse Mtn.....................9B2
White L.....................16C2
White L.....................26A4
White Lake.....................**16C2**
White Man Mtn.....................18D2
White Man Pass.....................18D2
White Pass.....................**80A4**
White Pass.....................80A4
White R.....................12C4
White R.....................18D4
White R.....................19D4
White R.....................52C3
● **White Rock**.....................**5C3**
White Spruce Cr.....................77C2
Whitecap Cr.....................14C2
Whitecape Gla.....................12D1
Whitecone Pk.....................35D3
Whitecrow Mtn.....................28A1
Whitefish L.....................47A3
Whitehorse.....................**80A1**
Whiteman.....................**16C4**
Whiteman Cr.....................16B4
Whitemantle Gla.....................13A1
Whitemantle Mtn.....................13A1
Whitepine Cr.....................28D4
Whiterocks Mtn.....................7B1
Whiterocks Mtn.....................16B4
Whiterose Mtn.....................28D3
Whitesaddle Mtn.....................24B4
Whitesail L.....................35D2
Whitesail L.....................36A2
Whitesail Reach.....................36A2
Whitesand L.....................24C3
Whiteshield Mtn.....................40C3
Whiteswan L.....................18D4
Whitetail Cr.....................18C2
Whitetail L.....................18C4
Whitetop Mtn.....................24B1
Whitetop Mtn.....................37B4
Whitewood Cr.....................16A1
Whiting Cr.....................35D1
Whittier Cr.....................38C3
Whitton Cr.....................23D2
Whitworth Pk.....................6B3
Whudzi Mtn.....................63B2
Whyac.....................**2B4**
Wichcika Cr.....................48D3
Wickaninnish B.....................1C-D3
Wicked L.....................55D2
Wicked L.....................56A2
Wicked R.....................55D2
Wicked R.....................56A2
Wickson Cr.....................12D2
Widgeon Cr.....................4B1
Widgeon Cr.....................5C2
Widgeon L.....................4B1
Widgeon L.....................5C2
Widgeon L.....................23C2
Wiggins Cr.....................26A2
Wigwam B.....................12A1
Wigwam R.....................10B3
Wild Horse R.....................9D1
Wildboy Cr.....................88B3
Wildcat Cr.....................29A3
Wilde L.....................57C3
Wilder Cr.....................57B2
Wilderness Mtn.....................23D3
Wildfire Cr.....................52B-C1
Wildmare Cr.....................57A3
Wildwood Heights.....................**2B1**
Wilfred Cr.....................2A2
Wilkie Cr.....................17C3

Wilkinson Cr.....................7D2
Willan Cr.....................25A4
Willan L.....................25B3
William L.....................11B2
Williams Cr.....................45A3
Williams L.....................25D2
● **Williams Lake**.....................**25D2**
Williams Lake R.....................25D2
Willie Jack Cr.....................71A1
Willis Cr.....................6D3
Willis L.....................16D2
Willison B.....................69C1
Willison Gla.....................69B-C1
Williston L.....................48B1
Williston L.....................55C2-D3
Williston L.....................56A3
Williston L.....................56C-D2
Williston L.....................64A-B4
Willoughby Cr.....................52C3
Willow Cr.....................54B1
Willow Point.....................**8D2**
Willow R.....................38D1
Willow R.....................39A3
Willow R.....................48D2
Willow River.....................**48D4**
Willow Valley.....................**57C3**
Willowbrook.....................**57D3**
Willowy Cr.....................47C2
Wilma L.....................16C4
Wilmer.....................**18C3**
Wilms Cr.....................69D2
Wilms Cr.....................70A2
Wilson Cr.....................1B2
Wilson Cr.....................17C4
Wilson Cr.....................80D4
Wilson Cr.....................81B4
Wilson L.....................17C4
Wilson L.....................26D4
Wilson Landing.....................**7C1**
Wiminasik L.....................53B1
Windermere.....................**18C3**
Windermere Cr.....................18C3
Windermere L.....................18C3
Windfall Cr.....................7D3
Windfall Cr.....................27D1
Windfall Cr.....................49A1
Windham.....................**59B2**
Windrem Cr.....................57A3
Windsor Cr.....................33D1
Windsor Cr.....................44B4
Windsor L.....................2C1
Windsor L.....................13C4
Windsor L.....................48B4
Windy Camp Cr.....................81B3
Windy Cr.....................26D4
Windy Cr.....................28B3
Windy Cr.....................57B2-3
Winfield.....................**16C4**
Winfield Cr.....................45C3
Wingdam.....................**39A3**
Winlaw.....................**8C2**
Winnifred Cr.....................8A1
Winslow Cr.....................5D2
Winter Cr.....................60B1
Winter Har.....................11B3
Winter Harbour.....................**11B3**
Winter In.....................43D2
Winter In.....................44A2
Winters Cr.....................7A3
Wistaria.....................**36B1**
Witch L.....................47B1
Witches Br.....................15C3
Witness Cr.....................18C3
Wittsichica Cr.....................47C1
Woden Cr.....................8B1
Woden Pk.....................8C1
Wokas L.....................1D1
Woking.....................**58D4**
Wokkpash Cr.....................75A3
Wokkpash L.....................75A-B3
Wolf Cr.....................9D1
Wolf L.....................2A1

Wolf R.....................1D1
Wolfe Cr.....................6D2
Wolfe L.....................12A4
Wollaston L.....................16C4
Wolverine L.....................26B1
Wolverine L.....................39A-B4
Wolverine L.....................73A3
Wolverine R.....................39B-C2
Wolverine R.....................49B1-2
Wonowon.....................**66A4**
Wood Arm.....................28A2
Wood L.....................16C4
Wood R.....................28B2
Woodall Cr.....................49A4
Woodfibre.....................**5B2**
Woodhaven.....................**5B3**
Woodhus Cr.....................1D1
Woodjam Cr.....................26B2
Woods L.....................16B3
Woods Lagoon.....................11D1
Woods Landing.....................**16D1**
Woodsdale.....................**16C4**
Woodyadilinka Cr.....................48D2
Woolsey Cr.....................17B1
Word Cr.....................25C4
Work Chan.....................33C1
Work Chan.....................43D3
Work Chan.....................44A3
Wormwold Cr.....................39A3
Worry Cr.....................62B2
Worsley.....................**58C-D1**
Woss.....................**12B4**
Woss L.....................12B4
Wragge Cr.....................17C4
Wrede Cr.....................63C4
Wriggle Cr.....................60A1
Wright.....................**26A3**
Wright Cr.....................48C4
Wright In.....................33D3
Wright In.....................34B2
Wright Pass.....................21C1
Wright Pks.....................69D3
Wright Pks.....................70A3
Wright Sd.....................34C3
Wuho Cr.....................9C2
Wutak L.....................36B-C2
Wutlus L.....................38A4
Wyclees Lagoon.....................11C-D1
Wycliffe.....................**9C2**
Wye Cr.....................3C3
Wyndham L.....................33D3
Wyndham L.....................34B2
Wynndel.....................**9B3**

Y

Yaak.....................**9D4**
Yaculta.....................**13A4**
Yahk.....................**9C3**
Yahk Mtn.....................9D3
Yahk R.....................9D3
Yakoun L.....................30D3
Yakoun L.....................32C4
Yakoun R.....................30D2
Yakoun R.....................32C3
Yalakom R.....................14C1
Yale.....................**6B2**
Yale Cr.....................6B2
Yalta Pk.....................75B4
Yankee Flats.....................**16C3**
Yanks Pk.....................39B4
Yard Cr.....................16D2
Yardley L.....................38D2
Yarksis.....................**1C3**
Yash Cr.....................74D2
Yatzutkin L.....................47C2
Yaza Cr.....................53A1
Yaza Cr.....................62A4
Yedhe Cr.....................74D3
Yedhe Ls.....................74D3
Yedhe Mtn.....................75A3

Yehiniko Cr.....................60B1
Yehiniko L.....................60B2
Yeka L.....................88B4
Yeko L.....................9C3
Yellow Cr.....................28A2
Yellow L.....................7B2
Yellowhead L.....................41A4
Yellowjacket Cr.....................40D4
Yeo I.....................22B1-2
Yeo L.....................22B1-2
Yeoward Cr.....................17A4
Yesshadle Cr.....................87D3-4
Yeth Cr.....................70C2
Yimpakluk L.....................37D3
Yimpakluk L.....................38A3
Ymir.....................**8D3**
Ymir Cr.....................8D3
Ymir Mtn.....................8D2
Yohetta Cr.....................13D1
Yohetta L.....................13D1
Yoho R.....................29B4
Yookwa Cr.....................12B4
Yorston L.....................25D2
Youbou.....................**2C4**
Young Cr.....................23C1
Young L.....................15C1
Young R.....................22D3
Youngs Cr.....................48B4
Yoyo.....................**77B2**
Yuen L.....................54B2
Yule L.....................35A3
Yuquot.....................**1B2**
Yuzkli Cr.....................39A3

Z

Zagoddetchino Mtn.....................60B1
Zakwaski Mtn.....................15B4
Zamora.....................**7D3**
Zancudo L.....................70D1
Zayas I.....................43B3
Zeballos.....................**12A4**
Zeballos In.....................1A1
Zeballos L.....................12A4
Zeballos R.....................1A1
Zeballos R.....................12A4
Zechtoo Mtn.....................61B1
Zelkwas Cr.....................38B1
Zenazie Cr.....................81C3
Zenzaco Cr.....................25B3
Zeues Cr.....................88D4
Zeues L.....................88D4
Zohin Cr.....................70B2
Zohina Cr.....................69D2
Zuciarte Chan.....................1B2
Zus Cr.....................86D3-4
Zus Cr.....................87A3
Zymagotitz R.....................44D3
Zymoetz R.....................45A3
Zymoetz R.....................45B2

Road and travel conditions can change quickly according to weather, type of road use and degree of maintenance. With the recession in B.C.'s forest industry over recent years, more and more of our back roads and bridges are in various stages of disrepair, and conditions get progressively worse. Some forest roads may be closed to the public during periods of industrial use or extreme fire hazard or they may be gated to protect industrial equipment used in the area.

If you are unaccustomed to back-road travel or unfamiliar with the area or route, consider contacting the nearest Forest District Office, fishing/hunting supply stores, gas stations, logging companies etc., about area conditions and possible road closures.
Although forest roads are often used by the public, they are built primarily for heavy industrial traffic. Travelling in a two wheel drive vehicle dictates that you stick to well used roads. Most logging mains are well maintained .

Road Deactivation

While operating your motor vehicle, ATV, motorcycle, snowmobile or mountain bike on forest roads, please consider the following:

The objective of road deactivation is to control water flow, prevent washouts and, wherever possible, maintain limited vehicle access. Road deactivation is a stabilization process, not necessarily a closure. Deactivation techniques such as cross ditching and waterbarring significantly alters the road surface making the road impassable for some vehicles and creating a driving hazard for the unwary road user.

Forest roads that are not currently being used for timber harvesting operations may have been deactivated. Keep a lookout for hazards but do not expect all areas to be fully signed at all times. Without road deactivation, unmaintained roads may suffer serious erosion and contribute to forest, stream and wildlife habitat degradation.

All Users Must Use Caution
It is essential that vehicle operators exercise the utmost care and caution in utilizing all forest roads to ensure your visit is a safe and enjoyable experience.

Observe all signs and obey them. They are there for your protection.

●	**WELCOME** . . . . .Inactive forest area road open to public at all times. Please drive carefully.
▼	**CAUTION HEAVY VEHICLES** . . . .Open to public traffic – Drive with extreme care and observe all signs.
⬣	**ACTIVE LOGGING AREA** . . . . . . .Public may drive here on posted hours on weekdays – open weekends & holidays.

Safe driving tips
Traveling on forest roads is somewhat different from traveling on public highways.
For your own safety, drive with extreme caution at all times.

- Check your vehicle, fuel and supplies before starting out.
- Obey all road and access signs (see below), they are there for your protection.
- Give logging and industrial traffic the right-of-way by moving to the nearest turn-out or pulling off the travelled right-of-way as far as possible.
- Allow overtaking traffic to pass.
- Follow radio controlled traffic, if possible.
- Drive with your lights on — especially under dusty conditions — to make yourself more visible.
- Watch for fallen rock, downed trees, blind corners and animals on the road.
- Stay with your vehicle if you encounter dangerous wildlife, particularly those with young.
- Park well off the travelled portion of the road if you must stop along the way.

Observe … Record … Report

The unethical angler is a threat to your fisheries resources and outdoor recreation. Violations of these regulations damage the resource and reduce fishing opportunities for all anglers.

Here's how you can help protect your resources.

OBSERVE:

Learn the current regulations. Some common violations are:
> *angling in "no fishing" areas*
> *using illegal fishing gear*
> *exceeding engine power restrictions or using power boats on waters where they are prohibited*
> *transporting live fish*
> *selling fish taken by sport fishing*
> *damaging fish habitat*
> *guiding for compensation without a guide's licence*

RECORD:

When you see ANY violation, promptly record details of the violation. Two **Observe - Record - Report** forms are provided on the edge of this page for your convenience. Fill out the front and back of the form. Take pictures if possible. (Note: wallet-sized copies of the **Observe - Record - Report** form are available at Fish and Wildlife offices throughout the province).

REPORT:

Take or mail your completed form as soon as possible to one of the following:
> Conservation Officer Service District Office (see list on back cover for the nearest office);
> RCMP Detachment;
> Department of Fisheries and Oceans; or
> dial 1-800-663-WILD (9453) … toll-free, 24-hours

You may remain anonymous if you prefer.

1-800-663-WILD

OBSERVE, RECORD and REPORT was developed in co-operation with the B.C. Wildlife Federation

---

Observe, Record and Report

PLEASE ACT IMMEDIATELY

With timely, accurate information, an apprehension and conviction can often be obtained without it being necessary for you to appear as a witness.

If you are willing to appear and testify in court, please complete below.

NAME _____

ADDRESS _____

CITY _____ PROV. _____

PHONE _____ POSTAL CODE _____

Immediately take this card to one of the agencies listed on this page, or mail it to one of the following:

Department of Fisheries and Oceans
General Investigation Unit
555 West Hastings Street
Vancouver, B.C.
V6B 5G3

B.C. Environment
Conservation Officer Service
Parliament Buildings
Victoria, B.C.
V8V 1X5

* * *

This program is sponsored jointly by the Department of Fisheries and Oceans (Canada) and the Ministry of Environment, Lands and Parks (B.C.) in cooperation with the B.C. Wildlife Federation and the people of British Columbia.

Observe, Record and Report

PLEASE ACT IMMEDIATELY

With timely, accurate information, an apprehension and conviction can often be obtained without it being necessary for you to appear as a witness.

If you are willing to appear and testify in court, please complete below.

NAME _____

ADDRESS _____

CITY _____ PROV. _____

PHONE _____ POSTAL CODE _____

Immediately take this card to one of the agencies listed on this page, or mail it to one of the following:

Department of Fisheries and Oceans
General Investigation Unit
555 West Hastings Street
Vancouver, B.C.
V6B 5G3

B.C. Environment
Conservation Officer Service
Parliament Buildings
Victoria, B.C.
V8V 1X5

* * *

This program is sponsored jointly by the Department of Fisheries and Oceans (Canada) and the Ministry of Environment, Lands and Parks (B.C.) in cooperation with the B.C. Wildlife Federation and the people of British Columbia.

OBSERVE - RECORD - REPORT

VIOLATIONS WITNESSED:

DATE _____ TIME _____

VEHICLE, VESSEL OR AIRCRAFT DESCRIPTION:
LICENSE NO. _____
PROV. or STATE _____
MAKE _____
MODEL _____
UNUSUAL MARKS _____

DETAILS OF VIOLATION: _____
LOCATION _____
SPECIES TAKEN _____
HOW TAKEN _____

LOCATION OF CARCASS (if applicable) _____
POLLUTION OR LITTERING _____
OTHER _____
_____

DESCRIPTION OF VIOLATOR: _____
NAME (if known): _____
SEX _____ AGE _____
HEIGHT _____ WEIGHT_____ EYES _____
HAIR _____ BEARD/MUSTACHE _____
PHYSICAL MARKS OR SCARS _____
CLOTHING (hat, coat, etc.) _____
PECULIARITIES _____
OTHER EVIDENCE (type of gear, etc)_____
_____

REMARKS: _____
WITNESS(ES):
Name   Address   Telephone
_____
_____

OBSERVE - RECORD - REPORT

VIOLATIONS WITNESSED:

DATE _____ TIME _____

VEHICLE, VESSEL OR AIRCRAFT DESCRIPTION:
LICENSE NO. _____
PROV. or STATE _____
MAKE _____
MODEL _____
UNUSUAL MARKS _____

DETAILS OF VIOLATION: _____
LOCATION _____
SPECIES TAKEN _____
HOW TAKEN _____

LOCATION OF CARCASS (if applicable) _____
POLLUTION OR LITTERING _____
OTHER _____
_____

DESCRIPTION OF VIOLATOR: _____
NAME (if known): _____
SEX _____ AGE _____
HEIGHT _____ WEIGHT_____ EYES _____
HAIR _____ BEARD/MUSTACHE _____
PHYSICAL MARKS OR SCARS _____
CLOTHING (hat, coat, etc.) _____
PECULIARITIES _____
OTHER EVIDENCE (type of gear, etc) _____
_____

REMARKS: _____
WITNESS(ES):
Name   Address   Telephone
_____
_____